The Complete Idiot's Reference Card

Top Ten Things You'll Need for B

1. A bike that is the right size for your body
2. A bike that has the saddle height properly adjusted for your leg length
3. A helmet that is the right size and that is properly adjusted to stay snugly on your head
4. A full water bottle or hydration system
5. A survival kit consisting of everything needed to repair a flat, including inner tubes and some means of inflating the tire
6. Gloves for comfort and to protect your hands in a fall
7. Eyewear to protect your eyes from the sun and from airborne dust, debris, and flying insects
8. Bike shorts with built-in padding for buttocks comfort
9. An outer shell jacket in case of dropping temperature or unexpected showers
10. Knowledge of basic bicycle operation and safe riding techniques

Ten Ways to Have Fun on a Bicycle

1. Road riding
2. Cross-country mountain bike riding
3. Downhill mountain bike riding
4. A club ride or group ride
5. A fast training ride
6. A leisurely solo ride on a bike path or in a park
7. Riding a stationary trainer while watching a TV show or movie
8. A tandem ride
9. A picnic ride
10. A bike tour

alpha books

tear here

Ten Specialties in Bicycle Competition

1. Road, road racing
2. Road, criterium racing
3. Road, individual time trial
4. Road, team time trial
5. Mountain, cross-country racing
6. Mountain, downhill racing
7. Mountain, dual-slalom racing
8. Mountain, hillclimb
9. Mountain, endurance racing
10. Mountain, trails

Ten Bicycle-Related Web Sites

1. United States Cycling Federation (USCF), www.usacycling.org/road/
2. National Off-Road Bicycle Association (NORBA), www.usacycling.org/mtb/
3. Societe de Tour de France, www.letour.fr
4. Velo News, www.velonews.com
5. Mountain Bike Resource, www.mtbr.com
6. *Mountain Bike Magazine*, www.mountainbike.com
7. Shimano, www.shimano.com
8. Campagnolo, www.campagnolo.com
9. SRAM/GripShift, www.sram.com
10. The WWW Bicycle Lane, www.bikelane.com

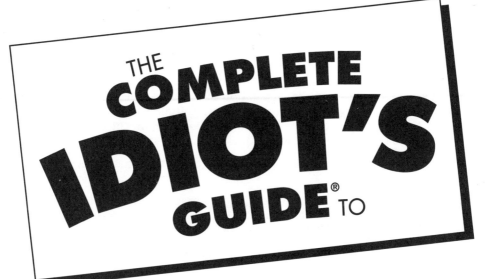

THE COMPLETE IDIOT'S GUIDE® TO

Cycling

by Vic Armijo

alpha books

A Division of Macmillan General Reference
A Pearson Education Macmillan Company
1633 Broadway, New York, NY 10019

Macmillan General Reference books may be purchased for business or sales promotional use. For information please write: Special Markets Department, Macmillan Publishing USA, 1633 Broadway, New York, NY 10019.

International Standard Book Number: 0-02862929-9
Library of Congress Catalog Card Number: 99-60669

01 00 99   8 7 6 5 4 3 2 1

Interpretation of the printing code: the rightmost number of the first series of numbers is the year of the book's printing; the rightmost number of the second series of numbers is the number of the book's printing. For example, a printing code of 99-1 shows that the first printing occurred in 1999.

Printed in the United States of America

Alpha Development Team

Publisher
Kathy Nebenhaus

Editorial Director
Gary M. Krebs

Managing Editor
Bob Shuman

Marketing Brand Manager
Felice Primeau

Acquisitions Editor
Jessica Faust

Development Editors
Phil Kitchel
Amy Zavatto

Assistant Editor
Georgette Blau

Production Team

Development Editor
Amy Zavatto

Production Editors
Christy Wagner

Copy Editor
Heather Stith

Cover Designer
Mike Freeland

Photo Editor
Richard H. Fox

Illustrator
Jody P. Schaeffer

Book Designers
Scott Cook and Amy Adams of DesignLab

Indexer
Brad Herriman

Layout/Proofreading
Angela Calvert
Julie Trippetti

Contents at a Glance

Contents

Appendices

Foreword

The Complete Idiot's Guide to Cycling is an odd title for a fantastic book. In my opinion, if you're riding a bike—whether you're new to the sport or a seasoned pro—you're far from an idiot! A person's active participation in bicycling can actually be considered a sign of intelligence. Why? Because it's a sport that gives back so much for everything you put into it.

While this may sound trite, I'm living proof that it's true.

I grew up in Norwalk, California, in a very humble (some would say "economically challenged") area near Los Angeles. For the kids in my neighborhood, opportunities seemed pretty limited. College wasn't a real option for most of us, so we were each left to find our own means of "breaking out." I made my escape on a bicycle.

Even more than most kids, I rode my bike everywhere while I was growing up. The sense of exhilaration and freedom it gave me was incredible. When I discovered BMX racing at age 13, I knew it was something I could excel at. And thanks to the help and support of my family, I did. With my mom as my mechanic and manager and my three sisters as my own personal fan club, I steadily moved up through the ranks. At the mere age of 15, I became the youngest professional BMX racer in the entire country.

My career soared when I switched to professional mountain bike racing in 1986. Suddenly, the boy who thought he might never see beyond the outskirts of Norwalk was traveling the world with the Volvo/Cannondale racing team, winning three U.S. National Championships, a silver medal at World Championships, a gold medal at the Pan American Games, and representing his country at the Summer Olympic Games.

More important than the medals or considerable financial rewards, though, are the rich benefits that cycling has brought to my personal life. The tireless support and sacrifice of my mother and sisters during the lean early years of my cycling career has created bonds between us that words are unable to convey. Cycling has even given me my lovely wife Jimena, whom I met at a race in Argentina.

So you see, it *is* true! Cycling can give you more than you'd ever imagined: improved health, new friends, the rediscovered joy of two wheels beneath you, and the wind in your face… These are just some of the benefits. Whether your goal is a slimmer waistline or a World Championship title, I can guarantee that you'll enjoy the ride. Have fun reading this excellent book, then strap on your helmet and climb on your bike. I look forward to seeing you out there!

—Tinker Juarez

Volvo/Cannondale Racing Team

Introduction

Every neighborhood seems to have that kid who if you hand him a football, it will fly off in a perfect spiral. Hand him a baseball and endanger the windows of houses three blocks away. Or slip a skateboard under his feet, and in a few minutes he'll be zooming and spinning up and down the block. I wasn't that kid. I still can't throw a football to save my life, my Little League career lasted one dismal season, and skateboards and I had a short but antagonistic relationship. Bicycles and I always got along, however. I was the wheelie champion of the neighborhood. Not only could I ride the full length of our street on the back wheel, but if the wind and stars were right, I could also turn around at the end of the cul-de-sac and wheelie all the way back in the other direction.

Since my days as the back-wheel king of Senwood Street, bicycles have almost always been in my life. There was that period when I focused on motorcycles and motocross (still two wheels though), but even then my desire to improve my fitness for motocross led me to buy my first "real" road bike. From there, it's been an unbroken span of over two decades of always having bikes, always riding, and nearly always racing.

Of all my life experiences, the vast majority of the most memorable are bicycle-related. And that fact is not because I'm a particularly gifted or successful racer—not at all. I wasn't blessed with lightning-fast reflexes or an above-average cardiovascular system. Sure, I've had a few decent finishes out of the literally hundreds of races I've entered over the years. But I have to train hard and race harder to be able to maintain my position as a mid-pack finisher. But the truly notable bicycle moments of my life involve the fun of riding, the beauty of a trail or destination, and the camaraderie of sharing a particularly grueling ride or race with friends.

Bicycling has taken me to many places, both literally and figuratively. It has been a common thread between me and some of the most warm and incredible people I've ever known. It has kept me more physically fit than most of my friends my age, and it has helped me to keep the fun-loving mental attitude of people much younger than I.

I know that the enthusiasm of the people I've met in this sport has been contagious— they certainly infected me. I'm hoping that the things I share in this book will also inspire you to enjoy a long, healthful, and safe life filled with lots of bicycles and lots of bicycle riding.

I hope that this book will instill in you the enthusiasm that will make bicycling a permanent facet of your life and that your bikes will never suffer the usual fate of forgotten exercise equipment. Whenever I see a nice bicycle suffering the indignity of being part of a garage sale (displayed right next to an unused Gut-Be-Gone or a practically new weight set), I can't help but wonder if its fate would have been different if its owner had only learned a bit more about bicycling. A little knowledge of the ways of bikes can go a long way toward making a new bike owner's first ride enjoyable enough for that new rider to want to make second rides, third rides, and nine hundred and fourteenth rides.

How to Use This Book

This book is laid out in a progressive fashion. I want you to be able to get a good grasp of each concept before building onto it with the information provided in subsequent chapters. I've divided the book into five sections.

Part 1, "Bicycle Fundamentals," covers such topics as the sheer fun of bicycling and the history of the hardware and the sport. It also provides information to help you to decide what type of bicycling is right for you.

Part 2, "A Shiny New Bike," helps you to choose a bike in the right type and size and to get that bike at a fair price. It also helps you in identifying some of the components of a bike and what they do. I've also included information on all the various accessories that you'll want to go along with your "fun on two wheels."

Part 3, "Pedal Time," will help you to master the intricacies of riding a modern bike, including shifting gears, braking, and steering. It also provides information on off-road riding techniques and survival tips for riding on city streets. Also included is information on getting the most performance from your body and a discussion of Spinning, the latest way to pedal in a group setting.

Part 4, "The Care and Feeding of a Bicycle," covers most of the technical and mechanical features of a modern bicycle. If you want to learn how to maintain and repair your bike, this section is for you.

Part 5, "Play Well with Others," illustrates that bicycling needn't be a solitary pursuit. There are several ways to enjoy the sport in the company of friends in races, group rides, fun rides, and tours.

I've also included a couple of appendices. Appendix A is a list of bicycle-related resources, and Appendix B is a glossary of the terms and cycling jargon you'll find in this book.

Extras

Throughout this book you'll find information that expands on the ideas in the main text. This data is easy to find, just look for the sidebars.

Miles of Experience

Learn from my mistakes and memorable episodes by reading these accounts of incidences that have taught me lessons.

Steer Clear

Here's my advice on things to avoid from a safety standpoint and things to avoid because they might cost you money.

Cyclebabble

These definitions of technical bicycle terms and cycling jargon pop up throughout the book.

Cycology

These tips and information provide an insider's glimpse into the world of bicycling. These explanations of concepts and bicycling practice and theory will make it easier for you to follow the rest of the chapter.

Acknowledgments

I first must thank the guys who prodded me into getting my first "good" road bike and who taught me the basics that carried me ever deeper into the sport. I don't know where Scott, Craig, and Chuck are today, but here's to you guys. I certainly can't forget Ray Blum, the grizzled old veteran without whom I may not ever have entered my first road race. I also need to express my gratitude to those folks who put on weekly rides and races: thanks to the dedicated folks at El Dorado Park, to the Saturday morning Chino Hills crew, and to every race promoter or fun ride organizer whose events I've enjoyed over the years.

I'm also indebted to Arnie Baker, M.D., who helped me with information on training and in putting technical physiological concepts into terms understandable by anyone. I want to express my appreciation to three-time U.S. mountain bike cross-country champion and '96 mountain bike Olympian Tinker Juarez, a rider with unparalleled determination, belief in himself, and tenacity—someone who I feel fortunate to be able to call a friend. I received a great deal of assistance from Patty Davidson and Bill Teel at Cannondale Bicycles. Although I've always known that Cannondale is on top of its game when it comes to clothing, accessories, and bicycles, it was great to learn that the people at Cannondale also meet such high standards.

I also extend thanks to the bicycle scribes Jacquie Phelan, Zapata Espinoza, Owen Mullholland, Maynard Hershon, Marti Stephen, John Wilcockson, Mike Ferrentino, and others who have not only inspired me to laugh and to ponder, but to also write about this wondrous sport.

I especially want to thank my permanent tandem stoker Kathy for her patience in this long project ("One more paragraph and I'll come to bed") and for her help in shooting many of the photographs appearing in this book ("That was perfect! Now hold still while I shoot six or seven more").

I wish to dedicate this book to the people whose efforts and exploits have made this sport so inspiring. I'm not only referring to the road racing heroes like Greg LeMond, Miguel Indurain, Eddy Merckx, and Fausto Coppi or to mountain bike stars such as Tinker, John Tomac, Ned Overend, Juli Furtado, and Susan Demattei, but to the real-life people who have used their joy from cycling and lust for life to kindle the spirits of those around them. I'm referring to personal heroes such as my friend Troy Rauh, a heart-transplant recipient who managed to return to racing at the expert level; my 60-year-old friend Dan Hanebrink, an engineer and racer who can still ride away from many racers one third his age; and to the late "Earthquake" Jake Watson, a downhill pro taken from us too soon and too tragically. In his short life Jake proved that a pro racer can still be a real person. He had just fulfilled his dream of being a fireman before his fatal accident. Those who didn't know Jake thought of him as a great big man on a mountain bike. Those of us that did know Jake knew that his heart was as big as his feet. And most importantly, thanks to all those riders who have focused their love of cycling into fund-raising rides to battle the scourges of diseases such as AIDS, cancer, multiple sclerosis, and diabetes. The joy of bicycling is not always a solitary pleasure—it is one that can be shared. And I thank all of those mentioned (and any of those over-looked) for sharing their love of this wonderful sport of bicycling.

Special Thanks to the Technical Reviewer

The Complete Idiot's Guide® to Cycling was reviewed by an expert who double-checked the accuracy of what you'll learn here to help us ensure that this book gives you everything you need to know about cycling. Thanks to John Flores for all his insightful input on this tome.

Bitten by the cycling bug in the mid '80s, John Flores has since sampled as many flavors of the sport as possible, from a very unsuccessful (yet fun) attempt at collegiate road racing, to loaded and unloaded tours of Colorado and the California coast, to regional duathlons (run, bike, run races), to mountain biking in Moab, and most recently, to 24-hour mountain bike racing in West Virginia. He especially enjoys long, steep, painful hills, where he can make the big burly grade-school bullies of his past really suffer.

Part 1
Bicycle Fundamentals

Because this book is in your hands, there's probably a new bike in your garage or living room. Perhaps that new bike is just in your thoughts. Whatever the case, welcome back. The fun you had as a kid has been waiting for you all along; I congratulate you on having the good sense to go looking for it.

I feel it only fair to warn you, however, that a bicycle is capable of sprouting far deeper roots than your average hunk of exercise equipment. If your bike does indeed work its magic on you, you might develop a full-blown case of cyclosis, *which is the urge to plan every weekend around rides or races and spend every spare dollar on bikes or accessories.*

Will you develop cyclosis? I certainly hope so. This first part of the book will spread the virus by letting you in on the fun and by helping you to avoid many of the mistakes most beginners make. There's no sense in resisting. Cyclosis can't be cured; it can only be treated. The treatment? Riding often and riding with a smile.

A. Bicycle   B. <u>Not</u> a
             bicycle

Chapter 1

Revisiting a Childhood Friend

In This Chapter

➤ Bikes aren't just for kids

➤ Benefits of cycling

➤ Magic rides and the cyclist's high

➤ What's a wafo?

How did you sleep that Christmas Eve so long ago when you just knew that Santa was going to finally bring you that bike you longed for? For many, the thought of that first two-wheeler still brings a smile. For those who continue to ride or have rediscovered bicycles, those joyful feelings are alive and well. Bicycle fun is most certainly not the sole claim of the very young.

A bicycle can bring a smile to even the most serious faces. Take the famed photo of Albert Einstein happily pedaling his bike, for example. The father of relativity isn't usually thought of as being a particularly bubbly kind of guy, but put him on a bike and look at the transformation! And then there's Richard Nixon, a man who may have had the most somber, granite puss of all time. Yet in a 1960 presidential campaign publicity photo depicting him and daughter Julie astride a pair of bikes, the broad smile on old Dick's face seemed sincere. If a bike can put a grin on an igneous mug like Nixon's, just imagine what a bike can do for you.

Greasy Kid Stuff?

I first felt the connection of my grown-up self to the kid on a *Stingray* on a crystal clear New Year's morning ride nearly 10 years ago. A large group of us had ridden mountain bikes to the top of Mt. Wilson, overlooking Los Angeles. Once there, we gathered for a group photo. It was then that I saw this group for who they really were. The riders included a dentist, an aerospace engineer, an anesthesiologist, a police officer, a firefighter, a supermarket chain executive, a philosophy professor, and a bike shop owner, but on that day I just saw a bunch of kids playing on bikes.

That day on Mt. Wilson, this group wasn't racing. We weren't there to impress a sponsor or land a racing contract, and we weren't out to prove who could climb the fastest (okay, maybe some of us were). Our ride up that mountain was about the sheer fun of being on our bikes on a beautiful, blustery winter morning and sharing the company of friends. There was no trophy presentation waiting for us at the top, only a spectacular view of greater L.A. and the ocean beyond. After all, the fun of bicycling is its own reward.

And that, dear readers (and riders), is what I hope you take away from this book. Sure, we're going to discuss many aspects of bicycles and cycling in these pages, including what to do if you are serious about taking the sport to a higher level. What I hope you learn, however, is that cycling is fun whether you're 7 or 87. Playing is a fundamental need. No one ever said from his or her deathbed, "Gee, I wish I would have spent more time at the office." Take some time from making a living and *do* some living. If you can make cycling part of the adventure, even better!

Cyclebabble

The Schwinn **Stingray** is a kids' bicycle from the early 1960s that continues to influence cycling. Its extremely strong 20-inch wheels gave it great maneuverability. As motorcycle **motocross** (dirt bike racing) became popular, kids began to outfit these bicycles with knobby tires so they could emulate their motocross heroes. Soon vacant lots across the United States sprouted dirt jumps and bermed (banked) turns, and the sport of **bicycle motocross** (**BMX**) was born.

Beat the Clock

As long we're on the subject of enjoying your life, let's take a minute and talk about extending it. Riding a bike can increase your fitness level, lower your cholesterol level, and decrease your chances of checking out early due to heart disease. And did I mention that riding a bike is fun, too? These health benefits make a great excuse to use on your in-laws the next time you're late for Sunday brunch: "Sorry ma. Just had to go ride that darn bike. Doctor's orders, you know."

Miles of Experience

The first real bike racer I ever met was a man who I was surprised to learn was then in his early 70s (he looked not a day older than 58). He had been an Olympic speed skater in the 1930s and later pursued a bike-racing career. Meeting him was a turning point in my life because he was the one who told me how to begin bicycle racing, how to train, how to pedal, and more. Of all the valuable things he taught me about this wonderful sport, the thing I remember most is when he said, "Time spent riding a bike is not deducted from your lifetime." As I consider all the people I've known in this sport who have had health, attitudes, and appearances of much younger people, I see how true his words were.

Take One Two-Hour Ride and Call Me in the Morning

In addition to improving your physical health, cycling improves your mental health. Psychiatrists routinely advise their overstressed, frazzled patients to get a hobby. Because entirely abandoning the lifestyle or job that landed these patients on the shrink's couch in first place usually isn't an option, cycling is a great way to relieve stress. It's relatively inexpensive and easy to do, and best of all, it's enjoyable.

Tired from a long day at work? Frazzled from a frustrating marathon meeting? Jump on a mountain bike and discover that it isn't your body that's tired, it's your brain. After a few minutes of having oxygen supercharged into your blood, that burned-out feeling is soon replaced with the invigoration that bike riding brings on so well. It freshens the mind and renews the spirit. After all, when you're busy making your way along a single-track trail or quiet back road, it's tough to stay upset about piddly problems like that lost order or the jerk who left you on hold.

I can't think of a better hobby for escaping life's pressures than riding a bicycle. Imagine being in the zone where only the trail or road exists and your mind doesn't stray to outside thoughts. That concentration and total immersion into the now is what's so invigorating about bicycling. When glancing at my watch while cycling, I've often been surprised to discover that far more time than I imagined had passed.

One caveat: Don't let your attitude stray from the smiley side. In our busy word-a-day lives, sometimes even our hobbies become stress factors. Some people begin to regard their bikes as mere pieces of exercise equipment instead of the wonderful toys they are. Don't fall into this way of thinking; take your bike outside and play!

There was no practical reason for me to wheelie alongside the edge of the Grand Canyon—it was just fun!

The Quest for the Magic Ride

Health benefits aside, there's one more reason for you to start pedaling: the sheer enjoyment of cycling. It's amazing to have one of those wondrous days when everything falls into place and riding a bike feels like the most natural and most enjoyable activity anyone has ever done. Some days you'll get out there, and the climbs will feel as though a little motor is hidden inside the bike and you're just along for the ride. Those who have experienced an effortless day will know what I mean when I say that it's one of the best feelings on earth. There's nothing like being strong, sharp, and at one with the bike and the trail.

I just got back from a great mountain bike ride, one that I'll remember for a long time. It wasn't terribly fast, and the trail was one I had ridden countless times before, but there was something exceptional about the trip. The weather was gorgeous, the bike was working well, and best of all, I experienced one of those rare rides where it seemed that I could do no wrong. Every hill was ridden a gear or two higher, every corner was railed just so, and every joyful wheelie went on forever. There were no flats, my last bottle-emptying swig of water came just as I was pulling in my driveway, and even though I had been riding for over three hours, I wasn't even the slightest bit hungry. It was perfect, just perfect. (With everything going my way, perhaps I should have bought a lottery ticket on the way home!)

Sometimes called the "runner's high," this phenomenon of endorphin-induced bliss is karmic payback for all those rides spent struggling and wheezing while contemplating selling the blasted bike and buying a set of golf clubs. True, unless you're one of those gifted few who can make a living as a pro racer, magic rides are rare, but that's what makes it so special when mere mortals like you and me and Joe Average get a taste of what our racing heroes call being "on." Unfortunately for me, those magic rides rarely seem to coincide with race day. Somehow it's always on some Wednesday afternoon training ride or a Saturday morning group ride that I feel like I could rip the cranks right off the bike or pedal my way up Mt. Everest.

Miles of Experience

On the flip side of magic rides are those times when a rider can do nothing right. It's best to listen to the symptoms. More than once I've heard riders begin a ride by saying they just weren't "with it," only to have the ride end in a fall. On days when you just don't feel as though you're at one with the bike, stay home.

What's frustrating is that following the experts' advice doesn't always produce a good day in the saddle. How many racers have followed the prescribed pre-race rituals of training, rest, and carbo-loading only to feel like they're dragging anvils behind their bikes on race day?

It's not always possible at first to judge how the day's ride will turn out. Some of the best rides don't always start out so great. I've had a lot of days where the first few miles of the ride have been a struggle, and I've had to fight the urge to go back home and see what's on *Oprah*. But sometimes after I break a sweat and warm up, the magic will begin to creep in.

There's no way of being sure when a magic ride will come. No one has quite figured out the secret of magic-on-demand. But one thing is for sure: The only way to have any hope of achieving bicycling bliss is to ride, ride, and ride some more. For the bike spirits bless only those who have earned it, and even then they bless you only rarely. If you have yet to experience being at one with the balance of steel, dirt, rubber, aluminum, oxygen, blood, and sweat, keep riding. Your magic ride will come.

What's a Wafo?

wafo (wa-fo) *noun* [mountain biker's lingo] 1: An individual who has difficulty understanding the purpose of another's leisure activities. 2: One who asks "Wafo?" as in "Wafo you ride those mountain bikes?"

Anyone who rides bikes, hang glides, bungee jumps, or wrestles alligators has met a wafo. Not that cycling exactly fits into the same category as those other extreme sports, but wafos perceive it that way.

Cyclebabble

The **Tour de France** is a three-week-long road race that has taken place in France each year in July since 1903. The overall route is usually more than 2,500 miles and attracts nearly 200 of the world's fastest pro racers. Each day, a racer's time for that day's race is added to a running total. The rider with the lowest overall elapsed time is the winner.

Cyclebabble

The **Kamikaze downhill** race at California's Mammoth Mountain Ski Resort took its name from the perceived suicidal tendencies of the competitors who routinely hit speeds in excess of 60 miles per hour on the 3.5-mile course that descended over 2,200 feet from its start at the top of the resort's 11,053-foot mountain. After the twelfth running of the Kamikaze in 1997, the relatively smooth and wide course was retired in favor of a narrower, rougher, and more technically challenging course.

Answering a wafo isn't easy. Saying, "I ride because it's fun" doesn't tell the whole story. I live in Big Bear, California, a mountain resort town that's a popular getaway destination for southern Californians. When I worked the rental counter at the local bike shop, I'd have groups in which there was invariably a friend, mother, or brother who wasn't too keen on riding (i.e., a wafo). I'd try to garner some enthusiasm for these apprehensive individuals by telling them what a great time they'd have, but my explanations were often met with a blank stare. The fun of riding has to be experienced to be understood.

For example, one Sunday morning a family from Arizona came in to rent bikes. Dad and daughter were anxious for their first mountain bike experience, but mom was skeptical. "Let's get this over with" was her attitude. We put them on some bikes and sent them to an easy trail, expecting to see them back within the hour.

Surprisingly, they stayed out for nearly three hours! On their return, mom was the most enthusiastic. She was bubbling over telling us about seeing a coyote and about the squirrels scurrying across the trails and how she couldn't remember when she'd had so much fun. She had jillions of questions and wanted to know about riding in Arizona. It was quite the contrast from three hours earlier when she thought it would be too much work. In the end she was glad that she hadn't gone shopping in the village instead.

Many wafos simply don't have a clear concept of what bicycling is really about. They may have seen the *Tour de France* or *Kamikaze downhill* on TV and think that all bicyclists are racers. Tell them you go road riding, and they picture a pack of 100 riders riding 150 miles in the Alps. Tell them you go mountain biking, and they envision downhill racers skirting the edges of cliffs at 55 miles an hour. No wonder they give an incredulous look and ask, "Wafo you do that?!"

Yet most mountain bikers will never even see the Kamikaze course, much less race, and only a select few of the world's pro road racers will ever ride in the Tour de France. Most bicyclists prefer the slower pace of casual fun rides. Enjoy the scenery, see wildflowers, climb to a peak for the views … good old-fashioned outdoor fun!

Experiences are what make life interesting. It takes a personal experience to discover cycling in the first place. So the next time you meet a wafo, don't waste your breath explaining because it's like trying to tell a stranger about rock 'n' roll. Instead, invite them to experience a ride. Let them experience the fun for themselves. Let them understand what it's like to not just view the scenery through a window, but to feel it, smell it, taste it, and be a part of it. Chances are they'll find themselves asking, "Wafo I didn't try this before?"

Which brings me to my final question: What are you doing sitting here in the house with a book on such a nice day? Why don't you and some of your little friends go outside and play?

The Least You Need to Know

➤ Bicycling is a completely acceptable form of exercise, but it's also great fun (but that can remain our little secret).

➤ The playtime fun of bicycling is its own reward.

➤ Cycling increases your fitness level, lowers your cholesterol level, and decreases your chances of checking out early due to heart disease.

➤ Don't let the wafos get you down.

Chapter 2

If You Build It, They Will Ride: The Beginning of the Bicycle

---

In This Chapter

➤ A brief history of the bicycle

➤ Mountain bikes: not just the latest trend

➤ A history of mountain biking as a sport

Did that jet airliner that you rode in to visit Aunt Gertrude last Christmas bear even a passing resemblance to the plane that Orville and Wilbur Wright flew at Kitty Hawk nearly 100 years ago? You'd certainly hope not. Bicycles, however, are a different story. Read on and see why in the world of cycling the old cliché rings true: The more things change, the more they stay the same.

Back to the Future

During the late nineteenth century, the bicycle represented the cutting edge of technology. Many of the most gifted engineers of the time spent their efforts on developing and refining bicycles and bicycle products. It was a prolific time in bicycle innovation. Many of today's concepts that are perceived as new inventions were first tried over a hundred years ago. Suspension forks, suspension frames and seat-posts, multiple gearing, and many other ideas that originated in that era had to wait for modern manufacturing and metallurgy to become practical and reliable products.

Take a gander at a modern road bike, and you'll find a machine with two equal-sized wheels that will likely have a classic diamond frame and a chain-and-sprockets drivetrain—much like the bikes designed and built in 1874 by an Englishman named

H.J. Lawson. True, old H.J.'s "safety" bike weighed somewhere in the 40-pound neighborhood and rode on iron wheels cushioned by a mere strip of rubber. But the basic configuration was such a sound concept that 125 years later, H.J.'s bike and the bikes ridden by today's racing heroes are easily recognizable as being of the same genus. Is there any other machine that has undergone such refinement, development, and distillation while still keeping its essence? (Maybe the bobsled, but let's not get too persnickety.)

Cycles of Cycles

The development of the modern-day bicycle didn't begin with H.J. Lawson. Rather, much like the designers of today, H.J. built his ideas upon the work of those before him. Just where and when the first bicycle was designed is the subject of endless debate. There's the well-known, yet oft-disputed, sketch attributed to Leonardo da Vinci (since it was crudely drawn and out of scale, experts surmise it was the work of a da Vinci pupil). Bicycle-like devices also are depicted in an ancient Babylonian sculpture where people are shown astride long poles with wheels at either end.

The earliest verifiable design is French carpenter Elie Richard's plans for a wooden two-wheeler, sketched in 1690. An example was built from those plans three years later by French engineer Jacques Ozanam. A contraption of similar design was marketed 100 years later by yet another Frenchman, Comte de Sivrac. Although Sivrac's machine enjoyed momentary popularity, its crude design consisted simply of a solid wooden beam with wheels attached at either end. A rider propelled the machine by paddling his feet on the ground to gain momentum. Although it was faster than walking, it lacked any means of steering. That subtle refinement was brought about later in 1816 by (you guessed it) another French tinkerer, J.N. Niepce.

Pedal Me This

Although Niepce's contraption had steering, it still lacked pedals—that development was introduced by Scottish engineer Kirkpatrick Macmillan. Macmillan's contrivance, with its two platforms connected to the rear hub by a long pair of arms, was indeed the first self-propelled bicycle.

To prove the viability of his invention, Macmillan rode over 70 miles from Thornhil, Dumfriesshire, to Glasgow. It is said that on his return ride he challenged a mail-coach driver to a race and won history's first bicycle race! (See Chapter 3, "Legendary Racers and Races," for more on the history of bicycle racing.) Still, the pedaling system was cantankerous, and overall the machine was heavy, ungainly, and, in the end, unsuccessful.

Riding High

French inventor (yes, another!) Perre Michaux is credited with building the first practical bicycle. Michaux's Velocipede had crankarms and pedals connected to the front hub, just as on a child's tricycle of today. Compared to Macmillan's machine,

Michaux's was lighter, easier to pedal, more reliable, and, ultimately, a commercial success. Michaux built only four machines in 1861, but the following year he filled orders for 142, and by 1865 he was producing over 400 of the wood and iron machines per year.

The front hub pedal placement of the Michaux machine caught on among other bike builders and was used during the next phase of bicycle evolution on bikes called *high-wheelers*. These bikes, with their large front wheel and tiny rear wheel, were popular from the 1870s to the 1890s.

A high-wheeler took its name from its very large front wheel. This large-diameter wheel enabled a rider to cover a greater distance with each turn of the pedals. Various wheel sizes were available with the only limiting factor being the length of the rider's legs. Also called *penny farthings*, after the largest and smallest English coins of the time, high-wheelers took a technological step forward with their all-metal construction and wire spoke wheels. Those spoked wheels and their solid, rubber tires provided a much more comfortable ride than previous bicycles. Performance-wise, these bicycles had some practicality as regular transportation. However, their price kept them beyond the reach of the average laborer because their cost was equivalent to about six months' wages.

Low Rider

The development of a practical drivechain was the biggest evolutionary step to Lawson's safety bicycle. This development allowed bikes to be built with smaller, equal-size wheels and to use gear ratios to keep the speed advantage of a high-wheeler. The smaller wheels also placed the rider much closer to the ground, which was a safer position.

Although these bikes were easier and safer to ride, their smaller wheels and shorter spokes didn't provide nearly as much shock absorption as the huge front wheel of a high-wheeler. That situation led to the 1890 development of pneumatic (air-filled) tires by an Irish veterinarian whose name is still associated with tires to this day. His name? John Boyd Dunlop.

Cyclebabble

In the 1930s, U.S. bike manufacturer Schwinn introduced bikes with wide 26" × 2.125" **balloon tires**. These tires were designed for comfort beyond the harsh ride offered by the 1"- to 1.75"-wide tires of the time. Forty years later, this type of tire led to the emergence of mountain bikes.

Cyclebabble

Clunkers is but one term used to describe the balloon-tire bikes that spawned mountain biking. Other names that have come and gone are ballooners, newsboy bikes, beach cruisers, strand cruisers, or just plain cruisers. Comparing sleek, fast road-racing bikes to the balloon-tire bikes used by the early off-road cyclists is akin to comparing a Ferrari to an old clunker jalopy, hence the name.

Dunlop's invention made bicycles far more comfortable to ride. As the popularity of bicycling increased, mass-production methods brought the costs down. Soon, the bicycle truly was a practical, everyday means of transportation that was affordable to the common man.

Take to the Hills! Mountain Bike History

The soaring popularity of mountain biking may appear to be just the latest fitness trend, but people have ridden bikes off-road since the beginnings of two-wheeled, people-powered transportation. To say that mountain biking was invented is false. Did the first cyclist who rode a high-wheeler on a dirt road invent mountain biking? What about the various armies of World War I, with their bicycle-mounted infantrymen, riding through the woods and back roads of Europe—did they invent mountain biking? Or did some Indiana farm boy aboard a *balloon-tire* bike invent mountain biking when he rode out to his favorite creek for some fishing and a swim?

Although no one can claim to have invented the sport, many people were involved in popularizing it, especially a core group of northern California cycling enthusiasts from the '70s.

Fat Tires and Flower Children

Reports of fat-tire bikes being ridden on the dirt trails of Marin go back to the '60s and even the '50s. By the early '70s, a group of off-roaders, "The Canyon Gang," were regularly riding single-speed *clunkers* on Mt. Tamalpais and even holding impromptu races. Word of these off-road pioneers reached the ears of the Marin road-racing crowd, drawing in names that are now recognized within the sport and industry for the bikes and products bearing their names.

After seeing three racers at a *cyclocross* race aboard fat-tire bikes with *derailleurs* and drum brakes, Gary Fisher (Gary Fisher Bicycles) cobbled together his own version of the mountain bike using a '30s era Schwinn Excelsior frame. More riders followed suit. As better and lighter components were bolted onto their clunkers, however, the limitations of the old Schwinn frames became apparent.

Meanwhile, road racer Joe Breeze (Breezer Bicycles) began exploring off-road riding with some of the

Cyclebabble

A **cyclocross** is an off-road event using road bikes equipped with narrow, knobby tires. A **derailleur** is a mechanism that causes a bicycle to shift gears by guiding the bicycle's chain sideways from one sprocket to another.

Cyclebabble

Before mountain bikes began to be mass-produced, practitioners of the sport had to cobble together their own bikes using old balloon-tire bikes and a selection of road bike parts and motorcycle parts. The 1930's Schwinn Excelsior favored by early mountain bikers was the basis for Joe Breeze's first Breezer, which used the same basic dimensions and angles but was made from much lighter tubing.

Canyon Gang. In 1977, Breeze, who had been building road frames, began building his first run of 10 Breezers, the first fat-tire bikes built specifically for off-road riding.

A year later, Breeze showed one of his bikes to local frame builder, Tom Ritchey (Ritchey Mountain Bikes). Intrigued by it, Ritchey built a few frames for himself and Gary Fisher. After building some more, Ritchey recruited Fisher to sell them. Business soared. A few Ritchey frames ended up in the hands of Mike Sinyard, founder of Specialized Bicycles. At least one of those found its way to Taiwan, where it served as the blueprint for the Specialized Stumpjumper, which was introduced in 1981. From then on, mountain bike production continued to multiply. Within a few years, dozens of brands entered the fray. And the rest, as they say, is history.

Long before such bikes were called "mountain bikes," riders like Joe Breeze took old Schwinn balloon-tire bikes and rode them on the trails of Marin County, California.

A Sport Is Born

In the beginning, there was *Repack*. What's that, you ask? Repack was the birth of downhill racing. "Some new mountain bike racers don't even know what Repack was," says pro downhill racer Jimmy Deaton. "Tell them about it, and they're like, 'What's that?' It's the downhill race that basically started mountain bike racing. It's why you have a mountain bike. 'Cause these guys went out and raced down this hill."

Repack is the name given to a dirt road north of Mt. Tamalpais, just across the bay from San Francisco. On October 21, 1976, a handful of Marin County riders took their clunkers to the now famous site where they held the first recorded race of what we

Cyclebabble

The act of removing the ball bearings from inside of a bicycle wheel's hub, cleaning them, and reassembling the hub with fresh grease is called **repack**. In the famed Repack downhill race, the first mountain bike race on record, the racers reached such speeds that the grease in their rear hubs would melt away, so the racers had to repack their bearings after each ride.

now refer to as mountain biking. The steep nature of that dirt road allowed the riders to reach such speeds that the grease in the bikes' old-style coaster brakes would vaporize from the heat generated from the friction of the internal brake. The riders therefore had to repack their bearings before making another run—hence the name of the legendary race and trail. The seeds of mountain bike racing grew from that all-for-fun, party-atmosphere event.

The Gear

Jimmy Deaton, one of the few original mountain bikers still competing, first raced the Repack in '83 and won. "I raced a 26" Powerlight BMX Cruiser. One-speed with a 43-tooth chainring," he recalls. "It had front and rear brakes—just BMX caliper brakes. Some of the guys had real mountain bikes. But that was about as good as it got back then. In my first race I wore Levis and a T-shirt and an old Bell helmet. The next time I wore BMX pants and a BMX jersey."

These days, downhill racers wear body armor similar to that used by motorcycle racers. "When Swiss rider Phillipe Perakis came over in '90 wearing all that stuff, we called him the 'Bug-man,'" Deaton said, "We thought he was odd for wearing all that, now every one of us is wearing it. I can't believe how we used to race in just cross-country Lycra. Sliding along at 50 miles an hour, 'Ooh, I'm losing some skin.'"

Carving Out a Course

The other side of the mountain bike coin is cross-country racing. Many of the original dirt riders were accomplished road racers. For those riders, powering their new toys up and down hills with their legs and lungs was just as much fun as letting gravity supply the velocity. Get a few of these types together, and it wasn't long before the lengthy rides they preferred became cross-country races.

Cyclebabble

Toe-clips are metal cages that bolt to bicycle pedals. They use leather straps to affix a rider's foot to the pedal to increase a rider's power output by allowing the rider to pull up as well as push down when pedaling.

Those early cross-country events were informal affairs—"Take the old creek trail to town, last one to the Burger Burp buys the beer." Spectator appeal was the last thing on a race promoter's mind. Races were for the racers and so they were usually an out-and-back or point-to-point format as opposed to the multilap events of today.

The first U.S. championship in 1983 was held in Santa Barbara, California. Steve Tilford was the first men's champion based on his win of the cross-country event.

(The first U.S. downhill championship had to wait another seven years when "Insane" Wayne Croasdale took the first title.) Over 15 years later, Tilford still competes at the U.S. national level, and in 1998, he earned the World Championship in the 30 to 39 age category. The first women's cross-country champion, Jacquie Phelan, a colorful character who sometimes goes by the name Alice B. *Toeclips,* is also still active in the sport as a journalist and women's mountain biking advocate.

Fitness was especially important in the late '80s mountain biking competitions when there weren't downhill specialists. Events were a multidiscipline format with an overall winner. Joe Sloup, another fast downhiller of the era, explains, "In order to walk away a winner for the weekend you had to compete in a whole bunch of different events. There was a cross-country, a hillclimb, sometimes a *Scot Trials* course, and a downhill event." Today it's the rare racer that competes in both cross-country and downhill. With the level of competition so fierce in both disciplines, doing both is just too physically exhausting for most riders.

Downhilling's Evolution

From that turning point of downhill specific equipment, downhilling has evolved tremendously. Bikes now have suspension systems with seven or eight inches of *wheel travel*, front and rear. Various rollers and guides keep racers from tossing their chains. Tires are huge and are even tubeless.

The attitudes of racers have changed as well. Gone are the casual days of sleeping in the van and partying all night—at least for the pros. Downhillers know that downhill racing is a serious business for dedicated athletes. "I always knew that. I always trained very hard," says Deaton, who was one of the first to adopt the training methods used by most of today's downhillers. "I based my training on track pursuit where you train for four- or five-minute races. That's what downhill is really, a pursuit over bumps and terrain."

Cycology

The United States Cycling Federation (USCF), the sanctioning body for road racing in the United States, once forbade its members to race in non-USCF events. This policy prompted USCF racers who also wanted to race mountain bikes to adopt pseudonyms for their dabbles in the dirt. Jacquie Phelan's racing alias, Alice B. Toeclips, is a takeoff on the name of the American literary figure Alice B. Toklas (1877–1967).

Cyclebabble

Scot Trials is a rarely seen off-shoot of motorcycle "Scottish Trials," an event where riders negotiate extremely difficult terrain. Unlike regular trials, where simply getting through a section is the goal and speed isn't a concern, in Scottish Trials the riders need to get over a section as quickly as possible.

Cyclebabble

Wheel travel refers to the amount of movement a suspension fork or rear suspension system will allow the bike to move before completely compressing the shock absorber(s).

Cycology

When downhill racing first began, most bikes had rigid frames with no shock absorbers. Although some bikes had rear suspension in the mid-'80s (the Hanebrink Shocker, for instance), it wasn't until 1989 that bikes with rear suspension were widely seen at downhill events.

Cyclebabble

Single-track is a term used to denote narrow off-road trails. Most hiking trails are single-track trails. Many riders consider this type of trail to be the most fun because the narrow width is itself a challenge and most single-track trails tend to follow a twisty, meandering route, which adds to the fun.

Back in the early days of downhill racing, about the only downhill event that carried much respect on its own was Mammoth's Kamikaze. That event, with speeds in the 60-miles-per-hour neighborhood and its dramatic backdrop against the High Sierras, is legendary. Yet it's as behind the times as a 1989 vintage mountain bike. Consider that the original Kamikaze had nine corners. The popular and highly technical course at Deer Valley, Utah, has 58 corners.

"The courses now are totally different," Deaton says. "You couldn't even attempt to ride the courses we have now with the bikes we had back in the beginning. These courses are way too difficult to ride on those old rigid bikes. The brakes weren't that good. Even some of the parts on the bikes would break off. Tires weren't that good. Rims weren't that good either. You could bend all that stuff real easy. We mainly raced on fireroads. I don't think we had any *single-track* or tight stuff until '86 or '87."

Looking at today's state-of-the-art bicycles and the highly evolved technology present in every one of their parts, it's hard to imagine what the next 100 years will bring. Will today's 18-pound, titanium-framed, 18-speed road bikes and 22-pound, carbon fiber, suspension-framed, 27-speed mountain bikes bear any resemblance to the bikes of the year 2100?

Mountain biking has grown and changed far beyond what most would have imagined back in '76. Yet it seems that the future holds even more changes. According to Deaton, "Tires are already changing (Michelin has the tubeless system), disc brakes are improving, and drive systems are probably going to change." Those of us who were around for the drastic advancement of motocross technology of the late '70s and early '80s look at what's going on now in downhill technology with a sly grin. Deaton is right—we're in for a heck of a ride.

The Least You Need to Know

➤ The earliest verifiable bicycle design is French carpenter Elie Richard's plans for a wooden two-wheeler, sketched in 1690.

➤ The late nineteenth century saw huge innovations in bicycle technology.

➤ Mountain biking isn't just the latest fad; it's been around since the late 1970s.

➤ The first official U.S. cross-country championship was held in 1983 in Santa Barbara, California.

➤ The future holds new and exciting innovations in mountain bike technology.

Chapter 3

Legendary Racers and Races

In This Chapter

➤ Road racing throughout history

➤ The mother of all races: the Tour de France

➤ Famous winners of the Tour and their grueling tales of victory

---

Human nature being what it is, the world's first head-to-head bicycle race probably occurred moments after the completion of the world's second bicycle. This chapter covers bicycle racing's fast and furious history. Hold on to your handlebars!

Spinning Wheels

As bicycle technology in the late nineteenth century continued to advance, riders soon saw beyond the practicalities of this two-wheeled invention, and bicycle racing was born. The first record of an organized race took place outside of Paris in 1868. The event was promoted by Perre Michaux's company to showcase its wares. (Remember him from Chapter 2? He's credited with building the first practical bicycle.) The event was a hit, and soon more races were scheduled. With most races boasting a purse of 600 francs or more, riders quickly realized that they could make a living by racing.

The first long-distance event was also in 1868. Organized by the French cycling periodical *Le Velocipede Illustre*, the race route was from Paris to Rouen, a distance of 83 miles.

Bicycle racing continued to grow in popularity, both in Europe and in the United States. U.S. fans and promoters favored the events held on a 160-yard track *velodrome*, but in Europe the road race was king. In 1891, the French cycling newspaper *Veloce Sport* promoted a 360-mile Bordeaux-Paris event. That race gained such favor with French sports fans that numerous imitators immediately put together their own races. Races such as Paris-Brussels, Paris-Camembert, Paris-Lille, Paris-Lyon, and other newspaper-promoted events were all spawned by Bordeaux-Paris.

Cycology

The winner of that first 1,200-meter event in 1868 was British rider James Moore. That same year, Moore emerged victorious again, this time in the first long-distance event. During this race, he gave a glimpse of technological improvements to come by riding a bike with solid rubber tires instead of the iron wheels cushioned with thin strips of rubber used by the other riders.

Cyclebabble

A **velodrome** is a specially built bicycle racing track characterized by a smooth riding surface and high-banked sides. Often compared to riding in a giant cereal bowl, riding in a velodrome enables a cyclist to go at top speed without having to slow for the corners.

Le Tour de France

It was yet another newspaper, the sports journal *l'Auto-Velo*, that conceived an event larger and more spectacular than any before: Le Tour de France. The newspaper's editor, Henri Desgrange, himself a former racer, saw that his paper's main rival, *Veloce Sport*, continually outsold *l'Auto-Velo*. Realizing that his competitor's success was due to being the promoter of the most popular bicycle races, Desgrange set himself to the task of one-upping his rival. The idea of a race that would go around France was tossed out by one of Desgrange's assistants. Initially dismissed as being too much, too crazy, the idea stewed in Desgrange's head, and by that evening, he decided to go ahead with the outrageous scheme.

In modern stage races such as the Tour de France, riders are members of teams consisting of nine riders. Each of these teams has a captain, who is the rider with the best chance of winning the event. The job of the other riders is to ride in support of the captain.

The captain will often ride closely behind his team-mates, letting them fight the wind resistance so that he can conserve his energy. The lowest-ranked riders on a team, called *domestiques*, are the worker ants. They're the ones who'll drop behind to the team support car to fetch water bottles, jackets, or whatever else the captain or higher-ranked riders may need. It's also not unusual for a support rider to give up his bike or a wheel to a higher-ranked team member when that team member has a flat or mechanical problem.

The first Tour de France, which began on July 1, 1903, had just six stages, but each was about 250 miles long! With such long stages, the riders rode around the clock, often finishing a stage well into the next day. Mercifully, Desgrange had scheduled rest periods of two to three days between the stages. Sixty riders began the 19-day, six-stage, 2,428-kilometer event, vying for a 3,000-franc share of the 20,000 francs up for grabs. Over half of the racers had dropped out by the third stage of the 19-day race. Only 21 of the original 60 starters finished the race.

The first Tour was a monumental success. Desgrange's race and its winner, Maurice Garin, "Le Ramoneur" (the chimney-sweep), had succeeded in capturing the attention of the nation—Garin by dominating the race and winning the first and last two stages (and taking home 3,000 francs for his trouble) and Desgrange for having successfully pulled off his outrageous vision. (As an added plus for Desgrange, another result of the Tour was the eventual demise of *Veloce Sport*.)

The 1904 race has been called the "Tour de France that was almost the last." Problems and scandals of that edition of the Tour had Desgrange questioning whether he would continue organizing the event:

> ➤ Protesters disrupted the event with barricades on the route.
>
> ➤ Racers and staff were attacked.
>
> ➤ Saboteurs dumped tacks on the road.
>
> ➤ Several racers, including "winner" Garin, were found to have not ridden the entire distances, having hitched rides in cars.

Cycology

In the early twentieth century, bicycle racing was almost as popular as America's most favorite sport, baseball. Nearly every major U.S. city had an indoor velodrome that hosted races to sell-out crowds. The biggest events were the six-day races held at New York's Madison Square Garden. Racers routinely earned purses for one night of racing that surpassed the annual earnings of the average U.S. working man. In 1926, Australian racer Alf Goullet was paid an appearance fee of $1,000 per night to race in New York—this at a time when pro baseball players were earning $7,500 a year.

The Tour Gets a Tune-Up

The Tour de France was fine-tuned in subsequent years. The stages were shortened to eliminate the dangers of racing into the night. Issuing a yellow jersey to the overall leader to identify him in the pack began in 1919, the first year back after a four-year break for World War I. Desgrange chose yellow to match the color of the *l'Auto* newspaper. In 1930, Desgrange changed the format from teams of individual racers to national teams. In 1961, trade teams emerged. These teams were sponsored by major corporations as a means of gaining publicity for products ranging from washing machines to sausage.

Cycology

After the top four racers of the 1904 Tour de France were disqualified for hitching rides and not completing the requisite distances of the race, the overall win was awarded to the fifth-place rider, Henri "The Joker" Cornet, a 20-year-old French racer.

The next time you find yourself grumbling over not having a low-enough or high-enough gear, consider that throughout its first three decades, the Tour limited riders to one-speed bikes. Even after the invention of the derailleur, Desgrange didn't allow it in his race. Instead, those racers who wished to race with a choice of gears were forced to use a rear *hub* with a pair of *cogs* on either side.

Switching gears meant dismounting, loosening the rear wheel, moving the chain by hand from one cog (sprocket) to the other, and re-tightening the wheel. If the desired gear happened to be on the other side of the hub from the one in use, the rider had to completely remove the wheel and flip it around before reinstalling it and placing the chain on the desired cog.

That system changed in 1937 when Desgrange reluctantly allowed derailleurs and three-speed cossets. Three years later, though, there was more to worry about than manual gear-switching. The Tour took a seven-year lapse while France dealt with the horrors of World War II.

Cyclebabble

The name for the Tour de France's famed yellow jersey in the native tongue of its sponsor is **maillot jaune**.

Cyclebabble

The center portion on which a bicycle wheel turns is the **hub**. A **cog** is the toothed sprocket found on the rear wheel of a bicycle.

And Now, Back to Our Regularly Scheduled Program

In 1947, France was anxious to return to peace and its national pastime, and the first Tour was held since the onslaught of World War II. Jacques Goddet of the sports daily *l'Equipe* replaced Desgrange, who had passed away in 1940. That year, 25-year-old Jean Robic won after overtaking Pierra Brambilla at the last minute. Brambilla was so disgusted with himself for losing the yellow jersey after having dominated most of that year's Tour that he buried his bike in his garden. Robic became one of the most popular racers of the time, usually wearing a leather helmet, which earned him the nickname "Tete de Cuir" (Leatherhead).

Today, there are several stage races like the Tour de France. Italy has the Giro de Italia. Spain's national tour is called the Vuelta de España, and the Swiss have the Tour of Switzerland. Unfortunately, there is no equivalent U.S. event. The Coors Classic event of the 1980s was on its way to such status before its untimely demise in 1988. The Tour de Trump (promoted by, you guessed it, Donald Trump) was later changed to the Tour Dupont (sponsored by the Dupont company), but it fizzled out a few years ago. U.S. cycling fans can only hope for some benefactor to put on a U.S. event. Regardless of which nations have or don't have a race, though, the Tour de France is still cycling's premier racing event.

The Legends

To look back at the history of the Tour de France is to stand in awe of the racers who defined their eras. Of the 84 Tours run since 1903, only 18 racers have won more than once. The following is a look at some the racers who stood out from the pack.

Lucien Petit-Breton

The first multiple-Tour winner was Lucien Petit-Breton of France, who won in 1907 and 1908. His first win came at the expense of Emile Georget, a rider who had dominated that year until being disqualified for finishing the Bayonne stage aboard a borrowed bike. Petit-Breton's 1908 victory was without dispute; he won five stages that year. He later wrote a book of his tour exploits, titled *Comment je cours sur route* (*How I Ride the Route*). Sadly, the popular star was a casualty of World War I.

Phillippe Thijs

When the first three-time winner, Phillippe Thijs of Belgium, took his first Tour victory in 1913, he did it with consistent rides, winning but a single stage. His anonymous method of winning that year was further overshadowed by the six stage wins of Marcel Buysse and of the legendary misfortune of fan favorite Eugene Christophe. On a stage in the Pyrenees Mountains, Christophe broke his bike's *fork*. In that era, the rules required the riders to be fully self-sufficient. Forbidden to receive outside help of any kind, Christophe walked 14 kilometers to the village of Saine-Marie de Campon, where he commandeered the local blacksmith shop. Four hours later, he rejoined the race on the fork that he repaired himself. Imagine Miguel Indurain or Greg LeMond doing the same. Unthinkable!

Thijs's 1914 win was again with consistent rides and a single stage win on the first day. He still had a fierce battle, taking the yellow jersey on the sixth stage and successfully defending it through the remaining nine stages. The Belgian's 1920 win was his most decisive, with four stage wins.

Cyclebabble

A bicycle's front wheel is attached to the **fork**. The upper section of the fork (called the **steerer tube**) is inserted through the front section of the bike and is then attached to the handlebar. A rider steers by turning the handlebar, which then turns the fork, aiming the wheel into the desired direction.

Jacques Anquetil

The first racer to tally five wins in the Tour was France's Jacques Anquetil, with his first victory in 1957 and four straight victories from 1961 to 1964. Anquetil, who once claimed his best training was "a few whiskeys, blonde cigarettes, and a woman," won his first Tour de France at age 23. He established himself as a threat early that year, winning the third stage in his hometown of Rouen, eventually taking the yellow jersey for good in the tenth stage. In the 1961 race, Anquetil established his dominance even earlier and more decisively. He won the first day's time trial and wore the yellow jersey for the remaining 19 stages.

The 1962 event was closely fought with Anquetil's main rival, Raymond Poulidor of France. With only two stages remaining, Anquetil took the lead at the Bourgoin-Lyon time trial.

With his first three Tour victories firmly in the record books, Anquetil used the 1963 race to silence those critics who resented his style of saving his energy for the time trials. Although a fall in the first day had him riding with both a sore elbow and knee, squelching thoughts of road-stage victories, he did manage to take the first time trial (with a margin of 1 minute, 38 seconds). In a mountain stage in the Pyrenees, he not only stayed with Spain's Federico Bahamontes and Poulidor, he also beat them in the sprint to the finish. Three days later, he took another sprint victory in Aurillac. He sealed his victory with a stunning ride on one of the most revered climbing stages in Tour history: Val d'Isere-Chamonix. On that day, he faked a mechanical problem and switched to a lighter bike for the climbs. At the rainy finish, he again out-sprinted Bahamontes.

Anquetil's final Tour victory in 1964 was perhaps his most difficult. He said he was still fatigued from having won the Giro de Italia (Italy's version of the Tour). Poulidor, on the other hand, was fresh and had been showing improved time-trial form. Anquetil's form was good but not dominating. He won the ninth stage in Monaco and the eleventh in Toulon.

A few days later on the rest day in Andorre, he stirred resentment among his rivals by appearing before a group of photographers and reporters, wineglass in hand. The next day, the field attacked early, and a breakaway escaped with Poulidor leading the fugitives. Anquetil managed to chase down and join the break. Poulidor fell while leading over the Col d'Envalira, handing the stage to Anquetil.

The two battled head-to-head again on the climbing stage of Puy de Dome. Although neither took the stage, Anquetil managed to increase his lead over Poulidor. In the final stage in Paris, Anquetil increased his margin to 55 seconds to win the Tour and Giro in the same year for the second time in his career.

Cycology

In the early days of the Tour de France, a rider had to finish the Tour on the same bike on which he started and perform any repairs himself. Later, when the luxury of having mechanics was allowed, the rules stated that a change in bikes was only allowed if a rider's bike had a mechanical failure. Although Anquetil's creative bending of the rules in the 1963 Tour was a violation of the letter of the rule, his competitors and the fans of the time saw his switching bikes by feigning a mechanical problem as a shrewd and clever move. Currently, a rider can switch bikes at will, and swapping to a lighter mount at the base of a mountain isn't uncommon.

Eddy Merckx

When Belgian Eddy Merckx won the first of his five Tours in 1969, he had already won several major races, including the Giro, all by the tender age of 24. His way of devouring his rivals earned him the nickname "The Cannibal." The way he took his first stage win at Ballon d'Alsace was to become typical of his style. Not content to merely win the stage, he crushed his opponents that day with a seven-minute victory. Later, he won the time trials at Divonne-les-Bains and Digne.

In the end, he annihilated the field, taking the Tour in his first attempt. He did so with a margin of nearly 18 minutes over second place! In 1970, he "did the double" by winning the Tour and the Giro in the same year. That year, his Tour win was punctuated by eight stage victories. In 1971, Merckx experienced his first serious challenge in the form of Spaniard Luis Ocana. In one stage, Ocana's attack left Merckx nearly eight minutes behind. Merckx's counterattack the next day proved ineffective. When Ocana crashed while leading down a rainy descent and later withdrew, Merckx inherited the overall lead. Yet he refused to don the yellow jersey that day out of respect to his failed rival.

Merckx began the 1972 Tour just as he had finished the last three Tours—in yellow by virtue of winning on the first day. He would end up with five stage victories that year and would have had six had he not raised his arms in triumph too early at the top of Mont Revard, where an alert Cyrille Guimard was able to sprint by the startled Merckx for the stage win.

The 1974 Tour de France is remembered as the year that Merckx was revealed to be mortal. Although he won eight stages, his dominance wasn't nearly as pronounced. He was even left behind by 38-year-old Raymond Poulidor on the Col du Chat. Merckx made up the time on the flat stages that followed to take his fifth and final Tour.

Bernard Hinault

As Merckx had done before him, France's Bernard Hinault (pronounced *ee-no*) won the Tour in his first attempt. Also like Merckx, he would establish a reputation for pushing the pace harder than necessary for mere victory, reveling in punishing his rivals. For that trait, he earned the nickname "The Badger." At his first Tour in 1978, he held his own through the first week before winning the eighth stage, a 59-kilometer time trial. Later, he emerged from the Pyrenees Mountains in second overall. In another time trial, this time a 72-kilometer grueler, Hinault took over the yellow jersey for good.

In 1979, Hinault set himself the task of not just winning the Tour, but dominating it. He did so by winning seven stages, but not without a fight. Holland's Joop Zoetemelk also wanted the Tour. By the ninth stage, Hinault found himself 3 minutes, 45 seconds behind Zoetemelk after crashing. Two days later, he took back 36 seconds by winning the time trial at Brussels Millenaire. By the fifteenth stage, he had the yellow jersey. With that jersey came a renewed confidence. With the lead securely in hand and with nothing else to prove, he still went for and took the stage win in the next to last stage of Nogent-sur-Marne and again the next day as the race concluded in Paris on the Champs-Elysées.

After dropping out of the 1980 Tour with tendonitis, Hinault returned in 1981 to race like a hell-bound train, winning five stages. He took the leader's jersey barely a fourth of the way through the Tour at the Nay-Pau time trial and never relinquished it. In defending his jersey, he pushed the event to a new average speed record.

With the 1982 Giro de Italia win already behind him, Hinault began that year's Tour determined to join the elite ranks of those who won both the Giro and the Tour in the same year. After he won the prologue, the remaining stages went uneventfully. Aside from Australian Phil Anderson taking the yellow jersey for eight days (with The Badger always within striking distance), there were no serious challenges to Hinault's quest. With a victory on the final day in Paris, Hinault's tally read four stage wins and 10 days in yellow.

Hinault's 1983 assault on the Tour ended before it began when a bout with tendonitis had him undergoing surgery two weeks after the Vuelta de España. The following year, he signed with the new La Vie Claire team, telling his new boss, "There's a 50 percent chance that I'll get back to the top and a 50 percent chance that I'll never be quite as good as I was before." He nearly made it back that first year, taking second in the 1984 Tour to his countryman and teammate Laurent Fignon.

The following year was to be his last Tour victory. He had already won the 1985 Giro and wanted to come back in the Tour to silence his critics. The 1985 Tour de France proved to be his most difficult. It started fine—he won the prologue time trial. After giving up the yellow jersey, he stayed within striking distance, hidden by the pack and protected by his team. He waited until the ninth stage to Strasbourg to take back the lead.

After the first mountain stage, his lead over his American teammate Greg LeMond had stretched to four minutes. Then he broke his nose in a fall at Saint-Etienne, which made breathing difficult. With his face blackened with bruises, he continued. Controversy came with the mountainous stage to Luz-Ardiden, where Hinault faltered. LeMond grudgingly obeyed team orders to slow his pace on the final climb so as not to put too much time on Hinault. LeMond eventually took second in the Tour, less than two minutes behind Hinault—a greater margin than he had given up on Luz-Ardiden.

Greg LeMond

LeMond's reward came the following year in 1986 when he took the first of his three Tour victories. Hinault had promised to reverse the teammates' roles of the previous year and work for LeMond. Yet on the eleventh day of that Tour, Hinault broke away on the day's tough mountainous route, putting five minutes on the pack. Hinault attacked again on the next day's stage to the ski resort of Superbagneres. He was unable to keep his brutal pace, however, and was eventually passed by a pack of riders that included LeMond. LeMond closed to within 40 seconds of Hinault that day.

Hinault's true intentions became clear a few days later when he again broke away, this time with the only other rider with a realistic hope of overtaking LeMond or Hinault, Swiss racer Urs Zimmerman. That proved to LeMond that Hinault was willing to go for the win, even at the risk of helping the team's rival. The next day's stage was the hardest of the 1986 Tour, with a mountaintop finish on the Col de Granon. Hinault was left behind on the second climb of the day. LeMond responded by attacking, eventually pulling an advantage of two and a half minutes on Hinault and taking the yellow jersey. It seemed that the war between the teammates was over.

The next day they rode together, crossing the finish line at the top of Alpe d'Huez, hand in hand. Yet at that day's press conference, Hinault hinted at ideas of retaking the lead at the time trial in Saint-Etienne. LeMond knew he had to do what few riders could ever accomplish—beat Hinault in a time trial. LeMond was strong and confident that day and, by the halfway point, had bettered Hinault's split time. It all came apart in the second half, though. First LeMond fell in a corner. He immediately remounted, only to discover that the front brake had broken and was rubbing on the wheel. After trying to reposition the brake, he stopped again to switch bikes, losing a total of 25 seconds to Hinault. The yellow jersey was still his, however, and three days later so was the 1986 Tour de France.

The 1987 season started uneventfully for LeMond. Although his enthusiasm for the sport had been soured by the acts of his teammate in the previous year's Tour, he was ready to put that behind him. That March in an early season Italian event, the Tirreno-Adriatico, LeMond was part of a 50-rider pile-up and emerged with a broken wrist. One month later while he was turkey hunting in northern California, his brother-in-law accidentally shot him. The shotgun blast had propelled over 60 pellets into and through his body, nearly killing him with a collapsed right lung and pellets lodged in his kidney, liver, heart lining, diaphragm, and intestines.

Weeks later, he emerged from hospital with over 30 shotgun pellets still imbedded in him. His body had deteriorated greatly, dropping from 151 pounds to a slight 137 with his muscle tone nearly gone. Still, he began the long climb on the road to recovery and racing fitness. Four months after being shot, he had already put back on much of the weight and had even made a couple of race appearances (more for contractual obligation than for competition) when he was once again hospitalized for an emergency appendectomy, ending any hope of salvaging the season.

In early 1988, he seemed to be approaching his form, taking second place in the Tour of the Americas and sixth overall in the Tour of Venezuela. But his season ended in July when problems with his right shin proved to be an infected tendon, which required surgery. No longer considered a favorite, LeMond entered his 1989 season having taken a huge pay cut. He rode well in the early season events in Europe and returned to the United States to race the inaugural Tour de Trump, where he placed an unimpressive twenty-seventh overall.

Health problems continued to plague him throughout the year, until a blood test showed an iron deficiency. An injection of iron supplements during the early stages brought no improvement. But after a second injection about halfway through the Giro, LeMond began to feel like his old self. He felt so good that by the final time trial, he decided to go all out. He finished second that day, 1 minute, 18 seconds faster than the Giro's overall winner, Frenchman Laurent Fignon.

A month later, LeMond began the Tour de France with greater hopes than he could have imagined during the Giro. Although he hoped to merely finish in the top 20 and to perhaps win a stage, in the end he would shock himself and the cycling world by winning his second Tour. He would have to fight Fignon tooth and nail to gain the yellow jersey, but in the end he emerged victorious in the most dramatic Tour de France finish ever.

That he could finish well was apparent in the prologue time trial when LeMond finished fourth, only six seconds off the winner's time. LeMond bided his time during the flat stages of the following days. He met his goal of a stage victory on the fifth day in a 45-mile time trial. It was there that he brought out his secret weapon—an aerodynamic handlebar extension, the type favored by triathletes. This U-shaped bar placed LeMond over the front wheel with his hands spaced closely together to reduce wind resistance. LeMond rode magnificently that day, catching and passing five of the riders who had started ahead of him at one-minute intervals. He put 56 seconds on Fignon that day and put himself in the yellow jersey.

LeMond was unsure if he could keep the lead, especially when the Tour entered the mountains. "I hadn't raced well in the mountains in three years," he later observed. He needn't have worried. He held on to the yellow jersey until the tenth stage, when Fignon attacked on the final climb to Superbagneres. LeMond followed Fignon's brutal pace, and Fignon backed off, only to attack again near the summit. LeMond gave chase, but faltered. "It was a tactical error on my part," LeMond said. "I should have kept my pace and closed in slowly instead of catching right up to him and going into oxygen debt." With a week to go before the finish on the Champs-Elysées, LeMond put himself back in yellow in the second of the three time trials where he beat Fignon by 47 seconds. But Fignon wasn't finished yet. On the climb to L'Alpe d'Huez Fignon led LeMond by 1 minute, 19 seconds, taking back the lead with a 26-second cushion. Fearing that LeMond could make up that slim margin in the final time trial in Paris, in the next stage Fignon broke away in the last 14 miles, winning the stage by 24 seconds and increasing his advantage over LeMond to 50 seconds. The press had written off any thoughts of LeMond making up the time deficit and winning the Tour. Fignon had told LeMond, "You rode a great race. My coach predicted this is the way it would finish, me winning and you second." LeMond quietly accepted Fignon's backhanded compliment. Meanwhile, the American rider had his own ideas of the Tour's ultimate outcome. He had recovered from the efforts of the mountain stages and was feeling strong and confident. Just how strong would be told on the final 15.2-mile time trial on the Champs-Elysées.

That day in Paris, Fignon was every bit as confident as LeMond and dismissed any notions that LeMond could make up 50 seconds over such a short distance. So assured was Fignon that he chose not to use the aerodynamic bars that had helped LeMond so in the previous two time trials. Fignon also eschewed the aerodynamic helmet he had used prior, choosing to let his ponytail flap in the breeze. Fignon began his fateful ride two minutes after LeMond. At the five-kilometer mark Fignon's coach, following in the team car, told Fignon that he was already 10 seconds off of LeMond's pace. Fignon picked up his cadence but by the 10-kilometer mark was a full 19 seconds slower than LeMond. Fignon began to panic. Meanwhile, riding ahead, LeMond kept his phenomenal pace. As he entered the Champs-Elysées he heard an announcement that he had a 35-second advantage on Fignon. He held his effort to the end, posting a time of 26 minutes, 57 seconds—a full 33 seconds quicker than the next best of the day, setting a new record for fastest average speed in a time trial, a record that still stands nearly a decade later. Looking up at the clock, he quickly calculated that unless Fignon crossed the line with a time better than 26 minutes, 49 seconds, LeMond had won the Tour. The magic number clicked by as Fignon was still 200 meters from the line. Greg LeMond had come back from near death just two years earlier to win his second Tour de France by eight seconds—the closest finish in the event's long history.

Greg LeMond endeared himself to the fans when he won his first Tour de France in 1986. When he came back and won it again in 1989 after nearly dying from a hunting accident, LeMond became a legend.

I had the good fortune to go to the 1990 Tour de France, traveling from stage to stage and seeing the race up close. LeMond proved he was a factor in this Tour on the eleventh stage when he took second on L'Alpe d'Huez, moving him up to third overall behind his French teammate, Ronan Pensec, and Italian Claudio Chiappucci. In the following day's time trial, LeMond put in a fifth-place ride while Chiappucci's eighth

Cycology

There's a story of LeMond as a teen-ager writing his life goals in a notebook. Among those goals were to win the Tour de France, the World Championship, and the Olympics. Politics kept him out of the boycotted 1980 Olympics, but he did achieve the other goals. Today LeMond owns a bicycle company and is a race-car driver. His latest goal? To race in the India-napolis 500. Can anyone doubt that he'll someday sit on the starting line in the Brickyard and hear "Gentle-men, start your engines!"

Cycology

Very few Tour de France winners have been much taller than 5' 9". It's a simple matter of the power-to-weight ratio; a smaller rider has less weight to haul up the mountains. Although the six-foot Miguel Indurain never had quite the climbing prowess of a smaller rider, he minimized his time losses to the pure climbers and more than made up for them with his phenomenal power in time trials.

place was enough to put the Italian in yellow. LeMond was able to take a huge chunk out of Chiappucci's lead in the following day's race to Saint-Etienne, where he and four others broke away, allowing LeMond to reduce Chiappucci's advantage to a mere 2 minutes, 34 seconds.

Three days later came the pivotal stage in the Pyrenees, which I was able to witness firsthand. On the lower elevations of Luz-Ardiden, the lead riders finally came through. Two of Greg LeMond's teammates led a small pack. Sitting in their draft was LeMond with Spanish rider Miguel Indurain drafting closely behind LeMond. "Indurain?" I thought. "Isn't he one of his team's sup-port riders? What's he doing near the front?" Little did I know that I was witnessing the setting of the stage for the following year's changing of the guard. Indurain took the win that day, with LeMond only seconds behind. But LeMond had achieved his true goal for the day—he had closed within five seconds of Chiapucci.

The next day, LeMond clinched his Tour de France win in the Lac de Vassiviere time trial. He rode to fifth place for the day, with a time that was 2 minutes, 21 seconds better than Chiappucci's, giving LeMond the yellow jersey by well over two minutes. The next day's ride into Paris was a mere formality; LeMond had won his third and final Tour de France.

Miguel Indurain

So, who was that nearly unknown Spaniard who shad-owed Greg LeMond up Luz-Ardiden in the 1990 Tour? In 1991, he let the world know who he was and what he was capable of doing. Miguel Indurain had always been a strong support rider for his teams. He showed promise in time trials, yet because of his large size (he's 6' 1" tall) and the limits that size placed on his climbing, he was never considered to be a threat for a Tour win. But between the 1990 and 1991 seasons, he shed over 20 pounds, entering the 1991 Tour de France at a svelte 162.

LeMond had been favored that year and started well, taking a close second to Indurain in the stage eight time trial and taking over the yellow jersey the next day. By week three, LeMond seemed destined for a fourth win—that is, until the race entered the Pyrenees and LeMond fell behind. By the second day in the mountains, Indurain had taken over the lead for good. In Paris, it was Indurain in the yellow jersey on the top step of the podium.

The following year, Indurain joined an elite group by becoming only the sixth rider to win the Giro and the Tour in the same year. The predicted Indurain/LeMond showdown never materialized. Although LeMond and Chiapucci did manage to lead a breakaway in the sixth stage, Indurain calmly sat in the pack, biding his time until the Luxembourg time trial. Indurain took over the yellow jersey and would wear it all the way to Paris, winning yet another time trial on the way.

With his second Tour de France win, Indurain established his formula for his next three Tour victories—finish well on the flat stages, ride conservatively in the mountains, and annihilate the field in the time trials. By the end of his career, Miguel Indurain left a legacy of achievements that may never be duplicated: five straight wins from 1991 to 1995. Even after his final Tour in 1996, where he struggled to keep the pace, he was able to add to his list of great achievements by winning the gold medal at the Olympic time trial a month later.

Cycology

Indurain drew some criticisms for his riding method, as well as his understated, enigmatic personality that had the press wondering if he was human. Indeed, he was often referred to as "The Alien" in print not just for his superhuman efforts, but for his detached, unexcited responses to his own exploits.

The Least You Need to Know

➤ The history of bike racing is rooted in the late nineteenth century, when cycling technology was vastly improving.

➤ The first organized bicycle race on record took place outside of Paris in 1868.

➤ The very first Tour de France was held in July 1903.

➤ The only American to ever win the Tour de France was the tenacious Greg LeMond, a true hero of the cycling world.

Chapter 4

Pavement or Dirt?

In This Chapter

➤ There are so many bikes; which do you pick?

➤ Finding the playgrounds: determining where you'll ride

➤ The different flavors of bicycles

➤ Some extra words about mountain bikes

What type of bicycling is for you? Are you psyched to explore secluded trails on a mountain bike? Are you geared up for some mountain bike cross-country racing or the thrill of downhill racing? Maybe you simply want to glide into town on a nice, relaxing bike path or lose yourself on some rolling back-country roads. Perhaps you want to try to get a little exercise into your busy schedule by commuting to work or school. There are many reasons to get on a bicycle, not the least of which is the fun and enjoyment of cycling. It's just about the most healthy addiction you can pick up.

Many riders start out casually in one type of cycling or another and soon find themselves trying other types. That's what happened to me. Hanging in my garage are a road tandem, a mountain bike tandem, a classic old road bike, a modern road bike, a touring road bike, my "good" rigid-frame mountain bike, my "beater" rigid-frame mountain bike that I take when traveling by airplane, a long-travel suspension downhill race bike, a front-suspension dual-slalom bike, a dual-suspension cross-country bike, a "cruiser" replica of a 1930s Schwinn for tooling down to the mini-mart, a 24-inch wheel BMX bike, and a 20-inch wheel BMX bike. There's also a utility trailer that can attach to any of these bikes for hauling camping gear or groceries. Then there's my girlfriend Kathy's bikes. I sometimes picture myself sitting in a room introducing myself to a support group, "My name is Vic, and I'm a bike geek." "Hi Vic!" the sympathetic group answers in unison.

Miles of Experience

When I bought my first "good" road bike in the early '80s, what I really wanted was one of those new mountain bikes. But my friends who were coaxing me into the sport were all road riders who insisted, "You don't want one of those heavy, clunky things. You won't be able to keep up with us." So I spent the next few years riding the road bike. When I finally got a mountain bike, I regretted not getting one sooner. Not that I didn't cherish every road mile I had ridden. I just wish that I'd begun my dirt experience earlier. Since then, I've made up for lost time and then some.

My point is that there's a different bike for every type of cycling (and I have just about all of them). One of those types of cycling could be perfect for you. In this chapter, I'll help you determine what kind of cycling is up your alley and which flavor bike goes with it. Or you could end up like me and want to try them all!

Where Will You Ride?

Before you hit the bike store, consider where you will be doing most of your riding. Will you be pumping over the Brooklyn Bridge to your job on Wall Street in downtown Manhattan, or will you be riding through country roads in France on a planned bike tour? Let's take a look at the options.

Steer Clear

Realize that not every patch of dirt is fair game for you and your knobby tires. Just because your local park has nice green hills that beg to be ridden doesn't mean that the local constabulary will agree with your intended use for the city's well-maintained greenbelt.

City

Some riders yearn to ride mountain bikes, but they live in an urban area and think that road riding is their only choice, especially if riding on off-road trails means a long drive out to the country. But love often finds a way; in New York City, for example, dirt-loving mountain bike riders who avoid city streets like the plague have managed to piece together a variety of dirt riding opportunities using various paths, abandoned rail routes, and parks. If they've succeeded in finding ways to ride on real live dirt in the pavement-and-high-rise capital of the world, chances are that there's suitable dirt in your city, too.

Road riding in an urban area has its own set of challenges. Riding on traffic-clogged streets amid harried motorists is a trial of nerves and luck that I'll leave to demented souls such as bike messengers. Those battle-wise individuals regard the occasional bouncing over the hood of a Buick as a mere fact of life.

Most cities have some less-traveled roads, however. Ask around. Other riders or bike shop employees can offer suggestions on riding options where you're less likely to become a hood ornament. Surprisingly, there is often excellent riding in the heart of major cities. Central Park in New York City is an ideal place for road riders to amass miles around the paved trails and roads. There may be a park, college, or other such area with lightly traveled roads in your area, too.

You can usually find an escape from the tangle of traffic at the edge of most major cities. By tossing the bike into a car and taking a short drive, you can often find quieter, safer roads. If you just can't stand the sight of concrete anymore, get out to the suburbs or the country to flee the hectic existence of the city. If you don't have a car, most modes of public transportation will allow you to bring a bike onboard for free or a nominal fee.

Steer Clear

Be realistic in choosing your in-town road riding routes. Avoid temptations to rationalize: "That bridge isn't that narrow," or "I'll only be in that gang-infested neighborhood for a few blocks." Recognize when it's smarter and safer to avoid certain routes or to begin your ride elsewhere.

Suburbs

Most of the U.S. population lives in suburban cities in the land of tract homes, shopping centers, schools, and strip malls. Road riding in the suburbs can be very enjoyable, especially if you learn the streets that are less traveled. Many suburban towns grew out of farmland and may still have nearly rural roads on the outskirts. Newer cities that sprung up all at once are often planned communities. If they were developed in the 1970s or later, chances are the city planners had the foresight to make the major roads wide enough to include a bike lane.

Some areas are especially bike-friendly. In southern California, for instance, many of the rivers have paved access roads that have been converted to bike paths. Other cities, such as Boulder, Colorado, have built specific bikeways. With such bike paths and bikeways, it's possible to ride long distances and not have to compete for road space with motorists. These types of systems also greatly increase the safety and practicality of using a bike as everyday transportation.

For off-road mountain biking opportunities, most suburbs have undeveloped public land nearby. Nearly any undeveloped wooded area, ridge, or waterway will have dirt roads or trails. Unless you live in Kansas, there's probably some highland nearby. Where are the TV and radio transmitter towers for your area? Chances are good that they're on some local peak, hill, or butte and that there's at least a dirt road to the top. Hopefully, there's a narrow trail, too.

Many cities have dirt trails or greenbelts running through town. Often they follow former railroad routes or were specifically planned for the recreation of the population. Make sure that it's legal to ride these trails, and be considerate of pedestrians and equestrians.

Country

Riders in rural areas are the most fortunate of all. Living in an area surrounded by quiet roads, a maze of off-road trails, and *fireroads* is the dream of many cyclists. In these areas, environment doesn't dictate the type of riding riders choose, and they can enjoy any type of riding that suits their liking or mood.

Cyclebabble

Dirt roads in forests and undeveloped lands are often called **fireroads**, because they were built to provide access to firefighters. They also serve as firebreaks.

I live in the mountains and have a variety of riding options. That's how I ended up with a garage full of bikes. I didn't always have all these riding choices. I used to live in the suburbs and did my best to enjoy my road bikes and mountain bikes with the roads and terrain from which I had to choose. My move to the mountains was directly related to wanting more and better places to ride. And I'm not unusual—I've known many other people who got into bikes, realized what a rut they'd gotten themselves into in a city, pulled up stakes, and moved out to where the air is clean and the stoplights are few. This fate may also befall you. Consider yourself warned.

Is there anything as elegant as a 20-pound machine capable of turning human leg power into speeds of over 30 miles per hour?

(Almost) All There Is on Two Wheels

Now that you've given some thought to where you plan on rolling those rubber treads, it's time for the fun part. Let's talk bikes!

Road Bikes

Most people are familiar with road bikes. People of and around the baby boomer era often call them 10 speeds. Older folks refer to them as English racers. Young boomers and Gen-Xers know about Schwinn Varsities. Of course, modern road bikes usually have 16 or 18 speeds, and the term English racer may seem odd considering that, compared to the Italians and French, England has been a minor player in bike racing history. The name probably stems from the 1950s, when Raleigh and a few other U.K.-based companies exported light-weight, low-priced road bikes to the United States Schwinn Varsities, introduced in the 1960s, were certainly bomb-proof and sturdy, but they're 40-pound anchors compared to the modern 20-pound road bikes.

Road bikes have been called "the most efficient means of human-powered transportation." Think about it; 20 pounds of metal and rubber can transform leg power to speeds of 20 or 30 miles per hour. Although few people in the United States use bikes for daily transportation, our country is still the world's largest bicycle market. Why? Fun, plain and simple. Bikes are a kick.

Touring Bikes

In the 1970s and early 1980s, before the mountain bike boom, the big surge in bicycling was touring, which means traveling self-sufficiently by bike with all the necessary camping gear and such carried on the bike. Touring never went away, and has regained popularity in recent years.

With its racks and panniers (saddlebags) packed with provisions and camping equipment, a touring bike is prepared to take on the world.

A touring bike doesn't look much different from a road-racing bike. A touring bike has a slightly longer top-tube and chainstays for increased stability. It has fittings on the fork and the rear of the frame for bolting on luggage racks and usually has space for three or more water bottle cages. The wheels and tires are wider and sometimes have

Cyclebabble

Panniers are bicycle saddlebags. Typically they have built-in hooks and buckles for securing them to the bike's luggage rack. They usually have handles for easy carrying off the bike.

27-inch wheels instead of the 700-centimeter wheels found on race bikes. The reason being that 27-inch tires can usually be found in any small town in a department store or hardware store, but 700-centimeter tires are usually only found in bike shops. When touring through a remote area, you want to be able to find a replacement tire whenever necessary.

The luggage racks are designed to work with saddlebags called *panniers*, which are removable for packing. When these packs are filled with camping gear, food, and clothing, and a sleeping bag and rack box are placed atop the rear rack, the cargo load might be 30 to 50 pounds. To handle that weight, a touring bike is equipped with a wider range of gears than a race bike, with the lowest gears being far lower.

Triathlon Bikes

During the triathlon boom of the mid-1980s, many athletes took up cycling as part of the sport of "swim-ride-run." In the beginning, a triathlete competed aboard standard road-race bikes. Well-heeled amateurs and sponsored pros soon began racing triathlons aboard time-trial road bikes. Without the long, stodgy traditions of road racing, the triathlon world soon developed bikes that were technologically superior to road racers' time-trial bikes. Aerodynamic handlebars were the first major development, followed by aerodynamic wheels and other advancements. Road racers have since adopted many of those developments.

A highly specialized triathlon bike with aerodynamic wheels and handlebars and a forward riding position gives triathletes that competitive edge.

Miles of Experience

A major factor for Greg LeMond in winning the '89 Tour de France was the triathlon handlebar he used, which put his arms ahead of him in an aerodynamic tuck similar to the hands-in-front position used by speed skiers. Although these bars had been popular in triathlons for a couple of seasons prior, pure road racers had ignored them. The year after LeMond's win, this type of aerodynamic handlebar was seen on the time-trial bikes of nearly every Tour de France racer.

One feature that is unlikely to catch on with road racers is the riding position of today's triathlon bikes. Realizing that a triathlete would become less fatigued with a bike-riding position that more closely duplicated the athlete's running position; triathlon bikes have a very upright, forward position.

Cyclocross Bikes

For decades, European road racers have used an off-road cycling sport called cyclocross for winter training. They use bikes similar to standard road bikes, but with knobby tires, mountain bike-type cantilever brakes, and a less-steep steering angle for stability. Cyclocross races are held on dirt hillsides and are usually about an hour long. The classic elements of cyclocross are as follows:

➤ Mud

➤ Sometimes snow

➤ Racers having to run with the bike hoisted on a shoulder on sections that are too steep to ride

Cyclebabble

Travel: A term related to bicycle shock absorber systems. It refers to the amount of upward movement the wheel can move in response to hitting a bump. The more travel a front or rear suspension system has, the bigger the bumps it can handle.

Although cyclocross has but a small cult following in the United States, the bikes have a unique, multiuse appeal that is starting to catch on. With its cantilever brakes, a cyclocross bike can double as a touring bike. The knobby tires may be too narrow and fragile for a cyclocross bike to be used as a mountain bike, but they do great on dirt roads and smooth trails. Replace the knobby tires with road tires, and a cyclocross bike is also a fine road bike. For a rider with a limited budget (or garage space), a cyclocross bike can suit many uses.

Before mountain bikes, there was cyclocross. Cyclocross racers compete on a dirt course aboard road bikes equipped with narrow, knobby tires.

Mountain Bikes

After 15 years of riding mountain bikes, I still find myself being surprised at the capabilities of these wonderful machines. Watch a mountain bike race on TV sometime, and you'll be amazed at how these bikes can take terrain far rougher and steeper than you can imagine. Yet of all the millions of mountain bikes that have been sold in the United States, very few are ever ridden on dirt. Most of them are ridden mostly on city streets. It's sort of like the soccer mom's sports-utility vehicle that has never and will never be put into four-wheel drive, much less go off-road. And that's too bad. There's nothing like the fun of exploring a mountain, valley, or river trail. The feel and exhilaration of following a twisting trail is very similar to skiing or motorcycle riding.

A mountain bike is truly in its element when it's on dirt. Practically any dirt roads or narrow trails are within the capabilities of a mountain bike. I'm often amused at the reactions of non-bike people I encounter on the trails. Many are astonished at seeing what kind of terrain a mountain bike can handle.

Mountain bikes have developed into four distinct types: cross-country, downhill, freeride, and slalom.

Cyclebabble

Cross-country bike: A bike intended for cross-country racing or off-road riding. Weight is a concern in cross-country racing, so most bikes of this type have only front suspension, although some racers and riders compromise weight for the added control and comfort of rear suspension, too.

Most mountain bike riders ride cross-country-type bikes with front suspension and a rigid frame.

1. A *cross-country bike* is the most common type of mountain bike. It's the type used for most riding and for cross-country racing. Most cross-country bikes have a fork with front suspension with a shock absorber system offering two to three inches of wheel *travel*. Some will also have rear suspension for even greater comfort and control, but most will be rigid in the rear. Low weight is important for a cross-country bike because the rider pedals it up hills as well as down.

2. A *downhill bike* is a highly specialized piece of equipment. Although as recently as 1992 a downhill racer's bike was no different from a cross-country racer's bike, downhill bikes have since evolved into purpose-built machines that are of little use for anything but downhill racing and riding. With front and rear suspension, six inches or more of wheel travel, wide tires, and *disc brakes*, these bikes can be ridden over terrain that most people would have trouble walking over. The high weight and high gearing of a downhill bike makes them impractical for riding uphill. Downhill riders and racers rely on chairlifts or trucks to get them to the tops of the hills.

Cyclebabble

Disc brake: A type of braking system consisting of a metal plate attached to the wheel hub and a caliper system that presses brake pad into both sides of the plate. The resulting friction causes the plate and subsequently the wheel to slow or stop. Disc brakes are more powerful than standard bicycle brakes.

43

With front and rear suspension providing six inches of wheel travel, a downhill bike can be ridden down the roughest, nastiest terrain imaginable.

With a bit less front and rear suspension than a downhill bike and just a little more weight than a cross-country bike, a freeride bike offers the best of both worlds.

Cyclebabble

A **downhill bike** is a bike used for downhill racing over rough, steep courses. A typical downhill bike has front and rear suspension with six inches or more of wheel travel. Downhill bikes usually have a chain-retention device and often have disc brakes.

3. *Freeride bikes* emerged as downhill riders realized that a 40-pound downhill bike is only good for going downhill. Many riders wanted a bike that was light enough to ride like a cross-country bike, but with the plush suspension and powerful brakes of a downhill bike. The freeride bike emerged with about four inches of wheel travel and a lighter frame and components. Freeride bikes weigh about 28 to 30 pounds. They're a bit tougher to get up a hill than a cross-country bike, but they are much more fun when you're bombing down the other side.

4. A *slalom bike* is used for dual-slalom racing, which is a form of racing that pits two racers against each other on duplicate, side-by-side, twisting courses filled with motocross-style jumps and turns. This type of racing was patterned after slalom ski racing and uses the same types of flags to mark the corners. A typical slalom bike uses a very small frame, a front suspension fork with about four inches of wheel travel, some type of chain-retention system, and a short stem with high-rise handlebars.

Cyclebabble

Freeride bike: A mountain bike with four to six inches of suspension travel and a full range of gears. It is meant for riding down rough terrain, similar to that found on a downhill course, while still being able to ride up hills.

Riding a Mountain Bike on the Road

There's a reason so many people buy mountain bikes even though they have no intention of ever going off-road. The upright riding position and big, cushy tires of a mountain bike give a far more comfortable ride than a road bike. The suspension forks and rear suspension systems that cushion the bumps, ruts, and rocks of a dirt trail can make the ripples and irregularities of paved terrain virtually disappear.

Cyclebabble

Slalom bike: A type of mountain bike used for dual-slalom racing. Generally a slalom bike has a small frame and only front suspension.

Miles of Experience

A few years ago, I was at California's Mammoth Mountain for a national championship mountain bike race. Parallel to the road to the race site from town is a pair of twisting, single-track trails. One is for riding up to the race venue, and the other is for riding down. One day as I rode a mountain bike up the up trail, I saw a rider on a road bike on the down trail. This guy was flying! Curious as to who could ride so fast on a bike so unsuited to the terrain, I cut over to the down trail and gave chase. It took over a mile of riding at my race pace to catch the guy. It turned out to be Casey Kunselman, a former national championship downhill contender who won several major events in the late '80s and early '90s. The difference in skill between riders like Casey and average riders like me is amazing. Casey's bike didn't even have knobby tires!

Currently there's an increase in the sale of road bikes. It's partly attributed to the large number of people who bought mountain bikes for riding on the road and then realized how much slower a mountain bike is compared to a road bike. That difference in speed is mostly due to the tires. Several factors cause off-road tires to have much more drag than road tires:

1. Knobby tread has much more rolling resistance than smooth tread.

2. Mountain bike tires are at least twice as wide as road tires.

3. Mountain bike tires are usually only inflated to 35 to 50 psi (pounds per square inch); road tires are inflated to 80 to 120 psi.

A road bike's tires are usually 700 centimeters in diameter by 20 to 25 centimeters wide (roughly, one inch wide). A mountain bike's tires are 26 inches in diameter and 1.9 to 2.35 inches wide. There are one-inch wide, high-pressure, road-tread tires designed for mountain bike wheels that can make a mountain bike ride like a road bike. The quick feel, acceleration, and increased top speed of these tires can be a real treat for someone who's been riding heavy, wide, knobby tires on the road. The ride with these narrow tires may be uncomfortable to some riders, however. For these folks, road-tread tires that are 1.5 to 1.75 inches wide are a good solution. The ride is much more comfortable with these tires, and you give up little of the speed of the one-inchers. Not a bad compromise.

Cyclebabble

A narrow off-road trail is called a **single-track**. The name is used to differentiate these trails from the wider trails used by motor vehicles called **double-track**, named for the side-by-side trails left by the vehicle's wheels.

Riding a Road Bike in the Dirt

Taking a standard road bike with smooth tread tires on an epic off-road adventure may sound like a recipe for disaster. Although I'm not suggesting that anyone take a road bike on a rock-strewn, root-infested, *single-track*, a road bike can do surprisingly well on smooth dirt roads. The rider just needs to be very careful about taking the corners. If you install a set of cyclocross knobby tires, a road bike can do quite well, although it still won't corner as well or ride as smoothly as a mountain bike. The steering is quicker than a cyclocross bike, and bumps and ruts need to be carefully avoided, but the performance can be better than most riders would guess.

The Truth About Hybrids

Shortly after the beginning of the mountain bike boom, manufacturers introduced hybrid bikes, which are a cross between a road bike and a mountain bike with a mountain bike's upright position and wider wheels and a road bike's narrower tires and higher gears.

Hybrid bikes were originally touted as bikes that could do it all, on-road or off-road. However, when it comes to a sheer performance comparison of hybrids versus pure road bikes or mountain bikes, it's obvious that hybrids do neither job well. There is a job, however, that hybrids do exceptionally well. If you're looking for a bike that's comfortable and easy to ride, if you want something to ride to the corner market, around town, for leisurely spins in the park, or to commute to work or school, a hybrid is an ideal steed. Hybrids deserve consideration for riders unconcerned about riding in the dirt or speeding down the road.

A hybrid bike is a comfortable and practical choice for running errands and casual-paced pedaling around town.

The Least You Need to Know

➤ The riding opportunities in your community may be more diverse than you realize.

➤ Living in an area suitable for many types of riding may be hazardous to your bank account and surplus garage space, but it's a lot of fun.

➤ Few mountain bikes are ever ridden on off-road trails.

➤ For casual, around-town use, a hybrid can be a better choice than a road bike or mountain bike.

➤ By switching to knobby tires your road bike can handle light off-road use. And putting narrow road tires on your mountain bike can turn it into a pavement speed demon.

Part 2
A Shiny New Bike

Getting a new bike is like getting a new pet. What kind of dog is right for you: a little cute ball of fluff, a huge mass of muscle and fangs, or something in between? Just as choices in man's-best-friend are dependent on the owner's personality, needs, and preferences, so are choices in bikes.

Before picking out a brand-new bike and bringing it home to stay, you need to first consider such things as what kind of riding you want to do, where you'll ride, and how much you'll ride. Just as bringing home a new canine companion also means getting all of the accoutrements (leashes, tags, dog beds, and so on), cycling involves buying a lot of extras. To enjoy your shiny new steed, you'll need an assortment of accessories, including a helmet, water bottles, and several tools. This section will help you to choose the bike that's right for you. It will also help you in getting to know that bike and choosing all of your needed accessories. This section will help you to save money on this cycling stuff, too.

Chapter 5

Knowing the Thingie from the Doodad: A Part-by-Part Description of Bicycle Components

In This Chapter

➤ Road bike components

➤ Mountain bike components

➤ The different materials used for frames

➤ Keeping the wheels on the bike

It has been said that the frame is the heart of a bike. If that's the case, then the various components are the other organs. After all, what good is a heart without kidneys, lungs, a spleen, and all the other assorted guts? Read on to learn about the various bits and pieces that work together to bring a bike to life.

Road Bike Parts Parade

Among very serious cyclists, road bike brand names are worn like badges of honor and defended almost to the death. The rider with a De Rosa swears that no bike is worth riding unless it's touched by Ugo De Rosa himself. Eddy Merckx riders don't understand how anyone could ride something not designed by the five-time Tour winner. If you speak badly of most any brand, there's bound to be a staunch supporter who'll squeeze you into the curb the next time he or she gets the chance. Before you can engage in any bike snobbery yourself, however, you need to learn the components that hang on some of cycling's favorite framesets.

Brakes

High-quality road bike brakes went relatively unchanged from about the mid-1960s to 1990. During that time most were of the "side-pull" design. A side-pull brake consists of a pair of aluminum calipers joined together at the center with a pivot that also serves as a bolt to mount the brake to the frame or fork. The cable passes through an extended portion built into one of the arms, and then attaches to the other arm. Pulling the brake cable causes the cable to pull on the brake arms, causing them both to pivot and push the brake pads into the rim. These brakes work and are fairly easy to install and adjust.

In 1990 Shimano introduced the dual-pivot road brake. They're actuated from one side with an interconnected cable in much the same way as side-pull brakes. These more modern brakes—as the name states—have two pivots, one for each brake caliper. Placing these pivots a couple of inches out from the center allowed each caliper to be made longer for more leverage and more powerful braking action.

The two biggest names in brakes, Campagnolo and Shimano, both use similar dual-pivot designs for greater leverage and stopping power. While you'll still find side-pull brakes on lower-priced road bikes, they're becoming rare as lower-priced dual-pivot brakes become available. Tektro has a version of the concept that has become popular for entry-level-priced road bikes.

One last word on brakes. These days most road bikes have brake levers that have built-in gear-shift levers. Most of Shimano's and Campagnolo's wares have combination brake/shift levers called STI and ErgoPower, respectively.

Crankset

The two arms that the bike pedals are attached to are called the *crankset*. The crankset is a very important component. That's where all the power to propel the bike is generated. You want to have a crank that's as strong and stiff as possible. Inflex or bending of the crank as you pedal translates into wasted effort and power. Again, the big names in this arena are Shimano and Campagnolo (or Campy, as it's sometimes called). Campy has long been known for strong, beautifully sculpted cranksets. Its philosophy has always been to make cranks stiff; if that means adding a few grams of weight, so be it. The Chorus and Record cranksets are two of the best-looking, best-performing cranksets to ever grace a bike. They're good enough for top pros, so they're definitely good enough for you. On entry-level bikes you'll find cranksets made by Sugino or Cyclone. While a strong rider or pro would notice the difference in stiffness of these budget cranksets as compared to a top-of-the-line crankset, as a novice rider you're not likely to feel much difference.

A couple of years ago, Shimano introduced a new DuraAce crankset that borrowed the hollow-spindle, bottom-bracket concept from its successful top-of-the-line XTR mountain bike group. Shimano also went with an XTR-like set of hollow crankarms.

Derailleurs

The *derailleurs* are the mechanical devices that guide the chain from one sprocket to another when the rider shifts gears. They were invented by Tullio Campagnolo (yes, him again). Although Campy still has a good share of the market, Shimano's DuraAce derailleurs have been popular among amateur and pro racers. Sachs also has a small but loyal following. And Mavic has introduced an electronically controlled derailleur that is intriguing. That French company had an earlier version a few years ago that ended in failure. So far the new version seems promising. So far, SRAM, the American company with a line of mountain bike derailleurs, hasn't entered the road bike market. My guess is that they're at least considering a move to pavement.

Some of the derailleur names of the not too distant past seem to be only memories: Galli, Simplex, Huret, and SunTour all have fallen victim to the giants of Italy and Japan.

Cycology

The debate of the merits of Shimano versus Campagnolo components is as heated today as it was over 25 years ago when Shimano introduced its top-of-the-line DuraAce road component group. Campagnolo fans are quick to point out that no racer has ever won the Tour de France aboard a Shimano-equipped bike. Although Shimano has occasionally held a slight technological advantage over Campy, Campy always catches up.

Forks

The portion of the bike that fits around either side of the front wheel and attaches it to the frame is the *fork*. Many frame builders also make steel forks specifically for their bikes—steel has nice vibration-absorbing qualities. Even those builders will sometimes use forks built by other companies, however. Carbon-fiber forks, such as those made by Kestrel, Kinesis, and Look, are popular optional choices. Carbon fiber can be even better than steel at absorbing vibration, giving a bike a very nice ride that's easy on the hands. Some riders, however, prefer the stiff ride of aluminum forks. They're willing to put up with a harsher ride in exchange for a bike that doesn't flex beneath them—flex that they feel robs them of power and efficiency. For myself, I prefer the comfort of a steel or carbon fork. I figure any possible slight loss in efficiency to a little flex is far outweighed by the hand-fatigue factor of a too stiff fork.

Pedals

Over a hundred years ago, cyclists realized that they could put more power to their wheel if their feet were firmly attached to the pedals. This arrangement allows a rider to pedal in a complete circle, applying power through the entire arc rather than continuously pushing down. During that time, the system of toe-clips and straps was devised.

A *toe-clip* is a metal or plastic cage that attaches to the front of a pedal and loops over the toe of a rider's shoe, extending up to the top of the instep. At the end of the clip over the instep is a metal loop. A leather strap with a spring-loaded buckle is threaded through this loop and through the pedal. When the rider places a foot all the way into the toe-clip, a slotted cleat comes into position over the rear plate of the pedal. The plate slips into the slot, and when the leather strap is pulled tight, the foot is firmly secured into the pedal.

Toe-clips and straps do have their drawbacks. When the straps are pulled tight, the rider usually goes down with the ship in a crash because there's little time to dislodge your feet from the straps in order to get off the bike before it hits the ground. Another downside to toe-clips and straps is that after a long day of riding with them your toes can go numb, and your feet will often ache the next day.

Miles of Experience

When I began riding my first real road bike with my first pair of real cycling shoes with real cycling cleats and toe-clips, I was very impressed with the huge power advantage of my new footwear over my old tennies. Locking my feet firmly in place was something that took quite a while to master, however.

I remember one instance where I stopped at the top of a hill waiting for a riding buddy. Not wanting to "clip out," I slowly circled while I waited. When he came into view, I stopped and balanced for a moment to say something snide and promptly fell over, rolling onto my back with my bike still attached to my feet and the wheels pointing to the sky. My friend nearly fell over, too—from spasms of uncontrollable laughter. When the new "clipless" pedals came out I rushed to be among the first to have them.

The popularity of toe-clips began waning in the mid-'80s. Virtually all racers and performance-oriented riders now use clipless pedals that click into place. They work very much like a miniature ski binding. These systems use metal or plastic cleats that bolt to the bottom of a cycling shoe. The cleats have small protuberances that mesh with the pedal to hold the rider's feet solid. To "click out," a rider merely needs to twist his foot, rotating the heel outward as though he were squashing a bug. The ease of getting in and out of these pedals gives them a huge advantage over toe-clips and straps. They have quickly caught on as riders have recognized their advantage in safety and comfort.

People who are long to this sport will remember the big, white, blocky clipless pedals that Bernard Hinault used back in '85. Those prototype Look pedals that everyone lusted for would hardly garner a glance in this the day of a dozen or more clipless road pedals. The large, triangular cleat used by those old looks is still around and is compatible with Campagnolo pedals and some of Look's pedals. Wellgo has a new road pedal that uses a cleat very similar to the old Look. Time pedals, introduced a couple of years after Looks, have a loyal following. Time pedals work only with a Time's own uniquely shaped cleat.

Shimano's SPD system, with a smaller cleat originally designed for mountain bike use, has been quickly adopted by the road bike crowd. Casual riders like being able to walk normally without sliding on the cleats. Today, a majority of road pedals use a SPD-type cleat. Ritchey makes a very nice and light road pedal, the Logic Road Pro. Wellgo has a few road models, and many riders simply use mountain bike pedals. Still, Shimano has taken the next step with its SPD-R system that, you guessed it, uses a completely new type of cleat.

Gear Shifters

Although some lower-priced road bikes still have shift levers mounted on the down-tube, most bikes have shift levers built right into the brake levers. When the shift levers-on-the-brakes idea was first introduced, many dismissed it as a gimmick. But it takes only one ride to realize the advantages of being able to shift without letting go of the handlebars.

Shimano introduced its STI Dual Control system on pro bikes in 1990. Campagnolo followed suit with its ErgoPower a couple of seasons later. Sachs has a version that's nearly identical to the Campy parts for use with Sachs derailleurs.

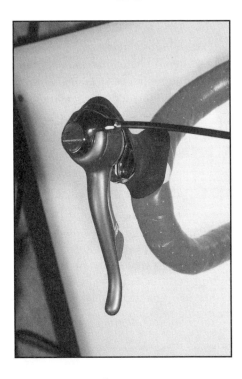

There's a lot going on in a Shimano STI lever assembly. On this right lever assembly, the big lever pivots back to push the brake, and it also pivots sideways to shift to a lower gear. The small lever behind the brake lever pivots inward to click to a higher gear.

Shimano's Road Bike Pecking Order

In each of the previous component categories except for forks, Shimano was named as a major player. It's the rare bike that doesn't have equipment from this Japanese giant, so here's a rundown of Shimano's road bike component groups:

➤ **300 EX:** The beginning level of performance-oriented parts. This stuff isn't glamorous or feather-light, but it works well.

➤ **RSX:** Features of higher-priced Shimano groups at a moderate price. The STI system with the shift levers built into the brake levers is an option, as is a triple crankset with three chainrings for a selection of ultra-low gears.

➤ **105-SC:** The beginning level of race-quality components. STI is available, and you can get 105-SC with either eight- or nine-speed cogsets. Appearance-wise it's very similar to Ultegra, with just a little more steel and plastic to trim costs.

➤ **Ultegra:** Used by some pros, the performance differences between Ultegra and DuraAce are minimal, with Ultegra weighing only a few ounces more. It comes in nine-speed, and the STI system is standard. You also have the option of three chainrings.

➤ **DuraAce:** Used by pros and folks with big budgets. The finish and quality is state-of-the-art. And Shimano finally realized that not every DuraAce customer is a top racer—you can now get DuraAce with three chainrings for people with more dollars than leg strength. Have a few extra bucks to spend? Get the special DuraAce Twenty-Fifth Anniversary Group with special laser etching. It comes in a commemorative case complete with numbered certificate. Cool.

Cyclebabble

When shopping for a bike, you may hear the term **gruppo**. This is merely a shop employee using the Italian word for "group." Back when Campagnolo ruled the bicycle component market, the cycling community referred to all component groups as gruppos.

Campagnolo's Rise Through the Ranks

Campy considers all of its parts to be made for serious racers. The question is, how serious? Since there's no set Campy retail price list for component groups, I looked at some of the custom bikes currently available and took an average of what the extra charges are from the frame builders to building a bike with the following Campagnolo groups. As you can see, Campy parts aren't cheap. But there's no disputing Campy durability and performance. And of course there's the beauty of Campy parts, too, which adds to the aura of the Campy mystique.

Group	Cost
Veloce	$500
Campy positions this group alongside Shimano's 105-SC. Veloce has ErgoPower (shifters built into the brake levers) and the bearings throughout the group are virtually identical to the higher-priced groups. The appearance is pure Campy with lot of polished parts. Veloce weighs a bit more than the current cream of Campy's crop, but performs as well as the top-line stuff of a few years ago. Need three chainrings for the hills? That's an option.	
Athena	$800
This group is aimed at Shimano's Ultegra market. Again you have ErgoPower, smooth Campy bearings, and your choice of two or three chainrings. The finish work is a step above Veloce, some of the parts are nearly indistinguishable from Chorus in appearance and performance. Only a metallurgist or gram scale would know for sure.	
Chorus	$1,000
Campy claims that in quality of materials Chorus is comparable to Shimano's DuraAce. The parts are elegant and attractive to say the least. And their performance is certainly at least on par with DuraAce. ErgoPower is standard; three chainrings is an option.	
Record	$1,580
According to Campy, the Record gruppo goes one step beyond Shimano's best. No corner is cut in Campy's quest to make this set of parts the most attractive and best performing money can buy. ErgoPower is standard, and you can get three chainrings if you want.	

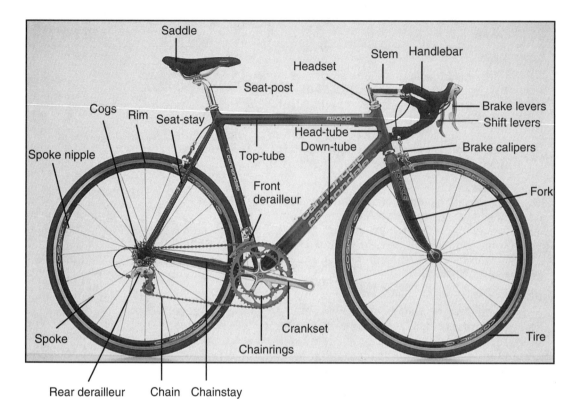

Anatomy of a road bike.

Mountain Bike Parts Parade

When you pick out a new bike, whether it's a Schwinn, a GT, or a McFurd, the brand name usually only refers to the frame. Other manufacturers usually make the rest of the parts, from the handlebars and saddle to the shifters and brakes. Making sense of all these parts can be difficult. So lean back and read on, we're going to discuss hardware.

Brakes

Prior to 1996 nearly all mountain bikes used "cantilever brakes." Cantilever brakes consist of a pair of brake arms with each one bolted onto either seat-stay. Cantilever brakes use two cables. One called the "straddle cable" connects both brake arms together. The other cable runs from the brake lever to the center of the straddle cable. The brakes are actuated by pulling the brake lever, which pulls the cable, which pulls the main cable, which pulls the straddle cable, causing the brake arms to pivot toward one another, driving the brake pads into the rims.

Since Shimano's introduction of *V-Brakes* a few seasons ago, brakes of that type have practically taken over the mountain bike market. Characterized by a pair of long, vertically mounted brake arms cable-actuated through an aluminum tube, V-Brakes have excellent stopping power. The brake arms are much longer than cantilever brake arms, giving these brakes much more leverage and, consequently, more power. Other manufacturers have adopted the concept (I won't say *copied* because there's a French patent for a similar design going back to the 1920s), but because Shimano has copyrighted the term "V-Brake," other similar brakes are referred to as long-leverage brakes or linear-pull brakes. The most successful emulators of the concept, Avid and Tektro, both have their brakes on many brand's bikes.

Cyclebabble

Although the name **V-Brakes** is a Shimano trademark, the term is often used to refer to any brand of brake that uses long brake arms and actuation via a side-mounted cable. With the arms about 25 percent longer than the arms of the cantilever brakes in use prior, V-Brakes have greater leverage and stopping power.

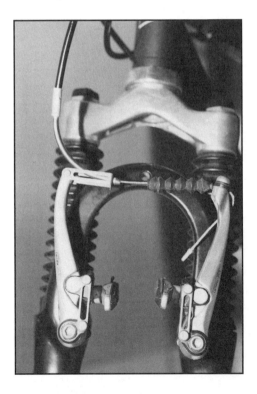

When Shimano's V-Brakes first became available in 1996, they set a new standard of stopping power for cable-actuated brakes. Since then, several other companies have adopted the concept, including Avid, Dia Compe, Tektro, and others.

As downhill racing continues to grow, such companies as Hayes, Hope, Formula, Rock Shox, and Magura have answered the call for powerful disc brakes. While disc brakes offer tremendous stopping ability, they're also very expensive, especially considering

59

that you'll need other new parts to go with a disc brake. You'll need a new hub that's designed with mounting brackets for the disc itself. If you get a hydraulic disc system you'll also need to get a hydraulic brake lever (your existing brake lever can be used with mechanical disc brakes). And lastly, not all frames or forks have the necessary mounting brackets to be compatible with disc brakes. So you may need a new fork. Until recently you might have also needed a new frame or to have yours modified by installing a disc brake bracket. However, Hanebrink Designs recently introduced the DU-1 system, a bolt-on assembly that allows a rear disc brake to be used on any bike. Cycle Therapy has a similar design, both consisting of a disc bracket mounted to a rod that connects to the existing brake bracket.

For the ultimate in braking power, disc brakes are the undisputed king. This Hope disc brake handles the stopping duties on my mountain bike tandem. Other brands of disc brakes are Coda, Hayes, and Magura.

Cranksets

If you remember from earlier in this chapter, the two arms that the pedals are attached to are together referred to as the crankset. This part is in many ways the heart of a bike. Stiffness and light weight are the goals of a crankset engineer.

Cyclebabble

The term **CNC-machined** refers to a manufacturing method whereby a computer-controlled machine carves a part out of a solid piece of material.

Most production bikes come with Shimano cranksets, although quite a few have Sugino cranksets. Sugino also makes cranksets for other companies, such as Ritchey and Specialized. Cannondale's Coda division has a new crankset design called Tarantula that shows promise.

A few seasons ago there was a proliferation of custom *CNC-machined* cranksets—cranks that were made by a machine that basically carved them out of a hunk of aluminum. The huge number of CNC-crank manufacturers has tapered off as consumers began realizing that some of them were poorly designed and made and that few offered any advantage over the forged cranks made by the long-established crank manufacturers. Most of the remaining CNC cranksets are good, although it's tough to beat the strength of the forged cranksets of Shimano and Sugino.

Derailleurs

The two big manufacturers for mountain bike derailleurs are Shimano and SRAM-GripShift. Shimano practically owns the derailleur market. Although a few companies make CNC-machined derailleurs (Precision Billet, Paul's Components, White Industries), these limited-production derailleurs are very expensive and are valued mostly for the novelty of running unique parts. For sheer performance, they're no match for Shimano or SRAM's products.

Shimano's XT rear derailleur is among the most popular.

The U.S.-made SRAM-GripShift derailleur is challenging Shimano's hold on the derailleur market.

Forks

Most mountain bikes come equipped with suspension forks. These days, cross-country mountain bikes have 60 mm to 70 mm of wheel travel, thanks to their improved suspension forks.

Freeride bikes typically have about 100 mm of wheel travel. All of the major manufacturers have forks for this market. Some use dual-crown designs similar to downhill forks, but with regular dropouts that work with a quick-release axle instead of motorcycle-style axle clamps. That's handy since you can remove your front wheel with just a flip of the quick-release lever instead of having to loosen eight axle-clamp screws and pull out your axle as you do on most pure downhill forks.

Rock Shox aimed its Judy 100 fork at the four-inch wheel travel freeride market. This 3.7-pound, single-crown fork is a popular choice for those riders who fit between the suspension cross-country crowd and the freeriders.

Long-travel downhill forks provide wheel travel ranging from 100 mm to 150 mm. The long-travel market also has brands that specialize in forks with 6, 7, and even 10 inches of wheel travel.

The giant of mountain bike suspension is Rock Shox, a company that introduced its first mountain bike suspension fork back in 1989. Manitou entered the suspension wars in '91, as did Italy's Marzocchi. White Bros. came out with a line of forks in 1997. K2's linkage fork has a loyal following, as does its new standard fork. Forks such as Foes, Bombshell, Bullet-ZZYZX, Hanebrink, and Risse are purebred racing equipment.

Cyclebabble

A **roadie** is a cyclist who rides a road bike.

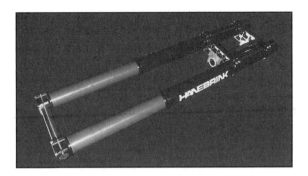

When Hanebrink Bicycle Components introduced this stout, triple-clamp, six-inch travel fork at a 1995 bicycle trade show, the major fork manufacturers called it "too much" and "too big" and generally dismissed it as a gimmick. However, by the beginning of the following race season, virtually all of the major fork builders had prototype forks similar to the Hanebrink fork for their sponsored pro racers.

Pedals

The huge surge in the popularity of mountain bikes was happening at about the same time that clipless pedals were being introduced to the road bike market. The mountain bike world had already improved upon road toe-clips, making them out of flexible plastic to withstand the slamming abuse that bent metal toe-clips. It didn't take long for mountain bikers to appreciate the advantages of the new clipless pedal being used by the *roadies*.

For over a hundred years, this was the state-of-the-art in pedals technology. Slip your foot into the cage so that the rear plate of the pedal aligns with the slotted cleat mounted to the bottom of your shoe, pull the leather strap tight, and your foot ain't coming out. This "ain't coming out" feature led to the development of clipless pedals.

The days of toe-clips and straps for mountain biking are practically gone. Clipless pedals with their easy-in, easy-out features and solid, locked-in security are the pedals of choice. Shimano dominates the clipless pedal market, but there are several other brands from which to choose, such as Wellgo, Ritchey, Scott, Coda, Exus, and Icon. These pedals are all similar in features and design to Shimano pedals. Look also has two off-road models that have enthusiastic fans. One model, the Moab, looks a lot like the early Shimano SPD but with a larger overall body. (It's the only pedal that three-time mountain bike champion Tinker Juarez will ride.) The other Look model, the Moab II, uses urethane bumpers instead of springs in its mechanism and has never widely caught on with the mountain bike public.

*On clipless pedals, the
small steel cleat engages
into the pedal mechanism
like a ski binding. Step in
and press down to engage
the mechanism; twist the
heel outward to disengage.*

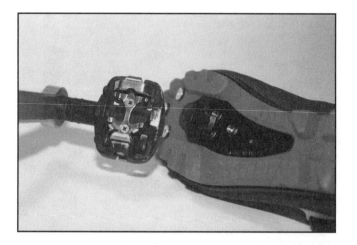

Time's off-road pedals have an equally loyal following. Its pedals are renowned for their ability to function well in muddy conditions. Riders with bad or sensitive knees also like the amount of "float" or free lateral movement that these pedals offer. Most other brands either hold a rider's foot rigidly in place or allow only a few degrees of lateral movement, causing any imbalance in the pedaling stroke to be transferred to the knee joint. Since they allow a rider to slightly adjust the foot position throughout the pedal stroke to avoid side forces, Time pedals can be easier on a rider's knees.

*Downhill racers and riders
who ride very technical
terrain like the platform
area of these DH clipless
pedals for times when
being clicked in isn't the
best option. They're nice
for riding to the store in
sandals or tennies, too.*

In the last few years, a new type of clipless mountain bike pedal has come to the forefront: pedals with a clipless mechanism surrounded by a large platform. Downhill racers and riders who enjoy severe terrain favor this type of pedal. The advantage is that in situations where a rider wants to have a foot free, he or she can click out and still have a surface on which to rest that foot. These pedals offer a big advantage on trails that have sharp turns and require a rider to extend the foot on the inside of the turn.

Gear Shifters

The two main players in mountain bike gear shifters are Shimano and SRAM-GripShift. Shimano's shifters, called RapidFire, use a trigger and a button for upshifting and downshifting duties. GripShift uses a system consisting of twist-grips similar to motorcycle throttles. You turn the grip until it clicks to upshift or downshift.

Both systems have their advantages and drawbacks. When a Shimano RapidFire system gets a little out of adjustment (as all shifters eventually do), choosing the right gear might take an extra click, and then the derailleur might be positioned a bit toward the next gear, causing the chain to rub and clatter. When a GripShift system gets out of adjustment and doesn't shift to the next gear, a rider can usually get it to go with just an extra little twist without ending up with chain rub or chain clatter.

Another important comparison is the ability to shift and brake at the same time. With Shimano RapidFire, a rider can brake with the middle finger while shifting gears with the index finger and/or thumb. The throttle-twisting motion of a GripShift system makes simultaneous shifting and braking nearly impossible. A GripShift user needs to anticipate his or her shifts and make them before braking. That's not too difficult in a racing situation where the rider knows the course, but in real-life riding, it sometimes leads a rider to find himself or herself in the wrong gear.

When it comes to shifting over a number of gears all at once, GripShift holds the advantage over RapidFire. With GripShift, a rider can twist all the way from the big cog to the small cog (or vice versa) with one quick turn of the grip. The chain and cogs might not like it, but the shifter can handle it. With RapidFire, a rider can downshift three gears at once with a hard push on the thumb button, but upshifting requires one pull of the trigger for every gear. Going from the big cog to the small cog will take seven pulls (eight with a new nine-speed system) instead of one quick turn of the wrist.

Cycology

For large manufacturers of bike parts, CNC-machining is a cost-effective way to make prototype parts for testing and development. When it comes time for production, however, the designs are forged, a process that uses heat and high-power presses to make a part. The reason for this is that CNC-machined parts are carved from a solid chunk of billet aluminum that has a grain structure. If oriented in the wrong direction, that grain on a part, such as a crankset, could possibly break. Forging parts is very expensive in small quantities, but in mass production, forging is far more economical than CNC-machining. No broken parts mean no returns. That's not to say that all CNC parts are inferior—there are some excellent parts available: cranksets, brakes, brake levers, hubs, and stems. And there's no denying the appeal of the high-tech "prototype" look of a CNC part. It's just that pound per pound (or ounce per ounce), a forged part can be made stronger.

A twist of the grip is all it takes to shift with GripShift.

Push the button or pull the trigger to shift with Shimano RapidFire.

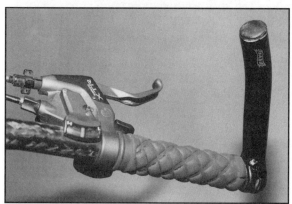

Shimano's Mountain Bike Pecking Order

As with road bikes, Shimano is a major player in the mountain bike component market. Here's a rundown of Shimano's mountain bike component groups:

➤ **Altus:** Budget-priced, entry-level bikes. You'll find lots of steel and plastic parts, very little aluminum. This stuff works well, is strong and durable, but compared to the high-priced parts it weighs a ton.

➤ **Acera-X:** Entry-level bikes. Still lots of steel and plastic, but a little more aluminum than Altus for a slight drop in weight. The performance is actually pretty good. It's a good set of work-horse parts.

➤ **Alivio:** The beginning level of performance-oriented parts. This is where the family resemblance to the high-priced groups stars. Still lots of plastic and some steel, yet there's more aluminum than with the lower groups, making it only slightly heavier than the STX parts above it on the price ladder.

➤ **STX:** Features of higher-priced Shimano parts at a moderate price. The overall shape and basic designs of STX parts are very similar to the component groups above it in price. Some of the cost savings of STX were had by using steel or plastic in place of the aluminum found on the better stuff. So while STX parts may work nearly as well as the higher-priced parts, they weigh more and will wear out quicker.

➤ **STX-RC:** STX with a few refinements. STX-RC is nearly identical to STX, but with a higher level of finish. Performance is identical to STX; cosmetics are a step above.

➤ **LX:** The beginning level of race-oriented parts. The performance is very near to the quality of the next in the line-up XT or the top-of-the-line XTR. However, the material quality of LX parts isn't quite as good as XT or XTR, so LX parts are a bit heavier and not quite as durable.

➤ **XT:** Used by some pros. This is almost as good as the top-of-the-line stuff. The overall finish isn't quite as pretty, but the performance is nearly identical.

➤ **XTR:** Used by most pros and folks with big budgets. A beginner doesn't need it, but there's nothing wrong with having the best if you can afford it.

Mountain bike anatomy.

A Material World

A variety of materials are used to build bike frames. What type of construction is right for you? Steel? Aluminum? Carbon fiber? Balsa wood? The ride, weight, feel, and price of a bike are all affected by what *tubeset* material the frame builder uses in making the bike. The following sections cover the advantages and disadvantages of the most popular frame materials.

Cyclebabble

Most bike frames are built by joining together metal tubes. The tubes that go into making one frame are referred to as a **tubeset**.

High-Tensile Steel

High-tensile steel is the most common frame material of lower-cost bikes in the $200 to $350 range. Although it's just a step above plumbing pipe, hi-ten (as high-tensile steel is frequently called) has a lot going for it. It's strong, relatively cheap, and simple to weld. Hi-ten does have its drawbacks, though. It's heavier than more expensive steel alloys, and it doesn't do much for quelling road vibration.

Chromoly

Further up the steel price ladder is chromoly. There are many grades of chromoly so you'll find it on bikes ranging from $300 or so on up to custom bikes costing $3,000 to $4,000. This blend of steel, chromium, and molybendum is lighter than hi-ten. Because it's much springier than hi-ten or aluminum, it gives a better ride. Although chromoly is heavier than aluminum, many riders favor the resilient ride of chromoly over the super-stiff ride of aluminum and are willing to have a slightly heavier bike in exchange for the more comfortable ride.

The weight and ride of chromoly are both improved with butted tubes, which are tubes that have thicker walls at the ends. This puts the strength where it's needed at the *weld* (or, in other words, that point where the frame tubes were joined by welding, while the rest of the tube has thin walls for more resilience. If a frame sticker says *butted tube*, that means that only one end of the tubes are butted. *Double butted* means both ends are butted; *triple butted* means there are three distinct wall thickness over the length of the tubes.

Other Steel Alloys

In recent years, steel alloys have been introduced that are a step beyond chromoly in strength, weight, and riding resilience. These wonder steels contain one or more of the following:

➤ Manganese

➤ Vanadium

➤ Titanium

Falling under this super-steel category are Reynolds 853, Dedacciai tubesets, Ritchey Nitanium, and some of Excel's tubesets. Frames made from these materials will cost more, but the ride and feel of bikes made from these super-steels is well worth the added expense if you plan on spending a lot of time in the saddle.

Titanium

Titanium is great stuff for building bike frames. It's also very expensive, it's rare to find a titanium bike for under $2,000, and some cost up to $5,000 or $6,000. Although it's one of the lightest metals, it also has a fatigue life up to five times greater than steel or aluminum. Titanium is very corrosion-resistant, so most frame builders using it leave their bikes unpainted because they can (and to show off what the bike is made of!). Finally, the ride of titanium is among the best in the business. It has the resilience and liveliness of a premium steel frame. I once heard a rider call his titanium bike, "The best steel frame I've ever ridden. One that I know I won't break." There's a lot of truth to that statement.

Along with titanium's big numbers in tensile strength and hardness, however, come big numbers in expense. A titanium tubeset costs much more than even a premium set of steel tubes. Titanium is also very hard on the tools used to cut and miter it, and the welding process requires special equipment. All that adds up. Expect to pay much more for a titanium frame than for a steel or aluminum frame.

Carbon Fiber/Thermoplastic

Some call carbon fiber and thermoplastics the future of bicycles. With the variety of ways that these materials can be used, they may be right. Carbon construction offers a variety of rides and characteristic and specific strengths, depending on how many strands are used, what direction they're wrapped, what shapes are formed, and what type of bonding agent is used.

Carbon got a bit of a bad rap in the early '80s, mostly due to some frames that had thin carbon tubes bonded into aluminum lugs. Flexy frames that bowed beneath the rider was a common complaint. And some frames suffered from delaminated lugs—that is, the glue failed, causing the cast aluminum fittings to come away from the frame tubes. Now, with better bonding epoxies and purpose-built tubes, some bikes of that type of construction perform admirably.

Probably a better application of the material are the *monocoque* carbon frames. Construction methods vary, but most of these frames are made by laying

Cyclebabble

Monocoque (pronounced *mon'-o-cock*) refers to a construction method whereby a structure is not made up of subcomponents that are joined together, but rather the structure consists of one singular shape. The front sections of a Trek Y-bike or Cannondale Raven are examples of monocoque construction.

sheets of carbon-fiber fabric into the two sides of a mold. Airbags are placed between the sandwiched layers. The lugs for the head-tube, bottom bracket, and dropouts are positioned before the mold is put under tremendous pressure and heat. After curing, out comes the smooth, swooping shape of a monocoque carbon frame. Frames of this type are usually noted for their lateral stiffness for efficient transfer of pedaling power, and excellent vibration damping for a comfortable ride.

Thermoplastic frames are made by wrapping a silicone bladder with a mixed weave of carbon fiber and nylon resin. The resulting shape is then placed into a mold for heating and pressurization. Both carbon and thermoplastic manufacturing are very expensive, so expect to hand over some big bucks for bikes made of these materials.

The front section of this Cannondale Raven is an example of monocoque construction.

Aluminum

Although aluminum is among the lightest metals, it's also a relatively soft metal. To make an aluminum frame as strong as other materials, a builder must use more material. That's why most aluminum frames are built with much bigger tube diameters than a steel or titanium frame. A fundamental rule of engineering is that when the diameter of a tube is doubled, strength is increased eight times. That's how some aluminum frames are able to get into the titanium weight range and still be plenty strong.

Price-wise, aluminum bikes start out at about the price of plain chromoly bikes. Premium aluminum bikes, such as those made of Easton tubing, are priced at and above the costs of premium steel, but still below titanium.

Aluminum is characterized as having a very stiff ride. Some riders, especially hard-core racers, look for this trait in a bike. They like the feel of having every bit of energy transferred into forward motion, not going into flexing the frame.

Most aluminum frames are made of 6061 grade aluminum. This grade has excellent weldability. Finished frames go through a heat-treating process that takes them almost to the melting point before being quenched in a liquid coolant. The other common aluminum, 7000 series, is slightly harder than 6061. It does not, however, need to be heat-treated to such a high temperature as 6061, so warping induced by heat-treating isn't as much of a concern.

A Word About Wheels

With the exception of department-store bikes with wheels held on with axle nuts, most modern bikes use quick-release levers to attach the wheels. These simple devices can secure a wheel to a bike every bit as tightly as axle nuts can, yet the wheel can be removed without tools—all it takes is a simple flip of a lever.

As wondrous as quick-release levers are, every year riders are injured when an improperly used quick-release lever pops open, causing a wheel to come loose. These accidents all could have been prevented had the rider followed the directions on quick-release lever use provided in the owner's manual. In all of my years of riding, I've never seen a properly secured quick release pop open.

Probably the biggest misconception on the use of a quick release is that the wheel is attached by twisting the lever as a sort of built-in wrench or single-sided wing nut. Although a wheel attached in this manner may seem secure, in reality a bump or jolt can, and often does, knock the wheel lose.

Cycology

Easton is now offering an aluminum-alloy tubeset using a secret formula from the former Soviet Union. The U.S. military was long puzzled by the performance of Soviet aircraft and at the ability of Soviet missiles to blast through ice caps and not lose their welded stabilizer fins. After the Cold War, it was revealed that Soviet aerospace had been welding structures that the United States would have made with CNC-machined parts. How did the Soviets do this? They added the element Scandium. When added to aluminum alloy, Scandium reduces the size of the grain and inhibits the material from recrystallizing when welded. Easton's newly developed Scandium alloy produces a bike frame that's 25 percent lighter than a titanium frame and has a ride that's less stiff than aluminum, yet not as flexible as titanium.

Miles of Experience

Seventy-three years ago, race bike wheels were held on with oversize wing nuts. Tullio Campagnolo, an amateur racer, was in a race called the Gran Premio della Vittoria. It was snowing, and Tullio got a flat. He hopped off and tried to turn his wing nuts only to learn that they were frozen in place. Frustrated, he uttered in Italian, "Bisogno cambio quelcossa," which in English means, "Something must change." Tullio cobbled up the first quick-release skewer in his workshop shortly after that day. The rest, as they say, is history.

Follow these simple instructions, and you'll be able to ride secure in the knowledge that your wheels will remain where they belong—on your bike.

When a quick-release lever is in its open position, the lever hangs free. On many quick-release levers, the word "open" is printed onto the lever and will face outward when the lever is in its released position.

To secure a quick-release lever, pivot the lever toward the hub. You should start to feel tension midway through the swing at the point where the lever is horizontal.

If you feel tension before the lever is horizontal, slightly loosen the nut on the other side of the axle from the quick-release lever. If tension begins after the horizontal point, tighten the nut slightly.

After you've adjusted the quick-release nut properly, pivot the lever all the way until it stops. It takes quite a bit of hand pressure to completely close the lever. Some levers have the word "closed" printed on the lever that will face outward when the quick-release lever is in its secured position.

The Least You Need to Know

➤ Most bike companies only make bike frames. Other companies make most of the rest of the parts.

➤ Don't believe your Shimano-loving friends that badmouth GripShift, and don't believe your GripShift-loving friends who badmouth Shimano. Both of these mountain bike shifting systems work well.

➤ Every frame material has its advantages and disadvantages.

➤ Used properly, a quick-release mechanism will hold your wheels as securely as axle nuts.

Chapter 6

At the Bike Shop

In This Chapter

➤ Department stores are for clothes and housewares, not bikes

➤ Bicycle shops: the place to buy

➤ Getting the most bike for the fewest dollars

➤ Making use of used bike lots

➤ Helpful things to know

Although in many ways a bicycle is a toy (and a wonderful one at that), it's also a very complicated piece of equipment. These days, most people own some type of expensive equipment. Some people are into computers, others have all the latest ski equipment, and music lovers often have thousands of dollars tied up in stereo components. Even the avid angler can go crazy on gadgets for the ultimate in fishing. How do expensive bits of hobby hardware relate to bicycles? People knowledgeable about computers, skis, stereos, fly-casting, and so on don't shop for the gadgets of their passion at K-Mart.

So where do you think the informed bicycle shopper looks for a new bike? That's right, at the local bike shop. For not much more money than the bicycles found in the toy department at Bargain-Mart, a real bike shop offers bicycles that are better made and much safer to ride.

Penny-Wise, Bike-Foolish

I know what some of you are thinking, "This guy is a hard-core bike geek used to riding all the latest high-end bikes!" True. But it doesn't take a bike expert to recognize that when compared to a "real" bike, it's no bargain to save a few bucks on a heavy department-store bike with poor shifting, woefully inadequate brakes, and cheesy components. Invest a little more and get a bike that works properly, and you'll probably end up riding more. A well-performing bike is just more fun to ride.

Miles of Experience

Many times during my days behind the bike shop counter I'd have customers bring department-store bikes to the service department saying, "It doesn't shift right, the wheels are wobbly, and brakes don't really work." It was hard to resist replying, "Yeah? No fooling!" Sure, we'd adjust their bikes and make them work better. But no amount of fiddling could ever make them work as well as one of our low-priced entry-level bikes. The funny thing is that after buying a department-store bike and paying for an hour or two of repair fees at a bike shop, those customers had as much invested in their bikes as the cost of one of those entry-level bikes. And their department-store bike *still* didn't work as well.

The Sum of the Parts

Although some volume discount retailers (those places that sell margarine by the pallet and toilet paper by the ton) sometimes carry decent-quality equipment, as do some sporting goods stores, poor assembly is the norm. Ask any bike shop mechanic about the assembly quality of bikes from volume discount retailers. Most will relate stories of brand-new bikes with improperly installed parts, inoperable shifting, dangerous brakes, and poorly positioned saddles and control levers.

Few of those high-volume vendors have sales staff knowledgeable on the technical aspects of modern bikes, such as using the gears or proper bike sizing. It stands to reason that folks with a real passion for bikes will usually end up in the bike industry, not working at MegaPrice.

Riding Without a Warranty

Here's the most interesting fact of all about buying a name-brand bike from a discount retailer: Although these bikes are identical to the ones at your local bike shop, they're often missing one important component—a warranty. That's right. The manufacturer's warranty on these bikes is likely null and void.

Because virtually none of the major bike manufacturers will sell bikes to volume discount retailers, those retailers often resort to gray market tactics to obtain their merchandise. Their usual scam is to have an overseas importer purchase a large quantity of bikes from a manufacturer and then divert them to the volume discounter. Virtually all name-brand bike manufacturer's warranties require that an "authorized dealer" assemble their bikes. Because the volume discounter is anything but authorized, the warranty is effectively terminated. If, when asked about a warranty, the discount retailer replies, "We'll fix it," remember that the same vice-grip mechanic who assembled it in the first place will likely be the one to work on it again.

The Helpful Folks Behind the Counter

Buying a new bike isn't like buying a new toaster. You don't just take it out of the store with no plans of ever returning. No, you're looking at a long-term relationship. If you're new to bicycling, you're going to need a lot more than just your shiny new bike. You'll need a helmet, bike shorts, gloves, frame pump, spare tubes, H_2O bottle, bottle cage, and so forth. Take it from me, the list is practically endless. Plus, your new scoot (that's bike geek speak for bicycle) is going to need a break-in adjustment and service throughout its life. Choosing the right dealer can make this whole process more enjoyable and economical.

I recommend looking for a shop that's involved with local races and rides, offers regular group rides, and has staff who are also enthusiasts and racers. Sure, Clem and Zeke's Lawnmower, Bike, and Key can give you as good a price on a bike as any other shop, but does Clem know how to rebuild a suspension fork or shock? Can Zeke properly fit a customer with the right size road bike? Do either of them know where the best local roads are or what tire works on the local off-road trails?

There's a lot to be learned about a shop by how it's kept. Look for a shop with clean bikes, orderly displays, and a clean, well-organized service department. Sloppy, haphazard displays and service departments are indications of sloppy, haphazard work habits.

Look around, visit a lot of shops, and ask your friends. The right shop and the right bike are out there waiting for you. Go find them and join the fun!

Saving and Spending Tips

Shopping for a bike is a lot like shopping for a car; bikes are one of the few retail purchases where bargaining is still widely accepted. You'll get the best deal if you make it clear that you plan on buying on the spot. Some shops give the sales staff the freedom to "get out the sharper pencil" (give a discount) in putting together deals. At smaller shops, try to deal with the owner or manager. Letting them know that you mean business and are also going to buy a load of accessories is a big help in getting a discount. But don't expect a drastic slash from the manufacturers' suggested price. The markup on bicycles is nowhere near the markup of most other retail items.

You can save more dollars by getting a leftover from the previous model year. Bikes have model years just like cars. And just like car dealers, bike dealers don't like to see any noncurrent models hanging around. Most bikes don't have many earth-shattering changes between their '98 and '99 models. Some models are even exactly the same; maybe only the paint or stickers are different. Or maybe the '99 road bike is an 18-speed instead of a 16-speed (or 27-speed versus a 24-speed mountain bike) or some other upgrade. There might even be enough savings in getting a leftover '98 to be able to upgrade to '99 specifications and still come out ahead. Ask your dealer about noncurrent inventory. You may not get your preferred color, but you can easily save big bucks.

Steer Clear

Beware of salespeople who try to talk you into buying the wrong size frame. Often the bikes leftover from the previous year are either the very large or the very small sizes. Getting the wrong size bike isn't a bargain at any price (see Chapter 7, "The Right Bike for the Job," for more on frame size and seat height).

Steer Clear

If a used bike seems to be priced too low to be true, the bike is probably hot. Look for the bike's serial number. If the number has been filed away, get the heck out of there. Ask questions, such as "Where did you buy the bike?" Be suspicious of sellers who offer evasive answers or don't seem to know much about the bike.

If you're planning on doing some upgrading and parts changing, it's smart do it right away, especially if the dealer says the bike you want is still in the box. That way there shouldn't be any additional labor charges for installing your preferred changes. Since they need to assemble the bike any way, it shouldn't make any difference if they're bolting on the stock parts or your upgrade choices. Most dealers will trade out the unwanted parts and give you some allowance toward your upgrades. You'll save time and money in the long run.

Above all, the most important thing to shop for is a caring, competent dealer who'll take the time to explain your new bike and how it works. There's no value in saving a few bucks by buying at a dealer who doesn't take the time to make sure that all your questions are answered. Look for the dealer who insists that you get the right size bike that's also right for your uses. Competent help after the sale will go a long way toward making up for a few extra dollars in price. It's hard to put a dollar value on service.

What About Used Bikes?

It's possible to save a lot of money by buying a used bike over buying new. But as with any used purchase, there's also the possibility of getting ripped off. Doing your homework and knowing about new bike prices and price points of components can help you spot the good deals. Recruiting a knowledgeable friend—perhaps the friend who conned you into this sport in the first place—is also a big help.

Newspaper classified ads or your town's local bargain-shopper paper are a good resource for used bikes. Cycling is like many other sports or hobbies. Newcomers sometimes get all excited and buy all the equipment and accessories and then lose interest. Finding someone who has gone this route in cycling can be a real gold mine. I've seen people get nearly new bikes for half the original retail price. As a bonus, the seller will often throw in bike accessories, such as a helmet, tools, cyclometer, pump, seat-bag, and gloves.

Bike races can be another source for used bikes because racers often take advantage of those gatherings of bike folks as a good opportunity to sell a bike. Be aware, however, that a racer's old equipment is often pretty beat up by the time a racer retires it.

With any used bike, be aware of the following:

Cycology

Although buying a used bike from an expert-level racer may sometimes not be a good idea, used bikes from sport racers and beginner racers can be real bargains. Some racers have more money than talent or desire and get new bikes every year.

➤ A good cleaning and paint touch-up can make a bike look new, obscuring the fact that the parts are worn out.

➤ A test ride is an absolute must.

➤ Anyone who won't let you take the bike for a spin around the block probably has something to hide.

During a test ride, check the shifting; does it click right into gear or does it sometimes take an added nudge or an extra click? It could need just an adjustment, or the derailleurs or shifters could be worn out. Worn derailleurs usually have excess side-to-side play. Grasp the lower cage of the rear derailleur and check to see whether the cage has more than a millimeter or two of free movement side-to-side. Check the front derailleur by grasping the cage (over the big ring) and pulling outward. Again, more than a millimeter or two of free play is an indication of excessive wear.

Look at the teeth on the chainrings. Looking down at a tooth from above, you should see that it's nearly the same thickness all the way down. If it looks as though its width has been filed to a point, then the chainring is probably worn out. Inspect the cogs for pitting on the chrome plating and for bent teeth or obvious wear.

Flip the bike upside down and grasp a wheel by the tire and apply side-to-side movement to check for free play at the hub. Free play indicates that the hub is worn or out of adjustment. Next, spin the wheels. They should spin silently and smoothly. Crunchy sounds indicate that the hubs at least need fresh grease and possibly bearings. As the wheel is spinning, watch the rim at the brake pads to see whether the wheel is straight. A little wobbling can usually be fixed; big bends or an out-of-round wheel are another story.

To check the bottom bracket, use your hands to lift the chain off the chainrings. Rest the chain inside of the small ring so that the cranks can turn freely. Check for free side play and then spin the cranks. They should spin silently, smoothly, and for several rotations. If they sound crunchy or if they bind and coast to a stop after only a few rotations, then the bottom bracket either needs servicing or replacing.

To check the headset, lift the front of the bike and turn the handlebars. Do they rotate freely and quietly? Position the bars as if the bike were heading straight ahead. If it feels as though there's a notch and the bars sort of click into the straight-ahead position, then the headset is worn out and needs to be replaced.

A few worn parts don't necessarily mean that a used bike is a bad deal. You just have to factor in the cost of parts and labor to the price of the used bike and the price of a new one. You may still come out ahead with the used bike.

Miles of Experience

Having a valuable bike stolen is aggravating and heart-breaking. Increase your chances of getting your bike back by taking down the serial number. It's usually located on the bottom bracket shell, on a rear dropout, or on the head-tube. Put that number, your receipt, and a photo of the bike in a safe place. Check your homeowner's insurance or renter's insurance to see if it covers your bike. Read carefully, because some policies only cover up to a certain dollar amount. Finally, write your name, address, and phone number on a piece of cardboard with a note reading, "If this bike was brought in by anyone other than me, it's stolen." Then laminate the cardboard with some clear packing tape and tuck it inside of the bike's seat-tube. I've heard of more than one bike owner retrieving a long-lost bike after having a mechanic discover such a note.

What About Mail Order?

Pick up nearly any bicycle magazine, and you'll find several advertisements for mail-order companies selling everything from helmets and inner tubes to complete bikes and suspension forks. The topic of mail-order companies is hotly debated in the bicycle industry. On one hand, they're the only alternative for cyclists living in outlying areas with no bike shop in town. On the other hand, catalogs can never top the hands-on customer service you get at a bike shop.

Mail-order companies often offer unbeatable prices. With their huge buying power, mail-order companies are often liquidation houses for a manufacturer's overstock. Several times I've seen prices on parts and accessories in mail-order ads that are lower than what a dealer pays when buying from their distributors. For parts or accessories that you or a friend can install, buying from a catalog may be the best deal price-wise. (Just don't expect your local bike shop to be very enthused about installing them.)

You can find some real bargains on complete bikes through mail order as well. When comparing prices, realize that when a mail-order house ships a complete bike it comes in a box "partially assembled" with the brakes and shifters already installed and adjusted. Usually it's up to the buyer to install the wheels, pedals, handlebars, seatpost, and saddle. If those chores are within your mechanical ability, fine. Realize, too, that a new bike will need a break-in service or two during its first few months of use as cables stretch and cause the brakes and shifters to go out of adjustment and spokes seat-in, causing the wheels to need truing. That service is usually included with the purchase of a bike from a bike shop, but they'll charge $25 to $45 for doing it on a bike purchased elsewhere. Factor in that cost before ordering a bike from a catalog.

Whatever you do, don't use your local bike shop as a resource for mail-order shopping. Having the shop's employees serve you in finding a shoe size or determining parts compatibility so that you can then mail order them is poor etiquette. How would you feel if someone used you and your livelihood to give business to your competitor?

Miles of Experience

One weekend at the bike shop, a young woman came in saying she was thinking about clipless pedals and shoes. I spent a good hour showing her several models of each and helped her try on a few different brands of shoes and explained the importance of proper cleat installation. She left without buying, indicating that she'd be back after payday. A few weekends later she walked in with a pair of pedals and a pair of new shoes under her arm. Assuming she had been in on one of my days off, I spent the next hour installing and setting up her cleats. When we were finished, she commented, "I'm sure glad I tried these on before I ordered them." "Ordered them?" I asked. "Yeah, I got them mail order. Well, thanks a lot," she said as she rode off. I stood there speechless. She had stolen two hours of my time. Shoplifting is a crime. Morally, I think that time-lifting is, too.

Ten Things the Bike Shop May Not Have Told You

Most bike shops are run by folks who are cycling enthusiasts themselves. Generally, they do a good job of explaining the basics to their customers. However, there is much they can miss in the short time it takes to write up your purchase and help you out to your car. Following are 10 things to keep in mind when purchasing your newly beloved bike:

1. Tires lose pressure over time. Rubber is semi-porous, so all tires, even car tires, seep air. It's just not as noticeable on cars because of their greater air volume. Add air to your bike tires every few weeks. If the bike sits for several weeks and goes flat, try reinflating the tires before deciding to replace the tubes.

2. There are two different types of valves found on tires: *presta valves* and *shrader valves*. Inner tubes with the small, skinny type of valve are called presta valves (some folks call them French valves). Shrader valves are the same type used on car tires and can be inflated with a standard bike pump or at the gas station. Most bike pumps can also do presta valves; unscrew the pump head and flip over the rubber grommet and valve depressor and presto, presta pump. Or get an adapter that screws onto a presta valve so that it will work with a shrader pump. Adapters are only a buck.

3. A kickstand on a mountain bike is not a good idea. Riding off-road means bumpy trails and hard jolts. Rough terrain can make a kickstand come down, dig into the dirt, and pole-vault the rider into the weeds. Kickstands also aren't pleasant things to tangle with in a crash. You can easily prop up your bike against a rock or tree. Just be sure to rest it by the rear wheel. If you rest it by the front wheel, the handlebar will turn and the bike will fall. Or just lay it on the ground to begin with, only not on the right side—you want to keep the chain out of the dirt, and you don't want to bend the derailleurs.

Steer Clear

Do not put a kickstand on any bike that will be ridden off-road. Kickstands are engineered to stay in their up position under the normal bumps of road riding, but they can come down under the harder jolts of off-road riding. Many riders have been injured when a kickstand has come down and dug into the dirt. If your bike has a kickstand and you like using the bike for off-road riding, remove it or at least secure it up for off-road forays.

4. Bike shorts are meant to be worn by themselves with no underwear. Wearing undies will only cause the very problems that bike shorts are designed to prevent: chafing and bunched-up fabric wedging itself into areas best not discussed at the dinner table.

5. Bikes with stickers that say "Designed in America" are *not* American-made. That red-white-and-blue sticker displayed on so many frames only means that some product manager sat in a U.S. office when he chose the color scheme out of a Taiwan manufacturer's catalog.

6. The grease on a new bike's chain isn't chain lubricant. A layer of light grease is applied at the factory for rust prevention. It's too thick to lubricate properly, and its stickiness attracts grit. Use a rag and citrus solvent (it's biodegradable and not as toxic as petroleum-based solvent) to take it off and then apply real chain lubricant.

7. Replace chains often. Chains are cheap compared to buying a complete drive-train. You can get much longer life out of the cogs and chainrings by replacing the chain every 500 to 1,000 miles. Don't wait too long. A fresh chain on worn teeth will skip and grind.

8. Helmet adjustment is crucial. A poorly adjusted helmet offers little protection and could cause injury. The shell should fit snugly; add thicker sizing pads if needed. It needs to sit level on the head, not tilted back like a bonnet. The plastic side pieces on the strap should be adjusted to rest right under your ears. The chinstrap should be tight; you shouldn't be able to tilt the helmet side to side.

9. Mountain bikes and road bikes aren't BMX bikes. The sport of BMX has been around for nearly 30 years, so when adults decide to get their first new bike since childhood, chances are those adults have some experience with bikes meant to be jumped and slammed about. Nearly any bike shop employee can tell tales of riders with BMX experience getting their first mountain bike and coming back that same afternoon with pretzeled wheels. With the exception of downhill race bikes, mountain bikes aren't meant for big aerials and sideways landings. Think about it, even though they're bigger and have far more equipment, mountain bikes and road bikes often weigh less than BMX bikes. So obviously they're not built as hefty. BMX maneuvers on a mountain bike need to be done as lightly and gingerly as possible—or not at all. BMX maneuvers on a road bike are downright stupid and will likely result in immediate wheel failure.

Miles of Experience

Few people realize that inner tubes are slightly porous and will lose air over time. Leave a bike sitting for more than a few weeks, and the air will seep out of the inner tubes. Every spring at the bike shop, we'd have folks bring in bikes with flat tires, saying, "It was okay when I put it away last October." If they weren't in a hurry, we'd inflate the tires and check them again the next morning. It's amazing how many people were pleasantly surprised to see "No charge" on their work order.

10. Yes, you want toe-clips or clipless pedals. Having your feet attached to the pedals will give you more power by enabling you to pedal in a continuous circular motion instead of just mashing down. Those using plain pedals run the risk of having their feet bounce off the pedals over rough trail. Intimidated by the thought of not being able to get out of the pedals? Try half-clips that fit just over the toes and don't have straps.

Mastering toe-clips or clipless pedals isn't that difficult. Getting out of toe-clips is as simple as pulling your foot straight back. Clipless pedals are even easier, just rotate your heel out as though you were squashing a bug. Set the spring tension to a low setting for your learning period. Consider going to a park or school to try them on some soft grass.

The Least You Need to Know

➤ For slightly more money, a real bike shop offers bicycles that are better made and much safer to ride than those found in the sporting-goods department at Bargain-Mart.

➤ A used bike can be a bargain, but know what you're looking at before forking over your greenbacks.

➤ Mail-order houses often have low prices, but don't expect your local bike shop to be thrilled about installing your mail-ordered parts.

➤ Don't use your local bike retailer as a means of trying on shoes, clothing, and so on and getting the sizes so that you can then buy them mail order. It's poor bike etiquette.

Chapter 7

The Right Bike for the Job

In This Chapter

➤ What you need to know to choose the right size and type of bike for you

➤ Choosing a mountain bike

➤ Setting the saddle height

➤ Women's bikes

➤ Don't let your bike let you down

If you've been through Chapter 4, "Pavement or Dirt?" you already know whether you want a road bike, mountain bike, or hybrid. The question remains, "How can I choose the right bike for my riding and budget?" Here are the three main factors to consider:

1. How often will you ride?
2. What is your budget for a bike?
3. How important is the pride of ownership factor?

I'm not going to go into a direct comparison of brands and models. There are so many brands and models that it would take a book at least as large as this one to do so. And such a comparison probably wouldn't help you much in choosing a bike anyway. The differences between different brands at a given price point are extremely slight, such as proprietary design features from one brand to another. Of course, each brand touts its approach as being "the best." Think about it, who makes the best car, the best TV, or the best wine? All the brands have their features that make them favorites, but are they "the best"? It's the same with bikes. Pick a price point and look around. There aren't any "bad" bikes as long as you buy from a bike shop (see Chapter 6, "At the Bike Shop").

Picking a Road Bike

If you are a road rider who plans to ride only once or twice a month, a low- to mid-priced bike ($400 to $600) will serve you nicely. With advances in bike technology, bikes in this price range perform as well as the more expensive bikes of 10 years ago, and the performance difference between these bikes and current high-end models isn't as great as you may think.

If you step up in price to the $800 to $1,200 range, the performance is even closer to the top-of-the-line models. In this range, the shifting systems and braking systems are lower-priced versions of the top-of-the-line components. The basic designs and functions of these budget-minded parts are nearly identical.

Cycology

If your personal finances dictate getting a budget model bike or a used bike, don't be discouraged about joining in on group rides or even racing. The performance of lower-priced bikes can be surprisingly close to the high-priced models. Keep in mind that a fit rider on a budget can often overcome the advantages of an unfit rider's gold card.

To make a rough comparison, when considering shifting performance, braking performance, and the speed attained for a given amount of rider effort, a $800 to $1,200 bike probably works at least 95 percent as well as a $3,000 bike. The difference is that the higher-grade components of the more expensive bike will still be working long after the lower-priced bike's parts have worn out. The high-end bike will weigh less, and its frame will have a better riding "feel." However, the subtleties of the more expensive bike's superior ride quality are too slight for a beginner rider to feel. Finally, the more expensive bike's frame will have an overall higher level of finish, such as hand-detailed metal work, hand-applied paint, chrome-plated detail work, etc.

Going beyond the $3,000 range of road bikes enters into the realm of the truly exotic. Performance gains for the extra money are usually very slight and barely perceptible to novice riders. This price range is the domain of titanium frames, titanium stems, aerodynamically shaped carbon-fiber or alloy frames, carbon-fiber forks and wheels, and other such exotica. This is also where custom made-to-measure frames come in. Can the average rider use the potential of all this wondrous equipment? It's not likely. Of course, for many riders, playing with and admiring the hardware is as much fun as riding. If you can afford to have the best, go ahead and splurge. For the average cyclist, though, there's no need to buy the top-of-the-line.

Cyclebabble

A suspension fork or rear-suspension system is said to **bottom out** when all of the shock or fork has been fully compressed and all of the suspension travel is used up.

Choosing a Mountain Bike

Determining price ranges for mountain bikes is a little more involved. Will you ride your mountain bike on-road or off-road? If the latter, you want a bike that has at least *front suspension*. You'll want *dual suspension* if you're planning on doing heavy off-road riding or are willing to have a bike that's a little heavier in exchange for added comfort and control. Let's take a look at both.

A mountain bike with front suspension can make rough trails more enjoyable to ride.

Front-Suspension Mountain Bikes

Although there are mountain bikes with steel frames, front suspension, and up to 21 speeds starting at about $300, the performance of those bikes is suited to only moderate speeds and terrain. This kind of bike is fine if that's the kind of riding you want to do. Keep in mind, though, that this kind of bike is heavy (usually 30 pounds or more), and the suspension forks are flimsy with very soft action. A small bump is all it takes to *bottom out* the suspension travel.

If you're planning on more spirited off-road forays, you'll want a lighter bike with better suspension performance. Stepping up to the $500 to $700 price range will put you on a bike with a performance level to match this kind of riding. These bikes are entry-level performance/race bikes. In this price range, the bikes usually have frames of higher-quality steel or even aluminum. They'll have 24 speeds and weigh about 28 to 29 pounds. The suspension forks are much better made and are adjustable to your weight and preference. The forks

Cyclebabble

Some suspension forks and most rear-suspension shocks have a hydraulic mechanism called a **damper** that controls the speed at which the shock or fork compresses and/or rebounds. The effect of the mechanism is referred to as **damping** (often mispronounced as *dampening*).

Cyclebabble

Clipless pedals are pedals with built-in mechanisms that work with special cleats bolted to the bottom of cycling shoes to firmly attach the rider's feet to the pedals. The mechanisms work similar to ski bindings. You press down to click in and twist the heel outward as though you were squashing a bug to click out. The name came about as a means of differentiating these pedals from the old style that secured a rider's feet with leather straps and toe-clips.

Cyclebabble

The parts on a bicycle that transmit the rider's rotation of the cranks to rotation of the rear wheel are collectively called the **drivetrain**. Included in the drivetrain are the cranks, front chainrings, chain, front and rear derailleurs, and rear cogs.

at this price range still aren't quite up to the performance of the good stuff, but they still work well.

For performance similar to that of the bikes used by experts and pros, plan on shelling out at least $850. For that kind of money, you'll get a 24-speed bike that weighs between 26 and 28 pounds. The frame will be made of premium-grade steel or aluminum. The bike will have a hydraulically *damped* suspension fork and may come with *clipless pedals*.

The upgrades in the $1,000 to $1,500 range include a few components with performance truly worthy of an expert racer. On bikes priced from $1,500 to $2,000, nearly all the components are of expert racer quality. The performance of bikes in this range is only marginally less than the bikes pros use. These bikes will have top-grade steel frames or premium-quality aluminum frames, 27 speeds, clipless pedals, high-quality suspension forks, and premium-grade saddles and tires and will weigh in at 24 to 25 pounds.

At about the $2,500 level, you'll find complete bikes worthy of a pro. In this pricing stratosphere, usually all of the *drivetrain* and braking components are of pro-level quality. Few frames are steel in this range. If they are, the frames are made from top-of-the-line tubes that rival the weight of aluminum. Bike weight is usually below 24 pounds, and all of the various pieces (tires, rims, saddles, etc.) are top grade.

Things get real interesting when you start looking at custom frames and component mixes. There are titanium frames that cost $2,000 to $3,000. Shimano's XTR pro-level component group retails for about $1,300. A super-light, pro-level suspension fork is $500 to $700. By the time a rider chooses handlebars, stems, pedals, tires, and wheels, it's not unusual for his/her custom creation to go beyond the $4,000 to $5,000 mark. No one ever said that quality was cheap.

A mountain bike with suspension on the front and rear provides more comfort and control on rough terrain.

Dual-Suspension Mountain Bikes

The minimum price for a mountain bike jumps dramatically when you're looking at bikes with front and rear suspension. Although there are dual-suspension bikes priced as low as the $500 to $750 range, the overall quality and performance of these bikes makes them suitable only for low-speed rides. For brisk-paced riding or beginner racing, look to bikes in the $900 to $1,200 range.

To get a lighter, better-quality bike that will hold up to a few seasons of regular riding or racing, look at the $1,300 to $1,600 range. That's where you'll find bikes that weigh between 26 and 29 pounds and have hydraulically damped suspension forks. Beyond that, the sky is the limit. There are dual-suspension bikes priced well beyond $5,000 and weighing as little as 20 pounds. They're great fun (for those who can afford them).

Downhill Bikes

Downhill racing is the fastest-growing form of mountain bike racing, but very few manufacturers sell complete ready-to-race downhillers. Most of the ones that do (GT, Kona, Schwinn, Specialized, Trek, Yeti) have price tags of $4,000 to $5,000. These bikes are fully capable of winning at the pro level. They have six to eight inches of suspension travel in the rear and six or seven inches in the front. Disc brakes are the standard for downhill rigs. These bikes also come with some sort of chain-retention system, and all of the components are the strongest, most stoutly built available to be able to stand up to the abuse of downhill racing.

Many other small manufacturers build downhill frames. Most of those frames are at least $2,000 to $3,000. By the time a rider buys a frame, a long-travel suspension fork, disc brakes, and all the other parts needed to turn a bare frame into a bike, though, they're up to $4,000 or $5,000.

Cycology

Several types of chain-retention systems are used to keep the chain from bouncing off due to the rough terrain encountered on a downhill racecourse. The most common is a pair of round plates mounted on either side of the chainring and a pair of rollers (similar to small skateboard wheels) mounted perpendicular to the plates at the top and bottom. The rollers bridge over the two plates to capture the chain between the plates. Other systems use nylon blocks with channels for the chain. These blocks are mounted above and below the chainring. Rollers similar to derailleur jockey-pulleys are sometimes used instead of blocks.

For riders who don't have that kind of money in their bike budget, nearly any mid-range dual-suspension bike can be modified to be a suitable bike for a beginner or sport-class downhiller. Although many of the mid-priced dual-suspension bikes have only three or four inches of travel, they can still work well for an amateur. Also, installing a longer rear shock can increase the travel on many of these bikes. For front-suspension bikes, more travel is also better. However, many amateurs do quite well with only four inches of travel. Suitable four-inch travel forks sell for $400 to $600; six-inch travel models range from $800 to $2,000.

The cantilever brakes on mid-priced bikes aren't nearly as strong as the disc brakes on a pro downhill bike, but they can do an adequate job for an amateur. About the only thing an amateur can't do without is a chain-retention system to keep the chain from coming off during the bouncing and rattling of downhill racing. These systems cost about $100 to $150. I've seen amateur riders take this approach and have a good performing downhill bike for under $2,000—even less when they've started with a used bike. Do these bikes perform as well as a custom downhill rig? No. But the difference in performance isn't so much that the riders can't have fun or even win in the amateur ranks.

Selecting a Hybrid

Hybrid shopping is much easier than evaluating road bikes and mountain bikes. With few exceptions, there aren't any high-end hybrids. Most fall into the $300 to $800 price range. As with road bikes or mountain bikes, investing more will get you a bike that's a little lighter and that has more durable components. Decide what you want to spend, get thee to a bike shop, and ride happily ever after.

Some hybrids come equipped with narrow knobby tires, implying that the bike is suitable for off-road use. These minimalist knobbies may be okay for low speeds on level, easy, dirt roads, but push beyond that, and you'll quickly reach their performance limits. Also, knobby treads don't work as well on pavement as a smoother road tread. They have higher rolling resistance and less traction, especially in cornering. If dirt riding is definitely not in your riding plans, have the bike shop swap the knobbies for street tires. You'll ride safer and a little faster for your effort.

Finally, if you're the type of person who appreciates the finer things in life and you can't stand the notion of parking a mere $700 bike next to your Bentley, fear not. Remember that I said that I wasn't going to go into specific brands and models? Well, I also said that there were a "few exceptions" to the $300 to $800 price range of hybrids. Because there are so few, I'm going to mention them:

➤ Mercedes Benz makes a extremely luxurious hybrid, complete with disc brakes and front and rear suspension.

➤ Cannondale has the Super V400 SRB. Based on the Super V line of mountain bikes, this bike has high-rise handlebars, street-tread tires, and a big, thick, cushy, coil-spring saddle that will end all complaints of sore buns.

➤ A few manufacturers make bikes styled after the bikes of the 1930s and 1940s. These cruisers often have Shimano's seven-speed Nexus internal hub shifting system. Breezer, KHS, Kona, and Electra all have very stylish cruisers that make great "around-town" bikes.

What's that? An off-the-rack hybrid is too gauche? Consider taking a high-end mountain bike and fitting it with high handlebars, street tires, and a cushy saddle. One well-known Hollywood actor took this approach to a $5,000 downhill race bike. That bike will probably never be used on a dirt trail. Instead it will lead its life riding around Malibu. Its sophisticated suspension system will only serve to make that actor a little more comfortable as he rides off curbs and over speed bumps. To purists it's blasphemy. To the casual rider with a taste for fine machinery, this approach is an exercise in fun and frivolity.

Women's Bikes

Some smart bike manufacturers are making bikes specifically sized for women. The companies have realized that women's bodies are built differently than men's bodies (smart cookies, those bike companies). Women have shorter torsos than men of their same height do, yet most bikes are built to male body proportions. Put a female on a bike that's sized by her leg length and the top-tube will likely be too long, stretching her out in an uncomfortable riding position. The solution is to build the bike with a shorter top-tube and shorter stem. That's the approach that Trek, Independent Fabrications, and Terry Precision have taken with their female-specific road and mountain bikes.

Terry takes the concept one step further with its Symmetry road bike. With the steeper head-tube angle of a road bike, shortening the top-tube can result in the rider's toes extending past the edge of the tire at the front of the pedal stroke. Terry solves this situation by using a 24-inch front wheel.

Don't confuse these bikes with what we as kids called "girl's bikes," which are bikes with no top-tube. With few exceptions, I don't recommend them. That type of frame (called *mixtes*) is from another age. The step-through design allowed women to ride in skirts back when no respectable gal would be caught dead in slacks or shorts.

A few manufacturers still have mixtes, mostly at the lower-price points. Mixtes are perceived as being easier to mount and dismount, which isn't necessarily so. True, with no top-tube, it's easier to step through the frame to get on or off, but it's even easier to get on a bike by leaning it over and swinging a leg over the back.

I discovered something quite funny about some of the mixtes. One day at the bike shop where I worked I happened to notice that the size 16-inch man's mountain bike that was parked right next to a 16-inch mixte mountain bike looked like it had a shorter top-tube. So I grabbed a tape measure and found that the distance from the seat-tube to the head-tube was a full inch longer on the mixte. So what advantage did that "woman's bike" offer a female rider? Let's see, the frame is far weaker, more flexible, and the riding position is too long. Great selling points, eh? Since then, I've checked a few other brands' mixte bikes and found most of them to also be longer than the same size man's frame.

There are two notable exceptions to my reluctance over mixtes. Terry Precision Cycles makes a fine mixte that's appropriately proportioned. Cannondale has four hybrid models, two of which have front suspension and suspension seat-posts for a real Cadillac ride. Both of these companies realize that some women feel more comfortable with a low top-tube. A spokesperson from Terry commented, "Many of our mixte customers grew up riding them. We're doing it strictly from a physical standpoint for older women who, for whatever reason, won't ride a 'man's bike.'"

Terry Precision Cycles specializes in cycling products for women. Terry's mixte model is popular among women who insist on a "woman's bike" with a step-through frame.

Choosing the Right Size Bike

Choosing a bike with the right frame size is critical to a rider's enjoyment and comfort. However, as any bike shop employee can tell you, many new cyclists have odd ideas regarding bike sizes. When asked what size bike they need, many customers will ask for a 26-inch. They no doubt recall that number from childhood when small kids rode bikes with 20-inch wheels and bigger kids rode "newsboy" bikes with 26-inch wheels. Bike size refers to the size of the frame, which is the length of the *seat-tube*. A bike size of 26 inches would be suitable for a giant like Dennis Rodman.

Choosing the wrong size bike can ruin the enjoyment of bike riding. And no, you can't make up for it by just raising or lowering the seat. Bikes are made proportionately. The larger size bike will have a longer *top-tube*, and a smaller size will have a shorter top-tube. A bike that's too small will put the rider in an uncomfortable, scrunched position. On a bike that's too big, the rider will have to stretch out too far—again, very uncomfortable—and the rider may have difficulty mounting and dismounting the bike.

Road bikes are sized in centimeters, with most major manufacturers offering sizes at two-centimeter intervals. Mountain bikes are normally sized in inches, with most bike makers offering sizes at two-inch intervals.

Straddle Up

The basic sizing method most bike shops use as a starting point is to have the rider straddle the bike's top-tube. On a road bike, if there's about an inch between the top-tube and the rider's crotch, the bike is roughly the right size. On a mountain bike, you're looking for two to three inches of clearance.

The straddle-the-bike method is rudimentary at best. Choosing a frame size is practically a science unto itself. Some custom frame builders specialize in making made-to-order frames sized specifically

Cyclebabble

Look under your saddle, and you'll see that it's bolted to the seat-post. You'll also see that the seat-post is inserted into the bike's frame. The portion of the frame that the post is inserted into is the **seat-tube**.

Cyclebabble

Sit on your bike and look down. That horizontal portion of the frame that extends straight out in front of you is the **top-tube**.

Steer Clear

Resist the temptation to take advantage of a bargain price on a bike that is the wrong size. A bike that's too big or too small will never be comfortable or enjoyable to ride. About the only exception is in cases where a bike is such a deal that the parts alone are worth the asking price. Pull off the parts, sell the frame, and buy the right size.

for the customer. These builders don't make standard sizes; each frame's dimensions and angles are based on measurements of the customer's body. Of course, these frames are not cheap.

To get a rough idea of frame size, straddle the top-tube of a bike. A road bike should have about an inch of clearance between the top-tube and the rider's crotch; a mountain bike should have two to three inches of clearance.

Many bike shops will have one or two staff members well-versed in the art of bike fit. They're usually very experienced riders and/or racers with a keen eye and a thorough knowledge of how a bike should fit. These experts can help a customer not only to choose the right frame, but also to choose the right width of handlebar and the right length of stem to custom fit the bike to the customer.

The Fit Kit System

Another avenue to bike fit is to visit a bike shop equipped with a Fit Kit system. This system consists of a set of measuring devices and procedures for taking a series of size measurements of a rider's legs, feet, torso, and hands. An angle-finder is used on the knee joint to help compute optimum saddle height. All these figures are run through a series of formulas (or fed into a computer) to calculate every variable in fitting a bike to the customer. The system determines frame size, stem length and how high it should extend out of the frame, handlebar size and width, saddle height and tilt, crank length, and more. A Fit Kit session takes an hour or so. Most shops charge about $50 for a fitting, but they will often deduct that if you buy a bike.

I went through a Fit Kit session 15 years ago when I was ordering a new bike. I had already spent several years riding a bike that had been sized by the straddle-the-top-tube method and had fine-tuned the riding position myself. The Fit Kit determined that the frame I had been riding was two centimeters too big and that my saddle was set too high and too far back and that my stem was also adjusted too high. My new bike was ordered, assembled, and built to the specifications of the Fit Kit. The very first time I sat on it, it just felt right. I still have that bike, still ride it regularly, and haven't adjusted its position one iota.

Another Use for This Book

You can precisely determine frame size yourself by taking an inseam measurement. This measurement is taken a little differently than the measurement a tailor takes:

1. Tape a piece of paper to a wall, just around hip level.
2. Take off your shoes. Choose a book that's an inch or two thick and hold the spine of it in your crotch, perpendicular to the ground.
3. Press the book slightly upward to simulate your body weight against a bike saddle.
4. Stand close to the wall, and mark the place where the spine is on the sheet of paper. Remove the book.
5. Measure the distance from the mark on the paper to the floor in centimeters and multiply it by .96 to get your road bike frame size. For a mountain bike, take the measurement in inches and multiply it by .59 to arrive at a frame size.

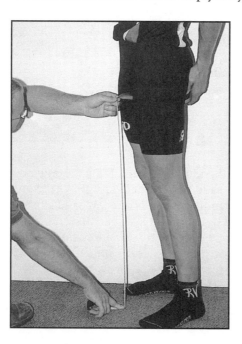

Taking an inseam measurement.

Saddle Height

Look at the riding position of an experienced rider or racer, and you'll see the rider's legs go almost to full extension at the bottom of the pedal stroke. Novice riders, however, often choose a saddle height that is far too low. With a properly positioned saddle, a rider can usually touch the ground only with the toe of one shoe. Riders with limited riding skills like to be able to put both feet firmly on the ground for starting and stopping. However, riding with the seat set that low robs the rider of a great deal of power. It also can tire a rider prematurely. Think about it: How long could you walk in a squat? Not long, unless you're a Cossack dancer.

When the saddle is set to the proper height range, the rider's leg will have only a slight bend at the bottom of the pedal stroke.

Despite the increased performance and endurance that a higher saddle position provides, some riders still prefer a low saddle height. Perhaps they take only very short rides a few times a year and like the stability and ease of a low saddle. It's hard to argue with that, except these folks still need to be careful about setting the saddle too low. Many riders position the seat all the way down with absolutely no seat-post extending out of the frame. By positioning the seat this low, a rider runs the risk of knee injury from bending the knees too far at the top of the pedal stroke.

The goal of setting saddle height is simple: Provide a position that allows the major muscle groups to work in their optimum range of motion. Achieving that means putting the saddle high enough so that at the bottom of the pedal stroke the leg is almost straight, with very little bend. How much bend is the optimum? That question has been a topic of endless debate among riders, racers, and coaches for the past hundred years. There are several methods and measuring formulas in use, and all have their followers and detractors. Yet they all are but guidelines to arrive at a starting point.

No matter which method a rider uses, he or she will get similar results. The debate of one method over another debates minor variances only. My personal saddle height was arrived at years ago at the hands of an experienced expert with a Fit Kit. But the following two simple methods arrive at saddle heights only a few fractions of an inch from what I've been using.

The quickest and easiest method for setting saddle height is to do the following:

1. Position the pedal at the bottom of the stroke and have the rider place a foot over the spindle of the pedal.

2. Raise the saddle until the rider's leg is at full lock with the foot held level Then when the foot is in the proper position (with the ball of the foot over the pedal spindle), the rider's leg will have only a slight bend and the saddle will be at the right height.

Cycology

Despite all the formulas and methods, seat height is still a personal preference. Eddy Merckx, one of the greatest racers of all time, is known for constantly experimenting with different saddle positions throughout his career. He was so particular about using different positions for different conditions that he sometimes raced with an Allen wrench stashed in his jersey pocket so that he could stop and change his seat position to match the terrain.

Another common method of setting saddle height is based on the same inseam measurement we used to choose frame size. Take that inseam measurement and multiply it by .96. The resulting number is the distance you want to set the center of the saddle from the center of the bottom bracket.

Whichever method you use to determine saddle height, have someone ride behind you when you first try it. If it looks as though your hips are rocking from side to side, the position is probably too high. Lower the saddle about $1/8$ inch at a time until the rocking goes away.

Also, if you've already been riding for several months and the height arrived at by either method is more than an inch higher than what you've been using, don't immediately go to the increased height. Your muscles are already used to the lower height, and you could pull or tear a muscle. Instead, mark your seat-post with a punch and a hammer to put a small dot on the post at the point where it comes out of the frame. Put the saddle back to the height you've been using. Raise your saddle $1/8$ inch each week until the post is back up to the mark.

A quick and easy method of determining saddle height.

For those riders who are still getting the hang of stopping, starting, and turning, by all means go ahead and ride with a low saddle while you develop skills and confidence. But first use the previous formulas to arrive at the ideal range, mark your seat-post, and slip it back down to where you're comfortable. Then before every ride, raise the seat a little. Eventually, you'll be at full height. After your riding skills have developed, you'll be able to appreciate the greater power, speed, and endurance that proper saddle height provides.

Male Rider Myth: You Won't Lose That Loving Feeling

Some of you may have heard the report of a urologist who appeared on TV's *20/20* a couple of years ago. He was announcing the results of his research, which indicated that riding a bicycle could lead to impotence. Before you toss this book into the fireplace, decide to forget all about this bike idea, and head out to go buy *The Complete Idiot's Guide to Macramé*, read on. (Incidentally, the doctor in question has since backed off of his stance, partially in response from critical and skeptical comments from other urologists.)

According to the urologist's original report, when a man sits on a bicycle seat, his weight can put pressure on the penile arteries, and that pressure can cause numbness and eventually impotence. Fair enough. However, a rider who experiences that type of pressure can easily rectify the situation. He can try to slightly alter his riding position.

Or he can purchase one of the new models of saddles with specifically designed cutouts or padding in the crucial area to completely eliminate the pressure.

The new cutaway saddles are comfortable right from the start. Terry, a company that has specialized in women's bikes and equipment, has been making women's saddles with cutouts for several years and was the first on the scene with the Liberator line of saddles for men. This patented selection of saddles includes the Liberator Pro, the Liberator Ti Race (a racing saddle with titanium rails for reduced weight), and the slightly wider Liberator Ti Comfort, which also has titanium rails. Since Terry led the way, T-Gear has introduced a similar design. Italian saddle makers Selle Italia and Selle San Marcos both offer saddles with a strategically placed soft section of gel pad.

Cycology

Go to any cycling event, and you will see that men make up the majority of racers and long-distance riders. Since there are other "recreational activities" that many men enjoy even more than riding, would so many men continue cycling if the incidences of impotence were anywhere near the numbers originally reported on *20/20*? I doubt it.

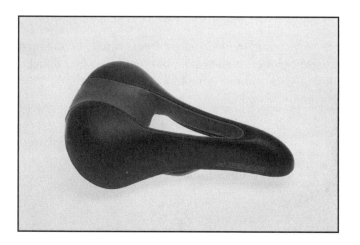

The pressure of the saddle against a man's crotch can cause penile numbness and impotence. Saddles with a cutaway such as Terry's Liberator can solve both problems.

Getting back to the issue of rider position, numbness can often be prevented by a simple saddle adjustment. In most cases, you want your saddle to be positioned level. Positioning it with an upward tilt will almost certainly cause pressure. A downward tilt is rarely desirable either. Riders who have experienced discomfort or numbness will commonly try to rectify the problem by trying a downward tilt. This can often worsen the situation because the position causes the rider to continually slide forward onto the nose of the saddle.

Having the saddle positioned too far back can also be a cause. A rider's body will try to compensate for a poor position. If the saddle is too far back, the forces of riding will continually cause the rider to slide forward onto the nose of the saddle. Riding a bike with a top-tube or stem that's too long can have the same effect. If you suspect poor fit, have someone in the know look at your riding position.

It's also important to occasionally stand up or to change position on a bike. Sitting locked into one position throughout a ride can numb more than just your penis. Slide back on the saddle and let your weight rest on your buttocks from time to time. Sit up with your hands on top of the handlebars or on the brake hoods.

Lastly, if riding your bike is causing you any type of physical discomfort, before going to a doctor who doesn't know bikes, get yourself to a bike shop or bike expert who knows bike fit. Millions of men have ridden bikes comfortably without going impotent. You can, too.

The Least You Need to Know

➤ Brand name isn't as important as intended purpose and budget.

➤ The right size bike is more comfortable (and more fun) to ride.

➤ Yes, the saddle is supposed to be *that* high.

➤ The reported incidence of bicycling-induced impotence is mostly an exaggeration by alarmists. If you are experiencing any pain or numbness when riding, a simple seat adjustment will keep you riding happily and healthily.

Chapter 8

Accessorizing

In This Chapter

➤ Gearing up for a safe ride from head to toe

➤ Outfitting your bike

➤ Making an emergency kit

➤ Special gear for women

➤ Bringing the kids along and using trailers

➤ Packing up your bike without scratching up your car

Choosing a bike is only the beginning of gearing up to ride. You'll need a few items other than the bike itself to help keep your riding fun, safe, and hassle-free. You also need to know a few things to stay happy and healthy on a bike.

Helmets: Keeping Your Brain Intact

Face it, bike riding can be dangerous, even lethal. The number one fatal injury to cyclists is head injuries. Wearing a helmet can prevent most of these tragedies. If you think helmets look nerdy, consider that every U.S. pro racer wears a helmet in competition, and very few choose to go bareheaded during training rides. Are you more skilled than a pro? I didn't think so. Wear a helmet, if not for your sake, then for the sake of your riding partners. None of your road-riding friends wants to sit roadside while your brains and blood seep into their new jersey, and none of your mountain bike buddies wants to haul your comatose carcass out of the woods either.

Don't put off getting a helmet. Your bike and helmet are a set. Probably all bike shop employees have had customers spend a sizable chunk of money on a bike and then say, "Oh, I'll get a helmet later." To which sharper shop employees ask, "So, when did you plan on having your first head-slamming crash?" There are two types of bike riders: those who have fallen and those who haven't fallen yet.

Miles of Experience

Being in a mountain resort area, the bike shop I worked in rented out a lot of bikes. We required all renters to wear helmets, and this policy drew mixed responses. I was always amazed at the parents who were pleased to hear that their kids would have to wear helmets, but didn't want to wear them themselves. "I'm not going racing. We're just going to ride the bike path," was a common excuse. I'll always remember one dad, who after grudgingly donning a helmet, had the thing save his skull. It seems he swerved too far to get around a skater, struck a curb, and launched himself over the bars and onto his head. His wife later brought back his cracked and smashed helmet. We kept it around for a couple of years because it was a great visual aid to demonstrate that *everyone*, racers and bike-path riders alike, needs a helmet.

The Price of Security

Good helmets start at about $50, and some go up to two or three times as much. The added cost for those above $50 is mostly styling and colorful graphics. The cheaper helmets in the $20 to $30 range are rarely very well made.

Cycology

Bell, one of the biggest names in helmets, once ran an ad that read, "If you've got a $10 head, get a $10 helmet." It was a rare example of truth in advertising.

Occasionally, you can find discontinued helmet styles at bargain prices. To be sure that you're getting good quality, look for a sticker inside the helmet. Helmets sold in the United States in 1999 and beyond must have an inspection sticker from the CPSC (Consumer Products Safety Commission). If you find a leftover 1998 model helmet that has a sticker from Snell or one that reads *ASTM-1447*, it's still a good helmet. These stickers show that this particular model of helmet has been tested and found to meet certain minimum standards regarding its strength and absorption of force. These ratings also pertain to the straps and buckles, because even the strongest helmet can't protect the wearer if the buckle fails and the helmet ejects on impact.

You Wear It Well

It's a pity how often I see riders who had the good sense to buy helmets render those helmets nearly useless by not taking the time to properly adjust them. A helmet should sit level on your head, not tilted back like a bonnet. The front edge should come about halfway down the forehead.

Helmets are meant to fit fairly snug with little room between the wearer's head and the inner shell of the helmet. Most helmets have removable pads so you can mix and match from a choice of pad thicknesses to customize the fit to your particular noggin. It's best to choose a model that fits fairly well without you resorting to extra-thick pads.

You may need to try several models or brands before finding a shell size that fits well. For my head, some helmets are made too short front to back. No amount of pad fiddling can make these helmets work for me.

Steer Clear

Do not continue to wear any helmet that has taken a hard impact. A helmet is designed to save your life by giving up its life. One hard blow is all it takes to compress the poly-styrene (Styrofoam) liner and to compromise the outer shell. A helmet that has taken one impact may come apart on the next spill. Some helmet manufacturers offer crash replacement for $15 to $20. There is no crash replacement policy on your brain.

A helmet isn't supposed to be worn like a bonnet (left); it's meant to sit level as shown (right).

Strap adjustment is also critical. Unfortunately, many riders wear helmets with the straps adjusted too loosely to do much good. During my days working in a bike shop, I had a favorite way to demonstrate the ineffectiveness of helmets with loosely adjusted straps: I'd walk up behind someone who was wearing a loose helmet and slide the helmet around to the side of his face. Imagine what could happen in a crash with such a poorly adjusted helmet! If you can get more than two or three fingers between the helmet strap and your chin, the straps are too loose.

Adjusting helmet straps takes only a few minutes. Stand in front of a mirror and place the helmet on your head so that it sits level. On each side of the helmet you'll find two nylon straps designed to buckle together under your chin. Each of these straps is two straps joined together by a small slider. These sliders are meant to be positioned just below each ear.

Adjust the two sliders as needed by sliding the strap through until they rest below each earlobe. To tighten the chinstrap, slide the strap through the buckle until the helmet is snug on your head. Check to make sure that the straps are also tight above the sliders. If you notice any slack, adjust the straps as needed. With the chinstrap buckled, try to move the helmet forward and back and side to side. A little movement is okay, but if the helmet moves more than an inch in any direction, it needs to be tightened.

Cycling Shorts Are Your Friend

One of the most common questions I hear from noncyclists is "Why do you all wear those tight, black shorts?" The answer is simple: comfort. Bike shorts are form-fitting to prevent chafing, and they have built-in padding for added bun comfort. Why are they usually black? As with many things in cycling, black shorts are a tradition, one that goes back a hundred years. Back then, riders realized that they could use their black shorts to wipe off their hands if they got them greasy.

Miles of Experience

These days, a cyclist in bike shorts can walk into a 7-11 or bagel shop without drawing a second glance. That wasn't the case before the cycling boom of the mid-'80s. Remember the scene in *Easy Rider* where Peter Fonda, Dennis Hopper, and Jack Nicholson sat in a small-town coffee shop while amused locals looked on, muttering insults about the "freak show"? That was about the response that Lycra-clad cyclists got in the early '80s. Thankfully, the days of having our bike shorts draw snickers are gone. When you enter a store or coffee shop wearing bike shorts nowadays, the only comments you're likely to get are "Where are you folks riding to?" or "Nice day for biking!"

First off, realize that there is a difference between real bike shorts meant for cycling and the ones sold as fashion statements. Nothing can take the place of real bike shorts with padding sewn into the seat and crotch. Ever ridden in jeans? On anything but a short ride, that thick denim seam is sure to cause problems in Australia (you know, "down under"). Nearly the same can be said of gym shorts or jogging pants.

Cyclists don't wear bike shorts just because they like black, shiny Lycra. Bike shorts have padding sewn into the seat, and the snug fit prevents chafing.

Bike shorts vary in price from $20 to over $100. Generally, the more panels of fabric that are sewn together to make the shorts and the better the fit, the higher the price will be. I like *bib shorts* with built-in suspender straps. They stay up well without a tight waistband.

Realizing that not all riders are comfortable appearing in public wearing form-fitting Lycra, several manufacturers make casual, loose-fitting shorts with an inner cycling short built in. These shorts provide all the comfort of regular bike shorts without also providing an anatomy lesson. This type of short is popular among mountain bikers and touring riders who like having pockets and an inconspicuous look.

Cyclebabble

Bib shorts are Lycra biking shorts that contain built-in suspender straps instead of an elastic waistband. These straps help keep the shorts up without the binding nature of elastic at the waist.

Not all bike shorts are form-fitting Lycra. Loose-fitting casual bike shorts are also very popular and comfortable.

Bike shop employees often neglect to tell customers one important thing: Bike shorts are meant to be worn without underwear. If you wear your usual skivvies or your favorite sexy briefs under your bike shorts, they're liable to bunch up into places best not discussed at the dinner table.

If you hear someone refer to the padding in bike shorts as chamois, you know that he or she is a long-time cyclist. Years ago, chamois (like the type you use on your car) was the material of choice for bike short padding. Before a ride, cyclists would prepare the chamois by rubbing in some lotion or Vaseline. As gross as that may sound, a well-lubed chamois was very comfortable, especially for a long day in the saddle. Although modern bike shorts use synthetic materials instead of chamois, if you're suffering from chafing, try using some lube on the pad. Your friends might think it an odd practice, but I won't tell them if you don't.

Cycology

Riders who experience numb palms or aching hands can get relief by wearing gel gloves. These gloves have special pads made of silicone gel built into the palm to relieve the pressure points that cause numbness and soreness.

Hand-to-Hand Combat

A pair of gloves with padded palms can take the hand-ache out of a long ride, but they're not just for comfort. Their real value is protecting your palms in a crash. I've seen crashes where riders have ground right through their gloves. Imagine what kind of damage would have been done without hand protection.

Gloves come in a variety of styles and types. The short-fingered variety are popular because they're not as warm and they provide a bit more dexterity. Some short-fingered models have crotchet backs and leather palms. The open weave provides added cooling and comfort. It can also create an interesting mottled tan on the backs of your hands that other cyclists will instantly recognize. Many gloves are made with terry cloth on the back—a handy means of sopping up sweat or errant snot (more on the cyclist's nasal clearing ritual later in Chapter 11, "Rules of the Trail").

Classic crotchet cycling gloves like these are cool (temperature-wise) and comfortable.

Long-fingered gloves are designed for added warmth or added protection. Motocross-type gloves are especially popular among mountain bikers and downhill racers. Their thick palms and plastic-reinforced backs provide serious protection. Other long-fingered gloves are designed for cold weather wear. Some are made like thin ski gloves and have an insulating layer sandwiched between an inner layer and an outer moisture/temperature barrier. For riding in extremely cold weather, I like the "lobster" type gloves. These mitten-like gloves have a pocket for the thumbs, another for the first and middle finger, and third for the ring finger and pinkie. They're plenty warm and provide just enough movement to work the brakes and shifters.

Fancy Footwear

Cycling is yet another sport that requires special footwear. Cycling shoes are made with very stiff soles so that virtually no pedaling effort is lost to flex. A little flex in the shoe from a soft sole may not seem critical, but a bit of flex on each turn of the pedals multiplied by 60 to 100 rpms (revolutions per minute) is a lot of lost energy. Also, riding with a flexible sole will make the bottom of a rider's feet ache from the shoe pressing into the pedal. As I discussed in Chapter 5, "Knowing the Thingie from the Doodad: A Part-by-Part Description of Bicycle Components," cycling shoes are also designed to accept cleats to work with pedals with toe-clips or clipless pedals.

Fit is critical. Cycling shoes should fit snugly enough that the feet don't shift around from the pedaling action, but not so tight that the feet hurt or circulation is hindered. The fit of cycling shoes varies from one manufacturer to another, so try on several brands of shoes before buying.

Miles of Experience

Shoes are such an integral part of pedaling and riding that many riders find a brand they like and then stick with it with undying loyalty. I know of one pro racer who used the same brand and model of shoe for several years. When his team was later contracted to another brand of shoe, he continued to use his favorite brand, costing himself tens of thousands of dollars in endorsement fees.

Soles for Sale

Prices on cycling shoes range from about $35 all the way up to $200 and sometimes more. Budget-price shoes usually have standard shoelaces. Step up in price, and you'll get shoes that fasten with Velcro straps or plastic buckles like the ones on ski boots; some shoes use combinations of laces and straps. Laces do a fine job of securing a shoe and can be adjusted to customize the fit, but be careful to tie them securely and tuck them in. I've seen a few riders crash from having a lace come untied and wrap itself around the pedal. That's why I recommend that if you get shoes with laces you choose a model that also has straps to contain the laces.

Parlez Vous Français?

Many cycling shoes are sized in European sizes; for example, a size 9 in U.S. sizes is size 43 in European sizing. Most shoe companies offer sizes all the way up to size 50, which is about a size 15. Riders with odd feet or very large feet can order custom-made cycling shoes from Lamson Cycle Shoes of Rifle, Colorado. Since 1988, Lamson has been making mountain bike shoes, road racing shoes, triathlon shoes, and touring shoes. These well-made shoes fasten with laces secured by Velcro straps. They're not cheap—a pair costs $550. Getting a custom fit isn't quick either; it takes a year from the time that Lamson receives a traced outline of your feet to get your shoes.

Racers prefer sleek cycling shoes with hard, stiff soles like the ones on the left. Less serious riders like the comfort and ease of walking with shoes like the ones on the right.

Eyewear

Eyewear not only looks cool, it also provides protection. Having grit or insects fly into your eyes can be painful and can even cause a crash. The UV protection of a good pair of shades will reduce eyestrain and lessen your likelihood of developing cataracts.

Whether you spend $14 for a pair of shades from the drugstore or 10 times that for some name-brand eyewear, be certain that the frames are designed for active use and that they won't bounce off while riding. My favorite driving glasses are terrible for riding because they constantly slide down my nose. Some riders use sport straps, but I've found them to be uncomfortable under a helmet and they tend to interfere with the helmet straps.

Steer Clear

Resist the temptation to not wear eye protection on cloudy or overcast days. Eyewear does more than protect your eyes from sun; it also serves to keep out debris and flying insects. Imagine the consequences of having your eyes water over from stinging debris while you're riding at a high speed.

Jerseys and Other Assorted Finery

Many people ride in a T-shirt or sweatshirt, but a cycling jersey can be far more comfortable and has many practical features. Cycling jerseys are made long in the rear so that they don't ride up while you are in the riding position. Jerseys have pockets on the back where a rider can easily retrieve snacks, glasses, wallet, and so on. Many jerseys have a long front zipper, allowing a rider to open the front of the jersey on hot days or close it up for cooler temperatures.

109

If you wear a T-shirt or sweatshirt in warm weather, the cotton fabric can become wet with sweat, making you feel uncomfortably moist and clammy. In cold weather, that moisture can make you uncomfortably cold, even dangerously so. Cycling jerseys are made of fabrics specifically designed to wick moisture away from the skin. Look for jerseys made from such fabrics as Coolmax, C-Tech, and Fieldsensor.

Cycology

If the comfort of a cycling jersey isn't enough to win you over, its utility is sure to. Riders quickly learn to love the sheer convenience of having their snacks, wallet, keys, and so forth secure in the out-of-the-way back pockets. A lot of people I know wear cycling jerseys for other sports where rear pockets are convenient: hiking, cross-country skiing, running, and riding horses.

Steer Clear

Beware of using rainwear that wasn't designed to be worn during strenuous activity. Although regular raincoats do a good job of keeping water out, they can be equally effective at keeping moisture in—moisture that you'll generate from sweating so much from pedaling and from trapped body heat. If you combine moisture against your skin with cold temperatures, you may develop hypothermia.

Many people picture bright colors and garish designs when they think of cycling jerseys. However, there's a large selection of simple designs, solid colors, and muted hues available for those with more conservative tastes. You don't have to look like a rolling billboard or pro racer, although replicas of pro team uniforms are still very popular.

Cold-Weather Wear

Short-sleeve jerseys and cycling shorts are fine for warm weather. But as temperatures drop, other bits of cycling wear can make riding more comfortable. Cold-weather jerseys have long sleeves (surprise!) and are made of thicker, warmer fabrics than their warm-weather counterparts.

It's very important to keep your knees warm when riding. I recommend covering the knees any time the temperature drops below 60 degrees. Knee joints normally release an internal lubricant during exercise, but cold weather inhibits these secretions. A pair of Lycra tights worn over cycling shorts is a good way to keep the legs completely warm. Leg warmers and arm warmers can help meet the challenge of riding in changing weather. They can be put on or peeled off as needed, and they stash easily in a jersey pocket.

Rainy-Weather Wear

Most cyclists are fair-weather riders who head for home at the first sign of sprinkles. Then there are those riders who like rain. Dedicated bicycle commuters who regard driving as a sin may not necessarily like rain, but they deal with it. Riders who live in Seattle or Portland have to ride in rain; otherwise, they would never ride.

Riding in standard rain jackets and rain pants not designed for exercise or cycling can be hot and uncomfortable. Cycling rainwear is made of breathable fabric that lets out body heat generated from riding, but doesn't let rain in. Some cycling rain jackets and pants are equipped with side vents that zip open for added cooling. Cycling rain jackets are cut longer in the back to keep the lower back and buns covered while riding. Read the label carefully. A jacket or pants with a label reading *water-resistant* might be okay in a light sprinkle, but to keep from being soggy, cold, and miserable in a downpour, you want garments that are rated as *waterproof*.

Leg warmers are handy in changing weather. Pull them on when it's warm; peel them off when it's not.

Inclement weather doesn't have to keep a rider indoors. A waterproof jacket such as Cannondale's Tempest can keep a rider dry and warm, even in the rain.

111

Cycling Essentials

Now that we've looked at what you need to put on yourself, let's take a look at what you need to put on your bike. These extras will make your biking experience the best it can be:

1. **Water bottles and cages.** Riding is exercise, and exercise requires rehydration. Even a half-hour spin can be too long without water. Those first few rides for someone not used to exercise can be strenuous enough without having to go thirsty.

Most bikes have at least two sets of screw holes to accommodate plastic or metal cages designed to hold water bottles. I prefer the plastic variety to metal cages. Metal cages can bend open with repeated use, making them prone to launching your bottle over a bump.

2. **Frame-mounted pump.** Most pumps can be easily changed to work on either presta or shrader valves (remember those from Chapter 6, "At the Bike Shop"?) by unscrewing the end and flipping the plastic fitting inside. Try using it at home to be sure you know how to use it. Don't count on CO_2 cartridges. They're great for races where their main advantage is speed, but most riders will only carry a cartridge or two. What will you do on your third flat? It happens.

A frame-mounted pump doesn't weigh much, takes up virtually no room, and can save you from taking a long, unplanned hike.

3. **Chain lubricant.** Dry chains squeak, shift poorly, and wear out your drivetrain. Get a bottle of chain lubricant and use it. An entire industry has been formed to cover the chain lubrication needs of cyclists. There are dry lubes and wet lubes, lubes with Teflon, lubes with wax, and lubes with various additives and miracle polymers that promise to increase your speed and walk your dog as you ride. For every type of lube, there are legion of riders who love it and those who hate it. No matter which lube you choose, remember to use it often and to first clean off the old lube and built-up lube before adding more lube. Chapter 17, "The Chain Gang," has more on cleaning your chain and sprockets.

4. **Flat repair/survival kit.** No one with more than half a brain would drive a car without a spare tire and jack. Why would anyone ride a bike miles from home and far from the nearest highway any less prepared? I hate to break this to you, but you are going to get flats. Lots of them. Accept this fact, and learn to fix flats. There is no bicycle equivalent of the Auto Club, so self-sufficiency is a must. A spare tube, patches, tire levers, and frame-mounted pump are the bare minimum. Read on to see what goes into the survival kits of the truly prepared.

Survival Kit

Assemble a survival kit that includes the following 14 (count 'em, 14) items:

1. **Something to put it all in.** A small seat-bag or fanny pack can hold a survival kit, but it's a tight fit. Some riders prefer a small backpack or one of the hydration packs that also contain a water bladder.

2. **Inner tubes.** Don't count on only a patch kit. Tubes are often ruined beyond repair. Carry at least two tubes.

3. **Patch kit.** Use this kit as a backup to spare inner tubes. Remember that once the tube of glue is opened the glue tends to dry out, so check it occasionally.

4. **Tire levers.** These levers are for opening up the tire from the rim to get at the offending leaky tube inside and for closing up the tire after putting in a new tube or patching the old one. Using a screwdriver is only asking for yet another perforated tube.

Steer Clear

Don't fool yourself into believing that you're not likely to get a flat just because your bike is new or your tires are new. Flats can and do happen at any time. Although I've sometimes had the good fortune of riding for months with no flats, I've also seen brand new bikes get flats on parking lot test rides. Be prepared. It's gonna happen. Put together a flat repair kit and know how to use it.

5. **Multitool.** Park, Wrench Force, Topeak, Ritchey, and others make tools with several functions. They're sort of the Swiss Army Knives of bike tools, combining an assortment of wrenches and such into one small tool.

6. **First-aid kit.** A kit containing a few bandages, a gauze pad or two, some aspirin, a few disinfectant towelettes, and a pair of tweezers can be a big help.

7. **Matches.** This one is mostly for mountain bike riders. Even the most experienced rider can get lost or have a breakdown keep them out overnight. A simple book of matches or a box of waterproof matches to build a signal fire or to keep warm can be life-saving.

8. **Cash.** Having a few dollars to get a bite to eat, buy a tube, or get a bike part sure is handy. Be sure to carry a couple of quarters or a phone card for a phone call. "But I'll call collect," you say. Fine, just hope you don't reach an answering machine. Those with calling cards need to either always have it with them, memorize the number, or have the number written on a slip of paper in their survival kit.

9. **Duct tape.** Wrap a long section of duct tape around a tire lever to store in your survival kit. Its uses are limited only by your own ingenuity. Use it to keep broken spokes out of the cogs, to boot a cut tire sidewall (see Chapter 16, "No Air in There"), or to secure a broken shoe buckle.

10. **Razor blade.** Keep a standard box-cutter blade in your patch kit box. You may need it for anything from cutting up a T-shirt to make an emergency bandage to cutting duct tape for trailside repairs. I once used one to cut out a length of fishing line that pulled up into the cogs.

11. **Chain links and/or Shimano pins.** Nothing can replace a link. Simply removing a damaged link can work, but with a too-short chain, you run the risk of damaging your derailleur or frame if you inadvertently shift to the big chainring and big rear cog. It's better to take out the offending links and replace them with the same number of fresh links. I like to keep a four- or five-link section in my patch-kit box. Those using Shimano chains need to also carry Shimano's special pins. Although it's sometimes possible to repair a Shimano chain without replacing the pin, it's not something that can be counted on.

12. **Spare cleat screws.** The cleats used with clipless pedals are tiny, so they're sometimes prone to backing out. Losing one can ruin a day. I know a rider who lost a right cleat when he was 25 miles out into the woods. After pedaling out basically one-legged, he had trouble with that left leg for

Cycology

The original multitool favorite is still the Cool Tool. It has the three most commonly needed Allen keys (a 4mm, a 5mm, and a 6mm), a Phillips screwdriver, a chain tool, an adjustable wrench with narrow jaws that will work on pedals, a spoke wrench, and a socket for crank bolts.

the whole rest of the summer. Drop a couple of extra cleat screws into your patch-kit box and be sure to also have a 4 mm Allen key to tighten them.

13. **Spare toe-strap.** If you haven't gone clipless, having an extra strap is handy. Straps sometimes break, and not being cinched in tight sure makes the climbs tough. A toe-strap can be handy even for clipless users. I've seen them used to hold a water bottle in place after the cage broke and even to hold a saddle in place after the clamp bolt on a seat-post broke.

14. **Emergency food.** Keep an extra stash of gel packets (see Chapter 12, "Your Bike's Engine" for more on gel packets) or energy bars in your survival kit for those inevitable times that you end up staying out much longer than planned. Anyone who rides much will eventually get lost or have an irreparable breakdown. Why add hunger on top of whatever misery is keeping you out late?

This small seat-bag can carry enough tools, spares, and food to keep a ride to remember from becoming one you'd rather forget.

Lock 'Em Up

An expensive bike is an inviting target to thieves. Some of these low-life scumbags are good at what they do. The best lock is never letting your bike leave your sight. Of course, that's not always possible. No lock is completely thief-proof, but thieves are basically lazy. Making your bike harder to pilfer by using a lock will hopefully make them move on to easier pickings.

The most secure locks are the U-type made by Kryptonite or Master. These locks have case-hardened shackles and unpickable cylinder lock mechanisms. Beware of cheap imitations. Many of those can be forced open with a crowbar, and some thieves have learned how to open them using a car jack. While U-locks are effective, they're also heavy and awkward to carry. Some riders who only need their lock at one location—perhaps at work or school—leave it there, locked to a pole or bike rack.

Cycology

What should you do if you don't have a lock with you and you have to leave your bike? Take off your front wheel and take it with you (with a quick release, this will only take a few seconds). You can also click your gear shifters a few times after you've stopped. That way, the chain will jump if anyone tries to pedal off. Of course, these tips won't stop the thief who tosses your bike into the back of his or her truck.

Kryptonite also makes the Kraits cable lock that uses the same lock mechanism as its U-lock. The heavy-duty braided cable is extremely tough and can thwart all but the most determined thieves. A Kraits lock weighs only 1.2 pounds.

Another alternative is to use a standard padlock and a Flexweave cable from Kabeltek. Flexweave cables are woven with more wire strands than standard cables. Sure, they can still be cut (eventually), but it would take a bike bandit a long, long time to chop through all those strands. These cables are plastic-coated, so they won't mar a bike's finish, and they come in several lengths. I use them to lock bikes on my truck's roof rack and to lock up all the bikes in my garage.

A cable lock is a good compromise between security and easy carrying.

Women's Department

Much to the joy of women cyclists, manufacturers are increasing their selections of clothing, saddles, and other accessories. Until recently, few bicycle clothing companies offered riding wear for women. That has all changed thanks to companies such as Shebeest, Koulius Zaard, and Terry that exclusively make women's cycling clothing. Some of the major companies have also gotten smart about meeting the needs of their women customers. Cannondale has an extensive line of women's wear. Trek has a large selection, too.

Thanks to these smart companies, women no longer have to settle for men's size small cycling clothing (which usually didn't fit very well). Now they can have cycling wear tailored to fit a woman's smaller waist, wider hips, narrower shoulders, and shorter arms. Whether a woman wants casual yet functional jerseys and shorts, racer-oriented wear, or anything in between, there's plenty from which to choose.

For comfort, it's hard to beat a one-piece skinsuit such as Cannondale's Liberator. They have a rear pocket and a comfortable seat-pad and come in three prints and three solid colors.

Terry Precision Cycling does more than clothing. Terry was the forerunner in saddles designed and shaped to be more comfortable for women. Most of Terry's saddles are made wider at the rear and with a shorter nose. The most obvious feature of a Terry saddle is a hole cut out in the middle of the saddle. The cutout is positioned to eliminate contact to sensitive areas. The Women's Liberator is one of Terry's best sellers. The Women's Liberator Lite has manganese rails instead of steel rails for reduced weight. The Women's Ti Racing Liberator has titanium rails for even lighter weight, and the shape is narrower at the rear to give the rider more freedom of movement.

Terry Precision Cycling invented the hole-in-the-saddle concept. Women swear by the comfort of Terry's Women's Liberator saddles.

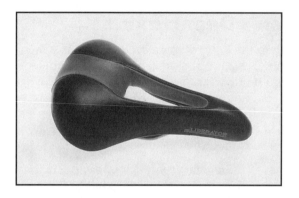

Terry also makes the T-Bar women's handlebar. The patented T-Bar has the classic road bike handlebar shape, but with indents in the bar at the brake lever so that a woman's smaller fingers are set closer to the brake levers. A selection of short reach stems is another popular item from Terry. These stems are made with longer *quills* so that the handlebars can also be set higher than is possible with a standard stem.

Cyclebabble

On a bicycle stem, the **quill** is the portion of the handlebar stem that fits inside the frame. A stem with a long quill allows the handlebar to be adjusted to a higher position by allowing more of the quill to extend out of the top of the frame.

Bringing the Kids

For riders with small children, bringing the kidlets along on a ride can be a lot of fun for everyone. For infants, toddlers, and youngsters not yet able to ride, I recommend the small trailers that are pulled behind an adult's bike. I strongly advise against child seats. There have been some real tragedies resulting from child seats. I witnessed one, and the image of that small child with the head injury will haunt me forever.

Miles of Experience

Kid trailers aren't just for kids. I know a racer who uses a trailer to bring her dog along on training rides. The dog loves it and gets excited about going for a ride as soon as he sees my friend hooking up the trailer. And she likes the company and the extra workout she gets from hauling the trailer and 40 pounds of mutt.

On a child seat, the child is firmly strapped in with his/her head being the highest point on the bike. If the bike falls over, the child's head swings down from about five feet high and can be the first thing to hit the ground. Although child seats are designed to extend outward and above to isolate the child from hitting the ground in a fall, that concept only works if the child is firmly strapped into place. Few kids will submit to being cinched in that tightly. Parents give in and only loosely tighten the belts, which creates enough movement to defeat the impact-isolation features of the child seat. Even if the child's head doesn't contact the ground, that's still an extremely hard jar to a tiny little body.

Several companies make child trailers; Burley, Winchester, and Cannondale are the market leaders. Be wary of cheap imitations sold at department stores. They're usually quite rickety, because the construction isn't near the quality of the major brands. Child trailers are priced at about $320 to $400. That's quite a bit more money than a $50 child seat, but isn't your child's life worth a few extra dollars? There's always used trailers. Trailers are sturdy little things, and considering most get used for only two or three years before they're outgrown, most are still in great shape before they're sold at a garage sale. Used child trailers often sell for about half the cost of a new one. Bike shops with a rental department often rent child trailers, which can be an economical way to go if you'll take the kids along only a few times a year.

Most child trailers are designed to fold flat and have quick-release wheels so that the trailer can be easily stashed in a car trunk or the back of a minivan. The hitch mechanisms on child trailers are designed to pivot so that the trailer remains upright even if the bike falls over. The only real danger is from motorists, but that's always a concern—trailer, child seat, or otherwise. Some child trailers have a plastic body; others use an aluminum framework covered in nylon fabric. Either type is easy to keep clean: simply turn on the hose and spray out the cookie crumbs and stray Gummi Bears.

Some kids are apprehensive about being strapped into a child trailer for the first ride or two. Most learn to love it. Providing snacks and a favorite stuffed toy can help the child feel more at ease about the whole proposition. Child trailers have clear plastic or screen canopies that snap over the front to keep out insects and such and to keep objects in. Use the canopy. Kids don't like being invaded by a swarm of gnats, and kids are also prone to tossing things just to see them fly. You don't want to discover at the end of a ride that the kid's favorite teddy bear is laying on the bike path four miles back.

For kids who are able to ride, but aren't yet able to keep up with Mom and Dad, consider Burley's *Piccolo* Trailercycle. Alley Cat and others make similar machines. These "half-bikes" have a rear wheel, pedals, and handlebars, but in place of the front wheel and fork, they have a hitch that attaches to an adult rider's bike. With one

Cyclebabble

Piccolo is the Italian word for "small."

of these in tow, the adult can pull the youngster along and not have to wait. It's a great way to teach kids to ride, too.

A kid trailer like this one from Burley is far safer than a child seat.

When kids are too big for a trailer but too young to keep up on their own bike, Burley's Piccolo Trailercycle is the answer.

Rack 'Em Up

Not all of our favorite rides begin at our front doors, so it's often necessary to transport bikes by car. Stuffing a bike into a trunk is one way. Shoving it in the back seat is another. There are, however, better ways that don't damage bikes or get grease on leather upholstery.

Among serious cyclists, roof racks are still the most popular means of automotive bike transport. That niche is filled nicely by such companies as Thule, Yakima, Graber, and others. Transporting bikes on a roof rack is handy because it takes advantage of space that would otherwise go unused, leaving the cargo area free for other items.

Using a roof rack is fairly simple: Pop off the bike's front wheel, slip the fork into the rack's fork mount, close the rack's quick-release lever, and strap down the rear wheel. This process can be a real balancing act with tall vehicles, however. The roof of my SUV has quite a few scratches from minor slips I've had while loading and unloading bikes. And with a rack full of bikes, gas mileage suffers.

Carrying a bike with one of the new "through-axle" suspension forks that use motorcycle-type axles isn't possible with a standard roof rack mount. There are two alternatives: The easiest is Hurricane's Fork-Up, a simple device that slips into the fork in place of the axle. It has metal extensions that are the same size and shape as the bottom of a standard bike fork, allowing a through-axle fork to mount to a standard rack. A Fork-Up runs about $40. With Yakima Racks' Anklebiter mount system, a bike with a through-axle fork can be mounted to a Yakima roof rack. The front wheel stays on the bike, and the system secures the bike by the crank. An Anklebiter rack mount is $100.

In recent years, rear racks that attach to a vehicle's trailer hitch have become increasingly popular. Their low height makes loading these racks very easy. There are several manufacturers and several models, carrying two, four, or six bikes. Low-priced hitch racks such as Rhode Gear's Backpacker sell for as little as $175 for a two-bike system. It can be upgraded to a four-bike system for another $120. On the budget-priced hitch racks, access to the trunk or rear doors is restricted. There are, however, several models that swing out of the way or tip back to allow entry.

Bauer's Revolution system has the swing-out-of-the-way feature. A two-bike carrier with locks runs $279.95. To carry four bikes, you'll also need the two-bike extension kit for $59.95. Hollywood's Destination 5GS uses a gas-shock tilt-assist system to pivot the rack down and out of the way of the door. It carries four bikes on the rack, and a fifth

Steer Clear

Roof racks make efficient use of space, but many cyclists have forgotten about having a bike up there and tried to drive into garages or under awnings. Once I was driving my SUV on a dirt road leading to a prime trail. One of the bike's saddles hooked on a tree branch, ripping the entire rack and three bikes right off the roof. A roof rack provides a great way to haul bikes, but you need to always be aware of low-hanging obstacles.

can go between the rack and the vehicle. The 5GS sells for $399.95. Reva Racks makes a rack that carries six bikes, or you can install optional adapters and haul 12 pairs of skis or 12 snowboards. The rack opens up to swing entirely out of the way of the rear door. It sells for $989.

The lowest-priced bike carriers strap onto the rear of a vehicle. They're often called trunk racks. Most rack companies make trunk racks. One of the easiest to use is the Bones rack from Saris. Its unique arch design fits over spoilers and keeps the bikes separated, and it's small enough to be packed along on trips to use on rental cars. A Bones rack costs $89.95.

Although trunk racks are handy, they can sometimes mar a car's finish. Bard Wyers Sports makes the Stealth +4 rack with a patented design that has no struts leaning on the vehicle. The Ski-Logic kit converts the rack to carry four pairs of skis. The Stealth +4 is priced at $119.

An alternative for SUVs with rear-mounted spare tires is Hollywood's Spare Tire Rack that mounts onto the spare. It carries two bikes and can be removed in less than a minute. The price is a low $90.

The Least You Need to Know

➤ Always use a helmet!

➤ Cycling gear such as bicycle shorts and specially made raingear isn't a trendy fashion statement; it's comfortable and functional.

➤ Women don't have to settle for wearing men's cycling wear; many manufacturers now carry a full line of women's cycling clothing, as well as bike parts contoured for women.

➤ When bringing the kids along, opt for a trailer rather than a child seat for better safety.

➤ Roof racks, rear racks, trunk racks, and spare-tire mounts are bike-carrying alternatives that will keep the chain grime off your leather upholstery.

Part 3
Pedal Time

They say that you never forget how to ride a bike. Which raises the question, "What if you never knew how before?" Sure, most folks can manage to pedal down the road, but there's far more to bicycling than just being able to remain upright.

After all my years of riding, the capabilities of bicycles still amaze me. With a merely average rider aboard, a road bike can often keep up with city traffic. Put that theoretical average rider aboard a mountain bike and that bike can cover incredibly treacherous terrain at surprising speeds. That a relatively simple machine that weighs a mere fraction as much as my body is able to do all this is remarkable.

However, these wondrous machines can't do any of these amazing feats on their own. It takes a rider with learned skills and knowledge and developed fitness. This section will help you to learn some of the things you'll need to tap into the amazing performance potential of a bicycle.

Chapter 9

Training Wheels

In This Chapter

➤ Why be a shiftless character?

➤ Going around the bend on a road bike

➤ Using a road bike's "whoa" levers

➤ Tricky mountain biking: bad weather, uphill, and downhill

➤ Dirty deeds: handling dirt trails when climbing

The simple act of riding a bicycle is something most people can do. We all learned to ride a two-wheeler when we were youngsters. The old cliché is true, "It's just like riding a bike; you never forget." However, riding a bike on city streets or off-road trails is far different from those long-ago days of tooling around the neighborhood on your first two-wheeler. To ride more enjoyably requires certain skills and knowledge. In this chapter, I'll go over some new and old skills to make your urban or off-road experiences as fun (and safe) as those first days on the two-wheeler.

Why So Many Gears?

Shifting gears on a modern bike is easy. Move a lever or twist a grip, and the bike will click right into gear without the fishing around for the right spot as on the bikes of old. Yet the abundance of gears on modern bicycles is one of the most intimidating aspects of cycling. I've seen many new riders scratching their heads in confusion as to why their new road bikes have 16 or 18 gears or their new mountain bikes have 24 or 27 gears.

One company banked on that shifting anxiety, using it to sell a ton of bikes equipped with automatic transmissions. Perhaps you recall that company's infomercials. That company eventually went out of business, much to the delight of those who recognized that the bike was overpriced, poorly built, and that the automatic shifting system really didn't work very well.

Actually, there's no need for automatic shifting bikes. The main points of shifting can be learned by anyone in just a few minutes. I've found the quickest way for new riders to learn shifting is to spend some time in parking lot with an experienced rider to take them through all the steps. Although it may take several rides before shifting becomes second nature, most people can catch on to the basics in 15 to 30 minutes, an hour tops.

The Shifting of the Gears

The concept of multiple gears is quite simple if you first understand *why* you need to shift in the first place. A reasonably fit person is most efficient at powering a bicycle when turning the pedals at least once per second. In cycling, revolutions per minute (rpm) is called the *cadence*. So one turn of the pedals per second is a cadence of 60 rpm (more on cadence in Chapter 12, "Your Bike's Engine"). As fitness improves, the ideal cadence increases. Racers commonly spin at 90 rpm. When a rider is spinning faster than the right cadence, it's time to shift to a higher gear. When a rider is grinding along lower than the right cadence, it's time to shift to a lower gear. Simple, eh?

Cyclebabble

Cadence is the revolution of your pedals per minute, or rpm.

A bike's drivetrain consists of the chain, two to three sprockets mounted on the crank, and eight or nine sprockets mounted to the rear wheel. The number of gears a bike has is the number of front sprockets multiplied by the number of rear sprockets. The old 10-speeds had two front sprockets and five rear sprockets: $2 \times 5 = 10$. A modern 27-speed mountain bike has three front sprockets and nine rear sprockets: $3 \times 9 = 27$.

Cyclebabble

A **derailleur** is a mechanism that moves side to side to carry a bike's chain from one sprocket to another. The movement is controlled by the rider's manipulation of a gear shifter.

There are also two mechanisms called *derailleurs*. One is mounted over the front sprockets, and the other is mounted at the rear sprockets. A derailleur derails the chain, moving it from one sprocket to another. Shifting gears is accomplished by moving the gear shifter, which moves a cable running to a derailleur, causing the derailleur to carry the chain to another sprocket.

Gear Shifter Options

Most mountain bikes have either GripShift shifters or Shimano RapidFire shifters. GripShift shifters are twist grips similar to a motorcycle throttle. These shifters have numbered indicators to show what gear the bike is in. The lower the number, the easier the gear. RapidFire shifters have a button located next to the rider's thumb and a trigger positioned in front of the handlebar for the rider's forefinger. They, too, can have numbered gear indicators with the lower numbers indicating easier gears.

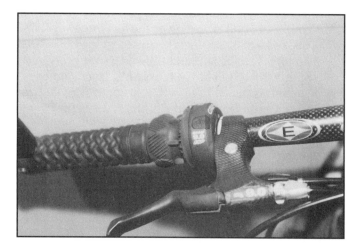

GripShift systems have a pair of twist grips similar to a motorcycle throttle. Turn them to shift gears.

With a Shimano RapidFire shifting system, gears are selected by pushing a button or pulling a trigger.

Older and lower-priced road bikes have a pair of shift levers called *down-tube shifters*. Located on the *down-tube*, the frame tube that runs down from the handlebars to the pedals, these levers don't have numbered indicators. They're still very simple to use. To shift on the rear cogs push the right lever forward for a higher gear—pull back for a lower gear. To shift from the small or middle chainring to a bigger chainring, simply pull the left lever back. Newer and higher-priced road bikes usually have either

Cyclebabble

Until the advent of shift levers built into the brake levers, most road bikes had **down-tube shifters**, simple shift levers mounted on the frame's **down-tube**, or the tube that runs down from the handlebars to the pedals. Some lower-priced road bikes still use them.

Shimano STI shifters or Campagnolo ErgoPower shifters. Both have shifting mechanisms built into the brake lever assemblies.

On the Shimano levers, the entire brake lever is both a brake lever and a shifter. You pivot the lever back to activate the brakes and pivot the lever sideways to shift. A second, smaller lever is mounted to the brake lever. It also pivots to the side and is used to shift gears in the opposite direction of the brake/shift lever. Some Shimano systems come with gear indicators, and you can add indicators to some of the systems that don't.

On Campagnolo's system, the brake lever is just a brake lever, but it has a side pivoting shift lever mounted onto it. To shift back in the opposite direction, a rider uses a small thumb-actuated button located on the side of the brake lever assembly. Campagnolo doesn't use gear indicators.

With a Shimano STI shifting system, the shift levers are built into the brake levers.

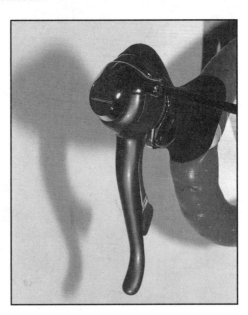

Back on the Chain Gang

Mountain bikes generally have three front sprockets or *chainrings*: a large sprocket called "the big ring," a medium-sized one called "the middle ring," and a smaller one called the "little ring." Because road bikes don't usually encounter the steep terrain of off-road trails, they generally have only two chainrings: a big ring and a little ring. However, some road bikes do come with triples (three chainrings) for those riders who prefer having a wider range of gears.

To demonstrate to yourself how these different chainrings affect the speed and pedaling of a bike, shift the bike onto the big ring and turn the pedals once to see how far the bike travels. Then shift it to the little ring and see what little distance the bike moves compared to the big ring. The big ring is used for high speeds, such as going downhill. The middle ring is for most level-terrain riding, and the little ring is for uphill travel. That's all there is to using the three chainrings, or shifting on "the front," as cyclists say.

Where shifting on the front is for those large changes in gear requirements (uphill, downhill, or level), shifting on "the rear" (moving the chain on the rear sprockets) is a way of fine-tuning the gear selection to stay within your ideal cadence. A bike's right shifter controls shifting on the rear sprockets (remember, "right for rear"). Many rear shifters have indicators, too, numbered one through eight or one through nine. Once again, the lower the number, the easier the gear.

Cyclebabble

The front sprockets of a bicycle are called **chainrings**. Mountain bikes have three chainrings: a small, a medium-sized, and a big chainring. Most road bikes have two chainrings.

When shifting gears, the derailleur moves the chain from one sprocket to another.

Suppose you start up a hill. After several shifts on the rear, the indicator is already at eight or nine, and you find that you still need a lower gear. Then it's time to shift to a lower gear on the front shifter. If that shifter is already at one, then you're already in the lowest gear. It works the other way, too. Suppose you start down a hill in the middle ring (indicator two on the front shifter), and as speed picks up, you've shifted on the rear until the indicator shows your highest number. Then it's time to use the front shifter to click it up to its highest number.

Those are the two extremes of what shifting is all about. All that middle ground is just fine-tuning to keep you in that ideal cadence. These basic concepts will get you through your first rides just fine. Don't be afraid to shift. The clunking and chattering sounds that sometimes happen when shifting are normal. You aren't going to break anything by shifting.

Road Bike Cornering

How does a rider steer a bicycle around a turn? Most people will answer that question with, "Turn the handlebar in the direction you want to turn." However, that's only one element in cornering. You may be surprised to learn that to initiate a turn, a rider first turns the bars very slightly in the opposite direction. This action is called *counter steering*, and its effect is to initiate the lean into a corner that causes the bike to turn. The faster you go, the more the bike will need to be leaned to stay on the intended path through the turn.

Use your brakes to slow before you get to the corner. Apply the brakes while the bike is upright, that is, before you lean it into the turn. When a bike is leaning, it's riding on a very small portion of the tire tread. In that limited traction situation, adding braking forces to the equation could add up to a skid—one that could immediately drop you onto the pavement. Also, braking in a turn causes the bike to want to spring upright from its leaning stance, which can force you to take the corner much wider than planned.

Cyclebabble

To initiate a turn on a two-wheeled vehicle, the rider must slightly turn the handlebar in the opposite direction of the desired turn. This effect is called **counter steering**.

To avoid falling from scraping a pedal on the ground while the bike is leaning in a corner, you should hold the inside pedal in the full upright position while coasting through the turn. It's safest to coast through a corner, because pedaling could cause a pedal to strike the pavement. Experienced riders and racers sometimes pedal through corners, but this skill takes a lot of practice and experience.

Miles of Experience

Despite their narrow width, road bike tires offer a surprising amount of cornering traction. However, unlike mountain bike tires or big, beefy motorcycle tires that give some warning before losing traction altogether, a road bike tire tends to let go all at once. I once received a very convincing lesson in this phenomenon while speeding down a twisty mountain road. I was in tight switchback corner going well over 20 mph when I looked up to see a motorcycle approaching head-on. The motorcyclist was attempting to pass a car and was in my lane! Hoping to avoid the motorcycle, I leaned my bicycle a little more to try to make the corner a little tighter. Suddenly I was on the pavement, sliding past the motorcycle's back wheel. I still carry graphic reminders about the limits of cornering adhesion in the form of shadowy scars on my right calf and right elbow.

To make a bike turn at speed, you need to lean it into the corner.

131

Road Bike Braking

Most bike shops assemble bikes so that the left lever controls the front brake and the right lever controls the rear brake (remember again, "right for rear"). Some riders, especially those with motorcycle experience, prefer to have their levers set up the other way around. That's fine. But realize that once you're accustomed to riding your own bike you may have trouble riding someone else's, especially in a panic stop. (And it would be a good idea to mention your "motorcycle style" brake if someone else rides your bike.)

Most of a bicycle's available stopping power is in the front brake, but many new riders fear using the front brake. Keep in mind that a flight over the front handlebars is a fate that only befalls those who use too much of *only* the front brake. For the most effective braking, apply both the front and rear brake together. By also applying the rear brake, you ask for less braking force from the front brake and erase the likelihood of locking the front wheel (and the rider taking a trip over the bars). When using a lot of front brake, brace yourself against the handlebars and slide back a little in the saddle to counter the braking forces that are pulling you forward. Using only the rear brake will greatly increase the distance needed to stop or slow and could result in a skid. Road tires are very narrow; skidding could cause you to lose control and could grind through the tire, causing an immediate flat.

Miles of Experience

I bought my first "good" bike as training for my sport of passion at the time: motocross. Having spent several years riding motorcycles (machines that have the front brake lever on the right side), I was surprised to learn that bicycles traditionally have the front brake lever on the left side. Very surprised. In fact, I nearly crashed in the bike shop parking lot on my first test ride. I had the bike shop assemble my new bike with the front brake lever on the right. I rode that way for the next 14 years until I took a job at a bike magazine. After having several near crashes from grabbing the wrong lever on magazine test bikes, I switched my front-brake lever to the left side. It took nearly a year to fully adapt.

I recommend that new riders practice hard braking in a vacant parking lot. Start out by practicing stopping from a moderate speed. Do it repeatedly, picking up a little more speed each time. Pick out a marker such as a paint stripe and use it as point to begin hard braking; see how much you can reduce your stopping distance. Once you're confident in that skill, try applying the brakes hard enough to cause the rear wheel to begin to skid. Once the wheel is skidding, releasing brake pressure to the rear wheel will keep you from wearing through the tire. Knowing what a skid feels like and how to control it is a valuable skill that you may need in the event of a panic stop.

Off-Road Basics

Riding a mountain bike is a bit different from riding a road bike. The rider needs to take a much more active role in keeping a mountain bike on track. Using these eight great basic mountain bike riding tips will keep you safe in the saddle:

1. **Bumps.** Sitting down over the rough parts will pound your tailbone and may cause a crash. Standing on the pedals in a crouch position allows you to use your legs as shock absorbers. Straightening the arms slightly to get more weight over the rear of the bike helps to keep you from getting pitched forward.

Cycology

When standing up for a bumpy section, don't extend your legs so that your knees lock. Keep your knees slightly bent to allow them to flex and absorb bumps.

To avoid a buttocks pounding, stand up over bumps and use your legs as shock absorbers.

2. **Body positioning.** Bikes are ridden, not driven. The rider who simply plops into the saddle and doesn't move around to control the bike will have very little control. Turning the bars to steer and maneuver is a minor factor in the control equation. Watch the pros. They're in a constant dance of standing to absorb bumps with their legs, leaning forward to weight the front wheel for cornering, moving back over the rear wheel to increase climbing traction, leaning into turns, and any combination of all these moves.

Cycology

Learning is usually easier with a visual aid. The next time you're flipping channels and come across a mountain bike race, sit back and pay close attention to how the riders position their bodies for the corners, bumps, and various changes in terrain. Watching a Supercross race is just as valuable because motorcycle motocross racers use the same types of body position as mountain bike racers.

Steer Clear

Avoid skidding the rear wheel. Not only does it take longer to stop in a skid, it also damages the trail. Don't give the anti-mountain bike crowd ammunition to use against us. Skidding also wears out tires, and tires aren't exactly cheap.

3. **The rear brake.** Increase front tire traction for cornering with a light touch on the rear brake to transfer forward motion into downward force on the front wheel. Using the rear brake will instantly bring the front wheel down if an out-of-control wheelie is about to dump you on your buns.

4. **The front brake.** The majority of your stopping power is in the front brake—don't be afraid of it. It will take much longer to stop by using only the rear brake, and you'll probably end up skidding. Learning proper front braking will make you a safer rider. Tales of being thrown over the handlebars are mostly exaggeration. True, simply grabbing a handful of left lever can launch you, but not if you get your weight back and brace your arms against the handlebars. New riders should practice front braking on level ground to get a feel for it.

5. **Wheelies.** Balancing on the rear wheel isn't just to impress your friends. Doing wheelies is also valuable for increasing rear wheel traction, lofting the front wheel over an obstacle, or riding through a puddle without getting splashed on. To loft the front wheel, yank up on the bars, pulling up and back with the upper body and apply downward torque to the pedals. Practice on grass to prevent bruised tailbones and remember the back brake will bring the wheelie down, as explained in tip 3.

6. **Rear-wheel unweighting.** This counterpart to a wheelie gets the rear wheel over the obstacle just cleared by the front wheel. Using this technique

increases the life span of the wheel. To unweight, rise up over the saddle and move slightly forward on the bike. Keeping your feet parallel to the ground, jump up slightly while lifting up and pulling the bike toward your butt. Clipless pedals or toe-clips really help here.

7. **Bunny-hopping.** This technique is useful for clearing ruts, obstacles, or even an otherwise unavoidable downed rider. Combine the techniques of tips 6 and 7 and focus on jumping straight up to lift the entire bike off the ground.

Bunny-hopping the bike in the air is a fun and useful skill.

8. **Brake lever position.** Some riders seem to think that brake levers should be positioned horizontally, but this position cocks the rider's wrists upward, resulting in muscle strain. Brake levers should be angled slightly downward so that when seated on the bike with hands on the grips, your wrist-to-hand junction is either straight or slightly cocked downward.

Steep Drop-Ins: Taking the Express Elevator Down

There's a sick feeling that mountain bike riders get when they look up at an ultra-steep trail, knowing that they're going to have to climb it. About the only worse feeling is when they look down at that same steep pitch, knowing that they're going to

Cycology

An easy way to learn to ride down steep pitches is to practice doing them with a low saddle height. Shoving the saddle down will lower your center of gravity and greatly reduce the "about to go over the top" feeling. Riders who thrive on riding steep stuff sometimes install a quick-release lever on the seat-post clamp so that the seat can be quickly lowered or raised as needed.

have to go down it. Riding off a steep drop-in doesn't have to be an eye-popping panic session. Knowing a few pointers can have almost any rider looking forward to the next chance to let gravity have its way.

Get Those Buns Back

The most important thing to remember when going down steep trails is to get your weight back. Straighten your arms, get up off the saddle, and hang your fanny back over the rear wheel. Having your weight back will help keep traction on the rear wheel while also lightening the front end so that the front tire can skim over ruts and ripples. Also, this rearward position can help keep you from doing a *faceplant*. However, don't hang off the back all the way. Leave yourself a little leeway so that if the trail suddenly gets steeper or if you hit something that's likely to send you forward, you can lunge back a bit to counteract it.

Cyclebabble

Faceplant: The act of falling off a bike and landing on your face. Experts advise against this practice.

Another technique to keep you from getting tossed forward is to brace your feet against the pedals by angling your ankles back a little. You want your feet to be pointed slightly upward so that the soles are perpendicular to any forces trying to toss you forward.

The trail is steep, but by keeping his weight back and bracing himself against the handlebars and pedals, this rider is in complete control.

Level Thinking

The dread that enters the hearts of most riders fearful of steep drop-ins is usually brought about by concerns over hitting an obstacle and getting launched over the bars, despite putting their weight back. Much of that fear can be relieved by taking a look at the trail, examining the surface, and imagining if any of its bumps, ripples, or ruts would be anything to be fearful of if the trail were level. Are there any holes, rocks, or square-edged bumps that are likely to deflect or stop the front wheel? If so, is there a smooth line around them? Keep in mind when choosing that line that there won't be much room for maneuvering on the trail, so you don't want to choose a line that's too twisty.

Things happen fast on steep drop-ins. Trying to flick a quick direction change may not be an option. Most of your steering will have to be done with body positioning and bike leaning. Trying to turn the bars can easily make the front end push and plow. Down you go. Look ahead, plan ahead, and make your line smooth and gradual.

Another anxiety-producing aspect of drop-ins is the steepness itself. But think about it; bikes are meant to roll. In fact, the faster they roll, the more stable they are. If there's nothing in the way, no bumps or ruts likely to cause a crash, and if there's enough run-off room, what's to keep you from rolling over the top of the hill and just letting 'er rip?

It's important to let the bike roll whenever possible. A wheel that's rolling will pass over a rut or bump, but a braking wheel will bounce and swap side to side. Use the brakes if there's some obstacle that mandates that you keep your speed in check, but use the brakes as lightly as you can. You want to avoid skidding. Locking up the back wheel can easily send the bike sliding sideways, sending you off your line—usually right into that rain rut that you were trying to avoid.

To keep your speed in control while still avoiding a skid, you'll need to use the front brake. "But that will launch me over the bars!" you say. Not true, as long as you do it carefully. Go easy on the front brake and let off if you feel the back end starting to lift. Watch the terrain carefully and let off as the front wheel is about to hit any obstacles. If you keep your arms straight and your weight back and are careful with that left lever, you'll soon realize how valuable the front brake is in controlling your speed, even on steep drop-ins.

It's also critical to stay loose and let the bike flow. Keep your arms and upper body relaxed, let your legs move up and down with the bike, and let it have some freedom to move around a little. Riding stiffly and rigidly can easily bounce you right off your intended line and into that rain rut.

Cycology

Remember how in driver's ed, your teacher harped on you to not focus on the brake lights of the car in front of you and instead to look at the horizon as a whole? The point was to get you to see everything that was going on and all possible obstacles that might present themselves. It's the same with bicycling: If you just look at the ground directly in front of you, you'll never see that crater or massive bump coming. Get a full picture of what's in front of you—it could save you from an ugly spill.

Sand: It's No Day at the Beach

Sand. No mountain bike rider likes it. It's nasty. It ranks right up there with steep hills and headwinds in the "least favorite things to ride" category. But like it or not, sand happens. Knowing how to deal with it can be the difference between grinding to a halt (or falling over) and skimming over the top.

Attack Your Enemy

The only way to beat sand is to charge it in a full frontal assault. To defeat the sand, you're going to need the smoother power output of a higher gear as you continue pedaling and trying to power your way over the top of the sand. So the first thing to do when approaching a sandy area is to upshift a gear or two higher than the one you would normally use for a given speed.

Just before your front wheel reaches the sand, get your weight back—way back. That means having your hands on the handlebars and not the bar-ends, and it means straightening your arms and hanging your buns off the back of the saddle to keep that driving rear wheel digging for traction.

Cycology

Any braking in sand needs to be done when the bike is still upright and aimed straight ahead. If you try to brake while leaning the bike or while trying to steer, the wheel being braked will slide out.

Hopefully, you'll be able to carry enough momentum to skim all the way to the other side of the sand. But on long sand sections or ones with deep, soft sand, you'll probably find yourself slowing down. Keep pedaling; otherwise, the front wheel will plow you right into the sand. Look for hard-packed areas that won't bog you down as much. Also, try yanking up on the handlebars to weight the rear wheel even more. Time those yanks with a lunge at the pedals as if you're trying to wheelie. This technique can often keep you rolling for those last few feet of sand. Remember, getting going again in sand is practically impossible, especially in deep sand.

Staying Straight

Ideally, because the front wheel should only be skimming the surface when you're riding over sand, steering input should be light and gradual. Don't try to force the front wheel into a precise chosen line. Sudden movements will only cause the front end to plow into the sand, causing you to bog down or stop. Instead, choose a path a foot or two wide and let the bike wander a little. Don't be alarmed when the front wheel deflects and veers off a bit. Let it have its way for the moment and then gently guide it back. The same goes for the rear wheel. It may slide around and fishtail some, but keep pedaling in order maintain traction. The bike will continue to go straight ahead, more or less.

Cornering

Cornering is another instance when momentum is your friend. When approaching a sandy corner, keep your speed up and avoid slowing yourself down with the brakes. The sandy surface is going to slow you down anyway. If at all possible, continue pedaling through the corner. Any last-moment braking on the sand should be done with the rear brake; front braking will cause the front to plow. Corner with a wide, sweeping arc. Attempting to square off the corner will probably just cause the front of the bike to wash out.

Riding in sand will never be particularly fun, but a few simple skills can keep it from being something to be feared.

Snow Riding 101

For riders living in places where it snows, winter often means it's time to hang the bike in the garage. It doesn't have to be that way. Riding in snow can be a kick and is a lot more fun than riding a stationary bike 'til spring.

When riding in snow, dress in layers so if it gets warm, you can shed some clothing. You'll be generating body heat, so if you're warm enough when you step out, you're overdressed. But bring along an extra layer, just in case.

Take care in choosing your clothing. Avoid cotton, especially as a first layer. Once cotton gets wet, it stays wet and gets bitterly cold. And it will get wet, either from perspiration or from falling in the snow. Start with something that can wick away moisture, such as polypro thermal underwear or Lycra tights. Then pile on other layers of cycling clothing, ski wear, or cross-country ski wear. And don't forget your feet. Wool or polypropelene socks with waterproof over-socks will keep your feet warm and dry.

Staying warm is the key to keeping snow riding fun. A balaclava such as this one from Cannondale can keep a rider's head and ears toasty warm. By wearing it over the mouth, a rider can also breathe pre-warmed air to prevent lung burn from chilled air.

Once your feet get cold, your body is soon to follow. Keep your dogs warm with oversocks.

If you're riding clipless pedals, find your old toe-clip pedals and bolt those on instead. You're going to be doing some walking and pushing. Clipless pedal cleats will pick up snow and jam up the works of clipless pedals, making it difficult to click in or, worse yet, impossible to click out. About the best pedal setup for snow is a set of platform pedals with power straps. For footwear, I use a pair of low-top Sorrel shoes. They keep my feet dry and warm and are easy to slip into the pedals.

Finally, along with your usual survival kit (tools, spare tubes, and so on), grab a small pack and toss in some snacks, a trash bag to use as an emergency poncho, and some extra clothes—having something dry to put on can be a blessing.

It's surprising how much traction there is in a shallow layer of white stuff. Even deep snow can offer good grip if it's been packed down by 4×4s, ATVs, or snowmobiles. Get in the tracks and go. Lowering your air pressure will increase traction. With the lower speeds of snow riding, you're not likely to get a pinch flat. Just be careful of buried rocks and square-edged bumps.

Riding in snow can be a lot like driving in it. Don't make any sudden moves if the surface is icy. On icy sections, it's important to keep the bike perfectly upright, keep it straight, and lay off the brakes. Failing at any one of these will land you on the ice in an instant.

Just because there's snow on the ground doesn't mean the bike has to stay in the garage. Snow riding can be big fun!

To keep your speed in check, look ahead and anticipate where the patches of traction are. Generally, if the surface is white, traction is good. Translucent or shiny surfaces are usually more slippery than greased Teflon. Keep your brakes from icing up by lightly applying the brakes occasionally to scrape off the ice and snow. You want to be sure that they'll work when you need them.

To keep momentum, again look for those precious patches of traction where you can get out a few good pedal strokes. Even when traction is limited, you can still maintain forward motion by pedaling with just enough force to keep moving and keep traction.

When you do get wheelspin, momentarily back off your pedaling force. If that's not enough, slide back on the saddle to weight the back wheel.

Riding in snow is much like riding in mud and sand; you won't be able to choose a precise line. Instead, select a general path that allows for the inevitable slipping and sliding. Chances are you'll take a tumble or two, but snow is soft. Right?

Mountain Biking in Rain, Mud, and Muck

In wet conditions, traction is rare. Mud robs you of momentum and makes it difficult to ride a straight line. Many sand-riding techniques also apply to mud.

Traction will vary with the amount of moisture. Damp soil usually has more traction than dry soil. A thin layer of mud isn't difficult to deal with either; your tires will dig down to the dry surface underneath. But when the mud gets thick, riding becomes tricky.

Mud riding means learning to control wheelspin. To avoid bogging down to a stop, you'll sometimes need to keep pedaling to churn through long after knobby-to-trail adhesion has gone. The bike will fishtail, but steer ahead and keep pedaling; it will straighten out.

The best way to tackle slippery sections is to gain speed where possible and carry that hard-earned momentum over the slippery patches. Pedal or at least get off the brakes where traction is better. Any lump of grass, dry sand, or gravel will offer better traction than mud. One of the trickiest conditions you'll ever encounter is a muddy uphill. Using the momentum-carrying technique is your best chance of making it up.

In deep mudholes, finesse goes out the window. Lean back, yank on the handlebars, and blast through. When faced with deep, bike-swallowing mudholes, the aggressive rider has a better chance of coming out the other side.

Cycology

Some snow riders swear by studded tires and tire chains. I agree that they can help in icy conditions, but they don't do much for plain old snow. Nokian makes studded tires, and some riders make their own using sheet-metal screws. They screw them through the tire from the inside of the tire casing and cover the screw heads with pieces of duct tape to keep them from puncturing the inner tube.

Cycology

A cycling computer with cadence function (pedal rpm readout) can be a big help when going uphill. A drop in cadence will show immediately—"Uh-oh, down to 68 rpms, time to pick up the pace"— but a drop in miles per hour won't show up until you've already slowed by 1 mph, which can indicate a drop of 10 to 20 rpms.

Trails that you think you know take on a different character when rain comes. Low patches become puddles, and gullies become streams. It's sometimes hard to judge just how deep a stream or puddle is. I know one rider who misjudged the depth of a stream, blasted into it, was tossed off, and nearly lost her bike. Luckily, she was able to reach out under water and grab a wheel. Stop and check the water before blasting through.

Here's a few more wet/muddy tips:

1. Avoid following the line of riders ahead of you. Their tire spray will blast your eyes, and when they fall (and they will), the limited traction on a wet trail may prevent you from stopping in time.

2. Lowering your tires' air pressure will increase traction. With the lower speeds of wet-weather riding, you're not likely to get a pinch flat. Just be careful on jumps and square-edged bumps.

3. Keep your water bottle in your jersey pocket where the drinking spout will stay clean.

Climbing

What was Sir Isaac Newton thinking? If not for that long-haired Brit's revelations on gravity, we'd be able to go up hills as easily as we go down them. Makes you wish old Isaac had never sat under that apple tree. Congress isn't likely to repeal the Law of Gravity any time soon, so we must learn to deal with it. The following sections provide a few tips for handling the downward pull when you're climbing up.

Road and Mountain Bike Climbing

Of all the skills and abilities that make up this wonderful sport, climbing is the one that commands the most respect. I've seen a lot of riders with experience in motocross, BMX, or some other speed sport get on a mountain bike or road bike and immediately be able to corner fast or speed down hills. Has anyone ever taken his or her first bike ride and instantly shown exceptional climbing ability? I've never seen it. Going uphill fast is something that comes with time.

The key to effective climbing is learning how to pace. Starting out in a big gear may seem heroic at first, but as fatigue sets in, your pace will drop, and you'll go anaerobic. It makes more sense to maintain a constant effort for the entire climb. A fit rider should be able to maintain a pedaling cadence of 65 to 75 rpms or more. Dropping below that pace may seem like the faster way up the hill, but unless the rider is one of those rare brutes able to power high, big gears, trying to "big ring" up a hill will result only in pumped up legs, elevated heart rate, and even injured knees. Today's road bikes are blessed with 16 or 18 gears, and mountain bikes have 24 or even 27 gears. Use them!

Standing up occasionally during a long climb will help ease the fatigue by using different muscles and putting your body weight to work for you. "Why not do the whole climb standing?" you ask. For a short incline, that's not a bad idea—one short power effort puts you over the top. But for a long grinder, standing the whole way can have the same effects as trying to push a big gear.

Standing while climbing can give a rider added power, but it's also very tiring.

Dirty Tricks

So far, I've covered the aspects of climbing that relate to pedaling and power output. If this chapter were only about road riding, we could quit there. But adding in the uncertain element of dirt and its varying degrees of traction brings skill into the equation. Mashing away at the pedals without regard to the trail surface can result in unwanted wheelspin and wheelies; either can carry riders off their intended lines. On dirt, a rider with good technique can outclimb a more powerful yet lesser-skilled rider.

Optimizing traction is very important. Think about it. When you're climbing, all the force needed to lift the weight of you and your bike is being transferred through the few tire knobs in contact with the ground. When traction is limited, getting back on the saddle to weight the rear tire will help keep the rear tire's knobby tread hooked up. For sections with even less traction, such as a deep dusty patch, a quick wheelie will help the tire dig for every iota of grip. When you approach a slick spot, pull back and up on the handlebars at the last moment.

Getting back in the saddle also has the effect of raising the saddle; as a result, the hip joints are further from the crank spindle for more leverage and are better able to take full advantage of the "stomping down" portion of the pedal stroke. Rocking the bike back and forth also helps squeeze out a little extra power.

Squeezing out a little more power is also one of the main advantages of putting *bar-ends* on a mountain bike. With your hands high up on them, you have more leverage to push against for the downward stroke of the pedals. Bar-ends are also effective in keeping the front end of the bike down. Holding onto the bar-ends and leaning forward will help ward off unwanted wheelies.

Only the very nastiest and steepest trails are unridable. So often I see riders get defeated mentally by looking all the way to the top of a climb and convincing themselves that it can't be done. Break down the climb into individual segments. For instance, concentrate on just making those first 10 or 15 feet. Once you've done that, look ahead and plan your attack for the next 15 feet. Before you know it, you'll be near the top.

Cyclebabble

Bar-ends are extension handles that are clamped onto the ends of mountain bike handlebars. They're positioned pointing forward and provide extra hand positions. They also allow the rider to place his/her weight further forward to counteract the tendency for the front wheel to lift under hard climbing efforts on steep hills. Bar-ends also provide slightly more power by allowing riders to pull upward with their arms while thrusting downward with their pedals.

Miles of Experience

Here's a tip that can earn you a few positions in a race or humble your friends on a weekend ride. Just before the crest of a long climb, click up a gear or more, stand up, and accelerate over the top. Sure, your heart rate will jump, maybe even get close to your max for a few moments. But realize that you have the downhill to recover, and that the riders behind you have just been demoralized. They're thinking, "Oh man. If he's feeling that strong, just let him go." Only you need to know that your heart is racing and you're seeing stars. Knowing when to attack the crest is something that comes with experience. It may be only 10 feet from the top or 50 feet if you're feeling strong. Coming out ahead on climbs is as much a mental game as a physical game. Knowing how to use your brain and your muscles can make a huge difference.

Climbing on a mountain bike takes more than brute strength. It also takes skill and finesse.

The Least You Need to Know

➤ Shifting gears is easy—just get out there and practice.

➤ Yes, you really do want to use the front brake.

➤ You don't have to hang up your bike in snowy or rainy conditions; you just need to be prepared for the terrain.

➤ When riding off-road, don't stiffen up if the trail gets unruly. Give your bike a little room to go with the flow in order to ultimately maintain control.

➤ Any fearless rider can go fast down a hill, but only the truly fit can ride fast up a hill.

Chapter 10

Rules of the Road

> **In This Chapter**
>
> ➤ Ride as you would drive
>
> ➤ Avoid becoming a statistic
>
> ➤ Eyes on your own work
>
> ➤ Because they're not looking for you
>
> ➤ Three tons of rage

In most states, bicyclists are required to follow the same traffic laws as automobiles. Abiding by these laws will make you a safer rider. Traffic laws are designed to allow all traffic to flow in a predictable manner. Cyclists who deviate from this flow make themselves unpredictable to motorists and put themselves in danger. In this chapter, I'll show you what you need to know to ride on the road safely and responsibly while still having fun.

Right as Rain

Although some riders may feel safer being able to see approaching motorists by riding against traffic, in reality this is one of the most dangerous things a cyclist can do. You *must* ride on the right side of the road with the flow of traffic. Think about being in your car and imagine you're about to turn in or out of a driveway or side street. Where are you looking? Chances are you aren't looking for a bike coming the wrong way, and you'll make your turn. If there's a wrong-way rider approaching, you'll drive right into that rider's path. It happens all the time and is one of the leading factors of fatal bike accidents.

Don't Get Injured at the Intersection

Don't go to the curb at intersections. Pulling up to the curb can do two things:

1. It can block the way for motorists, especially those attempting to turn right.

2. It puts you in a very dangerous place. A common bike-versus-auto accident is a cyclist being hit by a right-turning motorist who didn't see the cyclist positioned at the curb. A motorist making a right turn is usually looking to the left for opposing traffic.

When stopping for a signal or stop sign, position yourself to the right of the right front fender of the car waiting to go straight. That way, there's enough room for everybody. You've left enough room so that a motorist can turn right, and your intentions are clear to the motorist going straight. When the light does change, you can proceed immediately. A cyclist stopped at the curb may have to dodge right-turning motorists before proceeding.

Steer Clear

I've had people tell me that back in elementary school they were taught to ride against traffic. Of all the bonehead things a cyclist can do to put him- or herself in danger, riding on the wrong side of the road is among the most hazardous. Motorists are watching the normal flow of traffic. Anything traveling outside of that normal flow is easily overlooked.

Miles of Experience

Have you ever seen a road rider balancing his or her bike while stopped at a light? Riders do this to avoid having to clip out of their pedals and to be able to proceed the moment the light changes. Some years ago before clipless pedals, I was balancing at a light and evidently hadn't left enough room to my right for a motorist to make a right turn. Suddenly, the left front fender of an olive green Oldsmobile was against my hip, sending me sprawling onto the pavement. As I struggled to free my feet from my straps and toe-clips, I looked up to see the elderly lady at the wheel of the Delta 88. Before I could say anything, she yelled, "You shouldn't be on the road with those damn bicycles!" then she made her turn and drove off. Ever since then I've made extra sure to leave enough room for drivers turning right.

The quickest, easiest, and safest way to turn left at an intersection is to use the left turn lane just as you would when driving. Any of the alternatives would have you pull up to the curb, which of course leads to problems with motorists turning right. By positioning yourself in the left turn lane, you're in the field of view of motorists behind you who are also turning left.

To pull to the left turn lane from the right lane or bike lane, look back and wait for a break in traffic. Look the drivers in the face and signal your intentions by pointing left. Don't make your lane change too early, or you may end up with faster-moving traffic behind you.

Pull into the left turn lane and take your position in line. Locate yourself on the right edge of the left lane so that motorists behind you don't have to follow you through the intersection, but can make their turn to your left. Be ready to move as soon as the light changes.

Steer Clear

Although using the left turn lane is the quick and safe way to turn left, getting to that left turn lane can be tricky. Use some discretion and realize that sometimes there won't be a safe break in traffic for a bike to go from the right shoulder to the left lane.

Reading the Road

Keeping your eyes open to the road's surface and configuration can keep you out of trouble. Watch out for broken glass, sand patches, and other possible obstacles to your cycle.

Miles of Experience

Until I began riding highways and city streets on a pair of fragile inch-wide tires, I never had any idea how much broken glass is out there. In my years on the road, I've developed a habit of continually scanning all around me. I'm watching for traffic to my side, watching for traffic ahead, and also looking ahead at the road surface. Watch for sparkles, because that's almost always glass. Because most broken glass comes from bottles tossed out of moving cars, the "debris field" can be fairly long. Often there will be a path at the edge of the traffic lane that's been cleared by the passage of car tires. This clear path provides an easy way to avoid glass, but take a quick look over your shoulder before pulling into the traffic lane. Don't hesitate to stop if there's no break in traffic—there's no sense in getting clobbered while trying to avoid glass.

Another thing to watch out for is sewer grates, especially those with slats running in the same direction as the road. Although most cities now use grates with a grid pattern, older towns may still have grates with slats spaced wide enough to allow a one-inch-wide tire to drop in between. When that happens, the front wheel stops immediately. The rider, however, does not. If there are wheel-swallowing grates in your town, contact your city government and be sure to mention that several cyclists have been injured by such grates and have successfully sued cities and been awarded large cash settlements. Although your city council or mayor may not necessarily give a hoot about cyclists, you can bet they care dearly about the city coffers.

Reading the road also means looking out for things such as two lanes that merge into one, disappearing road shoulders, and so on. Sections of road that go from two lanes to one are especially perilous. What often happens here is that one motorist will try to overtake another before the lane disappears. As the two cars squeeze into the bottleneck, there won't be any room left for you and your bike. Watch ahead for situations like this and hang back behind the cars to avoid being squeezed off the road or into the curb.

Cycology

When a group of cyclists ride in a single-file line, only the lead rider has a clear view of the road surface and the road hazards ahead. It's common bike etiquette for the lead rider to call out and point out road hazards. All it takes to keep the whole pack aware is a quick hand gesture and a short word or two. If you're the lead rider, point to whichever side has the hazard and call out loud enough to be heard by the next two or three riders behind you. When you're one of those riders in back, you'll appreciate hearing: "Glass right"; "Hole left"; or "Sand!"

Reading the Drivers

When motorists scan for traffic, they're looking for other cars, not bicycles. Assuming that you've been seen just because you're right in a motorist's line of sight can be a fatal mistake. Read on to learn how to survive encounters with drivers who fail to recognize anything weighing less than two tons.

Motorists Who Don't See You

With few exceptions, most motorists don't want to injure and maim another human being. Making eye contact with a motorist will make it click in his or her brain that it's a living, breathing human astride that pesky bicycle. In those instances when a motorist looks back with a vacant stare, give a friendly wave to get his or her attention. Often when I've done this, the motorist's reaction has been one of surprise—I hadn't registered on his or her brain until the motorist saw my human hand waving. Remember to always remain cautious, even with a motorist who looks you right in the eyes. You still may not have registered, and he or she might still pull out right in front of you.

Motorists Turning Left

One of the scariest bicycle versus motorist encounters is to have a car turn left in front of you as you're traveling straight through an intersection. Usually these encounters are classic examples of the motorist not seeing the bicyclist. To reduce your chances of becoming a hood ornament, do everything you can to be seen. When you approach an intersection and see a motorist on the other side waiting to turn left, try to make eye contact as early as possible. You also want to make your intentions clear; so if possible, pull out slightly into the traffic lane so that it's obvious you're not stopping or turning at the corner. If eye contact with the left-turning motorist is established, point ahead to signal you're going straight.

Carefully watch the motorist and the vehicle for signs of movement. Watch the motorist's hands on the wheel. Although many motorists turn the wheel to the left before making a turn, that should also be taken as a warning that the driver is about to move—right now.

Be prepared to take evasive action should the driver decide to proceed in front of you. Your clearest path is usually to your right. You want to put as much distance between you and the car as possible. If you're not yet in the intersection or have just entered it, making a hard turn to the right can put you parallel with the car as it turns.

Realize that while you and I know that a bicycle has the same rights to the road as a car, many motorists refuse to believe this. They honestly don't understand that turning left in front of a bicycle is a moving violation and an endangerment to the cyclist.

Miles of Experience

I once had a motorist begin a left turn in front of me and then stop short in the middle of the intersection. I skidded to a stop just a few feet short of her right fender. In my anger of nearly being clobbered, I yelled out, "What are you doing? I have the right-of-way!" She replied, "No you don't. Don't be ridiculous. You're on a bicycle." Then she drove off, smug in her false conviction that she was right and I was wrong.

Motorists Pulling Out of Parking Lots

There's something about pulling onto a major street from a parking lot that seems to make motorists go brain dead. Bicyclists need to be extra aware when passing a parking lot driveway.

Motorists waiting to make a left turn out of a parking lot will often pull out partially into the road. They want to get a better view of oncoming traffic and want to get a head start. Unfortunately, this tactic also blocks that portion of the lane where bicyclists ride. If the motorist pulls out too far, it also leaves precious little room between traffic in the right lane and the motorist's front bumper. In these cases, your safest maneuver might be to whip a right turn into the parking lot, pull around the back of the motorist, and then turn back onto the road.

A motorist waiting to turn right out of a parking lot can be just as dangerous to a passing cyclist. They're usually watching for oncoming cars and can easily overlook a bicyclist in that narrow space between the right lane and curb. As always, try to make eye contact.

If possible, use the cars in the right lane to your advantage. The motorist is not going to make his or her turn into an oncoming car. So position yourself next to one of these cars as you pass in front of the motorist and avoid being in the gap between cars. The motorist might see the gap as an opportunity to turn and not see you.

Parked Cars

Cars parked at the curb can present a variety of dangers to a cyclist. First off, when riding past a line of parked cars, avoid veering right into the space between them. Although this may momentarily give you a little extra breathing room between yourself and the traffic in the right lane, it also puts you in a vulnerable position when the gap ends and you have to veer left back into the traffic lane. You could end up getting squeezed between traffic and a parked car or might even find out too late that a motorist has taken the entire right lane, which will then force you into the back of the parked car. Ouch. By staying partially in the lane and holding your position to the left of the parked cars, you'll force motorists approaching from behind to stay in the left side of the right lane, and you won't get forced into a parked car.

Another danger of a parked car is having the driver or backseat passenger open the door into your path. Always watch for occupied parked cars. Making eye contact isn't usually an option because the people usually have their back toward you. So watch their movements. Most people will lean to their left as they're opening a door. Also watch the edge of the door for movement. When approaching an occupied parked car, look behind you for a moment to see if there are any cars behind you or if there's a break in traffic that you can pull into for the moment you're passing the parked car. You want to have an escape route should that door swing open. If there is no escape route, slow down so if the door does open, you'll hopefully be able to stop in time.

Cycology

Here's another instance where riders in a pack need to look out for each other. Just as the lead rider should call out road hazards, he or she should also call out potentially dangerous cars. A few typical warnings are "Car door"; "Parked cars"; or just "Car." By the same token, the riders in back should alert the riders ahead of an approaching motorist with a call of "Car back."

If a door does open in your path and there's no room on your left to avoid hitting it, use both brakes hard (but avoid skidding), straighten your arms, hang your buns off the back of the seat, and brace for impact. Take some comfort in knowing that in most states it's the driver's responsibility to check for traffic before opening a door. The motorist or his or her insurance company will probably pick up your medical bills and pay for a new bike.

Hostile Motorists

Remember the big bully in elementary school who used to shake down smaller kids for lunch money? He's all grown up now (physically at least) and has a driver's license and car. Only now, he uses his big car to pick on the smaller road users. Over the years, I've encountered a few of these oafs. I've had drivers squeeze me toward the curb, I've had them pull into the bike lane and skid in front of me, and I've had them toss glass bottles in my path.

I've never understood what would cause a motorist to feel justified in terrorizing a cyclist. Perhaps some become annoyed at having to steer around a bicyclist. Others seem to feel that bikes don't belong on the road (I've had motorists scream, "Get off the highway!"), and some are just plain vicious.

There's not much that a cyclist can do about an aggressive, hostile motorist. A 24-pound bike and a Styrofoam helmet are no match for a few thousand pounds of steel and a big-block V-8. If you're confronted by an antagonistic driver, it's best not to answer with a challenge. Getting away from the motorist is the safest strategy. There's an old Japanese proverb, "Of the 36 plans, flight is the best." Following that logic can be as simple as turning down a side street or pulling into a gas station or shopping center. If your encounter is on a rural road, getting off onto the shoulder may be enough.

As far as getting help from the police, unless contact has been made, don't put much stock in that. Unless the officer sees the motorist in the act of terrorizing a cyclist, there's not much the officer can do. The police may not believe you anyway. I've known a few people who have reported aggressive motorists only to be met with skepticism.

I once had a truck driver purposely make a right turn in front of me (he looked me in the face and laughed as he did it), causing me to barely miss hitting his back bumper. A few blocks later when I saw him in a convenience store parking lot, I felt fortunate to see a police car in a gas station across the street. I flagged down the officer and told him what had happened. He told me to wait as he went to speak to the truck driver.

He returned a few minutes later, saying, "Well, he says he never saw you. You know, you have to realize that bikes are hard to see. If you're gonna ride on city streets..." and on and on he went about how I misunderstood the truck driver's intentions and how I shouldn't be too thin-skinned when a driver makes an honest mistake. Too bad there weren't any bicycle patrol officers around. They would have understood and believed.

Steer Clear

As frightening and aggravating as it is to be harassed by a hostile motorist, resist the urge to confront the motorist. Think about it. Would a reasonable person harass an innocent cyclist? Of course not. Who knows what other irrational acts this jerk might be capable of doing if provoked? Play it safe and try to relax and continue with your ride.

Don't Be Dead Right

Although most roads are legal for cyclists, that doesn't necessarily mean that they're safe to use. Roads with blind corners and narrow shoulders are best avoided. Some of the most beautiful rides imaginable are on the little-used back roads of the Pacific Northwest. But guess who does use these roads? Great big double-trailer logging trucks that are nearly as wide as the lane on which they're driven. Sure, you have every right to ride on these roads, and I doubt that any of the logging truck drivers want to run over cyclists. Trouble is, trying to convey that fact to several hundred tons of timber momentum is fruitless.

While riding aggressively and asserting your right to your piece of the road is often the safest way to deal with traffic, there are times when discretion is the better part of valor. When it's obvious that a motorist is not going to yield to your right-of-way, there's no point in insisting. Whether you're right or the motorist is right, you and your spindly little bike are no match for a steel fender. Hit the brakes and let the motorist have his or her way.

Miles of Experience

There's a road in my hometown of Big Bear, California, that's perfectly legal for bicycle riding. I, however, choose not to ride it. It has a few sections of long, gradual curves. Motorists commonly drive 50 mph and faster. The danger lies in the fact that because of the curve they can't see a cyclist going only 20 mph until they're right on him or her. And there's no escape route. The road was carved into the side of a granite mountain and the shoulder of the road is practically nonexistent. Learn to recognize the differences between legal-to-ride roads and safe-to-ride roads.

More Survival Tips

Here are a few more tips to keep you and your bike in one piece and out of the hospital:

➤ Pretend you're invisible. When riding in traffic, ride as defensively as you would if you were invisible because I've got news for you pal—you are. Yes, I've had drivers look right at me and then pull out in front of me. It's as if their mind's accident avoidance system didn't detect any Buicks or buses, so it assumed it was okay to proceed. Never mind that doing so would mean wiping out my innocent Schwinn and me. Grab a pencil and hold it in front of your eyes at arm length.

That's all it takes to completely block out a cyclist from across an intersection. So it's no wonder that drivers in auto-versus-bike accidents claim, "I didn't see him, officer!" Realize too that many motorists don't expect to see a bicyclist on the road. They may see, but the image doesn't register in their brains. The moment you assume that a motorist sees you is the moment you may become a hood ornament.

➤ As far as mountain roads go, listen, look, and be seen. Being seen on twisty mountain roads is much more important than being seen on a straight road. On a straight road, as long as you stay at the right edge of the pavement, even a motorist who doesn't see you isn't likely to hit you. But most mountain roads don't have much in the way of straight paths, and because few motorists can see around corners, a cyclist really can "come out of nowhere." Some may debate my method for being seen, but here it is: I ride out in the lane and listen closely for cars coming up behind me. As a car approaches, I glance over my shoulder every few seconds until I'm sure I've been seen—they can't help but see me out there in the lane—then I pull over to the edge of the pavement to let the motorist pass. I pull over well before they're close enough to have to slow down for me to reduce the chance of them becoming irate over my presence. If possible, I give a friendly wave as they pass.

➤ Reduce your chances of becoming a victim of "I didn't see him!" by increasing your visibility with brightly colored clothing. If you ride at dusk or at night, the law requires you to have a light and a rear reflector. Go one better with a flashing rear light, too. These lights use very bright LEDs (light-emitting diodes), and their flashing strobe effect makes them very noticeable without blinding motorists. Several brands and models of rear strobes are available; most are only around $10.

➤ Always ride single-file. I know it's tempting to want to ride alongside your riding partners. It makes it so much easier to talk while you ride. But it also takes up the whole width of the road shoulder and may even put you into the right lane where an inattentive motorist might hit you. Besides, too many motorists already resent having to swerve around us bicyclists. Why infuriate them more?

The Least You Need to Know

➤ Riding against traffic is one of the most dangerous things a cyclist can do. Go with the flow by riding as you would drive.

➤ Keep your eyes peeled for obstacles: Glass, sand, merging lanes, and parked cars all require you to be extra aware of your surroundings while cycling.

➤ Drivers aren't looking for bicyclists; never assume a car sees you.

➤ In a road-rage incident, a bicyclist is no match for a car or truck.

➤ Learn to mentally put up your own "No Bikes" signs on those roads that are legal for bikes, yet still unsafe for bikes.

Chapter 11

Rules of the Trail

In This Chapter

➤ In the beginning: making the rules up as we went along

➤ What you need to know to ride off-road safely and responsibly

➤ Tasting the wilderness without having it taste you

➤ Safety in numbers

When mountain biking first started, the established trail users didn't know what to make of the new arrivals. No one had foreseen the emergence of bicycles capable of being ridden on the same trails normally inhabited only by hikers and people on horseback. So there were no laws or statutes pertaining to where mountain bikes were and weren't allowed. As mountain biking became popular, many members of the established trail user groups took a "we were here first" attitude.

This "us against them" attitude grew throughout the late '70s and early '80s. Some of that swell of animosity against mountain biking probably came from established trail users associating mountain bikes with off-road motorcycles, a group that had by then been eradicated from many multiuser trails. Of course, some of the anti-mountain bike sentiment was justified thanks to a few thoughtless riders and their careless actions. (Yes, there is a fringe element of careless mountain bikers, just as there's a small percentage of equestrians and backpackers who are littering, illegal-campfire-building slobs.)

In the early '80s, land managers began closing trails to mountain bikers. Most of these closures were based on reports from the established trail users that depicted all mountain bikers as adrenaline-charged, wild-eyed speed demons. That image fits but a very small minority. Most mountain bikers are conscientious, responsible people who enjoy their outdoor experiences every bit as much as hikers and equestrians.

Miles of Experience

In a 1990 study by the Department of Earth Sciences at Montana State University, it was concluded that when compared to hikers, horses, and motorcycles, mountain bikes made no more of an impact to trails than hikers, and certainly less than motorcycles or horses. From what I've observed, mountain bikes often improve trail conditions, because the passing of several riders can act to roll out hoofprints and ruts. But as mountain biking has grown and established trail users (hikers and equestrians) have become understandably irate at the inconsiderate actions of a few thoughtless riders, trails are being closed to mountain bikes, and the prevention of trail erosion is given as a leading argument in favor of this decision. Today, many of my favorite trails are off-limits. Don't think that it can't happen in your area. It can and will if mountain bikers don't mind their manners and learn to share.

Unfortunately, these signs are far too common.

Can't We All Just Get Along?

Yes, we certainly can. It all comes down to common courtesy, common sense, and respecting the rights and safety of other trail users.

Currently, few trails are closed to mountain bikes without opposition from the mountain bike community, and mountain biking has been recognized as a legitimate form of recreation by other kinds of established trail users. Mountain bikers, equestrians, and hikers often find themselves working as allies in issues regarding new trails and trail maintenance. When it comes to picking up a shovel and investing some sweat into creating a new trail or maintaining an old one, other trail users know that mountain bikers can be counted on. Much of that success was brought about by IMBA (International Mountain Bicycling Association).

IMBA was formed at about the same time that trails were being closed to mountain bikes. It began as a coalition of California mountain bike clubs that got together to oppose trail closures. The philosophy of IMBA is that although the joys of mountain biking are based on freedom and fun, the rights of other trail users can be respected without detracting from the experiences of mountain biking. Riding within that philosophy is as simple as abiding by the following easy guidelines:

IMBA Rules of the Trail

1. Ride on open trails only.
2. Leave no trace.
3. Control your bicycle.
4. Always yield trail.
5. Never spook animals.
6. Plan ahead.

I talked with IMBA's executive director, Tim Blumenthal, about these tenets. He elaborated on each one:

1. **Ride on open trails only.** Says Blumenthal, it's common sense and shows respect for the law. Mountain biking's public image and

Cyclebabble

A **multiuser trail** is a trail that is open to several types of users, such as hikers, equestrians, and mountain bikers.

Steer Clear

Don't assume that you can talk your way out of being cited for riding a closed trail by claiming, "I didn't know bikes weren't allowed." Just as claiming you didn't know that campfires weren't allowed in a certain area won't get you out of an illegal campfire ticket, feigning ignorance of closed trails won't cut it with most rangers either. With any wilderness activity, it's up to the wilderness user to know the rules and regulations. Besides, poaching on closed trails makes us all look bad and will only hinder any effort to re-open that trail to mountain bikes.

credibility is injured when people disregard closed trail signs. Disregarding the law in a fit of civil disobedience never helps. Chances are, the person who owns the land on which you are trespassing will only view you as a scofflaw, not an upholder of justice for mountain bikers.

2. **Leave no trace.** Although it's nearly impossible to leave absolutely *no* trace that you've been on a trail (this goes for hikers and equestrians as well, so don't feel singled out), you can minimize your impact on it. As Blumenthal says, "Don't litter, stay on the trail, and don't skid corners."

   He elaborated: "The first one is simple. Don't toss dead inner tubes; don't toss PowerBar wrappers. It's the old backpackers' adage of 'pack it in, pack it out.' In fact, pack out more. If you find someone else's litter, pick it up."

   "The next one is aimed at new mountain bikers. They have a tendency to ride around obstacles. At IMBA, we're for keeping single-track as single-track and not riding around waterbars or downed trees, even if it means stopping and stepping over a log. Taking the easy alternative around will eventually widen the trail."

   "As far as skidding corners, mountain bikes generally are very low-impact on straight sections of trail and can be on corners, too. It's the unskilled and uncaring riders who create ruts in corners from skidding. It's a real art to negotiate a tight switchback without locking up the rear tire. It's easy to lock it up and just sort of slide around. What's challenging is having the bike-control skills to use the right combination of braking and body balance and positioning to get around the corner without skidding."

   "This may sound lofty and high-minded, but I think this rule is summed up in the idea that anything you do on this earth you do with future generations in mind. You want the land or the trail to be the same for them. It comes down to not being selfish, to being aware of the world and realizing that everything is interconnected."

3. **Control your bicycle.** When dealing with other trail users, use caution. You may have slowed from 17 to 10 mph when some hikers came into view, but they only see you careening toward them. Part of controlling your bicycle has to do with body language in the way that other trail users perceive you. That can be something as minor as using both your front and rear brake and not skidding. A rider showing smooth, precise movements looks safer and more controlled.

4. **Always yield trail.** "Yielding doesn't always mean stopping and getting off your bike. It means to slow down when you approach other trail users, establish communication, and pass safely," advises Blumenthal.

IMBA yield.

"Communication is key. If you're cruising along on a nice single-track and you approach some hikers who graciously step aside, be grateful. A smile and a thank you go a long way. Hikers have the right of way, so if they don't move, by all means stop and let them by. And always be cordial."

"As far as horses go, anything approaching quickly and quietly will trigger a horse's 'predator alarm.' A frightened horse can injure itself, its rider, or you. Let the person riding the horse tell you what to do—he or she is the one who knows the animal. The rider may tell you to go ahead and ride past or may ask you to dismount and walk. Yield to his or her instructions."

5. **Never spook animals.** Blumenthal says, "There are three categories here: domestic animals, grazing animals, and wild." As far as domestic animals go, be careful on urban

Cycology

Equestrians get upset at cyclists who spook their horses and rightfully so. Whenever you're cycling near equestrians, consider that a horse weighs a good 1,250 pounds or so and that having a horse rear up and fall can be fatal to the animal and its rider.

trails where people may be walking their dogs. Dogs and a spinning bike wheel don't mix very well.

The most common animal to encounter, however, is a horse. Advises Blumenthal, "Riders need to realize that some horses are comfortable with bikes and others are not. You need to be prepared." When dealing with those large, noble creatures, never pass from behind without the rider telling you to do so. When approaching a horse from behind, announce your presence well in advance. This does two things: 1) the rider knows you're coming and can communicate to you what to do, and 2) hearing your voice will let the horse know that you're just a human.

You may encounter grazing animals if your riding takes place out west. Cattle can become frightened and, in their haste to get away, injure themselves. That doesn't make a good case for mountain bikers sharing public grazing land.

According to Blumenthal, "Always be alert when in a grazing cattle area. They may be used to humans and may not be alarmed as you approach, and so they don't retreat as a wild animal would. Two of the worst accidents I ever saw were riders colliding with cattle. The riders broke their collarbones. It doesn't do the animal any good either."

There have been very few instances of wild animals attacking riders. However, a new trend for justification of trail closures is mountain biking's impact on wildlife habitat. Although there's no science that shows that cyclists as a group are having more wildlife impact than other trail users, you do still need to exercise caution. For instance, when you approach deer or wild turkeys, just give them space. Not getting too close and avoiding frightening them is just common sense.

6. **Plan ahead.** Know your route, have the necessary tools to repair your bike, be prepared for changes in weather, and wear a helmet. "Back in 1988 when the IMBA rules were written, we didn't want to say 'Wear a helmet.' I think now we would. Having a rider sustain a head injury can really hurt access. It freaks out land managers if a mountain biker gets a head injury; they think 'lawsuit,'" warns Blumenthal.

In addition, there are a few other areas where inexperienced riders err. One is not knowing their route and somehow thinking that a trail experience is almost like going to a theme park. People don't always understand the realities of where they are and therefore aren't prepared for rough terrain. Second, many riders forget to bring a jacket or extra warm clothes. In mountain areas where weather changes quickly, you must consider the possibility of rain or sleet. Third, you must be prepared with the proper emergency tools (remember the emergency kit I told you to make back in Chapter 8, "Accessorizing"?). For instance, it's nearly impossible to fix a broken chain without a chain tool.

Lions and Tigers and Bears, Oh My!

Does a bear live in the woods? You bet he does. So do mountain lions and sometimes snakes. When you're riding in wilderness, never forget that you're riding in someone else's backyard, and that someone may have claws, fangs, and an appetite.

Bear in Mind

If your favorite riding area is also the favorite habitat of *Euarctos americanus* (black bear) or *Ursus horribilis* (grizzly bear), you need to know a bit about these creatures. In real life, they're a bit more imposing than Yogi and Smokey.

Miles of Experience

In all of my years of riding the trails around my Big Bear, California, home, I've yet to see one of the big bears. Plenty of other riders in town have. Once I was waiting on a hilltop for a friend to catch up when he rode up breathless, saying that a black bear had bolted across the trail and down a ravine, "He was only about a hundred yards behind you!" my friend explained.

Bears are solitary creatures that generally want nothing to do with humans. Most will retreat from approaching humans. Problems with bears arise when humans inadvertently startle them. A bear's response to suddenly encountering someone in its personal space is to either make a bluff charge or to attack, so make noise when riding in bear country. A trail bell can be effective. A human voice is another good way to let bears know that humans are present. If you suspect that bears are around, sing loudly. Any song will do: the theme songs from the *Flintstones* or *Speed Racer*—whatever. You're less likely to startle a bear if you are making noise consistently along your ride.

If you do encounter a bear, stop immediately. A bear can sprint to 30 to 35 miles per hour in just a few seconds. So unless you're on a fast downhill trail and already have a sizable head start, trying to pedal away from a bear is rarely a good idea. Don't make noise or scream. Although bears will usually retreat in response to distant sounds, in close proximity noise may only provoke a bear.

If you can get the bear to see you as being submissive, it may graciously allow you to leave its territory. To a bear, eye contact is a sign of aggression, so avoid looking in the bear's eyes. Speak calmly, back away, and don't turn around.

If the bear does charge, stand your ground; bears will often bluff charge to test an opponent. The bear may veer off and retreat or charge again. Bears sometimes charge several times before attacking.

The way to handle an attack differs between black bears and grizzly bears. Unless you live in Canada, Alaska, or some of the northwestern states, chances are you won't encounter a grizzly. Grizzlies are much larger than black bears and are usually brown or honey-colored. If a grizzly attacks, don't fight. Playing dead works sometimes—fighting a grizzly unarmed *never* works. If you do play dead, the grizzly will likely bat you around, bite you, and maul you before moving on. Any way you look at it though, being severely injured still ranks ahead of being severely dead.

If a black bear attacks, it's survival time. Black bears don't fall for the playing dead game. Fight back with any weapon you can find: a rock, a knife, your bike. You can inflict a nasty gash with your bike's chainring by hoisting your bike by the handlebar and saddle and thrusting the chainring into the bear's face.

Some bear-attack victims have survived their ordeals by using pepper spray. Riders in areas known for bear activity should consider carrying a can. Keep in mind that standard pepper spray isn't nearly as strong as those rated for use on bears and may only enrage the bear. Personally, if it came down to having to carry caustic sprays to go for a ride, I'd find another riding area.

Here Kitty, Kitty, Kitty

Mountain lion encounters are extremely rare. Mountain lions (cougars, pumas, catamounts—they're all names for the same critters) are normally even more skittish about humans than bears are. There was one well-publicized attack in 1995 on southern California rider, Scott Fike. When Fike first saw the approaching feline, his first action was the right one: He yelled at the mountain lion and put his bike between himself and the lion. Animal experts say to make noise, stand your ground, and stare the mountain lion in the face while you try to back away slowly.

When the mountain lion proceeded to chew on Fike's bike tire, his next action was one that experts say is the wrong one: He ran. While it's difficult to meet up with Snagglepuss and not be terrified into "exit, stage right," running from a mountain lion triggers the animals predator-versus-prey response, which is exactly what happened in this case.

While trying to escape, Fike tripped and fell onto his back. Seeing the lion about to pounce and knowing that a mountain lion will try to go for the throat, Fike rolled onto his belly to hide his face and neck. Meanwhile, the mountain lion leapt on Fike, biting and clawing at his head. Experts say to fight a mountain lion, which is what Fike did. He shoved the animal back before smashing it in the head with a rock. After a few blows, the mountain lion backed off, and Fike was lucky to come away with relatively minor wounds.

Riders who regularly ride in areas populated by bears or mountain lions may want to learn more on this topic. I recommend reading *Self Defense for Nature Lovers* by Mike Lapinski or *Bear Aware* by Bill Schneider.

One Is the Loneliest Number

The old saying "there's safety in numbers" holds especially true for mountain bike riders. Consider the mountain lion attack story I just told you. Had Fike not been riding solo, it's doubtful that the mountain lion would have tangled with Fike. Consider the possible consequences of a solo rider suffering an injury while deep in the woods. One slip of a tire or one unexpected low-hanging branch can transform a rider into a crawler. Combine a rider who can't ride with dropping temperatures and the approach of night, and you have a formula for disaster.

Some years ago, I crashed hard on a solo ride, knocking myself out and separating a shoulder. Luckily I was able to hike out, although I don't remember doing so. Since then, I rarely ever ride off-road alone. When I do, I let someone know where I'm going, what route I'm taking, and what time I should be back. That's still a far cry from riding with a partner, but at least if I don't come out of the woods, they'll know where to look for me.

Cycology

If you already have a mountain bike and sport utility vehicle, your friends already consider you to be an insufferable yuppie. So why not get a cell phone to complete the ensemble? Besides, a cell phone could save your life should you crash during a solo ride. Heck, bring it along even on group rides. Being able to alert help in an instant will always be a good thing.

The Least You Need to Know

➤ When it comes to the variety of off-road trail users, your kindergarten teacher was right: We all need to share to get along.

➤ Let the IMBA rules of the trail be your guide.

➤ Be aware that you're riding in someone else's backyard—someone with fangs and claws.

➤ A grizzly bear may move on if you play dead, but a black bear will probably just maul you and eat you. Know your bears.

➤ It's best to bring a friend along if you're riding off-road. If going solo, make sure you tell a friend where you're going, what route you're taking, and when you'll be back.

Chapter 12

Your Bike's Engine

In This Chapter

➤ Keeping your body properly hydrated

➤ The lowdown on sports drinks and bars

➤ Getting the most out of your pedaling

➤ Cyclometers as a learning tool

➤ Health and hygiene tips

Up to now, I've given you all sorts of advice and tips on your bike, its parts, and all the extras to make your riding adventures great. There's one major part of the bike we haven't discussed yet, though—its engine. You are your bicycle's engine, and if you don't keep yourself in good working condition, all the cool, fancy bike gear in the world won't do you much good. In this chapter, I'll show you how to care for and get the most performance from you, your bike's engine.

Hydration: It Beats the Alternative

The human body is 70 percent water. The human brain is 75 percent water, muscles are 70 to 75 percent water, and blood is 90 percent water. Water is essential to every function of a human body. It's integral in the body's ability to regulate temperature, convert food into energy, and carry nutrients, glucose, and oxygen to all cells in the body, and it moistens oxygen for breathing. A person can go weeks without food, but when a person becomes dehydrated to the point of losing 20 percent of the body's water stores, death usually results.

Health experts recommend that the average person drink a minimum of 64 ounces of water each day. As the amount or intensity of physical activity increases, so does the body's need for water. In addition to preventing dehydration, fluid replacement is extremely important for optimum performance as well. As little as 3 percent dehydration can reduce recovery after an event.

Miles of Experience

One fine summer day some friends and I set out for a 100-mile road ride in southern California's Santa Monica Mountains. Knowing that temperatures were expected to be in the mid-90s, I became curious about what effect the heat would have on my body's ability to stay adequately hydrated, so I weighed myself before setting out on our ride. Throughout the ride, I continually gulped water, and by the end of our five and a half hours of riding, I had filled and emptied a 24-ounce bottle six times. Yet even after having made a conscious effort at hydration, when I stepped back on the scale at the end of the ride, I weighed a full five pounds less than I had that morning. Realizing that despite my best efforts my hydration level was still very low, I downed another six glasses of water over the next couple of hours.

It's important to stay well-hydrated during any form of exercise, especially in hot weather. Don't wait until you feel thirsty to drink up. By the time you feel the dry-mouth indications of thirst, you have already dropped about 1 percent of your body weight to dehydration. If you let your rate of dehydration continue to the point where your body weight has dropped by 5 percent or more, you're into the danger zone. Nausea, headache, loss of strength, and an inability for the body to regulate its temperature are the next likely occurrences.

Following these simple steps should keep you from experiencing the unpleasant effects of dehydration:

1. Start your ride well-hydrated by drinking up to 24 ounces of water a couple of hours beforehand.

2. Drink another 16 ounces or more of water 30 to 15 minutes before beginning your ride.

3. Constantly take sips of water throughout a ride. You want to drain at least one 16-ounce water bottle every 45 minutes to an hour—more in hot weather.

A quick and accurate way to gauge hydration is check the color of your urine. If you're well-hydrated, your urine will be clear or nearly so. Dark urine indicates dehydration. (Note that urine color may not be an accurate gauge if you are taking certain vitamins, such as B-12, because these vitamins will also darken your urine.)

Hydration Systems

Ever grab for your water bottle and end up fumbling it onto the road or trail? It's a hassle, especially during a race. Ever inadvertently suck on a trail-muck-encrusted water bottle? It's not a pleasant experience, especially in cattle country. Can you ever fit all the essentials into your seat bag or jersey pocket? Doesn't it always seem a bit too stuffed?

Thankfully, these problems have solutions: hydration packs. Two such products are a CamelBak or Cascade Designs' Platypus Hydration Systems. These products enable riders to carry their water and supplies on their backs.

A hydration system such as this Platypus Liquidator is a handy way to carry extra water, along with all your tools, snacks, wallet, and keys. Perhaps the biggest advantage of a hydration pack is that the convenience encourages more frequent drinking.

The CamelBak, the original "on your back" water-carrying system, has been around for a few years. It consists of a plastic water bag contained in an insulating fabric bag that straps onto the wearer's back. A plastic hose hangs over the shoulder. Need a drink? Simply pop the hose in your mouth and clench the bite-valve between your teeth. Several other companies make similar hydration systems, including Cannondale and Platypus. Hydration system users swear by them; they like having their water supply so conveniently available.

1993 Veteran Cross Country World Championship Bronze Medalist Pat Hadley is a long-time hydration system user. Known for being strong and consistent throughout a race,

Hadley partly attributes her endurance to her CamelBak, saying, "I look geeky, I know. But it helps me drink more and more often, maybe that's why I don't fade." Geeky looking? Perhaps that's why so few pros use CamelBaks—that and the fact that they tend to cover sponsors' logos on the backs of jerseys. Personally, I'll take being properly hydrated and feeling strong over looking a little different any day.

Miles of Experience

For long rides or races in hot weather, I'll use a hydration system for my water and also carry a bottle or two of sports drink on the bike. I've tried putting sports drinks in my hydration pack, but the inevitable drips and dribbles made sticky messes on my back and bike. Also, cleaning the sports drink residue from the hydration pack's reservoir is a real pain.

Liquid Lunch: What Sports Drinks Can Do for You

Go to any cycling event, running event, ball game, or your local gym, and you'll see people guzzling sports drinks. Names such as Body Fuel, Cytomax, Exceed, Gatorade, Powerade, and many others are familiar to most sports-minded people. But what are these drinks? What's in them, and how can they benefit active people?

During long periods of exercise, your muscles are being fueled by glucose (*glycogen* stored in the liver and muscles). These glucose reserves last for about 90 minutes of hard effort. When these glucose reserves run out, a rider can *bonk*, or experience a sudden loss of energy. Sports drinks are a good means to supplement those stores for increased performance. According to the American College of Sports Medicine, to improve performance an athlete should drink a sports drink containing 6 percent glucose every 20 minutes at a rate of 600 to 750 milliliters per hour.

Cyclebabble

Glycogen is the compound in which sugar is stored in the liver for release to other parts of the body.

What's in Them?

Most sports drinks contain varying amounts of complex carbohydrates (such as maltodextrin), glucose polymers, and simple carbohydrates, such as sucrose, fructose, and simple glucose. Both simple and complex carbohydrates are efficient at replenishing blood glucose reserves.

An added benefit of a sports drink is that the absorption of water from the small intestine increases in the presence of glucose and sodium—helping a rider to more efficiently metabolize water. Sports drinks also taste better than plain old water, which often encourages a rider to drink more. A gulp of fruit-flavored sports drink is much more appealing than a swig of water that's picked up a plastic flavor from the water bottle.

Sports drinks are also touted as an efficient means of *electrolyte* replacement. The electrolyte of major importance to athletes is sodium. The average American consumes 10 times the needed amount of sodium per day, so American cyclists are unlikely to deplete their sodium stores, unless they ride hard in hot weather for longer than five hours.

Ironically, beyond that five or so hours where a rider can use sodium at 500 to 1,000 milligrams per hour, none of the electrolyte solutions have nearly enough sodium. Most have only about 90 milligrams per liter—a liter being about the maximum amount of fluid a rider can comfortably drink per hour. In such cases, a rider is replenishing sodium at only 10 percent of the rate of depletion. The answer for long rides in hot weather is to build sodium stores beforehand by consuming salty foods and to drink plenty of an electrolyte-laden sports drink in the early hours of the ride.

Cyclebabble

To **bonk** is to run out of energy due to lack of caloric intake. That is, "I didn't eat enough this morning and bonked with 30 miles to go." This is also described as "running out of gas."

Cyclebabble

Electrolytes are substances suspended in a liquid solution that convey electrical impulses. In the human body, sodium, potassium, chlorides, and other substances act as electrolytes to carry electrical charges in the blood to the cells around them, allowing the cells to "talk" to each other.

Eenie, Meenie, Minie, Moe

It seems that every year there's a new sports drink on the market, and virtually all claim to be "the best." How do you select one? When you compare the proportions of essentials such as carbohydrates, calories, and sodium, most sports drinks are usually within a few percentage points of having the same concentrations of these ingredients. My advice is to find one with a flavor you like and that agrees with your stomach and stick with it.

My favorite sports drink is one that's available at any grocery store. It's a liquid, so it's very easy to mix with water without having to wait for granules to dissolve. It tastes great, and it has no chemicals, preservatives, or artificial colors. It's called grape juice. If you mix grape juice or nearly any other type of fruit juice with water (25 percent juice to 75 percent water), you'll have an inexpensive and tasty drink that compares favorably to nearly any sports drink. About the only area a juice mix might fall short in is sodium content. Solve that by mixing in a teaspoon of salt.

Riding Behind Bars

Most active people are familiar with sports bars. No, I'm not talking about the taverns with walls lined with autographed photos of sports heroes and big-screen TVs tuned to ESPN. I'm talking about those candy bar-like energy bars. PowerBars, the original brand of sports bar, were first introduced back in the late 1980s. They were sold mostly in bicycle shops and sports stores catering to runners and triathletes. Now you can find them at most supermarkets and convenience stores, often displayed alongside other brands such as Clif Bars, Torque Bars, and Edgebars.

What are these sports bars, and what do they do? Most bars are touted as being easy to digest and come in a wide variety of flavors and textures. Some are stiff and taffy-like; others are more like a slightly dry cookie. Most of these snacks contain a mix of complex carbohydrates (from such sources as unprocessed rice, oats, wheat, or glucose polymers) and, more important, simple carbohydrates (from such sources as fructose, honey, or corn syrup), which the body can readily and quickly turn into its main energy source: glucose. Sports bars also contain fat, fiber, vitamins, minerals, and protein. Most contain between 100 and 350 calories. Some are made with sodium and/or potassium to prevent *lactic acid* buildup in the muscles by improving the body's oxygen consumption.

Close cousins to sports bars are sports gels, such as Gu and PowerGel. These little doses of energy look like little packets of ketchup from McDonald's. Inside is a carbo and glucose goop with a consistency akin to partially set Jell-O. Tear one open and squeeze its contents down your gullet (be sure to also swig about eight ounces of H_2O), and you've just taken in about 75 to 100 calories. These little wonders usually cost about as much as a sports bar ($1 to $1.75), but they have only half to a third of the calories. Their advantages are being quick to eat and taking up very little room. The expense of gels makes it hard to recommend them for everyday riding, but they're sure handy for racing.

Convenience is also the main benefit of sports bars. Most have about 200 or so calories, with about 60 to 70 percent of those calories coming in the form of carbohydrates. The same can be said of bananas, bagels, or peanut butter

Steer Clear

Beware of mixing your powdered sports drink mix in a higher concentration than the manufacturer recommends. Having too much carbohydrate in the solution will inhibit the body's absorption of the water. Also, a highly concentrated mixture can also be hard on your stomach.

Cycology

Sometimes it's impossible to bring enough water and mixed energy drink for a long hot day in the saddle. Because going beyond a two-bottle ride means water stops, why not assure that you'll have plenty of glycogen and electrolyte replacement by dumping a few scoops of mix into a plastic, resealable bag? Bring the scoop along so you can properly measure out the right water/mix ratio.

sandwiches, but none of these would hold up too well stuffed into a jersey pocket or seat-bag. But do you want to know what does? Low-fat Pop-Tarts. Depending on which flavor you get (and there are several yummy flavors to choose from), Low-fat Pop-Tarts also have about 200 calories, and (you guessed it) about 65 percent of those calories are carbohydrates. They come in a nice foil packet that's easier to open than most sports bars, and the packet is resealable—well not airtight resealable, but fold the foil over and you'll keep out most debris and most larger insects. Best of all, they're about half the price of most sports bars.

Matters of the Heart

Keeping tabs on the old ticker isn't a bad idea if you plan to use cycling as your main form of exercise (or if you have even the slightest hint of competitive spirit). The way to do this is by maintaining a working knowledge of your *maximum heart rate*, or the number of beats per minute (bpm) that your heart pumps out during aerobic exercise.

A number of factors affect the maximum heart rate of an individual, including genetics and physical conditioning. So comparing one's heart rate to another person may not mean much because two individuals riding at the same effort could have vastly different heart rates. Elite athletes undergo clinical testing to determine their maximum heart rate, but the simple formula of 220 minus your age is a good starting point. For example, I'm 38, so my maximum heart rate should be about 182 bpm, because 220 – 38 = 182.

Cyclebabble

Lactic acid is an acid formed in the body as a by-product of metabolizing sugars for hard exercise. This acid can build up in the muscles, causing the soreness associated with muscle fatigue.

Cycology

For more information on hydration, sports drinks, and sports bars and how they all relate to cycling, pick up *The Ultimate Nutrition Handbook* or *Eating for Endurance*, both by Ellen Coleman, and take a look at the nutrition section of *Bicycling Medicine*, by Arnie Baker, M.D.

For maximum aerobic benefits, training should be at 65 to 85 percent of the maximum heart rate, which for me would be 118 to 155 bpm. For those looking to lose weight, a heart rate of 55 to 65 percent assures that the body is fueling itself mostly on stored fat. So, for example, for me to be in my maximum fat-burning range, I want to work out with my heart rate at 100 to 118 bpm.

Designing a full training program tailored to the individual takes the expertise of a professional trainer. But the following sample schedule is a good starting point for the average weekend warrior. The actual mileage or ride duration is up to you and will, of course, increase as your fitness increases. For example, for a rank novice a "long ride" might be only 10 or 20 miles. But for someone with more experience a ride of 50 to

100 miles would be in order on the "long ride day." Note, too, that this schedule includes a day with a "recovery ride" and another with "rest or recovery ride." A recovery ride is ride with a very easy pace—some coaches call this "taking your bike for a walk." Experts have found that such easy rides can help you to recover from previous days' efforts better than if just stayed home on the couch watching *Jeopardy*. Again, the duration of a recovery ride is dependent on you and your current level of fitness. For some, a 15-minute spin is appropriate, while a competitive racer might take a two-hour recovery ride.

Day	Activity	% of Maximum Heart Rate
Monday	Recovery ride	55–65%
Tuesday	Long ride	65–75%
Wednesday	Interval workout	Percentage changes throughout the workout
Thursday	Rest or recovery	55–65%
Friday	Long ride	65–75%
Saturday and Sunday	One day should be a rest day; the other a race or high-intensity race simulation workout	

Getting Technical: Heart Monitors

Most pro racers train and even race wearing a heart-rate monitor—a watch-like device worn on the wrist and a transmitter strapped over the chest. Many take the science of heart-rate monitor use to the extreme. Their trainers design meticulous workout schedules for these athletes specifying exactly where their heart rates should be at any given time.

Cyclebabble

Your **maximum heart rate** is the number of times per minute (bpm) that your heart beats when your body is exerting at its maximum sustainable output level. There's a thin line between that level of maximum performance and that point where you succumb to the fatigue of the effort and fall in a heap. That's why a heart-rate monitor is such a valuable tool.

Heart-rate monitors aren't just for elite athletes. Many weekend warriors use them, too. They're a great way to gauge your workout, your fitness, and your fatigue level. And you don't have to spend a fortune to have one—basic models sell for around $100. True, you can determine your heart rate by simply taking a pulse and doing some basic math. But that's not really practical during a hard ride. Besides, for many cyclists the hardware and gadgets are half the fun—a heart-rate monitor certainly falls under the category of cool, high-tech toys.

To effectively train with a heart-rate monitor, an athlete must first determine his or her maximum heart rate. For example, we previously figured out mine is 182 using a simple formula. I've used a heart-rate monitor for years, and experience has verified this happens to be a good number for me.

With the excitement and adrenaline of racing, it's common for racers to routinely reach the point where the body can no longer keep up with the muscles' demands for oxygenated blood. This *anaerobic threshold* is typically at 90 to 95 percent of the maximum heart rate. A heart monitor can help an athlete avoid hitting this threshold and maintain his or her maximum performance. For example, in a race, I need to stay below 164 to 173 bpm in order to avoid hitting my anaerobic threshold. Experience has shown me that I can consistently stay in the 160s when racing, but beyond that I run the risk of *blowing up*.

The only time you ever want to get into the threshold range is occasionally during training to prepare for the race situations such as the start, short steep climbs, and passing other competitors. Otherwise, stay in the proper range for the best possible performance.

Cyclebabble

No, **blowing up** isn't when a rider physically explodes and scatters body parts all over the race course. But it can feel that way. Blowing up is a term used to describe instances where a rider overexerts him- or herself, is unable to recover, and succumbs to fatigue; as in, "I tried to catch up to the leaders, went too hard, and blew up."

Monitor Madness

Thanks to monitors with data gathering and download capabilities, a rider and coach can transfer data from the heart-rate monitor after a workout or race to a computer to create a graph of the workout or race, showing the rider's heart rate minute-by-minute. Only a few monitors have this capability, and they're not cheap. Polar's top-of-the-line Vantage Night Vision $399 heart-rate monitor can store data, provided you spend an extra $499 for the Polar Advantage Interface System consisting of computer software and a device that plugs into your computer to transfer data from the heart-rate monitor.

A good value is Polar's $299 Cross Trainer Plus, which also functions as a cyclometer (more on these later in this chapter). The download system, the Interface Plus, is only $249. Or save another $30 with the Accurex Plus for $269. It doesn't have cyclometer functions, but it also uses the $249 Interface Plus.

For those without big-bucks contracts, Polar also makes other models, such as the Beat. This $99 unit has one function: determining heart rate. It doesn't even have any buttons; the unit automatically comes on when it's in range of the transmitter. The $139 Target and the $159 Pacer 97 share many functions; both give current heart rate, have clocks, and can be programmed to beep at a given high or low target rate. The Pacer also gives the amount of time spent above and below the target rates. Any of these three units are adequate for most riders.

Pedaling in Circles

If you ask most people how a bike is propelled, they'll likely say something like, "You push down on the pedals." And that's how many people pedal: They push down with one leg while leaving the other one relaxed, letting the downward push of the other leg raise the relaxed leg, and then they repeat as needed. *Mashing* on the pedals like this uses mostly just the thigh muscles. Although the thigh muscles are among the body's strongest muscles, using them exclusively will tire them out quickly. Besides, why would you want to ignore all the other muscles that can be put to use with a good pedaling form?

A rider can go faster, go uphill more easily, ride more efficiently, and put less stress on knee joints by pedaling 'round and 'round. Learning to develop a good *spin* isn't something that happens overnight, although it's often been said that it takes less time for a new rider to develop a good spin than it does for an experienced rider to unlearn poor pedaling form. Those of you who are new to the sport are in luck—you get to learn the right way the first time.

Cyclebabble

Mashing is the act of pedaling by pushing downward on the pedals. It's also a term used to describe pedaling a very high gear; for example, "I mashed up that hill."

Cyclebabble

Spin is the act of pedaling in a circle smoothly and efficiently.

Keeping It Smooth

A major factor in pedaling smoothly and with the most possible power is to apply pedaling power throughout the entire pedaling circle, especially during the upstroke. To be able to pull up during the upstroke, a rider needs to have either toe-clips or clipless pedals. (Remember those from Chapter 5, "Knowing the Thingie from the Doodad: A Part-by-Part Description of Bicycle Components"?)

To learn to apply force all the way around the pedaling circle, you must first visualize the four main segments of that circle:

1. Upstroke
2. Downstroke
3. Bottom
4. Top

On first analysis, it seems that to have a smooth upstroke arc you must pull upward. That's only partially true. As trainers and racers have learned, it's smoother and more efficient if you put more pedaling force into pulling back and only slightly up. This action causes the foot to more closely follow the arc of the circle without being forced into the curve.

The second segment of the circle is the downstroke. As you might assume, it's the most powerful portion of the pedaling circle.

The third arc of the circle is at the bottom. Novice riders tend to straighten the leg and nearly stop it abruptly at the bottom of the circle. To smooth out that jerky movement, you need to guide the foot to follow through at the bottom of the pedaling circle—think of the movement of a bull's foot as it scratches at the ground.

The final segment of the pedaling circle is at the top of the pedaling stroke. Just as with the bottom of the circle, the top can be another dead point in the stroke. You can smooth out this transition greatly by pedaling up and over the top—picture the movement of a foot stepping up and onto a stair step.

Put all the arcs together, and you'll have a nice, smooth spin. Be patient, though. Although thinking about and trying to pedal through all these segments will probably improve your pedaling form almost immediately, developing the even, machine-like form of a pro can take months, even years.

Another component related to smooth pedaling is foot position. The term *ankling* refers to having the foot level at the bottom of the pedal stroke, the heel slightly up for the upstroke, and the heel slightly down for the downstroke. Positioning the foot this way makes for smoother transitions in the dead spots at the top and bottom of the pedal stroke.

Cyclebabble

Ankling is the ability to keep your foot level at the bottom of the pedal stroke. It is the optimal foot position for attaining a smooth pedaling stroke.

The Quest for the Perfect Spin

A by-product of a smooth spin is an overall smoother ride. Watch an experienced rider, and you'll never see rocking hips or shoulders. The only movement you'll see is in the legs. Riders with a good spin are more easily able to ride a straight line because there are no jerky movements causing them to veer from side to side. A good exercise for developing a smooth spin is to try to ride a perfectly straight line by following a paint stripe.

One of the best ways to develop a smooth spin is to ride *rollers*. On rollers, any weaving, bouncing, or uneven pedaling will become immediately apparent. The other type of stationary trainers that have brackets to hold the bike upright have often been targeted as being bad for a rider's spin. They do tend to mask the clues of bad form. However, these types of trainers also make it possible to do one thing that can't be done on the road or on rollers—ride with closed eyes. I've found that by closing my eyes I become much more aware of my pedaling and can more easily concentrate on pedaling in a circle.

Cyclebabble

Rollers are a device used to ride a bicycle in place as a stationary bike. Rollers consist of three horizontal drums held within metal frame. Two drums are placed at the rear, and the third is placed at the front. The rear drums are spaced about a foot apart to cradle the rear wheel. A belt runs from one of the rear drums to the front drum so that the spinning of the rear wheel will also spin the front drum and the front wheel. Rollers don't have a brace to hold up the bike; instead the rider remains upright by balance and the gyroscopic effect of the spinning wheels.

Toe-Clips and Clipless

As mentioned in the previous section, attaching your feet to the pedals with toe-clips or a clipless pedal system is integral to efficient pedaling. Clicked in or clipped in, a rider's pedaling power output can be increased by 25 to 30 percent. Yet for some people, the fear of falling while locked to the bike greatly outweighs any benefits of increased power. And that's too bad. Learning to safely use toe-clips or clipless pedals is easy.

Fear of Clipping

Those with a real fear of being attached to the pedals can get a sampling of the benefits by first spending a few rides using half-clips. These abbreviated toe-clips curve around a rider's toes and don't have straps. Without straps, a rider can quickly and easily slip out when needed, yet can still get some of the benefits of toe-clips or clipless pedals. With half-clips, a rider won't be able to pull up with full force, but they're still more efficient than bare pedals.

Getting Up to Speed

Once you get over the initial fear of clipping, you can start to practice on the real thing. Generally, clipless pedals come from the factory with the retention mechanism set at medium tension. For riders new to clipless pedals or for small riders, this tension may be too stiff, making it difficult for them to release from the pedals. To learn to use clipless pedals, first loosen the pedal's release tension by turning the tension screws on the front and back of each pedal. The screws are usually 3 mm Allen screws. Turn each one counterclockwise twice and test the tension. If the tension is still too tight, try another turn at a time, being careful not to completely remove the screw (they're practically impossible to put back).

With most clipless pedal systems, all it takes to *click in* is to align the cleat over the mechanism and then push downward. Some are a little easier to engage if the foot is held with the heel slightly higher than the toe. Practice getting clicked in while standing still or while the bike is propped up against a wall or stool. Better still; set the bike on a stationary trainer so that it almost can't fall over.

Practice clicking in and clicking out for several minutes. Remember to keep your feet level when clicking out, using an outward twist of the heel as if you were grinding a cockroach into oblivion. Remember to not roll the feet to the side or pull the feet up—neither motion will cause the pedals to release.

Cycology

Since the introduction of clipless pedals nearly 15 years ago, toe-clips have gradually fallen out of favor. Although toe-clips were fairly inexpensive and did a good job of holding feet to the pedals, they sometimes did *too* good of a job. With the straps pulled tight, riders often stayed connected to the bike during falls. With the ski-binding-like mechanism of clipless pedals, a rider can release from the pedals with a simple twist of the foot.

After you're able to consistently click in and click out at will, it's time to try it while rolling. Find a park, schoolyard, or football field with nice, soft grass. Ride slowly on the grass and practice clicking in and out. Remember to stop pedaling as you click in or out. Realize that if for whatever reason you find that you can't click out, all you have to do is resume pedaling and you won't fall over.

Once you're confident about clicking in and out at will, you're ready to graduate to the real world of streets and trails. After a while, you may want to increase your pedals' tension because a loose setting can lead to unwanted pedal release. Increase tension evenly, counting the turns of all four tension screws.

Cyclebabble

To **click in** is the act of engaging the shoe cleat into the mechanism of a clipless pedal.

Cyclometers as Learning Tools and Training Aids

So now you know how to pedal in circles and your feet are solidly clicked in to your pedals. There's only one more element needed to get the most efficient power output from your pedaling: learning to spin a fast cadence.

As I've mentioned a time or three already, in cycling cadence refers to the number of times per minute a rider turns the pedals. Again, an average rider is most efficient when turning the pedals at a cadence of at least 60, or one revolution of the pedals per second. As your fitness increases, you will want to keep a higher cadence of perhaps 80 or even into the 90s and beyond.

Calculating your cadence in your head is pretty tough beyond 60 rpms, especially since the oxygen in your blood is likely to be busy in areas other than your brain. Don't strain your brain; get a bicycle computer with cadence function. Virtually all bicycle computers (*cyclometers*) have a speedometer function. It works by means of a small magnet attached to a spoke and an electronic sensor mounted to the fork or frame. As the wheel rotates, the sensor detects the magnet as it spins by, the computer then calculates the bicycle's speed based on how long it takes for each revolution of the wheel. The cyclometer display then shows the speed in either miles per hour (mph) or kilometers per hour (kph). The cadence function works in much the same way, except the magnet is mounted to a crankarm and the sensor is mounted to frame. Instead of calculating speed, the computer estimates the number of times the pedals are turned per minute.

The majority of cyclometers don't have a cadence function, so you may have to do a little shopping to find one. Sigma has a few models with cadence, and Cateye's Astrale model is a long-time favorite of mine. Many riders find that after they've used the cadence function for awhile they develop a pretty good feel for being in the right range and may even stop using their computer's cadence function. After all, the point of using a cadence function is to learn what it feels like to be spinning in the efficient range.

Cateye's Astrale computer is one of the few that can compute pedaling rpms.

No Achy Shaky Parts

For racers and riders that like long mileage, a certain amount of soreness is part of the equation. However, many of the aches, pains, and post-ride trembles common to new riders are mostly caused by riding stiffly and not shifting their riding position throughout the ride. Here are some tips for better riding comfort:

1. **Change hand positions.** Riders who complain of chronic soreness of the hands, neck, shoulders, lower back, or bottom are often riders who plop themselves onto the bike and hold the same position throughout the entire ride. Hand, neck, and shoulder soreness can be greatly reduced by constantly changing your hand positions on the handlebars. Varying your riding position helps fight fatigue by giving certain muscle groups a rest while certain others bear the load for a while.

2. **Relax those hands.** It doesn't take a death grip to hold onto or steer a bike. On the contrary, thanks to the gyroscopic effect of the spinning wheels, a bike will generally go in a straight line when left on its own. That's how a bike can be ridden with no hands.

3. **Use the wide variety of positions available on road handlebars.**
   ➤ **The tops.** Placing your hands on the tops (the straight section extending out from both sides of the stem) provides a comfortable upright position

that's nearly the same riding position as a mountain bike. More variation is available by moving the hands closer together or farther apart. Although riding on the tops creates a lot of wind resistance, it's also a great means of giving the lower back and shoulders a break.

➤ **The hoods.** Placing your hands on the brake lever hoods (usually with the hood positioned between the thumb and forefinger) is another fairly upright position that takes pressure off the back and shoulders. It's also a favored position for climbing because the hoods give a rider a firm grip to pull against while lunging a leg downward.

➤ **The hooks or drops.** Placing your hands in the tight curve of the handle-bars puts you in a low, aggressive position that's very efficient for fighting wind resistance. It's the favored position for going very fast. Although riding in the hooks can be tiresome, assuming this position can also be a welcome break and a good back stretcher for a rider who has spent several miles riding on the tops or hoods.

4. **Change head positions.** The position of a bike rider's head relative to the torso when he's on a bike is about the same as someone standing and looking up. How long could you continue to stare up at a tall building? Not long if you didn't vary your head position occasionally. You can avoid neck pain by riding with your head cocked slightly to one side. By alternating head positions to the middle and to the other side every few minutes, you give all the muscles in the neck a chance to bear your head's weight. Sore necks are very common to new cyclists. This soreness will pass as neck muscles grow stronger through the miles.

5. **Bend those elbows.** Riding stiff-armed gives rise to a myriad of problems. Holding the arms rigid causes the shoulders and neck to also become rigid, making them stiff and sore. Stiff arms also transfer the movement of the legs into the handlebars, making the rider weave; this action is very tiresome because going straight becomes a constant series of corrections. Riding with your elbows bent so that the forearms are nearly horizontal will make your entire upper body more relaxed. A relaxed upper body is the key to smooth riding. Watch the pros; their elbows are bent and relaxed; the only things moving are their legs.

After the Fall

It's often been said that there are two types of bike riders: those that will crash, and those that will crash again. Gravity, the limits of traction, and our own limited sense of balance all conspire to occasionally deposit us onto the dirt or pavement. When that happens, the lucky ones among us lose only a bit of skin. The less lucky may lose a month or three from work as shattered bones heal. Knowing what to do immediately after a fall may help lessen the pain and suffering of injury.

Taking Inventory

The adrenaline of crashing can easily mask the signs of injury. For many, the first reaction is to jump up and get back on the bike, but this action can further aggravate an injury. Instead, take a moment to check yourself over.

Pay attention to your body. Start from your head and work your way down. Is anything sore? Did your head hit the ground? Did you roll and strain your neck? Did one of your shoulders hit first? Hand and arm injuries are very common because it's hard to overcome the instinct to put your hands out to break the fall in a crash. So wiggle your fingers, rotate your wrists, open and close your hands, and move your arms to make sure everything is okay. How's your back? Any creaks or pain? Hips okay? Legs? Feet? Is anything scraped? Did you pick up any debris or thorns?

Road Rash

The most common injury among cyclists is skin abrasions, usually on the shins and knees or on the hips or forearms. Scrapes can be very painful, mainly because scraping away the top layers of skin exposes a large number of nerve endings. Bleeding usually isn't the main concern with scrapes, because they have more of an oozing than a flowing type of bleeding. The main concern is the chance of infection and permanent scarring from imbedded debris.

A scrape will usually have bits of the very dirt and grit that caused it. Getting rid of that immediately will save a lot hassle and pain later. Grab your water bottle (be sure it's water and not an energy drink) and blast out the wounds to wash out the crud. A well-prepared rider will have a small first-aid kit along that includes some kind of antiseptic or antiseptic towelette, a few gauze pads, and some adhesive tape or bandages (refer back to the emergency kit discussion in Chapter 8, "Accessorizing").

After rinsing out the scrape (and unclenching your teeth), open the antiseptic towelette or put some antiseptic on a section of gauze. If bits of grit still remain, gently wipe them out with the gauze or towelette starting from the middle and working outward. If the scrape is already clean, simply dab on some antiseptic.

It's important to then dress the scrape. Otherwise, grime may fling up into it, and the painful wound-cleaning process will have to be done again. The simplest means of dressing the wound is with a large self-adhesive bandage. Lacking that, or if the scrape is too big, resort to gauze and tape. Choose a section of gauze that's at least an inch bigger than the scrape. Place it over the wound and secure with tape. If the scrape is on the knee or elbow, be sure to tape the gauze so that it won't pull off from the bending of the joint.

When you get home, remove the dressing and inspect the wound again under a bright light. You want to be absolutely sure that all grit is gone. Letting the wound heal over foreign matter will result in a permanent "tattoo" and may also lead to infection.

Broken Collarbone

Suffering a broken collarbone is almost a right of passage for racers. Those crashes where the bike comes out from under a rider and deposits him on his shoulder are a most efficient means of snapping a clavicle. Just ask '96 mountain bike Olympian Don Myrah—he's done it five times.

So there you are on the ground. You can't move your arm, and there's a golf ball-sized lump on your shoulder that wasn't there before. A clavicle fracture isn't terribly serious; the healing time is only four to eight weeks. Your immediate concern, though, should be getting your injured self back home.

To stabilize a clavicle fracture well enough to be able to gingerly ride one-handed or to walk home, a sling is needed. A suitable sling can be fashioned out of a spare inner tube or by tearing up a T-shirt or jersey. When using an inner tube you may want to cut off the valve stem, for obvious reasons. Then, loop the tube over the wrist and bring the tube up over the opposite shoulder, around the neck and down to the elbow. Wrap the tube around the inside of the elbow and take up the slack so that the arm can rest horizontally. Tie a knot at the inside of the elbow.

Further stabilization can be had by if another tube is available. Cut the tube across so that it opens up into one long piece. Pass it through the underarm opposite of the break; bring around the back, around the outside of the arm, and tie tightly across the chest. You now have a sling and swath that will secure your tender shoulder almost as well as the one that the doctor will put on (and for which your HMO will be billed $137.50). Get yourself to a hospital as soon as possible and hope that it really is a broken collarbone and not a shoulder separation. Collarbones heal quickly and completely. Shoulder separations can take months to heal and often are never the same again.

A Half-Dozen Cycling Hygiene Tips

I don't doubt that your mother taught you well, but there are a few hygiene-related issues pertaining to biking that you need to be aware of. In the following sections, you'll find everything your mother told you, and then some.

Nose Blowing

When you combine vigorous exercise with cool wind and perhaps a bit of pollen, a runny nose is practically inevitable. Keeping a few tissues in a jersey pocket can be real handy when the nasal passages really get to flowing. However, stopping to honk into a tissue isn't a real option in a race or fast-paced training ride. Here's a tip: Learn to blow snot sans tissue. It's quite simple. Just lean out to the side, use a finger to close one nostril, and blow hard to blast out the other. Repeat with the other side. When applying this technique around other riders, always be aware of the prevailing wind and the position of riders around and behind you. Move to one side if needed. Your fellow riders will appreciate it. One more thing: You probably don't want to mention your mastering of this particular skill to your mom.

Answering Nature's Call

Whichever of nature's calls you're answering, bring tissue in a resealable plastic bag. If ever you realize that you need to do that thing that bears are known for doing in the woods, you'll be especially glad to have that wad of tissue. The plastic bag will keep it intact for use and should be used afterward for carrying the used tissue home. That's right. Every good backpacker knows not to leave or bury used tissue, and it holds just as true for cyclists.

Miles of Experience

I don't think I have to offer many tips to my male readers on the topic of urination, but here's one tip that you may find useful when it comes to wearing Lycra bike shorts. Instead of lowering the front of your bike shorts and exposing yourself to the world at large, it's possible to be a little more discrete by rolling up one leg of your shorts and pulling the elastic away from your leg.

Sunscreen

Melanoma is not pleasant. Always apply sunscreen to all of your exposed skin before a ride. Don't forget the tops of your ears and the back of your neck. Use a brand of sunscreen meant for use during exercise. It won't run off as easily as you sweat. For rides longer than a couple of hours, consider bringing along a small bottle of sunscreen to apply another layer at a rest stop. Apply it sparingly on the forehead so that you don't get a stinging mixture of sunscreen and sweat flowing into your eyes.

Contact Lenses

Dust, grit, and small insects can do painful things to the eyes of contact-lens wearers. That's why many switch to eyeglasses for outdoor activities such as cycling. However, because contacts can correct vision imperfections that eyeglasses can't, switching to glasses isn't always an option. For those riders, a pair of sunglasses that fit closely to the face can help keep debris (living or otherwise) from getting into the eyes. Riders who are particularly sensitive should consider wearing goggles to completely seal the eyes. They might also consider adding saline solution, a cleaning case, and a small vial of distilled water to their survival kits.

Get Out of Those Bike Shorts

What's the ideal environment for breeding bacteria? Those that remember their high school biology will answer "someplace warm, dark, and moist." What's it like inside your bike shorts after a long saddle session? You got it. By getting out of those shorts and into something clean and dry as soon as possible after a ride, you'll reduce the incidence of pore-clogging bacteria that cause saddle sores.

When you finish a ride or race, instead of going straight to the post-ride pizza feed, take a few minutes to clean up and change. Keep a wet washcloth and a little soap in a plastic bag. Duck into a rest room if you can or keep a large towel handy in your car to wrap around yourself as you clean up and change. Give yourself a quick sponge bath. Start by cleaning your face, then move on to your torso, arms and legs, and then finish up with your crotch area.

Shave Your Legs

Something that noncyclists are often surprised to learn is that most racers, and quite a few serious nonracing riders, shave their legs. No, not just the women—the men, too. There are several reasons.

Probably the most compelling reason is that in the event of a crash, the inevitable leg scrapes will be easier to clean without there being a jungle of leg hair. The hair itself can also cause infection to a skin abrasion. Having shaved legs also makes it easier and less painful to dress scrapes with gauze because the adhesive tape can be removed without taking along a swath of leg hair.

Many riders enjoy a deep massage to the leg muscles after a race or ride. It's a wonderful way to speed recovery and ease the ache of hard riding. Most massage therapists use massage oil on the muscles. Having a thick growth of leg hair complicates the massage therapist's work as hair goops up with oil. The hard pressure and long strokes of sports massage can also pull leg hair. Ouch!

Cycology

Having shaved legs is a sort of right of passage to the "society of those that ride a lot and may even race." Claims of reduced wind resistance have some merit, although the amount of time lost to aerodynamic drag caused by having hairy legs probably amounts to minuscule fractions of a second per mile. The real reasons have more to do with a rider showing a serious commitment to the sport. And it feels good to have a warm breeze blowing over hairless legs while pedaling down a nice, quiet road.

The Least You Need to Know

➤ Water is the elixir of life, and it will certainly help to sustain yours during long excursions.

➤ Sports drinks and sports bars are convenient ways to stave off hunger, as are fruit juices, bagels, and fresh fruit.

➤ Figure out your maximum heart rate to perform at your personal best.

➤ Your bike is one more aspect of your life that can be improved with a computer; a cyclometer can help you to get the most efficient power output from your pedaling.

➤ To get the maximum from your legs, don't push the pedals down; spin them 'round and 'round.

➤ Practicing good bike hygiene will make you a happy biker.

Chapter 13

Spinning Wheels: Indoor Workouts

In This Chapter

➤ Spinning classes: aerobics on a bike

➤ Getting a stationary workout at home

➤ Stationary tips from Dr. Arnie Baker

➤ How riding in place can improve your racing results

In the previous chapter, I told you about how to keep your bike's engine—that is, you—in good working condition. Now we're going to take that conditioning one step further. If you can't work out outdoors on two wheels, don't fret. You can keep that momentum going inside, too. In this chapter, we're going to keep those wheels turning at home and at the gym. Saddle up.

Circle of Friends: Spinning Classes

There are a lot of exercise bikes in homes across the United States. They get used quite frequently, too—mostly for hanging clothes and handbags or as perches for pet parrots. There are, however, thousands of exercycles being used for their intended purpose. They're being used in health clubs and gyms in classes called *Spinning* where riders gather to enjoy cycling to music in a group setting.

An instructor takes the class through a 40-minute session of a series of cycling exercises, including standing, sitting, sprints, and climbing hills. All the while, music is playing, and the riders are sweating as they ride at their own individual intensity and pace, and no one gets left behind.

The bikes used are Spinners made by Schwinn's fitness division. Unlike many exercycles that use unadjustable upright riding positions, Spinners duplicate the position of a road bike. That's very important for experienced cyclists because forcing the body to adapt to a drastically different riding position can cause injuries to muscles, joints, and tendons. With a Spinner, a rider can adjust the saddle up and down as well as frontward and backward. The handlebar height is adjustable, too, so smart riders with a measuring tape and knowledge of the dimensions of their real bikes can virtually duplicate the position of their bikes in just a few minutes.

Spinning programs can be very effective training. The group setting can be a huge motivator. The drills and changes in speed of a Spinning class duplicate a real ride with hills and varying speeds and are very effective at increasing cycling fitness and burning calories. The average rider at a Spinning class burns about 500 calories. It's no wonder that Spinning classes are catching on.

Cycology

Going to a Spinning class doesn't mean being subjected to booming decibel levels. Because the music is piped through individual headphones installed on the bikes, the volume is up to the rider.

Spinning classes offer great workouts within the comfort of your local health club. Some serious riders may discount their effectiveness, but I've tried them, and the intensity of the workout leaves me feeling as though I've spent twice as long riding on the road or trail. For me, a Spinning class will never replace the fun of real riding. But when the weather is bad or when the change of daylight savings time robs riders of hours to ride, Spinning classes are a great means to continue riding and to maintain fitness for the weekends or the coming of spring.

You say the aerobics class at your local health club just isn't your idea of fun? For bicyclists, a Spinning class is a good way to get a good aerobic workout in a more familiar fashion.

Spinning at Home

At most any bike shop you can find devices that can turn any bike into an exercycle. They're called *stationary trainers* or *wind trainers*. Stationary trainers come in various types, which use different means to create resistance:

➤ **A wind trainer** uses a small turbine like those found on old-fashioned window fans. The resistance on a wind trainer most closely duplicates the resistance of riding on the road.

➤ **Mag trainers** use magnets to create resistance. They're quieter than wind trainers, but their resistance progress is more linear than a wind trainer. That is, the effort increase needed to accelerate from say 15 to 20 mph is the same as the effort increase needed to accelerate from 10 to 15 mph. That's not how it is in real riding conditions. On the road or trail the faster you go the harder it is to increase your speed. A mag trainer's linear resistance allows you to reach artificially high speeds. You might feel proud about training at 30 mph, only to discover that you can't go anywhere near that fast on the road.

➤ **Fluid trainers** use a chamber of oil to create resistance. They do a fine job of duplicating the resistance levels of actual riding and are also quieter than wind trainers, but they cost much more.

Most stationary trainers attach to the rear of the bike. A sturdy frame keeps the bike upright, and the rear tire presses against a small roller. A rider can then mount the bike and ride it just as they would an exercycle.

A stationary trainer is a very valuable tool to help you make better use of limited time. Regardless of weather, you can always get in some quality saddle time. When time is limited, a trainer workout can be much more effective and efficient than going for a ride. After all, how good of a workout can you get in an hour on a real ride? If you're starting in town, by the time you ride to a suitable trail or open road you've had to stop for traffic and stoplights and probably haven't even gotten a decent warm-up. Before you know it, it's time to turn around. That's not even taking into account the time that can potentially be lost to a flat tire. On a stationary trainer, every one of those 60 minutes can be put to good use.

By riding a trainer just two or three times during the week, a rider or racer can keep fit and even gain fitness to make weekend rides and races much more enjoyable and successful. All it takes is a few hours set aside each week. Some riders make it part of their morning routine or schedule their trainer riding to coincide with their favorite TV shows—"*Law and Order* and pedaling and sweating." Other riders keep a trainer and bike at work and get in a daily workout on their lunch hour. If you want to improve your cycling fitness, you'll find a few hours somewhere in your week.

This simple device can turn any bike into an exercycle. Thirty seconds is all it takes to set a bike into this Trakstand model from Blackburn.

If you find that you enjoy the experience and benefits of riding a stationary trainer, you may want to think about getting an old beater bike just for stationary training. Your stationary trainer beater bike needn't be anything fancy, as long as it's the same size as your regular bike, you can duplicate your regular position, and it has cranks the same length as your regular bike.

The frame could even be one that someone cast off because it was slightly bent or crash-damaged. You or some of your riding buddies may have enough cast-off parts to build the frame into a complete bike. Bolt on that old heavy seat-post that you replaced with a light alloy post, the same with those steel handlebars and stem. Those old wheels that won't stay in true won't be hitting any bumps on the trainer, now will they? You don't even need to put brakes on the bike. If you're smart, frugal, and are a bike pack rat (or know a few), you can build up a beater for practically nothing.

Another reason to consider a beater bike, other than economical factors, is that regular sessions on a trainer can put strain on your real bike's frame. Because it's being held rigidly in place, the side-to-side forces that would only cause harmless swaying on the road are being put right into your frame. Also, the gallons of sweat that will drip onto your bike aren't going to do its finish any good, especially if it's a steel bike. Constantly steering straight ahead will wear out a headset in no time as well.

The Doctor Is In

For all the benefits of stationary trainers, many riders still unfairly regard them as torture devices for masochistic riders who spend their time sweating indoors instead of riding on real roads or trails. That's only true for riders who grind along at a constant speed. It needn't be that way. Just ask renowned cycling trainer Arnie Baker, M.D., of San Diego, California. Dr. Baker's training methods include extensive use of stationary trainers. His programs have workouts with varying efforts and pedaling rpms that take away the drudgery of riding a trainer and make it fun.

He may look like a nice guy, but Dr. Arnie Baker can make you suffer. Follow his 12-week stationary trainer program, and you'll be able to inflict even greater suffering on your competition.

Among the loyal charges trained by Dr. Baker who follow his stationary trainer workouts are several veteran and master road racers and three-time U.S. mountain bike champion Tinker Juarez. As well as being a very successful trainer, Dr. Baker is quite an accomplished road racer himself. With five U.S. championships and five U.S. time-trial records to his credit, it's obvious that Dr. Baker practices what he preaches.

Dr. Baker advocates using stationary trainers for training specific cycling strengths. "There are elements of fitness that you can isolate on a trainer to hone and fine-tune better than anywhere else," he said. "You need to separate the parts and work on those parts to make a better whole. While there's nothing that can simulate riding on trails for technical aspects and handling skills needed for mountain biking, as far as fitness,

191

if you're concentrating on where your bike is going, you're not separating out the specific aspects of fitness. On the trainer, you can decide what aspect of fitness you want to work on and concentrate on it. Consider a runner. He can go run on the street or on the beach. But if he wants a precise workout and wants to time it and evaluate it to know exactly what he's doing, he goes to a track."

Dripping Sweat on Arnie's Patio

In his book *Smart Cycling*, Dr. Baker provides a 12-week series of workouts. This schedule of workouts is structured to gradually build fitness and, once a certain level of fitness is attained, to build on certain cycling aspects such as leg speed, power, climbing, and sprinting. For several years, Dr. Baker has held twice-a-week group training sessions on stationary trainers using his 12-week program. These sessions are sort of a Spinning class aboard actual bikes. However, Baker's workout programs are much better suited than Spinning classes to people who want to specifically improve their cycling strength. "Spinning is a good aerobic exercise," Dr. Baker said, "but it's not cycling- or racing-specific."

Among this group of riders dripping perspiration on Dr. Arnie Baker's patio is a three-time U.S. mountain bike champion and several road and time-trial champions.

During each session, Dr. Baker leads the group through warm-ups and intervals of specific power output and pedaling rpms designed to focus on particular cycling aspects. Sprinting, endurance, leg speed, and proper spinning form are all developed during the 12 weeks of sessions. Even climbing ability can be developed on a trainer by increasing the load resistance and raising the front of the bike so that the muscle groups can work in the climbing positions encountered on the trail.

I made a trip to visit Dr. Baker and to take in some of his trainer sessions. I hadn't spent much time on stationary trainers. I've always spent my stationary time riding *rollers*, a type of trainer that doesn't clamp the bike rigidly in place. Instead, a rider places the bike on a set of drums that requires the rider to maintain balance to remain upright. I had always had the doctrine of "rollers for perfect spin" pounded into my head. Dr. Baker agrees with that credo to a degree, "But rollers aren't as versatile as a trainer. Most of the time some of your effort is going toward maintaining balance. On a trainer, you can focus on the effort, even close your eyes and concentrate if you want. Try doing that on rollers."

The gradual warm-up portion of Dr. Baker's session wouldn't have been any problem on rollers, but it's doubtful I could have reached the intensity of effort needed for the intervals. Even if I had, at such highly anaerobic levels of effort, I probably couldn't have stayed upright anyway. As Dr. Baker later pointed out, "Even with stationary trainers, every year someone manages to fall during a session."

Thankfully, I stayed on my bike. At the end of the hour-long session, I realized that I had been through one of the most intense bike workouts imaginable. Dr. Baker's leadership along with the group atmosphere had inspired me to push myself much harder than I ever would have on my own. Judging by the numerous time-trial record-holders who attend Dr. Baker's sessions, these sessions obviously work.

"I can't say enough about how riding a wind trainer has helped me," said Tinker Juarez, a rider noted for keeping an insanely grueling training schedule. "On days when I wake up to see it's raining, I can still get in my hard training. And there's no hiding—Arnie can watch my trainer workout or read my heart-rate monitor and know exactly how I'm doing in my training. It works. No question. For the average rider, the good thing is they can get a workout at home—not everyone is comfortable in a group setting, especially people just starting out who maybe think they're too heavy or not fit enough. At home they can ride while watching their own TV or listening to their own music and build up their fitness in private."

Dr. Baker's training sessions can be duplicated by anyone with a stationary trainer and a copy of his book *Smart Cycling*. According to Dr. Baker, dozens of trainer sessions are held each week across the country. Perhaps you could gather up a few of your friends and start your own sessions, too. The sessions outlined in the book follow the same 12-week schedule that Arnie uses in the sessions at his home. They vary week by week with increased intensity and speeds to coincide with your increased fitness. And they help you to build specific cycling strengths such as leg speed, power, sprinting, and hill-climbing. Follow the 12-week program and you'll be fit, trim, and ready for a season of fun riding or racing. This same program has worked for top pro and amateur racers, so it will certainly work for you, too.

Using Your Stationary Trainer to Warm Up

Warming up before doing a hard effort is very important. Try to sprint or climb a steep hill before your body has warmed up and you're inviting a stress injury. On a casual ride or fun ride warming up is easy—just ride at an easy pace to begin with and increase gradually as you break a sweat.

There's no gradual warming up in a race, however. Races start out hard and fast. The pack explodes from the starting line with no gradual buildup of speed. "Yet I'm amazed at how many riders don't warm up—especially mountain bike racers," Dr. Baker revealed. "Tests have shown that at the start, racers often put out three or four times the power output of what they'll average over the race. To have the body ready for that kind of effort, it's important to warm up." That's where a stationary trainer comes in. "You can do your warm-up without distractions and don't have to be worried about where to go," Dr. Baker observed.

Dr. Baker explains how to do a pre-race warm-up with some riding and some trainer work. "Start very slowly. The first 30 minutes, just get on the bike and noodle around. Find out where the start is, find the porta-potties, go to registration. Do whatever. Then start a half hour of structured work on the trainer."

Dr. Baker gave me an outline for a warm-up that I now use for racing. This same outline will work for you or any rider regardless of fitness level. Just be sure that for the hard three-minute efforts you shift into a gear that's high enough to make you work hard enough to reach your max heart rate.

➤ Use a moderate gear for the first eight minutes, starting out at 90 rpms and increasing by 10 rpms every two minutes.

➤ After another two minutes of easy spinning, switch to a hard gear and a three-minute effort at 80 rpms.

➤ Follow this with two more three-minute efforts: one at 85 rpms and one at 90 rpms.

➤ Downshift for another two-minute easy spin.

➤ Follow this with three minutes in a moderate gear at 85 rpms, then three minutes at 110+ rpms, and then three minutes at 80 rpms.

"The basis is three or four efforts at threshold heart rate," Dr. Baker explained. "Some of the efforts with lower muscles demand spinning more to get the heart to race levels without tiring out the muscles. Most important are the efforts of three minutes with high power output at the effort that you'll race at. If you don't get there before, how can you expect to get there right off the start?" Dr. Baker's warm-up has me sweaty with muscles primed and ready to go.

How close to a race should a warm-up end? "The closer the better," Dr. Baker said. "Although if you do a 20-minute spin in the morning, it will help you even hours later." The timing of a warm-up is a tricky balance that will vary from race to race. Staying on your trainer too long may mean having to line up at the back of the grid. You have to ask how many places you'll lose if you're not there at a certain time. In a perfect world, you have your race bike sitting on the line, and you put your stationary trainer with another bike right next to the front row and warm up on it until there's 15 seconds to go. Then you hop on your race bike, and you're off!

Miles of Experience

Long ago I learned the importance of a pre-race warm-up. However, it wasn't until Dr. Arnie Baker suggested it that I began doing my warm-ups on a wind trainer. Looking back, I should have thought of it long before. Twice at road events I got flat tires miles from the starting line while warming up, causing me to miss the start of my race. At a mountain bike race, I narrowly avoided a head-on collision with another rider doing his warm-up, which surely would have made me miss my start. Countless times my warm-ups have been interrupted, shortened, or forgotten about when I've happened across friends and spent the time chatting instead of pedaling.

The Least You Need to Know

➤ Despite nay-sayers, Spinning classes and stationary trainers are great fun—and a great workout.

➤ A Spinning class can improve your overall fitness.

➤ To maximize the cycling-specific aspects of a Spinning class, bring a measuring tape and take the time to duplicate your regular riding position.

➤ You can do your own stationary workout at home.

➤ A stationary trainer can be a big help on race day.

Part 4
The Care and Feeding of a Bicycle

I've known many cyclists who never work on their bikes, not even for the most basic maintenance or repair. They only touch their bikes to ride them. Hang around any bike shop on a Saturday morning, and you'll probably see several people bring bikes in to have flat tires repaired—something that I can teach anyone to do in just 10 minutes.

It's a shame that these riders are so intimidated by their machines. Most basic bike mechanic skills, including flat fixing, are very simple to learn, not to mention the fact that a rider who doesn't know how to fix a flat tire will sooner or later find himself or herself walking home. This section will help to assure that you won't end a ride with a long walk. It will help you through the basics, including advice on what tools you'll need, and detail some of the more advanced mechanical skills that might interest those with nuts and bolts on the brain. Anyone can fix a flat, clean a chain, and do minor adjustments. You'll see.

Tool Time

For those who are mechanically inclined, doing basic maintenance on a bike can be almost as much fun as riding it. As with any piece of equipment, working on a bike is much easier with the proper tools. By proper tools, I mean wrenches and sockets in the right sizes. In this chapter, we'll take a look at the basic tools needed to do minor repairs and adjustments to your bike.

The Right Stuff

Using an adjustable wrench or pliers on a bicycle's small nuts and bolts is barbaric and ruins nuts and bolts. When I've worked in bike shops, the standing rule in the service department was "Anyone found using pliers, vice grips, channel locks, or an adjustable wrench on bicycle nuts and bolts shall submit to three blows upside the head with the offending tool."

You may already have many of the tools needed to work on your bike. Unless you're going to disassemble hubs and bottom brackets or replace a headset, you can complete most bike maintenance jobs with merely a selection of metric Allen wrenches, metric open-end wrenches, metric sockets, and a couple of small screwdrivers (one standard

Cycology

Aside from a few specialty tools, most of the mechanical work on a bicycle can be done with wrenches you may already have. With a set of Allen wrenches in sizes from 2 mm up to 8 mm and a selection of open-end wrenches in sizes from 6 mm to 15 mm, you can do just about every mechanical chore short of installing a bottom bracket or headset.

Cyclebabble

Remember the bike pump your dad kept in the garage when you were a kid, the one that looked like a dynamite detonator? That's a **floor pump**. The good ones can pump up bike tires to very high pressures (150 pounds per square inch and more) and have fairly accurate built-in pressure gauges.

and one Phillips). If you already have these tools and would like to tackle other maintenance chores, you can get most of the other tools you'll need for about $150 to $200.

Flat Fixing and Tire Care Essentials

In Chapter 8, "Accessorizing," I discussed the items needed to fix a flat on the road or trail. I recommend keeping a duplicate set of flat tools at home with your other tools. That way, your survival kit always stays together, and you won't accidentally leave something behind on your workbench.

You already know that you need a set of tire levers and a patch kit, but for your home flat-fixing kit, you also want a good *floor pump*. Using your frame-mounted pump for everyday inflation jobs will wear out your pump and take much longer than using a good floor pump. A quality floor pump can be had for $30 to $50. In those price ranges, most will have a built-in pressure gauge. The more you spend, the more accurate the gauge is. However, even the best built-in gauges aren't as precise as a good hand-held gauge.

The last item in your tire tool list isn't really a tool, but it's still important: a container of baby powder. Whenever you mount a new tire or change a tube, sprinkle in a bit of powder to keep the tube from sticking to the tire. Without it, you'll often find that the inner tube has adhered to the inside of the tire, making it difficult to pull out. Worse yet, when the tube is stuck this way, movement of the tube in the tire from bumps and such can cause the tube to chafe, resulting in a flat. These types of flats are particularly insidious, because there are often several tiny, hard-to-detect holes. Sometimes they're spread out over an area too large for even the biggest patches.

Wrenches in the Works

Most quality bicycles use Allen head fasteners. To be able to loosen and tighten these nuts and screws, you'll need a range of Allen wrenches. Allen wrenches come in three flavors:

1. A set of various wrenches sized in a pocketknife tool

3. Three wrenches sized on a Y-wrench

3. Loose L-shaped wrenches

Miles of Experience

Being a former Cub Scout, I tend to follow the credo of "Be prepared." My workshop tool collection is nearly as extensive as a bike shop's. And the toolbox that I take to rides and races is nearly as complete as my shop. With so much money invested in tools, I've taken precautions to keep my tools from "walking away." Each tool has my initials painted on with bright red paint. No one can dispute ownership if I spot a bright red "VA" in his or her toolbox.

Each kind has its advantages and drawbacks. A pocketknife-type set is handy because it prevents you from losing any individual wrenches. Sometimes, however, you won't be able to fit the whole bulky tool into tight spaces to get at the nut or screw you're trying to work on.

A pocketknife-type set of Allen wrenches keeps all the sizes in one handy tool where they're less prone to getting lost than loose wrenches. They won't rattle around in your seat-bag either.

A Y-wrench is handy because it has the three most commonly needed sizes: 4 mm, 5 mm, and 6 mm. However, the wrist-twisting motion used with a Y-wrench is hard on the wrist, especially when you're trying to get something really tight or loosen something that already is good and tight.

With a Y-wrench, the three most common wrench sizes are right in the palm of your hand.

Steer Clear

The bargain-basement models of combination wrenches that sell for half the price of good ones are often inaccurately sized and are made of inferior materials. If you use these, you'll soon have a bike full of rounded-off bolt and nut heads. The same goes for those one-size-fits-all miracle wrenches you see on late-night TV. Forget about them.

Loose L-shaped Allen wrenches are the easiest to use. They can fit into all the tight spots, and they're long enough to get good leverage. I have a set with extra long handles that I use when I want something really tight. The drawback with loose wrenches is that they're thin and small, which makes them easy to lose. They seem to disappear like socks in a dryer. Fortunately, they're fairly cheap; most sizes you'll need are only 25¢ to 50¢ at your local hardware store, and they're even cheaper when you buy them in a set. Pick up a few of each size, and don't sweat it when one gets lost.

Don't scrimp when you buy your combination wrenches. You can find good-quality, hard-chromed sets made of drop-forged steel for around $20.

Even if you have a Y-wrench and a pocketknife set, you still want a complete set of loose Allen wrenches. They're much better at getting into tight spaces.

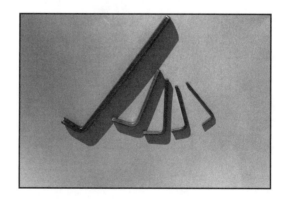

Tools for the Mildly Ambitious

If you're the type of person who likes to do handy jobs around the house, you probably have the aptitude to take on bike maintenance chores beyond simple lubricating and bolt tightening. For this, you'll want a few more bits of hardware:

➤ **Workstand.** Most bike maintenance and adjustment jobs are much easier to do when the bike is placed in a bicycle workstand. A workstand brings the bike up to a comfortable working level so you won't have to stoop over, and it allows the wheels to spin and the drivetrain to fully function.

Several companies make consumer model workstands; Blackburn, Park, Ultimate, and most others are priced between $150 and $250. Some fold up so they can be easily stowed in a vehicle to take on a trip or to a race.

Cycology

Although most of the fasteners on mid-priced to high-end bicycles are Allen heads, entry-level models have regular nuts and bolts. To work on these bikes, you'll need a set of open-end wrenches in sizes from 6 mm to 15 mm. You should get a set of combination wrenches, with each wrench having an open-end on one end and a box-end on the other. The box-end is particularly helpful for nuts and bolts that have been rounded off a bit. However, in tight spaces you can't always get a box-end over a nut or bolt.

Miles of Experience

For the budget-minded, a length of rope or a motorcycle-type tie-down strap can do a nice job as a workstand. Tie the rope or hook the tie-down to a garage rafter and tie it or hook it to the bike's saddle. I have a nice workstand in my garage, but for many jobs I prefer using a tie-down. With a tie-down, it's much easier to hoist the bike, and the bike can also be raised higher than it could with a workstand. This height can be a big help when you're working on the drivetrain. A rope or tie-down can also work at a race or event—just find a tree with a sturdy branch.

➤ **Cable cutters.** Get a set of cutters that are meant for bicycle use. Your diagonal cutters or lineman's pliers that do such a nice job on baling wire and speaker wire are not up to the task of cutting bicycle cable or cable housing. Most bicycle cable and housing is made of stainless steel or galvanized steel strands—really hard stuff. Your diagonal cutters or lineman's pliers might do an adequate cutting job if they're new, fresh, and sharp, but they won't stay that way once you start using them on bike cable. The truth is that they'll probably barely manage to cut the cable or housing. Poorly cut housing leaves jagged edges or can sometimes blossom out, leaving an inch or two of unraveled end and sometimes ruining the cable.

By putting a bike in a workstand, you won't have to stoop over your work. You can also test and adjust all systems because the wheels will spin and the drivetrain will function.

A motorcycle tie-down or even just a hunk of rope can work just fine as a workstand.

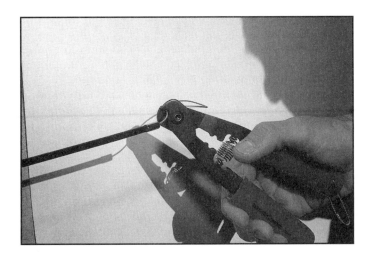

Try cutting cables or housing with your wire cutters, and you'll end up with dull cutters and poorly cut cables and housing. Instead, use a set of cutters like these from Wrench Force.

➤ **Third-hand tool.** Adjusting the cable tension on brakes and derailleurs is a fairly simple job that can be a chore without a third-hand tool. This tool holds the cable firmly in place and allows you to apply as much tension as you want before you tighten the cable's fixing bolt. A third-hand tool eliminates the frustration of trying to hold the cable with your hand or with pliers while trying to tighten the fixing bolt with the other hand.

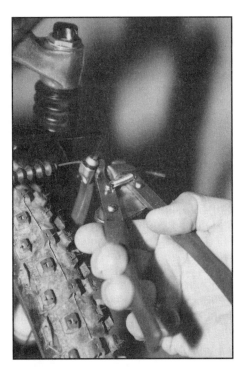

With a third-hand tool, you can set the tension on cable without having to hold the cable in your teeth.

➤ **Mallet.** Some think this tool is too barbaric for bike use. In the wrong hands, it can be, but it's not nearly as lethal as a hammer. A mallet is an easy way to coax end-caps into handlebars and bar-ends. It can be an easy way to apply a bit of added force to a wrench to loosen a particularly stubborn nut or bolt. It can smooth out big dents in rims without scarring the braking surface. It's handy for persuading stubborn stems or seat-posts to come out. And it can be used to ward off bothersome hangers-on who like to watch over your shoulder as you work.

➤ **Spoke wrench.** Although using this tool to its full potential is a skill that takes time to master, even in the hands of a novice it's very useful. With a little patience, most anyone can replace a broken spoke or relieve his or her wheels of minor wobbles. For more information on using this tool, read Chapter 19, "Beyond the Basics: Learning to Fix Some Bigger Problems."

➤ **Hacksaw.** When it's time to replace worn or lost bolts, it's practically impossible to get the right length from your local hardware store. But you can usually find them a little longer. No worries; just cut them down. Be sure to get a hacksaw with a quality blade—most of the bicycle bolts and things you'll need to cut are made of pretty hard stuff. A hacksaw is also handy for cutting down handlebars or chopping off excess seat-post.

➤ **File.** After you've cut a bolt, handlebar, seat-post, or cable housing, you'll need a file to smooth out the rough burrs.

➤ **Razor-knife.** The uses for this tool are nearly endless: cutting off old grips or handlebar tape, stripping back the plastic on the end of a cable housing, cutting off the tip of a tube of patch cement or grip adhesive, opening packages, cutting excess zip-tie, and so on.

➤ **Shock pump.** If you have a suspension fork such as a Rock Shox Sid, an old Rock Shox Mag21, a Marzocchi Super Fly, or Cannondale Fatty, or a rear air shock such as a Fox Air, Stratos, or Cane Creek, you need to be able to add air. Your tire pump isn't going to cut it on your shock. It probably won't generate enough air pressure, and it's likely the fitting will let out all the air when you try to take it off. Rock Shox's forks need a pump with a needle like the pumps used to blow up basketballs. Rock Shox's own pumps come with this needle, or you can put a standard ball needle on another brand of pump. Fox's shock pump works well and is sturdy and small enough to take along on a ride if you want to experiment with different pressures. The Fox pump will also work on any shock or fork that uses a standard shrader valve.

➤ **Needle-nose pliers.** No, they're not for tightening bolts. They're for feeding cables into tight places on shifters, for twisting wire onto a handgrip, and for holding a small nut in place while you thread in a screw. They're for any job calling for something small to be held, pulled, or twisted—anything but nuts and bolts, that is.

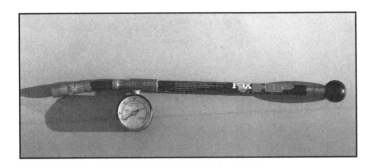

If you have an air shock or air fork, you need a good-quality shock pump.

➤ **Pedal wrench.** To install or take off pedals, you need to turn the wrench flats built into the spindle just inboard of the pedal platform. A pedal wrench is a 15 mm wrench with thin jaws to fit onto a pedal's narrow wrench flats. A standard 15 mm wrench is usually too thick to fit between the pedal platform and the spindle. You can save a few bucks over getting a $25 pedal wrench by taking a standard 15 mm wrench and using a file to shave it down to a thinner profile.

A pedal wrench has narrow jaws to fit onto a pedal's narrow wrench flats. It's also good and long for the added leverage you want to get pedals nice and tight and to loosen them once they are.

Many pedals can also be installed and removed with an Allen wrench because most pedals have a 6 mm hex head built into the end of the spindle. To install a pedal with an Allen wrench, thread the pedal into the crank by hand and insert the wrench into the hex head from the backside of the crankarm. Remember that you're turning the screw from the opposite side, so it needs to be turned in the opposite direction from normal. Also keep in mind that a right pedal is a right-hand thread and a left pedal is a left-hand thread, but when you're working from the backside, this is effectively switched. The drawbacks of using an Allen wrench instead of a pedal wrench is that a short Allen wrench won't have nearly the leverage of a long pedal wrench. You may not be able to loosen pedals that have been on for a long time or were installed good and tight.

207

Pedals can be installed or removed with a 6 mm Allen wrench. Remember that because you're working from the backside you need to turn the wrench in the opposite direction you would if you were using a pedal wrench.

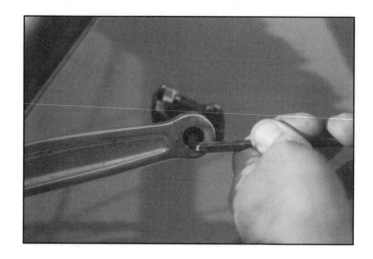

Lubricants

Even if you plan on having your local bike shop do all of your bike's adjustments and mechanical service, you should at least get a bottle of chain lubricant and learn how to lube your chain (see Chapter 17, "The Chain Gang"). If you clean and lube your chain every few rides, your chain and sprockets will last longer, and your bike will shift better.

Cycology

Although you can find most of your standard tools (Allen wrenches, screwdrivers, combination wrenches) at your local hardware store, you need to visit a bike shop to purchase specialty bike tools such as a pedal wrench. Look for brands such as Wrench Force, Park, or Hozan. If you're a real tool nut, get Campagnolo tools. They cost a bundle and are almost too nice to use, but boy, are they well made.

There are several types of lubricant: dry lubes, wet lubes, spray-on, and drip-on. Each type has those who swear by it and those who swear at it. I've yet to find the "perfect" lube. The wet ones last a long time, but they tend to attract grit and dirt. The dry ones keep the chain clean, but they don't last as long. Lube choice is up to the rider.

A popular brand of chain lube that many riders love is Tri-Flow. Personally, I think it's great for lubricating cables. It's thin, so it seeps in well. It also has Teflon particles, so it's really slick. But it's so thin that it attracts and holds the very smallest particles of dust and mixes into thick, clay-like grime. This grime builds up on and between the chainring and cog teeth and on the rear derailleur's jockey-pulleys. When we'd see a bike with a severe case of buildup at the bike shop, we'd say it had a severe case of "Tri-Flowsis." We'd cure this malady by removing the chain, chainrings, cogs, and rear derailleur and dropping them all in the solvent tank for a good scrubbing.

Realizing that thin oils either don't stay on or combine with dust to form a contaminating goo, some riders resort to using motor oil. This is a bad move for a number of reasons. First off, motor oil has a lot of nasty caustic chemicals added to it. Detergents in the form of solvents, sulfur, and other compounds designed to do good things to the inside of a motor can do bad things to the outside of a human. And motor oil is so thick that it attracts not only the fine particles of dust, but also big chunks of grit and small pebbles, turning your chain into a goopy, filthy mess of sludge in no time.

Finally, everything you've just read about house-hold oil, WD-40, Tri-Flow, and motor oil is to be disregarded should you discover that you're out of chain lube just before going for a ride. Using any of these is still better than running a dry chain. Of course, there was the guy who coated his chain with axle grease. If faced with a decision between staying home, riding a dry chain, or lubricating it with axle grease, my suggestion is to either stay home or put up with a squeaky chain.

Even if lubricating your bearings is beyond your mechanical ambitions or capabilities, you still want to have a small tube or tub of grease for other jobs. Get a brand name of bike grease, or if you already have automotive grease, go ahead and use it if it's a lithium type.

Any time you remove your stem or seat-post, be sure to apply a light coat of grease to the contact areas before putting them back in. No, grease won't make your stem or seat-post slip down, but it will make it easier to get them out the next time. This is especially important on a steel frame to prevent the post or stem from rusting in place from water and sweat that seep into your frame. It's a good idea on aluminum frames, too, for although aluminum doesn't rust, it still oxidizes in the presence of water and can grab hold of your stem or post.

Steer Clear

Be sure to use chain lube and not just household oil. Although the light oil you use around the house may work well to fix squeaky door hinges, it's too thin to do the job of lubricating a chain. Definitely don't use WD-40 as a chain lubricant. WD-40's formula has a high percentage of solvent, so it does a good job as a chain cleaner, but it isn't very good as a lubricant.

Cycology

Companies that make bicycle lubricants invest fortunes in developing their products. It pays off; most chain lubes, cable lubes, bearing grease, and cleaners from these companies work far better on bikes than household or automotive products do. Look for brands such as Finish Line, Pedros, Phil Wood, and Shimano. For bearing grease, it's tough to beat Campagnolo.

Dab a little grease on your seat-post, and you won't have to resort to dynamite the next time you need to take it out.

If ever you remove your pedals, you should also put a dab of grease on the threads of the pedal spindles, too. They'll thread in easier, the steel spindles won't damage the threads of the softer aluminum crankarms, and the pedals will be easier to remove the next time. In fact, just about any screw or nut on your bike can benefit from a little dab of grease before being put back in. Just remember to use it sparingly; you don't want globs of goo oozing out from all over your bike.

The Least You Need to Know

➤ Adjustable wrenches should only be used on your bike as a last resort.

➤ Raising the bike up to a comfortable work level will make any job easier.

➤ Your inner tubes don't like chafing any more than you do.

➤ Your bike likes a little oil and grease now and then.

Chapter 15

Garage-Majal

> ### In This Chapter
>
> ➤ Instruments for the bike surgeon
>
> ➤ Up on the rack
>
> ➤ "Oooh, tool panel!"
>
> ➤ Becoming the envy of every bike mechanic
>
> ➤ Bicotic State University

Let's get one thing straight right off: This chapter isn't for everyone. But if you were one of those kids who managed to take apart and put back together every one of your toys, if you hyperventilate with delirium at the sight of a Snap-On tool truck, or if the thought of having an excuse to buy lots of shiny new tools excites you, you're in the right place. We're gonna talk tools and workbenches; we might even get around to power tools and solvent tanks. If you love to tinker, this chapter is for you.

Tools for the Truly Ambitious

With these tools and equipment, you'll rival a bike shop's service department:

> ➤ **Axle clamp.** This handy little device makes servicing wheel bearings a breeze. Place it over your wheel's axle and place the axle clamp in a vice; the wheel will be held horizontally, and the axle won't turn as you open the hub.
>
> ➤ **Ball peen hammer.** Sometimes you just have to get a little medieval on your bike. Use this tool carefully and sparingly.

➤ **Bench vice.** Use it with an axle clamp to hold a wheel in place while you service the hub, or use it to hold anything that needs to be filed or cut. Be sure to place some cardboard or a shop rag between the vice's jaws and the part you're working on.

➤ **Bottom bracket tools.** Unless your bike is old or an extremely low-budget model, chances are it has a cartridge bottom bracket. In this case, all you need is a Shimano bottom bracket tool—they're about $12. If your bottom bracket is the old style with adjustable cups, you need a hook spanner, a pin spanner, and a fixed-cup spanner.

➤ **Cassette lock-ring tool.** It's the only way to remove or tighten the lock-ring on a cassette cogset. You'll need a chain-whip, too.

➤ **Chain-whip.** You need one to remove a cogset cassette. Wrap the chain-whip around the biggest cog to keep the cassette from turning while you loosen the cassette's lock-ring. If you have an older bike with a *freewheel* and want to change cogs or disassemble the freewheel for servicing, you'll need two chain-whips: one to hold the biggest cog and the other to thread off the smallest cog. Chain-whips usually sell for about $10 to $15.

➤ **Cone wrenches.** If you're going to service hubs, you'll need a set of cone wrenches to loosen or tighten the bearing cones. The common sizes are 13 mm, 14 mm, and 15 mm. The jaws are extra thin to fit into the very narrow cone nut slots.

➤ **Crank-puller.** If you take an aluminum crankarm and bolt it tightly onto a tapered steel bottom spindle, that puppy is on there solid. Simply taking out the bolt isn't going to get the crankarm off. You need to spend about $15 to $20 for a crank-puller.

➤ **Derailleur tab alignment tool.** Bending a derailleur tab is easy: Crash a bike onto its right side or snag a derailleur on a branch, and you've done a fine tweaking job. To get it back in line, you need this handy tool. Take off the derailleur, thread in the tool, and use the rear wheel to check the alignment. Use the leverage arm of the tool to bend the tab back in line.

➤ **Freewheel removers.** If you have an older bike with a freewheel cog cluster, you'll need the right type of freewheel removal tool. Brands include Suntour, Shimano, and Regina, and types include two prong, four prong, and splined. Take your wheel to your local bike shop and have the people there get you the right tool.

Cyclebabble

A **freewheel** is an assembly containing a set of rear cogs and a ratchet mechanism. The entire assembly screws onto the threaded end of a rear hub. Unlike a cassette cogset and cassette rear hub that has the ratcheting mechanism built into the hub, the ratcheting mechanism on a freewheel is contained within the freewheel body.

Screw the crank-puller into the crank and then turn the handle. As the center portion presses against the spindle it will force the crankarm off.

You can try to straighten a derailleur tab by eye, but the only sure way of knowing it's straight is to use a derailleur tab alignment tool.

➤ **Headset wrenches.** Although most bikes now have threadless headsets, older mountain bikes and some new road bikes still have headsets that screw onto a threaded steerer tube. For those, you'll need two headset wrenches: one to hold the adjustable cup and the other to tighten the locknut. Most road bikes use one-inch headsets. Older mountain bikes with threaded headsets use one-inch or $1^1/_8$-inch. And some, such as early '90s Fishers, have $1^1/_4$-inch. If in doubt, take the bike to your local bike shop.

➤ **Headset press.** Anybody that has ever tried to install headset cups by tapping them in with a mallet will appreciate how easy it is to use a headset press. Simply set the cups in place, position the tool, and turn the handles. Presto, your cups are in straight and tight. This tool is fairly expensive (about $105), but it's worth it for hardware junkies. As an alternative, you can make a reasonably functional press using about 20 inches of threaded stock, a stack of washers, and a couple of nuts.

The Park headset press sells for about $105. If you're halfway handy, you can cobble up a do-it-yourself press for about $10. The do-it-yourself model isn't as quick or easy to use, and you need to be careful to not get the cups in crooked, but it can do the job.

Cyclebabble

Headset races aren't competitions for riders wearing personal stereos. A headset race is a metal ring with a machined-in groove for the headset bearings. In the case of headsets with needle bearings, the headset race is cone-shaped.

➤ **Headset race punch.** The lower *headset race* needs to be pushed all the way onto a steerer tube until it bottoms on the fork crown. If you leave the slightest gap, the race will settle in, and your headset will come loose when you ride the bike. Slam the headset race into place with a headset race punch. They're about $15.

➤ **Headset cup remover.** Before installing a new headset, you must first remove the old headset cups. Tapping them out with a punch can work, but it doesn't always work, and it's easy to slip and damage your frame. With a headset cup remover, you put it in place, and one well-placed hammer swing has the cup jangling around on the floor. Flip the bike over and do the other one, and you're done. A Park headset cup remover costs about $29.

➤ **Snap-ring pliers** (inside and outside). Snap-rings are those little round metal clips you find inside of forks, on some bottom brackets, and on some suspension pivots. They're open at one end and have two little holes to accept the pins on a set of snap-ring pliers. The ones on forks or bottom brackets sit inside of a recess; they're inside snap-rings and need to be squeezed down for installation or removal. The ones that fit on the outside of a pivot shaft are outside snap-rings and need to be spread apart for installation or removal. Each type needs a different tool. You can get snap-ring pliers at any good tool store or automotive store. They're about $15 to $25.

Steer Clear

If you try to install snap-rings with regular pliers or pry them off with a screwdriver, you're going to ruin them or send them flying to some dark corner of your garage, never to be seen again.

Miles of Experience

It was the night before a mountain bike race, and I wanted to give my bike an extra thorough pre-race preparation and decided to remove, clean, and lubricate the cartridge bearings in my bottom bracket. The bearings were held in with snap-rings, and not having snap-ring pliers, I pried the snap-rings out with a small screwdriver. When I removed the second snap-ring, it sprang into the air, bounced off my workbench, ricocheted off the garage wall, and landed somewhere in a stack of firewood. It was already well into the evening, so any thought of buying a new snap-ring was out of the question. I began unstacking pine and juniper wood in my search for the escaped snap-ring. I finally found it two hours later. The next day on my way home from the race I stopped by an auto parts store and bought two snap-ring pliers and a few spare snap-rings.

➤ **Star-nut setting tool.** If you don't get the headset star-nut in perfectly straight in the steerer tube, the nut is sure to work its way loose, making your headset also come loose. Escape that fate with a star-nut setting tool; they're about $15.

➤ **Stereo.** Some would define the word *tool* as "any implement or instrument that facilitates the performance of a mechanical chore." How long could you work in your garage without some music or talk radio to break up the monotony? I know the first thing I do after flipping on the light in my workshop is to turn on the radio. My little AM/FM cassette unit set me back a full $5 from a garage sale. I hooked up some old speakers to it, and it now does a fine job of filling my shop with classic rock and talk show hosts spouting conspiracy theories.

➤ **Torque wrench.** Read the owner's manuals on bikes or forks and you'll often find torque specifications on how many inch/pounds to tighten certain nuts and bolts. These specs are especially important on things such as fork crowns where you have steel screws going into aluminum; if you overtighten the screws, you'll strip the crown.

➤ **Wire brush.** Sometimes a good, stiff wire brush is needed to get all the grit and grunge off of a chain, cogs, or chainrings, especially if they've been caked over with clay-based dirt. That same clay can build up and harden between the knobs of your tires, too. A wire brush can get it out.

➤ **Wheel truing stand and dishing tool.** You can do minor wheel truing jobs with the wheel on the bike. But to get it perfect (or nearly so), you need a truing stand. Truing stands hold the wheel solidly and have built-in reference indicators to find the wobbles. Consumer models from Park or Wrench Force are priced between $50 and $100 and are fine for most garage mechanics. If you're a tool nut, a shop-quality truing stand runs about $200. You also need a dishing tool, a device that measures the position of the rim relative to the hub. If you tighten too many spokes on one side, you can pull the rim off-center. A dishing tool detects this problem. It's also used in building a wheel to make sure the wheel is built on center.

Cycology

Most of the bike tools on this list aren't the standard stuff that your local bike shop is likely to have in stock for sale. However, that shop would be happy to order them for you. You might be able to save money on these tools if you order them all at once, especially if you have a considerable list of needed tools. Try to do a little wheeling and dealing with the shop owner or manager.

Workstands

In the last chapter, I talked about consumer model workstands. But if you're a serious hardware aficionado, you've probably noticed the heavy-duty steel workstands in the service department of your local bike shop. With few exceptions, most shops use Park workstands, which have a massive steel base, a chrome pedestal, and a clamp arm.

The clamp arm of a Park workstand swivels a full 360 degrees, so the bike can be placed at any angle to make it easy to work on any portion of the bike. The clamp arm's jaws are adjustable to fit over any size of seat-post or frame tube, and the jaws are padded to keep the clamp from marring the bike. The classic workstand with two arms that allows two mechanics to use the same workstand is called the PRS double arm and sells for about $520. The single-arm model, the PRS 3, sells for about $300. Park also has a bench-top model with a bracket that bolts onto any level surface. It uses the same clamp arm as the upright workstands and sells for about $200.

Shop-quality workstands like these are long-term investments that are well worth the money for the serious mechanic. There are shops that have been using the same Park workstand for 20 years or more. These workstands are built like tanks and can take a beating. Their weight makes them extremely stable. That's important when you're torquing hard on a bike with a stuck bottom bracket cup, for instance. Try some medieval pounding and twisting with most consumer workstands, and the bike and workstand could end up on the floor—you might even break the workstand.

Park also has a line of accessories for its workstands. A rotating tool caddy that mounts on top of the workstand has compartments to hold your most commonly used tools. The tool tray that mounts halfway up the pedestal is a handy place to keep screws and parts and such as you work on the bike. The tray also has slots to hold small tools such as chain breakers and Allen wrenches.

Peek into nearly any bike shop's service department, and you'll find a Park workstand just like this one. If it's good enough for the pros, it's good enough for you.

The Tool Panel

When you work on a bike, few things are as frustrating as coming to a standstill because you can't find a needed tool. That's why most bike shops keep their tools organized by hanging them on a wall of pegboard, also known as a tool panel. Well-organized shops have their tool panels organized in a specific manner and have the outline of every tool painted onto the pegboard. That way a mechanic can tell at a glance not only that a tool is missing, but what tool it is. Shops that use the tool panel method of organization are usually pretty strict about having every tool back in its place. That way, no tools get lost or "walk away."

Is there any question of which tools go where? A well-organized tool panel can make bike chores a real pleasure.

Many shops base the arrangements of their tool panels on the system taught at the Barnett Bicycle Institute, a bicycle mechanic school located in Colorado Springs, Colorado (more on Barnett later). Included in the curriculum of Barnett's course titled "Managing the Service Department" is a complete list of all the tools needed to run a bike shop service department and a diagram of how to arrange those tools on a tool panel. Barnett's tool arrangement is based on a tool's frequency of use, grouping of tools used for a specific task, and space efficiency. This arrangement is also based on years of mechanics' experiences. I've had the pleasure of borrowing some workstand time in a shop arranged by a Barnett graduate, and what a joy it was. Every tool was right where you'd expect it to be.

Few home mechanics are going to invest in all the tools that a bike shop needs. Having several thousand dollars' worth of bike tools just doesn't seem practical for the do-it-yourselfer. However, a home mechanic can still benefit from having his or her tools arranged on a tool panel. For the home mechanic, that arrangement is something that will come from trial and error.

Miles of Experience

Before I put up my tool panel, I kept all my tools in a three-drawer toolbox. Although I was able to grab the box and take everything to a race or ride, finding the right tool was always a pain. It always seemed that any wrench or tool I needed was invariably buried under a dozen other tools.

Getting Organized

To lay out a tool panel, you'll need at least one 4 × 8 foot sheet of pegboard and enough pegboard hooks for the amount of tools you have. You can find pegboard hooks at your local hardware store. Near the hooks you'll also find pegboard racks designed to hold screwdrivers. These racks also work well to hold handled tools such as cable cutters and pliers.

Before going to the hardware store to get your hooks and such, make a list of your tools and think of how each one will be hung so that you can make a shopping list of hooks. Tools such as hammers and mallets are going to need two hooks each, one on each side of the handle. For a tool that will hang crooked with only one hook (such as a hacksaw), use two hooks to make it hang straight and to use your space more efficiently. Try not to hang more than one tool on a single hook. It may not sound like much trouble to have to move one tool to get to the one behind it, but it can be a real annoyance in the middle of a job—especially on a job that's not going well anyway.

I've found that the best way to hold loose Allen wrenches is on a magnetic bar. Just set the wrench on the bar, and it's put away. You might not find a magnetic bar at your average hardware store. Try a large tool shop or tool catalog or have your bike shop order one for you from United Bicycle Supply.

Staying in the Lines

If you plan on painting the pegboard with outlines of your tools, paint the pegboard white or gray before attaching it to the wall. When you have your pegboard painted and have all your hanging hardware, nail up the pegboard and start laying out your tools. Place all of your frequently used tools down low in easy reach and the seldom-used tools up high. If your first effort at arranging the tool panel seems awkward to use, experiment a bit and try something different. It may take a week or more to finally arrive at an arrangement you're happy with.

219

When you're sure you're done changing things, you're ready to paint your outlines. Actually, you might want to use marking pen instead of paint. It won't be as dark, and you might use up a pen or two before the job is done, but it will be a lot easier and quicker than paint. If you do use paint, don't try to paint around the tools. Instead, use a pencil to draw your outlines, then take down all the tools and paint over the pencil lines. It will come out neater, and you won't get paint on your shiny new tools.

Once you begin working from your tool panel, you'll wonder how you ever put up with digging for tools in a cluttered toolbox. There's something about having a tool panel that makes the whole work area stay neater and more organized. Any bit of chaos just seems ludicrous next to the precision of a tool panel.

If your garage has become the gathering place for all your friends to work on their bikes, you'll find that your desire to keep a tidy tool panel is contagious. When friends see how neatly arranged your tools are, they'd feel awfully guilty if they left any tools lying around on the workbench. When every tool has an obvious place, it's hard not to want to put each piece back where it belongs.

The Extraneous Stuff

You could probably do without the items on this list, but they make working on bikes much easier and a bit more fun. If your bike maintenance chores are easier to do, you'll have more time to do other chores around the house. Feel free to use this excuse when you ask your significant other for the checkbook before heading out to the hardware store.

➤ **Air compressor.** With a good, powerful air compressor (three horsepower or more), you can inflate a road tire up to 100 psi in just a few seconds. Getting a mountain bike tire up to the usual 40 to 45 psi is just as quick. Get an air nozzle, too, and a compressor becomes a handy way to remove grips. Just force the nozzle under the inside edge of the grip and give it a blast of air, and the grip will inflate slightly. You can then slide it right off the handlebar.

➤ **Bench grinder.** Use it to quickly remove the burrs from a freshly cut length of cable housing

Cycology

Having a nice tool panel isn't going to miraculously erase sloppy work habits. Make it standard practice to return each tool to its rightful place as soon as you're done using it. Once you begin setting tools on the workbench, thinking, "I'll probably use this again today," you'll defeat the whole idea of a tool panel. Remember that a tool panel's purpose is help you avoid digging around in a pile of tools.

Cycology

An air nozzle is also a quick way to "sweep" the floor and get dust and cobwebs out of the corners of your garage. To justify the $200 to $400 cost of a compressor to your significant other, claim that you really want it to run a paint sprayer and that this summer you're finally going to paint the house, fence, doghouse, or shed. "Yeah, that's it. It's not just for the bike work area. I promise!"

or screw. Most grinders can hold two grinding wheels, so you might want to remove one and put a wire wheel or polishing wheel in its place.

➤ **Electric drill.** It's not often needed, but when it is, nothing else can take its place.

➤ **Electrical tape.** Use this multipurpose item to secure excess wire on a cyclometer or to secure the ends of handlebar tape. Its uses in creative repair are nearly unlimited; it will even work in place of a rim strip in a pinch.

➤ **EZ-Outs.** Even the most careful mechanics will sometimes break off a screw. Removing the broken screw is easy if some stub is left protruding. But if there isn't anything to grab onto, you need an EZ-Out. EZ-Outs look kind of like drill bits with a reverse spiral. To use one, you first need to drill a hole into the broken screw using a drill bit that's a little smaller than the screw. Then you choose an EZ-Out that's the right size for the hole and screw it into the hole by turning the EZ-Out counterclockwise. Once it has a good bite on the screw, keep turning it, and the screw will back out. Most of the screws used on bikes are small, so a selection of small EZ-Outs will handle most broken screw-removal chores. Get 3 mm, 4 mm, and 5 mm EZ-Outs, and you'll probably have all you'll ever need.

➤ **Metric taps.** I've seen a lot of parts get thrown away because of stripped threads when all they needed was a thread tap. You can often find complete sets of taps with sizes from about 3 mm all the way to 13 mm or 15 mm for less than $60. They come with a handle, too. Pick up a bottle of tapping oil, and you're set.

➤ **Multidrawer bin.** Never, ever throw away any usable nut, screw, bolt, or washer. Separate them by type and keep them in the drawers of a multidrawer bin and guaranteed, sooner or later, one of those little bits of metal will save the day for you. These bins are also a handy way to keep other parts organized: loose ball bearings, computer batteries, headset spacers, and so on. When I first got mine with 24 drawers, I wondered what I was going to do with all of them—now I have two bins and will probably soon get a third one.

➤ **Parts washer.** Most bike shops have a commercial solvent tank for cleaning parts. Unless you're running a bike shop out of your garage or also do a lot of work on cars or motorcycles, having a regular Safety-Cleen tank at home probably isn't practical. Finish Line's EZ-Pro Parts Washer is a good alternative for the home mechanic. It's a plastic tank that uses a simple pump trigger to spray Finish Line Ecotech degreaser, a petroleum-based degreaser that, surprisingly, is biodegradable.

Cycology

Finish Line recommends its petroleum-based Ecotech Degreaser over its citrus degreaser because the citrus product can damage certain rubber and neoprene parts, such as the seals and O-rings in suspension forks.

The EZ-Pro Parts Washer holds a mixture of 32 ounces of Ecotech and a gallon and a half of water. When the solution gets too murky to use, pop on the tank's cap and take the whole thing to your nearest oil-recycling center. You don't want to just pour it in the flowerbeds; the solvent is biodegradable, but all the grime and such floating in it after a few months' use isn't. The EZ-Pro Parts Washer sells for $39.95 and comes with one 16-ounce bottle of Ecotech Degreaser. It will work with one bottle of Ecotech, but it works better with two. Another bottle will set you back $19.95. For more information, check out Finish Line's Web site at www.finishlineusa.com.

➤ **Shop vacuum.** Keeping a neat and clean work area makes every job go easier and smoother. With a shop vacuum, you quickly clean up the dirt, grit, and grime accumulation before it takes over. Get a wet/dry vacuum, and you can even use it to clean up spilled liquids.

The Necessities of Life

This list is of those items, supplies, and sundry parts that anyone who rides a lot and/ or works on bikes frequently is definitely going to need. If you fit this description, you may as well have these things around. You're gonna need them all sooner or later, so you may as well save yourself a few trips to the bike shop.

Miles of Experience

I don't know if I hold the world record for trips to the bike shop in a single day, but I know that I'm at least a contender. On one single afternoon, I went to the bike shop for a tire and inner tubes, only to return a half hour later after I discovered that I also needed a rimstrip. I was back soon after I broke a spoke while truing a wheel. Had I thought to check the bike's shifting earlier I could have saved a fourth trip by picking up a cable and housing. Of course, I had to go back anyway when I realized that the ferrules from the old cable housing were too warped to reuse. Nowadays, I keep a good supply of all this stuff and more.

➤ **Brake cables and shifter cables.** I like to keep a couple of each on hand. If you have a tandem, be sure to get the extra long cables you'll need for the rear brake and rear derailleur.

➤ **Brake cable housing and shifter cable housing.** It takes about five to six feet of each to completely recable a bike. I like to keep at least that much around.

➤ **Cable end-caps.** If you leave a cable without an end-cap, the cable will unravel, ruining the cable and leaving needle sharp strands that will poke you—and they hurt. End-caps come in a bottle of 500. That should last a while.

➤ **Cable-housing ferrules.** Any time you replace housing, you need to install fresh ferrules. Sometimes they get bent, too, which can make your shifter or brake cable bind. They come in a bottle of 250, so you shouldn't run out of these too soon.

➤ **Chains.** Murphy's Law states that anyone who rides a lot will one night discover that his or her bike's chain has a nasty kink in it. This discovery will invariably occur long after the local bike shop has closed.

➤ **Fork oil.** Find out what weight oil your fork uses and keep a bottle handy. Even the best-maintained fork loses a bit of oil with use, and it's nice to be able add a little as needed. You'll definitely need some fresh oil when you do a major fork overhaul. If you like to fiddle with things, you might also get a bottle of the higher-weight oil and/or the next lower weight. You just might prefer the performance with a higher or lower oil viscosity. See your owner's manual for oil weight, capacities, and tuning instructions.

➤ **Inner tubes.** They're fairly cheap, and having them on hand can save you a trip to the bike shop. Buy them by the dozen, and you might even be able to save a dollar or more each.

➤ **Rim strips.** Have a couple of those rubber strips that go around rims to protect the inner tubes from the spoke nipples. They crack and rot with time, and when one breaks, you're sure to get a flat.

➤ **Sandpaper and steel wool.** Use them to renew brake pads by roughing up the surfaces after they've been glazed over from use. Use them to clean brake pad residue off your rims. They're also good for removing surface rust from parts or to smooth out paint chips on your frame before retouching it.

➤ **Shop apron.** After you have grease and grime ruin a few T-shirts or jeans, you'll appreciate the value of a shop apron. Slip one on and save your clothes. Most have a front pocket or two that are handy places to set a tool or two when you need a free hand. You can find shop aprons at bike shops. The bike shop models are usually silk-screened with some brand of bike or bike accessory—other than that, they're the same as the cotton variety found at hardware stores.

➤ **Shop rags.** Get a bag of the classic red mechanic's rags or just use some of your old T-shirts.

➤ **Tires.** Keeping a tire or two around can save the day if you discover a torn bead or sidewall the night before a ride or event (another occurrence that always seems to happen after the local bike shop has closed).

223

A Master's in Bike Mechanics

Many bike shop mechanics mastered their skills through trial and error, with a few lessons from the more senior mechanics thrown in for good measure. The story usually goes something like this: As a 13- or 14-year-old kid, the future mechanic began hanging around the bike shop. Figuring that if the kid was going to be around he might as well be useful, the shop owner or service manager began having the kid sweep the floors and empty the trash in exchange for first dibs on the worn-out tires and punctured inner tubes. Eventually the kid moved up to washing bikes. If the kid showed any inkling of mechanical aptitude, eventually he or she was allowed to do flat repairs or unbox new bikes for the mechanics to assemble.

Of course, that soon led to doing some of the assembly and then finally doing an entire assembly. After the kid put in a couple of summers and after-school hours in this manner, the other shop employees gradually began referring to the kid as "one of the mechanics," probably shortly after the service manager gave the kid a hand-me-down shop apron. It took another year or two before the kid was allowed to work on the expensive stuff. By then, the transfer of skills by osmosis was nearly complete and the obscure craft of bicycle wrenching had once again been passed onto another practitioner.

It's a lovely story, but there's a better way to learn to work on bikes: the Barnett Bicycle Institute and the United Bicycle Institute. Both offer efficient means of training that are far more appealing to someone who isn't a pimply faced teen and isn't interested in serving an apprenticeship while working for minimum wage and bike parts. Many of the best mechanics in the country received their training from United or Barnett, including some of the mechanics working for pro race teams.

Both schools offer a range of classes. Barnett's basic overhaul and maintenance one-day course is $100. For those who want to learn it all, Barnett's 12-day course on bicycle repair and overhaul offers a full 60 hours of instruction. Included in this course is instruction on every bicycle component, including suspension forks. Graduate from this course, and you'll be able to troubleshoot and repair practically any bike malady. Barnett also has courses on bicycle assembly, wheel building, and suspension theory and service. To find out more about Barnett Bicycle Institute, call 719-632-5173 or check its Web page at www.bbinstitute.com.

United Bicycle Institute of Ashland, Oregon, has a one-week course for $495 that covers such topics as fitting a bike; overhauling bottom brackets, headsets, and hubs; wheel truing; and several other skills. The two-week course on professional repair and shop operation costs

Cycology

Working on bikes isn't rocket science. However, many of the skills used to work on bikes are specific to only bikes. Not much of what you know about working on cars or even motorcycles will apply to bikes. You can learn by trial and error—and likely break a few parts and have a few malfunctions as you learn—or you can benefit from the experience of professionals and attend a school like Barnett or United.

$995 and includes a component-by-component study of bicycle repair with instruction on every bike part. Although this course is designed for people seeking a career in bicycle mechanics, United reports that a number of their students are passionate cyclists who just want comprehensive instruction on working on bikes. United also has a full selection of other courses, including wheel building and suspension. To contact United Bicycle Institute, call 541-488-1122 or see their Web page at www.bikeschool.com.

The Least You Need to Know

➤ The more specialty bike tools you have, the more jobs you'll be able to do.

➤ Organizing your tools takes only a few square feet of pegboard and a few dozen pegboard hooks.

➤ Keep a supply of parts that you know you're eventually going to need, and those night-before-the-ride wrenching sessions will go much smoother.

➤ Mechanics who go to a bicycle mechanics school don't have to spend years learning their skills.

Chapter 16

No Air in There

In This Chapter

➤ Flats are a fact of life

➤ The necessary implements for flat repair

➤ How to turn a flat tire into a few minutes of inconvenience, instead of a long walk home

➤ Foiling the flat-tire gremlins

Picture yourself on a bright Saturday morning out for a well-deserved ride. Suddenly, you hear that unmistakable "pfffffft." It's your turn for the flat-tire gremlins to strike. It's not personal; they get us all eventually. How the rest of your Saturday morning goes depends on you and your preparation. Will you be on your way again in just a few minutes? Or are you in for an unplanned hike? In this chapter, I'll show you how to fix a flat and be on your merry way in no time.

On the Road to Nowhere, but Not for Long

Fixing a flat is simple. All you need is a new tube or a patch kit, tire levers, a frame pump, and some easily mastered skills. Don't be intimidated by the process. Anyone can learn it in a few minutes. I like to see new riders learn flat repair right from the beginning. I've helped a lot of friends and family get into this sport, and I try to make it a point to take them through the flat-fixing drill before letting them take a solo ride.

Serious racers practice their flat-fixing skills. Some pros can do the whole process in two or three minutes. For them, getting a flat doesn't necessarily end their race. At a national championship mountain bike race at Mammoth one year, champion Ned Overend got a flat in the first lap, fixed it, and went on to win!

Miles of Experience

Unless you like to ride through broken glass or buckthorns, the chance of getting a flat on any given ride is solely dependent on luck. I've gone weeks and months without a flat and have had five in a day. When it's your turn to get a flat or six, don't fret or get upset. Just put in a fresh tube and move on, secure in the knowledge that you've made your sacrifice to the flat-tire gremlins and maybe, just maybe, they'll leave you alone for awhile.

Flat Repair Kit

The items that every rider should carry to fix a flat can easily fit into a seat-bag or fanny pack:

1. **Two tubes.** Go to your local bike shop for at least two tubes in the right size for your bike. Be sure to get the right valve. The skinny type (some call them French valves) are presta valves. The thicker automotive valves are shrader valves.

2. **Tire levers.** While experienced hands can usually fix flats with only two or even one lever, I recommend carrying a full set of three. Tire levers sometimes break, especially with tight-fitting tires.

3. **Frame pump.** A frame pump is a small air pump designed to be carried on a bike. It's worth its weight (usually about a half-pound) in gold. They're easy to carry, and they're reliable. Realize that because a frame pump is designed only for trailside/roadside repair, it takes a hundred or more strokes to get a tire up to full inflation, so you'll also want a floor pump for home use.

4. **Patch kit.** Patches are time-consuming, and it's not always possible to find all the holes at the trailside/roadside. I recommend putting in a new tube and taking the punctured one home to be patched later. But you still want to carry patches as a backup system for those inevitable rides with multiple flats.

Steer Clear

Many times I've had novice riders ask about those aerosol cans that are supposed to fix a flat and inflate the tire at the same time. The truth is they work ... sometimes. Other times they succeed only in filling your tube with goop and emptying themselves of their aerosol and your wallet of $6.99. Learning to fix a flat the conventional way is much more reliable and, in the end, cheaper.

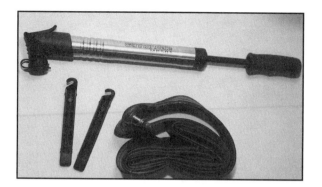

With just these few items, you can fix a flat tire in just a few minutes.

5. **Presta valve adapter.** A valve adapter weighs practically nothing, costs about a buck, and enables you to inflate presta tubes with a standard pump or even a gas station airhose.

6. **CO_2 cartridge inflator** (optional). Cartridge inflators are the quickest way to reinflate a tire. Two- or three-minute flat repairs wouldn't be possible without them, so I definitely recommend carrying them in races. But they're also very expensive and are sometimes tricky to use. Just about all riders have wasted cartridges by not quite having the fitting on the valve straight and sending four bucks' worth of CO_2 blowing into the atmosphere instead of into the tire.

Step-by-Step Flat Repair

Fixing a flat is as easy as following the steps in this section. I strongly recommend that you practice them at home before venturing out for your first long ride. None of the steps are difficult, but some may take a couple of tries to get the knack. If you master flat-fixing at home, you won't end up sitting by the side of the road frustrated over being stymied by a flat tire.

Release the Brake

To get the wheel past the brake pads, you must release the brake to its open position. All brakes are not released in the same manner, however:

Steer Clear

When using a CO_2 cartridge, avoid touching the cartridge's bare metal. When the compressed gas rushes out, the temperature of the outside of the cartridge quickly drops well below freezing. Touch it, and your skin will stick to it and also freeze. I once saw a rider stick a finger to a cartridge, and when he felt the sting of frozen skin, he flung the cartridge away, taking a few layers of skin with it.

Cycology

Patch glue can quickly dry out once its tube has been opened. Be sure to seal the cap tightly and also check your glue once in a while. Where would you rather find out that your glue has dried up: in your garage or 19 miles out?

To release the cable on V-Brakes, slip the end of the aluminum cable tube out of the clip.

➤ **V-Brakes.** With Shimano V-Brakes (or other such long-leverage cantilevers), use a finger and thumb to grasp the horizontal metal clip extending from the top of the left brake arm. While grasping the aluminum cable tube with the other hand, pull the tube to the left and the clip to the right. When the end of the tube clears the slot in the clip, raise the tube upward.

➤ **Cantilever brakes.** For older-style cantilever brakes, grasp the cable an inch or so up from where it slips into the notch on the left brake arm. Pivot the left brake arm up until the cable end clears the slot on the brake arm.

➤ **Road brakes.** The brakes on road bikes are simple. Look for a small lever on the left side of the brake caliper. Flip it up. You're done. Some Shimano brakes from the late '80s and early '90s have a button up on the brake lever, as do some current Campagnolo levers. Press it and the brakes pop open.

Steer Clear

Never use a screwdriver as a tire lever unless you like to ruin tires and inner tubes. The sharp edges of a screwdriver can rip into the bead of a tire, especially a tight-fitting tire. Avoid puncturing yet another tube: Get some tire levers and save your screwdriver for loosening and tightening screws.

Opening the brake caliper on a road bike is simple; just flip the lever.

Release the quick-release lever, pivot the rear derailleur back, and the rear wheel will practically fall out.

Remove the Wheel

For the rear wheel, first shift the chain onto the smallest cog. Open the quick-release lever. For bikes with enclosed dropouts or forks with safety tabs, you'll then need to loosen the quick-release lever by holding the nut and turning the opened lever

231

counterclockwise a few turns. Grasp the rear derailleur and pivot it back. Lift the rear of the bike by the rear derailleur to raise it a few inches. Use the opposite hand to give a slight tap on top of the rear tire. That should make it drop out of the frame. If not, use a little more force and a slight side-to-side motion. Once the wheel is off the bike, lay the wheel on its side and depress the valve stem to remove the last of the air.

To get to the punctured inner tube, you'll need to use tire levers to open the tire.

Cycology

Some tires have casings made of Kevlar, the same miracle fabric used to make bulletproof vests. Kevlar tires are strong, light, and more resistant to flats and sidewall damage. However, the same strength that makes them so tough also makes it hard to open them to fix a flat. Some racers make them easier to open by mounting the tire and inflating it and then deflating it and opening the sidewall. Repeat this five or six times, and the tire will become much easier to open.

Open the Tire and Remove the Tube

Insert the end of a tire lever between the tire bead and the rim. Be sure to place the tire lever with the curved end pointed down so that it hooks the edge of the tire bead. Pry the lever over and attach the hook end of the lever on a spoke. Insert a second lever one or two spokes over from the first lever. Pry it over and then try to slide it further along the rim. If the lever doesn't move easily, hook it on a spoke and use a third lever.

Reach into the tire and grasp the valve stem (on presta valve tubes, remove the stem nut). Work the valve out of the hole in the rim. Pull the tube out of the tire and inspect the tube for obvious punctures or damage.

Check the Inside of the Tire

Usually, whatever punctured the tube didn't hang around. Still, look inside of the tire casing for protruding thorns, glass, staples, and so on. If none are obvious, carefully run a finger inside the tire. Do it slowly to avoid scratching your fingers on tire shrapnel. Remove whatever caused the puncture.

Install the New Tube and Close the Tire

Slightly inflate the tube to give it some shape. A few pumps from a frame pump is usually sufficient. Pull the tire bead open at the valve hole; work the valve stem into the hole. Place a hand in the tire with your fingertips positioned over the side of the tube. Slide your hand along the rim and tire, tucking the tube down into the rim. Work your way around the wheel until the entire tube is tucked in.

Steer Clear

Never leave a dead tube on the trail. It gives the rest of us a bad rep. In fact, pick up any that you see.

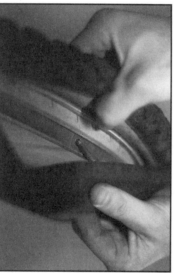

Put a few pumps of air in the new tube to give it some shape, slip the valve stem into the rim's valve hole, and tuck the tube inside the tire.

Try to close as much of the tire as you can by hand to avoid pinching the inner tube. You may need to use a tire lever for the last few inches.

Starting at the valve stem, push the tire bead into the rim using your thumbs. Work a few inches at a time, alternating sides so that the last few inches of open bead end up opposite the valve stem. Some tires are possible to close completely by hand, but on tight-fitting ones, you'll need to use a tire lever for the last few inches. When using a lever, be careful to not pinch the tube. Inspect the bead for pinched inner tube or unseated areas. Check the bead at the valve stem. If the bead isn't quite seated, press the valve stem into the rim while squeezing the bead at the stem.

Inflate the Tire

Pump up the tire. If you're using a frame pump, stop as the tire begins to get hard to check the bead. A tire that's slightly unseated at low pressure can blast off of the rim once it's up to full pressure. The tube usually pops when that happens. That's why for everyday use, I recommend manual pumps over CO_2 cartridge inflators. With cartridges, full pressurization of the tube is almost instantaneous, making correction of the bead impossible. Cartridges are great for racing where seconds count, but pumps are more reliable and quite a bit cheaper.

To put the wheel back where you found it, position the axle under the dropout, pivot the derailleur back, set the chain on the smallest cog, and slip the axle into the dropouts.

Cyclebabble

Booting a tire refers to placing a reinforcement inside the tire at the hole.

Reinstall the Wheel

Raise the bike to vertical, holding it up from the rear. Center the wheel between the brake arms and see that the chain is lined up above the smallest rear sprocket. While pivoting the derailleur back, lower the bike down so that the chain lowers onto the smallest sprocket. Set the bike down completely onto the axle. Grasp the quick-release skewer from both sides and guide the axle completely into the frame dropouts. Close the quick-release skewer. Spin the wheel to be certain that it's in the frame straight. Reconnect the brake cable.

Finish Your Ride

Gather up your tools. Make sure your get your valve caps and so on and that your seat-bag or pack is closed and secure. Be extra certain to grab your dead tube. Leaving a dead tube at the side of the road is littering. Leaving a dead tube at the side of the trail further sullies our reputations with those who don't want us on "their" trails, giving them more ammunition to be used against us bikers. When you're all gathered up, pedal off into the sunset, smiling smugly at your own foresight and preparation.

Miles of Experience

I don't remember when I last bought a tire lever. Every year I manage to find a few on the trail. No doubt riders who rode off in a hurry after fixing a flat left them behind. I also have a nice collection of tools and a couple of Quickfills, all found as gifts from the trail.

The Hole in the Wall

There are many ways to put a cut or hole in a tire sidewall or casing. Running over glass, hitting a rock or root, and even the short time spent riding while the tire goes flat after a puncture can all inflict sidewall or casing damage. When a tire has such damage, the tube will balloon out of the hole and immediately pop. Simply putting in a fresh tube won't solve the problem. You need to *boot*, or fix the hole. Otherwise, the new tube will balloon out the hole and suffer the same fate as the first tube. A mylar PowerBar wrapper makes an excellent boot. Duct tape works well, too, as does a dollar bill. I once found myself without any of the above, yet I was able to get myself rolling again with a piece of vinyl I found among the roadside debris.

To boot a tire, place your dollar, wrapper, or whatever inside the tire. Center it over the hole, setting it so that it sticks out on both sides of the tire. If you don't let it protrude out both sides, it may push out when the tire is inflated. Insert the tube and reinstall the tire onto the rim. When the tire is inflated, you can trim away excess material so that it won't slap against the frame. Once

Steer Clear

It's understandable to be in a hurry to fix a flat during a race or when the rest of the group is riding away. But don't get into so much of a hurry that you forget to reconnect your mountain bike's brake cable. Riders have crashed and even been injured after hastily riding away with a brake still disconnected.

underway, you'll probably feel that there's a low spot in the tire at the boot because the tire can't expand to its full shape at the boot. This is normal.

By using a dollar bill or other suitable material to boot a torn sidewall, a smart rider can ride home instead of hoofing it.

Flat Prevention

Products designed to prevent flats are practically an entire industry. There are tubes of goop that get squeezed inside of an inner tube so that the goop can seep into and seal small holes. There are strips of urethane plastic designed to be placed between the tire and tube to serve as a puncture barrier. There are tires with a layer of Kevlar built into the tread. And there are super-thick "thorn-proof" tubes.

The goop products, of which there are several, work fairly well on small holes. On a mountain bike trip in the Arizona desert, I tried the leading goop called Slime, an appropriately named lime-green, mucous-like product. While other riders suffered several cactus needle-induced flats, I rode all week without a single puncture. It wasn't until later when I removed my Slime-filled tubes that I saw that both tubes had several pin-sized green dots of hardened Slime. Cactus needles had poked in, and Slime had done its job by oozing into and sealing the holes. The drawback to goops is that they add weight (eight ounces per wheel), and in the event of a large puncture, $5 worth of goop blasts out of the tire, usually onto your bike and clothes.

Of the urethane strips, Mr. Tuffy is the best known. These strips provide good protection against most common road debris, but they are still no match for truly nasty stuff like nails, large tacks, or big hunks of glass. Their drawbacks are their weight (still less than

Steer Clear

Although booting a tire can get you home, it's only a temporary fix. Don't ride on a booted tire any longer than necessary. If the boot fails, the tube will instantly blow out. If that happens at high speed, you're going down, especially if it happens to the front tire.

goop products, and they won't make a mess) and that they tend to make a tire ride somewhat harsh, especially high-pressure road tires that can already rattle your fillings.

Some riders swear by "thorn-proof" tubes. Personally, I don't believe they're very effective. Sure, they're at least twice as thick as a standard tube, but the way I see it, 9 out of 10 of the thorns, bits of glass, and so on that would puncture a standard tube are big enough to also pop a thorn-proof tube. Considering that they cost twice as much and weigh twice as much, I don't see their value.

I would say that the only sure-fire way to never get a flat is to always keep your bike indoors and never ride it, but I once had a brand-new, unridden tire blow out in the middle of the night, seemingly all by itself. No, the only way to avoid flats is to not have a bike at all.

Actually, there are ways of never ever getting a flat. A few companies make airless tires that use foam rubber material to approximate the feel of an inflated tire. One company makes foam inserts to use in place of inner tubes with standard tires. But none of these products ride very well. They're very heavy, squirm around when cornering, and are very difficult to install. I suppose they would be acceptable for very slow riding by riders who don't care about the poor ride or vague cornering. Now that you know how to fix a flat, you don't need them anyway.

The Least You Need to Know

➤ You, me, and the cyclist down the street will all get flats.

➤ Never, ever, I mean never, leave a dead inner tube at the side of the road or trail.

➤ A torn tire sidewall doesn't necessarily mean you're walking home. You can temporarily fix it for only a buck.

➤ Thorn-proof tubes aren't.

Chapter 17

The Chain Gang

In This Chapter

➤ Long live the chain: how this little gadget keeps your whole bike moving

➤ How to keep your chain clean and lubricated

➤ When and how to replace a chain

➤ How Shimano chains differ from others and how to replace them

---

It's quite a job we ask of our chains. That a small, narrow-gauge chain is able to sustain all the power that propels a bike down the road or trail is quite remarkable. Factor in the side-to-side motion that chains go through when gears are shifted and the grunge and muck they're subjected to, and it's a wonder they last as long as they do. Over the years, engineers have attempted to come up with a better means of transferring power from the pedals to the rear wheel. They've built bikes with driveshafts like a car, and they've tried rubber belts, nylon belts, and cable drive. Yet none of these has proven to be as efficient or reliable as a chain. In this chapter, I give the chain its due. You will learn how to take care of your chain and how to fix it or replace it when the time comes.

Chain Reaction

The parts of a bicycle chain are quite simple. They consist of a series of *inner plates*, a *chain pin*, and *outer plates*. The chain pin is a rivet that has been pressed into both outer plates. The pin glides smoothly through the inner plates and the *roller*.

All chains have a slight amount of side-to-side play. This lateral movement is necessary so that the chain can flex sideways to shift gears. After miles and miles of use, the chain pins wear, causing the chain to "stretch." Chain stretch isn't from the plates getting longer; it's the accumulation of the slight amount of play in each of the 110 to 120 chain pins. A stretched chain also has more side play, which will adversely affect shifting.

The parts of a chain.

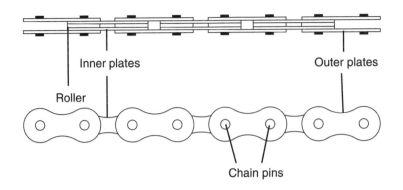

Roller · Inner plates · Outer plates · Chain pins

Rub-a-Dub-Dub: Removing Chain Grit and Grime

The average bike chain is continuously subjected to an environment of abrasive grit and old greasy lubricant, along with some rust-causing moisture thrown in for good measure. The life span of a chain can be greatly increased by minimizing that destructive grit and by keeping the chain well-lubricated.

1. Chain cleaning: A clean chain is a happy chain. Chains shift better and last longer when they're not carrying a bunch of abrasive grit, which is exactly what happens when new *lube* is added on top of grungy old lube. How often you should clean your chain depends on your riding conditions. A road rider who rides on nice dry, nondusty roads can go a long time without cleaning a chain.

   On the other hand, if you're a mountain bike rider who rides in muddy or dusty conditions, you might find it necessary to clean your chain after every ride. A general rule of thumb is if you don't want to touch your chain with your thumb lest you get it all greasy and grimy, it's probably time to treat that chain to a bath. Here's how to clean a chain and its associated parts:

   ➤ Get a scrub brush and a bucket and mix water and some dish soap or bio-degreaser such as Finish Line, Pedro's, or Simple Green. Shift the chain to the large chainring, hold the sudsy brush next to the chain on the chainring, and pedal backward. Next, hold the brush along the bottom of the chain and pedal backward.

   ➤ If grunge remains, use a small screwdriver to pick out stubborn grime from the nooks and crannies.

Cyclebabble

The **outer plates** are the series of hourglass-shaped metal pieces you see on the outer side of the chain. The **inner plates** are the series of hourglass-shaped metal plates set inboard of the outer plates. The **rollers** are the little cylindrical parts that fit in between the sprocket teeth. On a fresh, clean, and lubricated chain, the rollers are free to revolve against the teeth as the chain passes over the sprockets.

➤ Take one of your old toothbrushes (or your roommate's new one), dip it in the sudsy water, hold it against the inner side of the chain (the side that touches the sprocket teeth) just above the lower pulley of the rear derailleur, and pedal backward.

2. Running a clean, freshly scrubbed chain over dirty teeth doesn't make much sense. Grab that bucket, brush, and toothbrush again and use them on the sprockets. Wipe the chainrings and use the toothbrush to clean between the teeth.

   Remove the rear wheel and use a rag to floss the cogs. Use that small screwdriver again to gently remove any of the stubborn bits of grit.

3. Your chain is made of steel. Your cogs and possibly your chainrings are steel as well. If you leave them wet, they'll rust. Take a dry rag and wipe off any remaining moisture.

Cyclebabble

In bicycle jargon, **lube** is short for **lubricant**, which is any oil, grease, or other slippery stuff used to reduce friction on moving components, such as **chain lube**. Lube is also short for the verb to **lubricate**, as in applying oil to a component such as a chain or control cable.

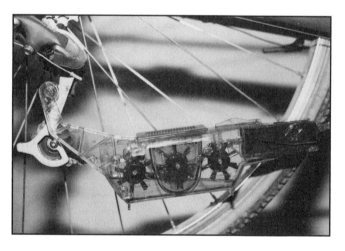

A chain-cleaning machine such as this one from Finish Line can make chain-cleaning chores quicker and easier.

Chain Lubrication

Only add lube to a clean chain. If you don't have time for a complete scrubbing, at least wipe the chain down before applying more lube. A quick spray on the inner side (the side that touches the sprockets) of the chain while pedaling backward is fine if you're in a hurry, but if you take your time when lubing a chain, you'll use less lube and your chain will attract less dirt.

I like to lube a chain the night before a ride to give it a chance to seep into the rollers and between the plates. Point your lube bottle at the inner side of the chain and slowly pedal backward so that each roller gets a small drop. Let it stand overnight and then wipe off any excess from the outer plates.

All types of chain lube go on wet. Some stay wet; others dry and leave a lubricating, waxy residue. A dry lube stays clean and doesn't attract dirt, dust, and debris as wet lubes can. However, dry lubes have a tendency to flake off with use and don't stay on the chain as long as wet lubes. That's why I usually use dry lubes only on my road bikes or on a mountain bike for short rides that will be dry and relatively dust-free.

For riding in wet, muddy conditions, you want a lube that will stay on as long as possible. It's hard to beat a wet lube for longevity. Some are specially formulated for inclement conditions. These foul-weather chain lubricants have a thicker viscosity to help them stick to the chain.

> ### Cycology
>
> There are several brands of chain-cleaning machines. Most are similar in design and function. The chain passes through the machine in a reservoir of citrus-based solvent. The user pedals the bike backward, driving the chain through the solvent and driving the machine's rotating brushes. They do a great job, are fast and easy to use, and run about $20 to $40.

When to Replace a Chain

I've seen bike chains last well over 5,000 miles, although I recommend changing them about every 1,000 miles because a worn chain will also wear out the sprockets and cogs. Most chains cost between $10 and $30, which is relatively cheap compared to the $75 to $100 it costs to replace front chainrings and the $30 to $70 cost of a fresh set of rear cogs.

> ### Steer Clear
>
> If you use a thick lube in dusty conditions, the lube and dust particles will soon mix together to form a thick, abrasive paste. Stick to dry lubes or light-viscosity wet lubes for dusty trails.

A symptom of a worn-out chain is when no amount of derailleur adjustment can get the chain to shift smoothly. Chains stretch and develop excess side play from use. When the derailleur tries to guide a sloppy chain sideways to shift, it only succeeds in taking up all the chain's side play. However, this condition could also be a symptom of a worn derailleur or shifter. The only sure way to tell is to check the chain; it's usually the first to go.

To accurately check a chain for wear all you need is a ruler. Hold the ruler along the side of the chain and line up the zero mark to the edge of one of the chain link rivets. On a fresh chain, the 12-inch mark will also line up at the edge of another link rivet. If the 12-inch mark is more than a millimeter or two beyond the edge of the other rivet, the chain is stretched and is ready for the scrap heap.

If you're the type who likes to have every tool imaginable, pick up a chain gauge. A chain gauge is a handy little workbench item consisting of small, rectangular metal plates with a pair of metal teeth on each edge spaced about four inches apart. To check a chain's condition, hold the tool in line with the chain and insert the teeth between two sets of chain outer plates. The tool's teeth should fit snug. If there's any gap between the teeth and the chain's rollers, the chain is stretched and worn and should be replaced. Rohloff and Park both make chain gauges. If your local bike shop doesn't have one in stock, it'll be happy to order one for you. Chain gauges are only about $20.

Aside from the wear of sheer miles, chains also need replacing if they've been badly twisted or damaged. Sometimes it's possible to replace only the damaged links if the chain is fairly new. But if the chain has been in use very long, the new links might not get along with the cogs that have already worn in to the old chain.

Removing a Chain

The chains used on road bikes and mountain bikes don't have a "master link" like the single-speed bike you rode as a kid. On a multispeed bike, the chain needs to be able to flex side to side to shift gears. That flex would make a master link pop off. To remove or install a chain on your road bike or mountain bike, you need a special chain tool designed to press in or out one of the chain link pins.

➤ **Step 1.** Many bike mechanics find that it's easier to remove a chain if it is first taken off the front chainring. That way you won't be fighting the rear derailleur as it tries to pull the chain back.

➤ **Step 2.** Set the chain into the outside notch of the chain tool. The inner notch of the tool isn't for chain removal; it's for adjusting tight links.

243

➤ **Step 3.** Turn the tool's handle to drive the chain pin out. Ideally, you want to push the pin out just far enough so that a small nub of the pin protrudes inboard of the outer plate. This little nub of pin will ease reassembly, because the nub will snap into the roller hole of the inner plates, instantly aligning the plates.

➤ **Step 4.** Flex the chain slightly to separate it.

➤ **Step 5.** Pull the chain out of the rear derailleur, being certain to pull it by the end with the protruding link because this link won't fit through the derailleur.

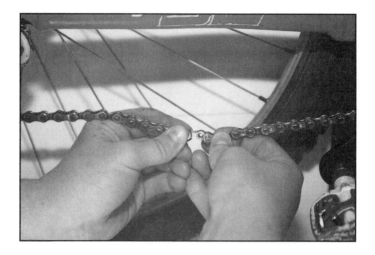

Determining Chain Length

If you're reinstalling the same chain, skip to the following "Installing a Chain" section, but if you're installing a new chain, you will first need to determine the proper length of chain for your bike. An easy way is to line up your new chain next to the old chain.

The method I use is to make the chain just long enough so that it can be shifted to the biggest rear cog and the biggest front chainring. Although this gear combination shouldn't be used (the severe chain angle is hard on the chain and sprockets), you want to be sure that the chain is long enough in case you do inadvertently shift to this combination. A shift to this combination with a chain that's too short can damage a derailleur or the *derailleur hanger*. The following steps should get you through this process without a damaged derailleur or derailleur hanger:

➤ **Step 1.** Use the shifters to position the derailleurs over the biggest rear cog and biggest front chainring.

➤ **Step 2.** On a new chain, one end will have a link pin set into one outer plate, already positioned to be pressed in with a chain tool. Set this end over the big chainring so the end of the chain is wrapped over the top of the chainring.

Cycology

Some tools (such as Park Tool's CT-3 or CT-5) are designed so that if you turn the handle until it stops, the pin will be driven out enough to remove the chain, but not completely out. Read the directions on your particular tool to see whether it has this feature. If it doesn't, take care to watch the pin position. If the pin is driven completely out, it's nearly impossible to put it back, and you'll have to shorten the chain or replace the ruined link.

➤ **Step 3.** Hold the chain in place on the chainring with your right hand while guiding the other end of the chain through the front derailleur and rear derailleur with your left hand (see "Installing a Chain" for photographs on guiding the chain through the rear derailleur).

Cyclebabble

The **derailleur hanger** is the portion of the frame that the rear derailleur attaches to. It's on the right side of the frame just behind the notch for the rear axle. On some bikes, the derailleur hanger is replaceable so that a bent or broken hanger doesn't mean an expensive repair job—simply bolt on a new one.

➤ **Step 4.** Grasp the end of the chain coming out of the rear derailleur with your left hand and pull it toward the chainring. Drag the chain toward the other end that's on the chainring. As you do this, the lower jockey-pulley of the rear derailleur will pivot forward. Pull the chain taut until the derailleur has pivoted as far as it can.

Determine which pin from a set of inner plates will line up with the outer plates of the other end of the chain. You need to keep track of that pin, so mark it with a crayon or hold that pin tightly with your left hand while you insert it into the chain tool to remove the extra links.

➤ **Step 5.** Turn the handle of the chain tool clockwise to press out the pin.

➤ **Step 6.** Flex the chain to slightly to separate it.

Installing a Chain

➤ **Step 1.** With the chain already cut to length, position the chain so that the protruding pin is toward you. Don't set it on the front chainring, you'll do that after the chain's ends have been connected. For now, you want the slack.

➤ **Step 2.** Guide the chain through the front derailleur.

➤ **Step 3.** Guide the chain through the rear derailleur by first setting the end under the forward jockey-pulley and under the rearward jockey-pulley.

➤ **Step 4.** Bring the two ends of the chain together and slip the inner plate end into the outer plate end.

➤ **Step 5.** Set the chain into the chain tool with the protruding pin lined up with the tool's pin-driver.

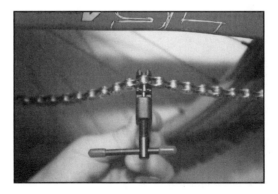

➤ **Step 6.** To press in the chain pin, turn the handle of the chain tool clockwise until it stops. Then turn the handle a few turns counterclockwise to release the chain from the tool.

➤ **Step 7.** Inspect the link that was joined to be sure that equal amounts of pin are protruding from each side. It should look just like the neighboring links. If too much pin is showing on one side, you'll need to use the chain tool to adjust this. You'll need to insert the chain into the inner notch on the chain tool, so first turn the handle counterclockwise to make room. Set the chain in the inner notch with the protruding pin positioned toward the tool's pin-driver. Turn the handle clockwise to push in the pin.

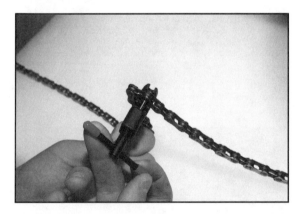

➤ **Step 8.** Grasp the lower section of chain and guide the chain onto the front chainring.

Finding and Fixing a Stiff Link

Sometimes the link that's been joined will be stiff at the pin. Always test the chain after installation by turning the pedals backward and watching the chain as it exits the derailleur. A stiff link will come out of the derailleur slightly pivoted over.

To loosen a stiff link, hold the link as shown in the following figure and flex the chain back and forth a few times. After doing this, test the chain by again pedaling backward. Repeat this process if needed.

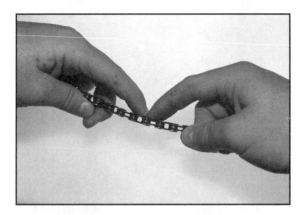

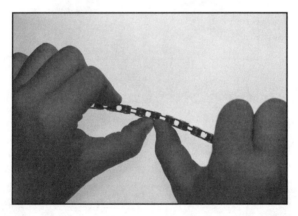

Removing and Replacing Shimano Chains

Now that you know all about replacing chains, I'm going to throw you a curve. Working with Shimano chains involves a few extra steps. First off, to tell whether your chain is Shimano, look on the outer plates for the markings *IG* or *UG*; either one is Shimano.

Shimano "peens" the pins on its chains. That is, the pin has been struck on the end with a tool that leaves two horizontal, parallel lines on the ends of the pins. This step puts a very slight flair on the pins, making them less likely to work loose. When you remove a Shimano chain by pressing out one of these pins, that slight peening is destroyed. So when you disconnect a Shimano chain, you need to completely press out the old pin and replace it with a special Shimano pin.

Shimano's replacement pins are about twice as long as the original pins. They're scribed in the middle so that once the pin is in place, the extra section can be snapped off. Also, one end of the replacement pin is smaller than the other. You put the smaller end into the chain when you're ready to reconnect it. The pin will press in most of the way by hand. Use your chain tool to press it in the rest of the way. Break off the extra length of pin. Some chain tools have a special notch for this, or you can use pliers.

The Missing Link: Chain Repair

It's rare for a chain to break under normal use. Most cases of chains coming apart during rides are caused by improperly installing the chain in the first place or by improperly adjusted derailleurs tossing a chain where it doesn't belong.

A poorly adjusted front derailleur can cause a chain to shift off the chainrings and end up wrapped around the bottom bracket spindle or caught between the crankarm and big chainring. A maladjusted rear derailleur can jam a chain between the small cog and frame of the big cog and the spokes. Any of these calamities can severely twist a chain and usually happens when you're miles from home. Keep a chain tool in your survival kit, and you won't have to walk home.

To fix a twisted chain, closely inspect the damaged area and use your chain tool to remove the offending links. Remember that you can only connect a chain by joining an inner plate link to an outer plate link. If you've had the foresight to keep a short section of extra chain in your survival kit (and extra pins if you have a Shimano chain), use that section to replace the damaged links. If you don't have extra links, realize that after removing the bad ones your chain will be too short. So be certain not to use the big chainring—otherwise a shift to one of the bigger cogs can damage your chain or derailleur hanger.

Replacing Cogs and Chainrings

It's not always easy to tell when a cogset is ready to be replaced. Chipped chrome, snagged teeth, and visible wear are indisputable signs that a cogset is ready for retirement. However, more than once I've inspected a cogset that looked nearly new and declared it to be good for one more chain, only to have the newly installed chain *skip and jump*, clearly demonstrating that the cogset was indeed worn out.

Cyclebabble

When you discuss bicycle chains and sprockets, **skip and jump** refers to the tendency of a chain to slip off worn cogs. Usually the chain will move to and from an adjacent cog.

Steer Clear

When inspecting cogsets and chainrings, don't mistake short teeth and grooves for wear. Many cogsets and chainrings, particularly those from Shimano, have special ramps, pick-up pins, and short teeth that are designed to improve shifting. If in doubt as to whether something is worn or was designed that way, compare it to a new part.

Rohloff and Hozan both make cog wear indicator tools. These simple tools consist of a short section of chain attached to a lever and handle. To use one, set the chain on a cog and push on the handle. If the chain stays on, the cog is good; if the chain pulls off, the cog is worn out. This is another one of those tools that your local shop probably won't have in inventory, but it can order one. A cog wear indicator tool runs about $20.

Chainrings are easier to judge. When the teeth start to wear into a hook shape, they're done. Actually, they're beyond done. Chainrings should be replaced before they get to this point. Continuing to use worn chainrings will cause rapid chain wear, which will in turn accelerate the wear of the rear cogs as well. To determine if a chainring is ready for the scrap pile, look at it from above. On a fresh chainring the teeth are the same thickness from the tip to the curved portion between the teeth. Teeth that have filed themselves thinner at the tip are showing the early signs of wear. Teeth that are starting to become curved are in the advanced stages of wear—scrap heap time.

Cycology

Sometimes when I'm replacing both a cogset and a chain I won't just toss 'em in the trash, especially if they were still working okay together. Instead I'll place them in a box together, knowing that I could use them again in a pinch. Having these matched sets around can sometimes keep you riding if you ruin a chain and discover that a new chain won't get along with your used cogs.

The short teeth, grooves, and ramps on these cogs and chainrings are supposed to be there. They improve shifting performance.

Removing a Cogset

Cogset removal is one of those jobs that sounds intimidating, but is really quite simple if you have the right tools (a *chain-whip*, a cogset cassette tool, and a 24 mm wrench or a large adjustable wrench). With those tools and just a little bit of know-how you can remove a cogset in just a few minutes…

➤ **Step 1.** Remove the quick-release skewer by holding one side and turning the other side counterclockwise. Insert the cogset cassette tool into the lock-ring. Reinstall the quick-release skewer to hold the tool in place.

➤ **Step 2.** Place the chain-whip over the large cog and the wrench onto the cassette tool as shown in the following figure. A chain-whip is a tool used in removing a cogset. It consists of a long steel handle with a length of bike chain attached.

➤ **Step 3.** Hold the chain-whip firmly to keep the cogset from turning while turning the wrench counterclockwise to loosen the lock-ring.

➤ **Step 4.** Remove the quick-release skewer and the lock-ring.

➤ **Step 5.** Lift off the cogset. On most cogsets, the larger cogs are all connected, with the smaller ones being either individual or sets of two. There may also be spacers in between the cogs. Be sure to note the order of any spacers.

Installing a Cogset

➤ **Step 1.** On the *freehub*, locate the spline that is wider than the rest. A freehub is the ratchet mechanism in a rear hub that allows the rider to coast. It is cylindrical and has splines machined into the body to accept a cogset.

➤ **Step 2.** On the cogset and any individual cogs, locate the large spline opening. Usually it is marked with a little triangle stamped into the metal.

A spline is a keyway or groove in a metal part. They are used to keep two metal parts aligned so that one doesn't rotate against the other. On bicycles the cogset and freehub have splines that mesh so they can rotate as a unit.

➤ **Step 3.** Line up the large spline openings on the cogset to the large spline on the freehub and slide the cogset, individual cogs, and any spacers onto the freehub.

➤ **Step 4.** Thread on the lock-ring by hand.

257

➤ **Step 5.** Insert the cassette lock-ring tool and tighten it with the 24 mm or adjustable wrench.

Cycology

While replacing chainrings and cogs isn't cheap, it is an opportunity to change your bike's gearing. Do you need a higher gear for that long, fast downhill? Or would you like some lower gears to get up that steep hill? In either case, your local bike shop can advise you on what chainrings or sprockets to get.

Removing Chainrings

To replace chainrings on a bike with only two chainrings, all you need is a 5 mm Allen wrench and perhaps a screwdriver or chainring nut spanner. For bikes with three chainrings, you're going to need to remove the crank to get to the small chainring, so you'll also need a crank-puller.

➤ **Step 1.** Place the 5 mm Allen wrench into one of the chainring bolts and turn the wrench counter-clockwise.

➤ **Step 2.** If the nut also turns, you'll need to hold it with a screwdriver or a chainring nut spanner.

➤ **Step 3.** Remove all the chainring bolts and nuts.

➤ **Step 4.** Remove the chainrings.

Removing an Inner Chainring

On bikes with a third chainring, the small chainring is bolted to the inner side of the crankset. To remove this chainring, you'll first need to remove the crankset:

➤ **Step 1.** Remove the crank bolt by turning it counterclockwise. Most new bikes have crank bolts that require an 8 mm Allen wrench. Older bikes have bolts that need a 15 mm or 14 mm socket wrench.

➤ **Step 2.** Some crank bolts also use a loose washer, so be sure that the crank bolt and the washer are both out before inserting the crank-puller.

➤ **Step 3.** Dab a little grease on the threads of the crank-puller.

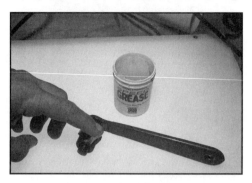

➤ **Step 4.** Thread the crank-puller into the crank by turning the large nut clockwise. Use a wrench to get it good and deep into the crank.

➤ **Step 5.** Turn the crank-puller's handle clockwise to remove the crank.

➤ **Step 6.** Remove the crankset.

➤ **Step 7.** Use a 5 mm Allen wrench to remove the chainring screws of the small chainring.

Installing Chainrings

To install chainrings, you basically reverse the steps of removing chainrings. Here are a few hints to make the job go a little easier.

➤ **Step 1.** Position the second-largest chainring behind the crank spider and slip a chainring nut through the chainring and the spider.

261

Steer Clear

Be careful not to overtighten the chainring screws; they're aluminum and may snap if you turn them too hard.

➤ **Step 2.** Position the big chainring in front of the crank spider. Dab a little grease onto the threads of a chainring screw, slip it through the chainring, and screw it into the chainring nut that you already positioned in step 1.

Repeat steps 1 and 2 for the other chainring screws, but tighten them just with your fingers. You'll cinch them all down with a wrench at the end, but for now you want them to be able to move a little, so it will be easier to insert the last few screws.

➤ **Step 3.** Tighten all the chainring screws with a 5 mm Allen wrench. Use a screwdriver or chainring nut spanner if necessary.

➤ **Step 4.** Position the small chainring over the screw holes on the inner side of the crank.

➤ **Step 5.** Dab a little grease on the threads of a chainring screw and then slip it through the chainring and screw it finger-tight into the crank. Repeat with the other screws and then use a 5 mm Allen wrench to tighten them all the rest of the way.

➤ **Step 6.** Slide the crank onto the bottom bracket spindle.

263

➤ **Step 7.** Tighten the crank bolt.

Don't follow the above instructions if your cranks are '96 or later Shimano XTR, XT, LX, or STX-RC. Your chainrings are all bolted together and held to the crankset by a lock-ring. To remove chainrings from one of these cranksets, you need to remove the crankset and then remove the lock-ring before removing the chainrings.

Got all that? Great. There's nothing to it, it just takes a little practice. If you forget, just keep referring back to this chapter. Just remember to keep this book next to your tools!

The Least You Need to Know

➤ Although many have tried, no one has been able to create anything better than a chain for transferring pedaling power to the rear wheel.

➤ A clean chain will live longer and happier than a dirty chain.

➤ A chain tool can save you from a long walk.

➤ Chains are relatively cheap; cogsets and chainrings aren't.

Chapter 18

Mechanical Basics

In This Chapter

➤ Your bike likes a bath

➤ Things to look for and hopefully not find

➤ Basic maintenance you can do at home

In the 100-plus years of their existence, bicycles have evolved into fairly sophisticated machines, so much so that I know professional auto and motorcycle mechanics who are too intimidated by the intricate workings of their bicycles to work on them themselves. Fear not. Aside from the inner workings of a Shimano shifter, bike parts are quite simple. They have to be to be as reliable as they are. There are many minor maintenance tasks and adjustments that you (yes you!) can do at home.

A Clean and Happy Bike

I've seen riders who seem to regard a filthy bike as proof of all the miles they've done. But a layer of filth and grunge can hide serious problems and discourage you from doing basic maintenance. Bike washing should be the first step in doing bike maintenance. Who wants to work on a filthy bike? Even if you're not going to work on the bike yourself and are taking it to your local bike mechanic, do the mechanic a favor and wash the bike first. Your mechanic's appreciation may be expressed in some added care in doing your work.

Take a bucket of water and squeeze in some dish soap, preferably one of the grease-cutting brands. Add a squeeze of degreaser or Simple Green for added grease-cutting power. Spray the bike with a light mist from top to bottom. Be careful not to spray with pressure toward the axles, headset, or bottom bracket—you don't want water getting to the bearings. Dip a sponge or rag into the soapy water and scrub the bike, again from top to bottom. Don't forget to scrub under the seat.

Maintenance begins with a thorough scrubbing. You never know what problems might be hiding under the dirt and grime.

Take a stiff-bristled scrub brush to clean the cogs, chainrings, chain, and mechanisms of clipless pedals. To really get the chain clean, shift the chain onto the big chainring and hold the sudsy brush against the chain and turn the crank backward. To clean the underside of the chain, hold the sudsy brush against the chain between the two little gears on the rear derailleur (they're called *jockey-pulleys*) and pedal backward. This method won't get the chain as clean as the solvent and brush method discussed in Chapter 17, "The Chain Gang," but it's quicker, and if you do the soap-and-suds thing first, the solvent-and-brush session will go much quicker.

There's no need to worry about your chain rusting from the sudsy water as long as you apply chain lube soon after washing it. Rinse the bike with light pressure and dry it with an old towel (or your roommate's terry cloth bathrobe).

Ready for Inspection

Once the bike is clean, it's time for a thorough inspection. If the bike has been through a lot of miles since its last major service, have a pad and pencil handy to make a list of things that need attention. That way you won't forget what you need to do, and if you're taking the bike to a shop for service, you've already written your own work order. Start with a meticulous examination of the frame. Carefully look for something you hope you won't find: cracks. Inspect every weld for hairline cracks. Flip the bike over and check it from the underside, too. Do not ride a bike with even minor cracks. Take it to the dealer for warranty work or to a competent frame shop for repair.

Next, inspect the tires for cuts or damage that may have been hiding under a layer of grime. Spin the wheels to see that they're straight and turn smoothly. Look for bent spokes or dented rims.

Inspect the brake pads for wear. Most pads have a wear line molded into the side of the pad. When they're worn down to the line, replace them. Check the braking surface for debris, such as asphalt, metal, or hard grit, that becomes imbedded in the pad and, in turn, puts deep gouges in your rims. Check the condition of the brake cable, especially at the point where it clamps to the brake arm, because that's where the cable gets pinched and smashed and, consequently, also where it breaks. Breaking a brake cable means no brakes. And that's a bad thing.

Move on to the crankset. Check that all the chainring bolts are still there—they sometimes fall out. Inspect the chainring teeth for wear and bent teeth. Road bikes rarely get bent teeth, but it's common on mountain bikes, usually caused by rocks and such being tossed up by the front wheel or from riding over logs and rocks.

Paint Touch-Up

A bike's paint is subjected to a lot of abuse, especially on a mountain bike. Crashes, chain-slap, and rocks flung up by the tires all take their toll on that paint job that you so loved in the showroom. Chipped paint is only a cosmetic worry on aluminum bikes, but it's a more serious concern on steel bikes—rust can ruin a frame.

Model paint found at toy and hobby stores is available in a variety of colors and is easy to apply with a small brush. Automotive touch-up paint is another choice. Start with a clean frame and be sure to remove any loose chips or rust before beginning your touch-up work. A stiff wire brush, sandpaper, or steel wool will work to clean off rust.

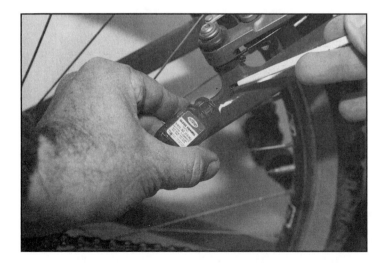

You can touch up minor paint chips with a brush and model paint.

Waxing

To keep your bike looking new and shiny, there's nothing like a good coat of wax. A waxed bike is easier to clean because dirt and grime simply rinse off. I like to use a good-quality car wax. It only takes a few minutes to apply a layer of wax to a bike's frame, so I'll often do it two or three times to give the frame a nice gloss. For in-between major waxings, it's hard to beat household furniture polish. "It cleans while it shines," as they say, and does a great job of waxing painted or anodized surfaces.

Mountain Bike Handlegrip Replacement

The easiest way to remove old, torn, faded grips is to shove an air compressor nozzle under the edge and give it a blast. The grip will inflate slightly and will slide off easily. Persistent twisting and pulling usually works, too. The only solution for stubborn grips is to just cut them off with a knife.

To install new grips, spray clear acrylic spray paint into the grip and slip it onto the bar; the wetness will make it slide on easily, and when it dries it will make the grip adhere to the bar. Let it set for an hour or more to dry. For added security, twist on a piece of safety wire. This is a trick used by most pros to keep the grips from sliding off in wet weather. Be sure to tuck the cut ends of the wire into the grip to keep the points from digging into your palm.

For those who regularly ride in wet conditions, there's nothing like contact cement or 3M weather strip adhesive to securely bond the grips to the handlebar. It's available at any automotive store. Motocross racers have used "gorilla snot" for years. It's messy to work with, but it sure holds.

Road Bike Handlebar Tape Replacement

A couple of fresh rolls of handlebar tape can do wonders to dress up the appearance of a road-weary bike. Handlebar tape comes in several types: vinyl, padded vinyl, cloth, or cork. Cork is hard to beat for comfort, but it's also more expensive than the other types. All types come in a wide variety of colors to match your bike or tastes.

Removing old handlebar tape is simple. First, remove the handlebar end plugs. Some pry out; others have a Phillips-head screw in the end of each plug that needs to be loosened. Next, peel off the adhesive tape that holds the handlebar tape to the handlebar near the stem. Unwind the handlebar tape off the handlebar. Some types of padded handlebar tape may leave behind a few chunks of foam-like material. Scrape these off with a knife or razor blade.

When you remove the new tape from its package, you may find a couple of sections of handlebar tape cut into three- or four-inch sections. These sections are meant to go around the handlebar and tuck under both sides of the brake hoods. If you don't have pre-cut sections, take a razor knife or large scissors and cut a couple of sections of tape to use. Otherwise, you'll end up leaving a gap of exposed handlebar at the brake levers.

Proceed as follows:

1. Start your wrapping job at the end of the handlebar. The first wrap around the bar should overhang the bar by about $1/8$ inch. That first wrap should go straight around the bar so that no bare handlebar is exposed.

2. Angle the next wrap so that it covers the first just short of halfway. Remember to pull on the tape as you wrap so that it goes on tight, but be careful not to pull too hard on vinyl or cork tape because they can tear.

3. Continue wrapping and covering the previous layer by half its width.

4. When you get to the brake lever, peel back the rubber brake hood and wrap the tape all the way up to the brake lever's mounting clamp. Wrap the tape around the other side of the clamp and continue wrapping.

5. Hopefully, you'll reach the stepped portion of the handlebar before you run out of tape. If you come up short, unwind the tape and try again using a little less overlap.

6. When the tape is wrapped on straight and complete, use one of the pieces of plastic adhesive tape that came with the handlebar tape to hold it in place. Sometimes the adhesive tape matches the handlebar tape or has some striped color design. Another alternative is to use a matching or contrasting color of plastic electrician's tape.

7. At the handlebar end, tuck the $1/8$ inch of overlapped tape into the handlebar and press in the handlebar plug. The plug may need a little coaxing with a mallet. Tighten the plug's screw if it has one, repeat all the steps on the other side of the handlebar, and you're done.

Hey, You Got a Screw Loose?

Compared to mountain bikes, a road bike leads a charmed life. More than once I've ridden a road bike all season without ever having to tighten a nut or bolt. Mountain bikes, on the other hand, live a life of constant jolts, vibration, and pounding. I've had saddles creep lower from loose seat-post screws, water-bottle cages fall off, headsets rattle loose, brake levers move up from loose clamps—you name a threaded part, and I've seen it come loose. Occasionally going over the screws and bolts on your bike is a good idea; having components fall off your bike isn't.

Most of the fasteners on a bike are hex-head or Allen screws. Most of those screws are 4 mm, 5 mm, or 6 mm in size. Most bike shops sell three-way wrenches shaped like the letter Y that have all three sizes. Or you can get individual Allen wrenches separately at most hardware stores; they're less than 50¢ each.

Beware of overtightening. Riders who are prone to giving every nut and bolt a slight turn before every ride will eventually have a bike full of overtightened nuts and bolts. Overtightened nuts and bolts are prone to cracking, usually when you're far, far from home.

Fixing Creaky Cranks

Few things in cycling are as annoying as suffering up a climb and having the added aggravation of creaking cranks. As if you're not hurting enough already, you have to listen to squeaks and creaks all the way up. Aaaaagh!

To tighten most modern crank bolts, you'll need an 8 mm Allen wrench, a size that unfortunately usually isn't stocked at your local hardware store. Don't ask me why, but I've checked with a number of hardware stores, and they've all had 7 mm and 9 mm wrenches, but no 8 mm wrench. Go figure. Your bike shop does have them, and they cost only about $4 or $5. Older cranks need a 14 mm or 15 mm socket. The ones in the socket set you use for working on your car might work, provided the socket walls are thin enough to fit into the crank's bolt recess. If not, you can find a wrench with both sizes at most bike shops for about $10.

To tighten crank bolts on most bikes, you'll need a 8 mm Allen wrench.

If creaking continues after a good tightening, try removing the crank with a crank-puller and applying grease or anti-seize to the spindle. If creaking continues after you grease the spindle and tighten the crankarms, the bottom bracket cups may be the real culprits. In that case, look in Chapter 19, "Beyond the Basics: Learning to Fix Some Bigger Problems," under "Becoming a Spin Doctor: Bottom Bracket Maintenance and Replacement."

Cable Lubrication

Clean cables allow a bike to shift and brake better. To free up the shifter cables for cleaning, start with the rear cable. To get enough slack to release the cable from the guides, follow these steps:

1. Shift into the smallest rear cog.

2. Manually lift the chain up to the largest cog.

3. Press the rear derailleur in to align it with the large cog. You'll then be able to pull the cable free.

4. Pull the sections of housing back to expose the inner wire and wipe the wire with cleaning solvent. Use light oil like Finish Line, Tri-Flow, or Pedro's Syn Lube on the sections of wire that are usually covered with housing.

For the front cable, shift to the smallest chainring. Pull the front derailleur outward to get slack, pull the housing away from the cable guides, and then clean and lube.

Getting the needed slack from brake cables is easy. Simply release the cable as you would when removing a wheel. Clean and lube the cables the same as you did with the shifter cables.

To lube cables, you first need to release them from the frame's cable guides.

Gimme a Brake

As brake pads wear, you'll find that you need to pull the brake lever farther before the brake starts to work. It's very easy to adjust for brake pad wear and only takes a few seconds.

On mountain bikes, each brake lever has barrel adjusters located at the point where the brake cable comes out of the lever. When you turn this adjuster counterclockwise, the adjuster screws out of the lever, taking up slack in the cable and tightening the brake. Some adjusters have a larger diameter ring threaded onto the adjuster. This lock-ring is designed to keep the adjuster from moving from vibration. You must first loosen the lock-ring before turning the adjuster. Once the adjustment has been made, tighten the lock-ring back down so that it butts up to the lever assembly.

Road bikes don't have lock-rings, and the adjuster is located on the brake caliper. Other than that, the adjustment method is the same.

Shifter Adjustment

The shifting systems of today's bikes are wonders of modern technology. Through the miles of dirt and muck, they continue to click off hundreds and hundreds of clean, trouble-free shifts. Occasionally, though, they'll go out of adjustment. In most cases, it's just a simple matter of cable stretch.

Since the rear derailleur is used more than the front, it's usually the first to show signs of cable stretch. The main symptom is a hesitancy to shift to a lower gear. If choosing a lower gear takes an extra nudge of the shifter or even a second click and your derailleur is still fresh, the problem is probably just cable stretch.

Look on your rear derailleur at the point where the cable housing enters the derailleur body. The end of the housing fits into a barrel adjuster. Turn that adjuster one turn and test the shifting. Turn the adjuster one turn at a time until the bike will properly shift to a lower gear. Then make sure that the bike will still shift up to a higher gear. If it doesn't, then you've overadjusted and need to turn the adjuster back in. You may have to go back and forth a time or two until the shifter shifts up or down without hesitation.

If you find that the front derailleur won't quite take the chain to the big ring, or that it does but the derailleur rubs on the chain, the problem is usually cable stretch. Front derailleurs don't have a barrel adjuster like a rear derailleur. But look on the front shifter where the cable comes out of the shifter and you'll find a barrel adjuster there. It's similar to those on brake levers. Turning the adjuster counterclockwise will screw it further off the shifter, taking up cable slack. Try about a turn at a time and test the shifting before trying another turn. Continue as needed.

If either shifting system needs more adjustment than the adjusters can provide, you'll need to loosen and readjust the cables.

By using the rear derailleur's adjuster, you can tune your shifting without tools.

Cleaning and Lubing Clipless Pedals

The mechanisms and springs of clipless pedals are dirt and grime magnets, and pedals with crusty workings can be difficult to click out of. Cleaning away built-up filth is easy—just scrub it out with a stiff brush and some sudsy water or cleaning solvent. Mountain bike pedals take a little more work to clean because small twigs, pebbles, and mud all seem to find their way deep into the inner recesses. Look under the pedal mechanisms at the points where the cleats enter. Bits of the aforementioned foreign matter imbedded in there are usually the culprit when the pedals are hard to engage. A small screwdriver or lengths of stiff wire are handy tools to pick out imbedded debris from a pedal's workings.

After the pedals are scrubbed and picked of all grime and imbedded stuff, they need to have their mechanisms and engagement surfaces lubricated. Chain lube works well, especially some of the thicker, wax-based lubes. Drip lube into the workings and into the engagement surfaces. Wipe off any excess lube that may get onto the body of the pedal. Otherwise, your foot can easily slip off while trying to click into the pedal.

The Least You Need to Know

➤ You take a shower before you go to see the doctor, don't you? Give a dirty bike a bath before taking it to see the mechanic.

➤ Tight screws are good and can prevent a breakdown. Overtightened screws break, causing a breakdown.

➤ You can make minor adjustments on brakes and shifters without tools.

➤ Dirt is usually the culprit when clipless pedals are hard to click into or out of.

Chapter 19

Beyond the Basics: Learning to Fix Some Bigger Problems

In This Chapter

➤ The steering committee: how your headset keeps you moving in the right direction

➤ Knowing when it's time to part with your headset

➤ Fixing the bottom bracket

➤ Silence is golden: getting rid of the creaks

➤ The spinning wheel: hub maintenance and wheel truing

Headset Maintenance and Adjustment

A bicycle's *headset* has a thankless job. Not only is it expected to pivot smoothly to turn the bike, it's also required to tolerate the forces transferred to it through the fork every time the front wheel hits a bump. The two types of headsets are threaded and threadless.

With threaded headsets, the steerer tube of the bike's fork is threaded, and the adjustable cup and locknut screw onto the steerer tube to adjust and tighten the headset. The handlebar stem for a threaded headset has a lower quill that is inserted into the steerer tube. The stem is affixed to the bike by turning a screw (expander bolt) located on top of the stem. This screw is attached to an expander wedge, which is a triangle-shaped nut. The expander wedge is drawn up the screw as the screw is turned, jamming itself between the stem quill and the inner walls of the steerer tube.

The parts of the quill type of stem used with a threaded headset.

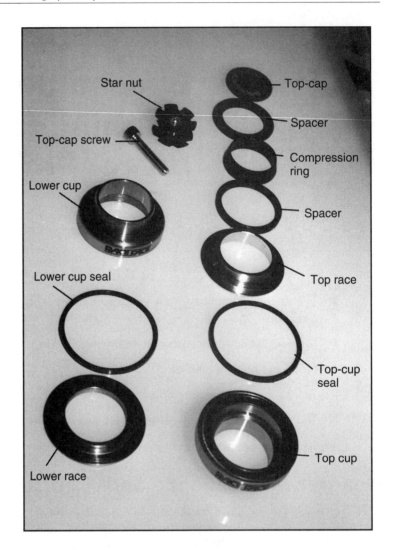

Star nut

Top-cap

Top-cap screw

Spacer

Compression ring

Lower cup

Spacer

Top race

Lower cup seal

Top-cup seal

Lower race

Top cup

Cyclebabble

A **headset** is the bearing assembly that attaches a bike's fork to the frame and allows the fork to pivot when you turn the bike.

The threaded type of headset was the standard for virtually all bikes until about 1992, when threadless models were introduced. On threadless headsets, the steerer tube is not threaded, and the stem has no quill. Instead, the stem clamps onto the end steerer tube. To tighten the headset, a small nut called a *star nut* (or *Star Fangled Nut* as it's sometimes called) is inserted into the steerer tube and is tightened via a screw inserted through a cap atop the stem and steerer tube. The stem being clamped atop the headset is what holds the system tight.

The advantage of a threadless headset is that servicing and adjustment can be done with just a 5 mm Allen wrench. Because a threadless system doesn't have a quill, expander wedge, or headset locknut, it's also lighter than a threaded headset and stem.

This little doodad is a star nut. It's used to tighten a threadless headset.

Servicing and Lubricating a Threadless Headset

To service a threadless headset, you'll need a 5 mm Allen wrench for the headset top-cap. The 5 mm may also work for the stem clamp bolts, although many stems use 6 mm Allen bolts. You'll also need a rag or two and some grease. Read on for my 12-step program to a happy and smooth-working headset.

➤ **Step 1.** Remove the front wheel and place the bike in a workstand, or hang the bike from the saddle so that it's up off the ground. If it's a mountain bike, disconnect the front brake cable at the brake lever.

➤ **Step 2.** Loosen the stem clamp bolts and the top-cap bolt and remove the stem. Be sure to hold the fork while removing the stem, or the fork might fall out onto the floor.

➤ **Step 3.** Remove the top cap and any spacers and washers (be sure to note their order—you'll need to put them back the same way). Guide the fork out of the frame.

➤ **Step 4.** Remove the lower headset bearings from the fork and the upper headset bearings from the upper headset cup. While most headsets have the bearings set into a metal or plastic cage, some have loose ball bearings. If yours has loose bearings, be sure to count them as you remove them.

Cyclebabble

A **star nut**, or **Star Fangled Nut**, is a star-shaped nut consisting of two rows of steel spring petals emanating from a threaded hole at the center. These nuts are designed to wedge into a steerer tube, allowing them to be used to tighten a threadless headset.

➤ **Step 5.** Use a rag and a splash of citrus solvent (it's biodegradable and not as toxic as petroleum-based solvents) to clean all the grease off of the bearing races and the bearings.

➤ **Step 6.** Inspect the bearings for pits, chips, and nicks, and replace the bearings if you find any such wear. Also inspect the bearing races and cups. If they're pitted or grooved, you may need a new headset. I say "may" because a headset with visible wear on the races often will continue to work smoothly for a long time.

Cyclebabble

Headset race: A headset has two "races," which are metal rings upon which the bearings ride. Races have grooves around their circumference so the bearings can roll smoothly. The races fit inside of the upper and lower cups.

➤ **Step 7.** Flip the bike upside down and dab grease into the lower headset cup. Liberally coat the lower bearings with grease and set them into the lower bearing race. Be sure to set the bearings so that the balls contact the bearing race; setting them in upside down will ruin the headset.

➤ **Step 8.** Flip the bike right side up (be sure to hold the fork) and dab grease into the upper headset cup. Liberally coat the upper bearings with grease and set them into the upper bearing cup. Again, be sure to set the bearings so that the balls contact the bearing race; setting them in upside down will ruin the headset.

➤ **Step 9.** Set the top-cap, the spacers, and washers onto the steerer tube. Place the stem onto the steerer tube, being certain that none of the control cables got twisted while the stem and handlebars were hanging around.

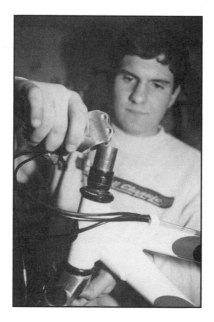

➤ **Step 10.** Place the top-cap atop the stem and screw in the top-cap bolt.

➤ **Step 11.** Tighten the top-cap bolt by turning it clockwise. While the headset is loose, you will be able to jiggle the fork back and forth quite a bit. This freeplay will diminish as you tighten the headset. As you tighten the top-cap bolt, jiggle the fork with every turn or two of the wrench. Continue tightening until the freeplay is nearly gone. At this point, turn the top-cap bolt only about $1/16$ of a turn at a time, checking for freeplay and that the fork pivots smoothly between turns. Continue $^1/_{16}$ of a turn at a time until the freeplay is gone. If you over-tighten the top-cap bolt and the fork will not pivot easily, loosen the bolt $^1/_{16}$ of a turn and pivot the fork several times. Repeat until the fork will pivot smoothly.

➤ **Step 12.** Install the front wheel, straddle the bike, and line up the stem with the front wheel. Tighten the stem clamp bolts and reconnect the front brake. Straddle the bike and apply the front brake while jiggling the bike forward and back to check that the headset is good and tight. Any knocking sounds or freeplay indi-cate that the headset isn't quite tight. Loosen the stem clamp bolts and repeat the sequence of $^1/_{16}$ of a turn at a time.

Servicing and Lubricating a Threaded Headset

To service a threaded headset, you'll need some grease, a 6 mm Allen wrench to loosen the stem, and a pair of headset wrenches. The size of those headset wrenches will depend on your headset. Most road bikes use a one-inch headset (no, you don't use one-inch wrenches); you'll need a pair of 32 mm headset wrenches to work with this headset.

Although most modern mountain bikes have gone threadless, if you have a bike made prior to 1992 or 1993, it probably has a threaded headset. In the late 1980s and early 1990s, three different headset sizes were in use. There were mountain bikes with one-inch headsets (Ritcheys and Bontragers still use them), others had $1^1/_8$-inch headsets, and some (most notably Fishers) had big $1^1/_4$-inch headsets. For bikes with $1^1/_8$-inch headsets, you'll need a pair of 36 mm headset wrenches. For 1¹/₄-inch headsets, you'll need a couple of 40 mm headset wrenches.

➤ **Step 1.** Loosen the stem by placing the 6 mm Allen wrench in the top stem bolt and turning the wrench counterclockwise. With the stem bolt loosened, hold the front wheel firmly between your knees and turn the handlebars to free them from the headset. If the stem hasn't been removed for a long time, it might be a bit stubborn. If this is the case, take a mallet and tap on the stem bolt to knock the expander wedge free. The stem should then lift out easily.

➤ **Step 2.** Remove the front wheel and place the bike in a workstand, or hang up the bike from the saddle so that it's up off the ground. If it's a mountain bike, disconnect the front brake cable at the brake lever.

➤ **Step 3.** Loosen the headset by holding the top race with one headset wrench while turning the locknut counterclockwise with the other headset wrench. Remove the top nut and any spacers or washers. Be sure to hold the fork while removing the top race, or the fork might fall out onto the floor.

Cycology

Sometimes a threadless headset becomes stubborn about staying adjusted. Often the culprit is a star nut that's been overtightened. Torque down too hard on a star nut, and the end of the petals will deform. Tighten it again, and it won't hold fast against the inside of the steerer tube. As you ride, bumps and jolts cause the faulty star nut to climb up the steerer tube, causing your headset to come loose. When this happens, it's time for a new star nut. Star nuts are only a few bucks. You'll also need a star nut setting tool, which costs about $20 to $25. Or have your local bike shop replace the nut for you.

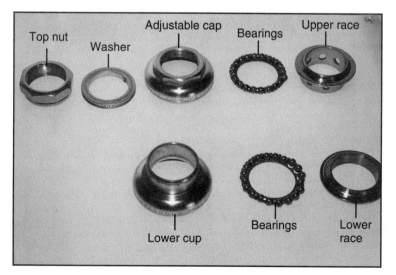

Parts of a threaded headset.

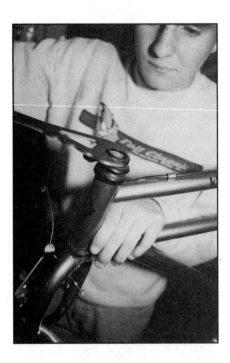

Cycology

Why do headsets that are sized in inches need wrenches sized in millimeters? Inch sizes refer only to the diameter of the fork's steerer tube. However, the headset's top-cap and locknut are sized metrically—just like every other bicycle nut, bolt, or screw. So why aren't steerer tubes sized in metric measurements? Over the years I've posed that question to various bicycle engineers and have never heard the same answer twice. The best I can offer is, "Because they're in inches."

➤ **Step 4.** Remove the lower headset bearings from the fork and the upper headset bearings from the upper race. While most headsets have the bearings set into a metal or plastic cage, some have loose ball bearings. If yours has loose bearings, be sure to count them as you remove them.

➤ **Step 5.** Use a rag and a splash of citrus solvent to clean all the grease off of the bearing races and the bearings.

➤ **Step 6.** Inspect the bearings for pits, chips, and nicks; replace the bearings if you find any such wear. Also inspect the bearing races. If they're pitted or grooved, you may need a new headset. I say "may" because a headset with visible wear on the races often will have some life left.

➤ **Step 7.** Flip the bike upside down and dab grease into the lower headset race. Liberally coat the lower bearings with grease and set them into the lower bearing race. Be sure to set the bearings so that the balls contact the bearing race; setting them in upside down will ruin the headset.

➤ **Step 8.** Flip the bike right side up (be sure to hold the fork) and dab grease into the upper race. Liberally coat the upper bearings with grease and set them into the upper bearing race. Again, be sure to set the bearings so that the balls contact the bearing race; setting them in upside down will ruin the headset.

➤ **Step 9.** Thread the top race onto the steerer tube. Set the spacers or washers atop the top race and thread on the locknut.

➤ **Step 10.** Place the stem into the steerer tube, being certain that none of the control cables got twisted while the stem and handlebars were hanging around.

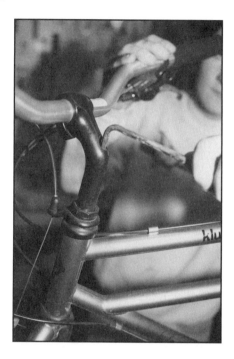

➤ **Step 11.** Tighten the top race by turning it clockwise. While the headset is loose, you will be able to jiggle the fork back and forth quite a bit. This freeplay will diminish as you tighten the top race, so jiggle the fork with every turn or two you make on the top race. Continue tightening the top race until the freeplay is nearly gone. At this point, turn the top race only about $1/16$ of a turn at a time, checking for freeplay and that the fork pivots smoothly between turns. Continue tightening the top race $1/16$ turn at a time until the freeplay in the fork is gone. If you overtighten the top race and the fork will not pivot easily, keep loosening the bolt $1/16$ of a turn at a time until the fork pivots smoothly.

➤ **Step 12.** Hold the top race in place with a headset wrench while tightening the locknut with the other headset wrench. Turn the fork to test that it turns smoothly without binding and without freeplay. If it binds, it's too tight; if it still has freeplay, it's too loose. Loosen the locknut and try again.

➤ **Step 13.** Install the front wheel, straddle the bike, and line up the stem with the front wheel. Tighten the stem bolt and reconnect the front brake. Straddle the bike and apply the front brake while jiggling the bike forward and back to check that the headset is good and tight. Any knocking sounds or freeplay indicate that the headset isn't quite tight. Loosen the locknut and repeat the sequence of tightening it $1/16$ of a turn at a time.

When to Replace a Headset

A well-maintained and well-adjusted headset will last a long time. However, sooner or later all headsets are ready for the scrap heap, usually because they've developed what bike mechanics call *indexed steering*, which is a permanent notch to the steering when the wheel is pointed straight ahead.

Indexed steering happens because a bike spends the vast majority of its time being ridden in a straight line. The ball bearings in the headset spend most of their lives sitting in about the same spot on the headset races and cups. The cumulative forces of vibrations and bumps cause the bearings to wear into the races and cups on these spots; eventually, they have slight indentations in line with each of the bearings. Point the front wheel straight ahead, and the ball bearings each drop into their own little pockets.

To detect indexed steering, lift the front of your bike and point the front wheel a few degrees away from straight ahead. Give the handlebar a gentle nudge so that the front wheel swings toward the straight-ahead position. If the wheel stops and seems to settle in at the straight-ahead position, your headset has probably had it. To confirm this, hold the wheel at the straight-ahead position and slightly turn the handlebars. If the handlebars are resistant to turning away from the straight-ahead position—if you can feel the ball bearings having to "climb out" of their little cubbyholes—then a visit to your local bike shop is in order. It's new headset time.

Becoming a Spin Doctor: Bottom Bracket Maintenance and Replacement

In the olden days (prior to about 1991), most bicycles came with bottom brackets that used a separate spindle, ball bearings set in metal cages, and a pair of bearing cups, with one cup being laterally adjustable. Although these types of bottom brackets worked quite well, working on them required at least three special tools and a degree of finesse in adjusting the cups that was sometimes beyond the proficiency of the average garage mechanic. If you set the bearings too loose or too tight, they'd quickly reduce themselves to junk.

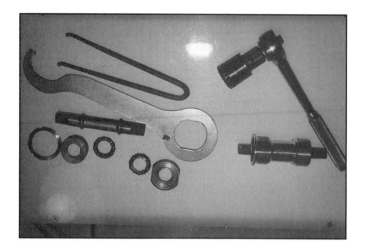

On the left is a standard bottom bracket and the tools needed for servicing (left) and a cartridge bottom bracket and its tool. Which would you rather change?

Then came the cartridge bottom bracket, which contained the spindle and bearings all in a single metal cylinder. Cartridge bottom brackets are very simple to work on—there's no adjusting involved because a cartridge system is fully self-contained with sealed bearings. You'll need a Shimano bottom bracket tool (about $12 to $20) and a $3/8$ ratchet handle.

To remove a cartridge bottom bracket, first remove the cranks using a crank-puller (see instructions on crank removal in Chapter 17 under "Removing an Inner Chainring"). Insert the bottom bracket tool into the bottom bracket on the right side of the bike (the side with the sprockets and chain) and turn the tool clockwise (it's a left-hand thread) until the bottom bracket comes out. Then insert the tool into the left-side, nondrive cup and turn the tool counterclockwise (it's a right-hand thread) until the cup comes out.

If you were removing the bottom bracket to replace it, be sure that your new one is the same size. Bottom brackets are sized by bottom bracket shell width and spindle width. If you're unsure, take your old bottom bracket with you to the bike shop.

To install a cartridge bottom bracket, first dab a little grease on the threads of the *bottom bracket shell*. The grease will help it to screw in a little

Cyclebabble

Bottom bracket: The bearing assembly and shaft that the cranks turn on. A bottom bracket consists of a pair of bearings and a shaft called the "spindle." Each end of the spindle has a threaded hole to accept the crank bolts that attach the crank arms to the spindle.

Cyclebabble

A **bottom bracket shell** is the lowest point of the bicycle frame and contains the bottom bracket.

285

easier and will lessen the chance of the bottom bracket developing an annoying creak. Look at the cartridge for markings that show left and right. Position the cartridge in the bottom bracket shell, insert the bottom bracket tool into the cartridge, and turn it counterclockwise (it's left-hand thread) to tighten it into the shell. Tighten it all the way down until it stops. Then insert the nondrive cup into the other side and turn it clockwise (it's a right-hand thread) to tighten it. That's it! There's no further adjusting or anything.

Installation or removal of a cartridge bottom bracket is easy.

Stop That Creaking!

In bicycling, few things are as annoying as a squeak or creak. Among the most common of these aggravating noises is a creak or squeak with every turn of the pedals. These sounds usually come from the bottom bracket, and thankfully, they're usually easy to cure.

Sometimes the creak is caused by the crankarm slightly flexing on the spindle. Many bike mechanics routinely apply grease to the bottom bracket spindle before installing the crank to prevent these creaks. However, I usually don't grease spindles because that extra bit of slipperiness can allow the spindle to slide on too far, causing the hole in the crank to enlarge. I'll make an exception to this in cases of creaky cranks, but I'm careful to not overtighten the crank bolts.

If greasing the spindle doesn't cure the creak, the next likely suspect is the interface between bottom bracket cartridge and the bottom bracket shell. Sometimes the threads in the bottom bracket shell and the cups don't quite match. In those cases, no amount of tightening will stop the play that causes creaking. Take some plumber's Teflon tape (the white stuff used to seal pipe threads) and wrap a layer around the cup threads before reinstalling.

Hub Maintenance and Adjustment

Bicyclists tend to forget their *hubs*. As long as the wheels are turning, the average rider will give them little thought and will spend money and maintenance time on other concerns, such as a new saddle, new handlebars, and titanium nuts and bolts. Meanwhile, the grease inside the hubs continues to deteriorate thanks to the grit and dirt that has worked past the seals. I've encountered people riding on wheels that sound like a pair of coffee grinders. If you let all that destruction continue, the hubs can be completely ruined. And that's too bad, because servicing hubs isn't difficult or even very time-consuming.

Miles of Experience

A racer competing in the entire NORBA National Championship mountain bike series brought her bike into the shop where I worked. She had just returned from a rainy, muddy race in Vermont and only had a few days at home before jetting off to the next event. She told us to put on fresh cables and a fresh chain and to replace the bottom bracket, but she said nothing about servicing the hubs. When we pulled off the bottom bracket about a cup of murky water spilled out! Knowing that the hubs couldn't be much better, we opened them and found more murky water. We cleaned them out and put in fresh grease and bearings. Had she continued to ride on these wheels she would have surely ruined a very expensive set of hubs.

The hubs on most bikes are the conventional, adjustable-cone type. They consist of the following parts:

1. **The hub shell.** The hub shell is the main part of the hub. It's the metal spool that the spokes connect to and that the axle goes through. Inside of each end of the hub are the bearing races, a pair of smooth channels in which the ball bearings roll.

2. **The axle.** The axle fits inside the hub and extends out of either side to fit into the slots on the frame or fork.

3. **The bearings.** The bearings are either loose ball bearings or ball bearings contained within a ring-shaped cage.

Cyclebabble

The **hub** is the center portion of the wheel that contains the axle and upon which the wheel spins. The hub is connected to the spokes, which are connected to the rim.

287

4. **The bearing cones.** The cones are nuts with tapered ends. The cones thread onto the axle, and the bearings sit between the cones and the bearing races of the hub.

The parts of a hub.

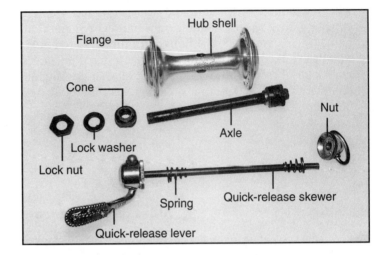

Hubs should be cleaned out and treated to a serving of fresh grease at least once a year—more often if you ride in wet, muddy conditions. It's also a good idea to check hubs any time the wheels are off the bike. It's simple to do: Hold onto the wheel by both sides of the axle and give it a good spin. It should spin silently and smoothly. Any audible grinds, ticks, or creaks are sure signs that the hub is at least ready for fresh grease and possibly new bearings. Also, pay attention to how it feels as it spins. Sometimes the early signs of internal grit can be felt in the fingertips before any audible symptoms arise.

It's easy to tell whether a hub needs servicing. Just spin the wheel and listen.

Another thing to check for is axle freeplay. The axle should turn smoothly without detectable sideplay. To check for this, grasp the axle and try to move it side to side. Any movement means that the cones need to be tightened.

To service a hub, you'll need a pair of *cone wrenches* to loosen and tighten the cones. Although cones come in sizes ranging from 12 mm to 17 mm, generally the cones on a front hub are 13 mm, and rear hub cones are 15 mm. You'll also need either a 15 mm open-end wrench for a front hub or a 17 mm for a rear hub, plus a small screwdriver, a couple of clean rags, some grease, and possibly some fresh ball bearings.

Cyclebabble

Cone wrenches are open-end wrenches with very narrow jaws designed to fit onto the flats of a bearing cone.

To check for axle freeplay, try to jiggle the axle from side to side.

Scrubbing the Hub

To disassemble and clean the hub, follow these steps:

➤ **Step 1.** Place a rag on a flat surface and rest the wheel on its axle on top of the rag.

➤ **Step 2.** Place the cone wrench on the flats of one of the cones (either side will do) and use an open-end wrench of the appropriate size (usually 15 mm for the front hub, 17 mm for the rear hub) to loosen the locknut by turning it counterclockwise.

➤ **Step 3.** Take off the locknut and the washer beneath it.

➤ **Step 4.** Turn the cone counterclockwise by hand or with the cone wrench to remove it.

➤ **Step 5.** Reach under the wheel to hold the axle while tilting the wheel slightly upright. Then remove the axle assembly. Do this over the rag so that any bearings that fall out will hopefully fall onto the rag and not roll across your workbench and fall behind your lawnmower. Count the ball bearings and make sure there's an equal amount from both sides. If any bearings are lost, your local bike shop can look up the correct number of bearings.

➤ **Step 6.** Use the screwdriver to pry out the dustcaps. These don't have to come out, but it's easier to clean the races and reinstall the bearings without the dustcaps in the way.

➤ **Step 7.** Clean all the parts. Use citrus solvent and a brush. Or if you're single (or really brave), put it all in the kitchen sink and scrub it all clean with dish soap and a brush.

➤ **Step 8.** Once all the parts are shiny clean, examine them. Inspect the bearings, looking carefully for chips or pits. Replace all the bearings if any show damage. Inspect the cones. If any bearing surface is pitted or has a worn groove, replace them. To check for a bent axle, roll the axle on a flat surface and watch for wobbles. Never reinstall a bent axle.

Picking Up the Pieces

To reassemble the hub, take your freshly cleaned parts (or new ones from the bike shop) and lay them out so that you know where every piece is. You're ready to begin.

➤ **Step 1.** Put a nice glop of grease in the bearing races. Don't worry about putting in a little too much—it'll squeeze into place. When you're all done, you can wipe off any excess that oozes out.

➤ **Step 2.** Place the bearings into the races. The grease will hold them in place. Be sure to put the right amount in each side.

➤ **Step 3.** Press in the dustcaps. Be sure to get them straight, or they'll drag on the axle as the wheel turns.

➤ **Step 4.** Smear grease all over the axle and slide it into the hub, being careful not to knock out any of the bearings.

➤ **Step 5.** Grease the cone and screw it onto the axle; slip on the washer, and then screw on the locknut.

➤ **Step 6.** Tighten the cone down by hand until it feels as though the wheel could spin smoothly. Hold the cone with the cone wrench and tighten the locknut by turning it clockwise with the open-end wrench. Then spin the wheel to check it. If it's too tight or too loose, loosen the cone and try again. Don't be surprised if it takes several tries to get it right. I don't think I've ever gotten it on the first attempt.

Wheel Truing

A bicycle wheel is a wondrous thing. The strength of these lightweight assemblages of aluminum rims and steel spokes is amazing. Consider that an average front mountain bike wheel weighs only about two pounds, yet it can endure your weight plus the abuses of rutted trails, rocks, roots, and bone-headed maneuvers. Alas, even the best wheels eventually succumb to these evils and develop wobbles.

Most minor wheel bends and tweaks can be cured with but a few minutes of attention from an educated hand wielding a spoke wrench. *Wheel truing* is an acquired skill. I've encountered people that have asked; "Don't you just tighten the spokes?" To answer that, I usually respond, "To tune a guitar, don't you just turn the tuning keys?" Neither skill seems difficult when watching a master, but the knowledge of which key or spoke to tighten represents hours and hours of experience. Do it wrong, and you'll only make things worse. An old joke around bike shops is that the best way to drum up business for the service department is to give away free spoke wrenches. But fear not. A novice wheel truer can tackle minor wobbles by knowing a few basic tips. Read on to learn a bit about the black art of wheel truing.

All you'll need is a spoke wrench and a rubber band. If you have a truing stand, your job will be easier. Otherwise, just leave the wheel on the bike. There are five different sizes of spoke nipples, so be sure to use only the right-size spoke wrench. Either get a wrench that has all the different sizes, or take your wheels to your local bike shop and have them determine which size you need. Don't get a cheap spoke wrench; spoke nipples are made of pretty soft stuff (either brass or aluminum), and a poorly sized wrench can strip a spoke nipple. I prefer Park Tools wrenches. They fit well and are color-coded for the various sizes (size .127 is red, size .130 is green, and so on).

Cyclebabble

Wheel truing is to straighten a bent wheel.

Miles of Experience

People sometimes become confused as to why a spoke is tightened by turning the spoke nipple counterclockwise. "Isn't it always righty-tighty and lefty-loosey?" Usually, it is. And no, spoke nipples aren't left-hand thread. But here's the deal: A spoke nipple is basically a female screw threaded onto the end of a spoke. If you were to tighten the spoke nipple from the end that has a screwdriver slot, you would turn it clockwise. However, because you usually tighten spokes from the other end, you need to turn the spoke nipple counter-clockwise to tighten it. Confused? Okay, take a ketchup bottle and look down on it as you tighten the top with your hand. Your hand turns clockwise, right? Now flip the bottle upside down and tighten the top again. From your vantage point (looking at the bottom of the bottle), your hand turns counterclockwise this time. Got it? Good!

➤ **Step 1.** Place the wheel in a truing stand, or lacking that, flip the bike upside down so that the wheels can spin.

➤ **Step 2.** If the wheel is in a truing stand, set the lateral feeler a few millimeters from the side of the rim; if the wheel is still on the bike, hold your spoke wrench a few millimeters from the rim. Spin the wheel slowly and watch whether the rim contacts or gets closer to the lateral feeler or the spoke wrench.

➤ **Step 3.** Determine how much of the wheel is affected by the wobble. Sometimes wobbles are localized to only one or two spokes or may be spread out to four or six spokes. Mark the midpoint of the wobble by looping a rubber band around the middle spoke.

➤ **Step 4.** Your goal is to tighten spokes to pull the rim away from the side that's rubbing. Spokes are set in the rim so they alternate—one spoke comes from one side of the hub, and the next one comes from the other side of the hub. You want to tighten the spoke that comes from the hub on the opposite side from the side of the rim that's rubbing. Start with the spoke that's at the middle of the wobble. Tighten it (turn it counterclockwise) only $1/4$ of a turn. Then do the same with the spokes on either side, remembering to skip a spoke so that you're tightening a spoke that comes from the hub on the opposite side from where the rim rubs.

➤ **Step 5.** Rotate the wheel slightly to check your progress. If needed, continue to pull the rim away from the wobble by tightening the appropriate spokes $1/4$ of a turn at a time.

➤ **Step 6.** Check the spokes on the side of the wobble. Pulling the rim away from them may have made them too tight. Check them by tapping them with the spoke wrench. If the sound from tapping them is much higher pitched than the rest of the spokes, they're probably too tight. Loosen them $1/4$ of a turn at a time and then rotate the wheel slightly to check your progress.

You may need to tighten and loosen spokes a few times before you get it right. Unless you drastically overtighten a spoke, you aren't going to break or ruin anything. In a worst-case scenario, you might pull your rim off-center or make your wheel worse. If this happens, at least you learned a few things. Throw in the towel and take the wheel to your local bike shop. If you ask, most shops won't object to having you watch as they true your wheel. If they're not too busy, they might even hand you a spoke wrench and supervise as you do it yourself. Of course, they'll probably still charge you the normal service rate, but it might also be the last time you ever pay to have a wheel trued.

The Least You Need to Know

➤ Headsets thrive on TLC—make sure you take care of yours.

➤ Hubs need TLC, too.

➤ All the nuts and bolts on a bicycle are metric, even on one-inch, $1^1/_8$-inch, and $1^1/_4$-inch headsets.

➤ Bottom brackets don't have to be noisy; creaks can easily be fixed.

➤ Bicycle wheels are strong but not invincible.

Part 5
Play Well with Others

Although riding alone can be calming and relaxing, there's something to be said for the fun of riding with other people. You can share the enjoyment of a particularly scenic road or trail, converse while riding, or spice up the ride with a bit of friendly competition ("Last one to the lunch stop buys!").

There are many ways to share the fun. Many riders join cycling clubs or go on regularly scheduled shop rides. Some riders plan their entire vacations around bicycling. Others go on charity rides, raising money for worthy causes while enjoying an afternoon or a week in the saddle. Then there's racing, which opens up a whole other list of group riding possibilities. This section will help you to decide what type of group riding will best suit you.

Chapter 20

Go for a Ride?

In This Chapter

➤ The more the merrier: why group rides are so great

➤ The Society of Enthusiastic Pedalers: different rides for different folks

➤ Riding after dark

➤ Launching a new ride

➤ Do your part: fun rides that serve a higher purpose

Sharing the fun of the ride with a large pack of riders or even just a small group of friends is loads of fun. Whether it's a group ride with a pace that's casual enough to allow conversation and joking or a *hammer-fest* that's more of an unofficial race than a ride, there's truth to the adage, "the more the merrier." Read on to find out more about the different types of group rides you can participate in.

Let's Get This Shop on the Road: The Shop Ride

Many bike shops have regularly scheduled road rides and/or mountain bike rides. There's a long tradition of Saturday and Sunday morning rides that begin and end at a bike shop. Depending on the shop's location, the rides themselves may not start at the bike shop, but the shop might still be where the riders meet to determine the day's ride before everyone piles into cars and heads to the start of the ride. Enthusiastic shops sometimes have several rides scheduled throughout the week. Perhaps your local bike shop has a weekday afternoon ride, or a women-only ride, or even a mountain bike

Cyclebabble

To **hammer** is to ride very hard and fast; for example, "I got a flat and had to hammer to catch up to the group." A **hammer-fest** is a group ride with a very fast pace.

night ride if the riders have powerful lighting systems (more on that later in this chapter).

Some rides become very popular. As the number of riders grows, it often becomes necessary to divide the ride into a fast group and a slow group (or fast and faster, because few riders like being called "slow"). Whether your local ride is divided or not, beginner riders rarely need to be concerned about being left behind. It's likely that other riders will be going about your same speed. If you or your group does begin to lag behind the rest, chances are good that they'll wait, especially on a mountain bike ride. No one wants you to get lost, and cyclists are generally a pretty caring and supportive bunch.

Members Only: The Club Ride

There are several different types of bicycling clubs: road racing clubs, mountain bike racing clubs, nonracing clubs for road or dirt, singles clubs, couples clubs, tandem clubs, senior citizens clubs, Christian clubs, gay clubs, and many, many more. Becoming a member of a cycling club offers camaraderie, often a full schedule of off-the-bike social events, and, best of all, a full calendar of club rides.

Club rides vary as much as the clubs themselves. Whatever type of riding suits you, there's a club that can fill your needs. Larger clubs often offer a full menu of rides from hard-paced training rides to casual picnic rides. Distances can vary, too, from short rides of only an hour to all-day rides in excess of 100 miles.

Some of the most fun rides are special-occasion rides that end in a picnic or barbecue. The really fun clubs look for any excuse for these types of rides: a founding member's birthday, a major holiday, Millard Fillmore's (thirteenth president of the United States) birthday. I've attended a "Who cares about football?" ride on Superbowl Sunday. Whatever the reason (or excuse), there's nothing like four or five hours of riding to work up an appetite for a good spread of food and to enjoy chilled beverages (adult or otherwise).

To find clubs in your area, your bike shop is the best source. Also check with regional cycling newsletters. Local newspapers are sometimes a good source; look under community or sports activities.

One, Two, Three, GO! The Training Ride

Riders with racing ambitions or even just a penchant for speed should think about finding a local training ride. These rides differ from most shop rides in that they're basically ridden the same as a race. The pace is furious, and there's no waiting for stragglers. Do a few of these, and not only will your speed increase, but your ability to ride in tight formation will improve as well.

Many bike shops and cycling clubs have training rides in their regular ride schedules. Participants in these rides are often divided into groups by ability and speed. In areas of the country with active racing populations, there are regularly scheduled training rides that have no shop or club affiliation—they've just been around for years. Finding out about the latter type of ride isn't always easy because the long-time participants are sometimes secretive about their training rides. They'd like to keep their ride for experienced riders and not have to instruct novices. However, the only way to know for sure if you're up to one of these training rides is to try one. There's no shame in riding at the back of the pack. In fact, until you develop the speed and confidence to ride elbow to elbow with dozens of other riders, that's the safest place to be.

Whether you're fast enough or skilled enough for the ride is something you'll soon learn, sometimes within the first mile or two. But even if you do *get fired out the back*, hang in there and finish the route. You might even join up with a few other riders that dropped behind. Ride with them and try to keep a fast pace. Next week, try it again. In time, you might even be able to hang with the main group.

If you're intimidated by jumping into the deep end and going on a fast-paced training ride, consider lowering your sights by joining a local race team and training with riders closer to your own speed and ability. Even if you just want to improve your speed and riding skills and have no aspirations of ever racing, being a member of an amateur team is a great way to learn more about the sport.

Areas with active racing opportunities often have dozens of teams. Some are sponsored by local bike shops or businesses; others are affiliated with organizations such as the YMCA or a school or college. Although some teams are exclusively for expert-caliber racers, many have members in all racing categories; there are even teams just for novices.

Cyclebabble

To **get fired out the back** is cyclist lingo used to describe when a slower rider drops behind the main pack of riders.

Being on a team offers many advantages. You'll have a large group of other people to ride with, and you're likely to ride more—it's hard to blow off a ride when you know that you'll later have to face those teammates who did go out and train. You'll also benefit from the knowledge of the more experienced riders. These seasoned racers can be particularly helpful in such things as evaluating your riding position and your pedaling spin and in teaching you about racing tactics or how to ride in a pack. Riders on shop-sponsored teams are often offered discounts on equipment, bikes, and mechanical labor. Last, but not least, being on a team will save you money on race day, because riders who are *unattached* usually have to pay an extra $5 or $10 for a race entry.

Cyclebabble

To be **unattached** in cycling doesn't have anything to do with your marital status; it's a term used to denote racers who are not members of any race team.

Cyclebabble

Breakaway is a group of riders who have managed to get ahead of the main pack. It can also be used as a verb, indicating an attempt to ride away from the main pack; for example, "Our team is going to try to breakaway at the top of the last climb."

Cycling is usually thought of as being an individual sport. Although that's true of mountain bike racing and of road time trials, in road racing it is extremely rare for an individual rider with no team affiliation to win a race. Team members work together in many ways, such as allowing one rider to spend most of the race riding in the draft of the other team members so that rider will be stronger for the sprint at the finish. Or if one or more team members is in a *breakaway*, the rest of the team might attempt to slow the pace of the main pack.

To learn about local teams, ask the folks at your bike shop. Or, better still, go to a local race. At the race you're sure to find out which local team is the strongest (just count the team jerseys) and which teams cater to novice racers (count the team jerseys in the novice categories).

Working on Your Night Moves: Riding After Dark

Being able to ride only on weekends is the curse of many. Sadly, for the average nine-to-fiver, riding after work is only an option in the summer months when the sun doesn't set until 8 p.m. There are answers to this dilemma, and they come with rechargeable batteries. I'm talking about bicycle lighting systems; these wonderful inventions open the possibility of riding enjoyably and safely long after the sun sinks below the horizon.

Many are spooked by the very thought of riding at night, but those who have tried it consider it one of their most fun cycling experiences. There's something magical about riding your favorite, familiar roads and trails after dark. They seemingly take on a whole new appearance. For the off-road set, the chances of spotting wildlife, especially nocturnal creatures such as coyotes, raccoons, and owls, are greatly increased after dark. It's not at all unusual to look off the trail to see a pair of beady eyes shining back.

For road riding at night, it's safest to choose a route with wide road shoulders. You'll still need a lighting system; however, if the route is well lighted with streetlights, a standard bike light may be sufficient. Most standard lights run on standard batteries (AA, C, or D cell) and do a fair job of lighting the road surface. Their main purpose on well-lighted roads is to make a bike more visible to oncoming motorists. To alert motorists approaching from behind, it's a good idea (and the law in most states) to have at least a rear reflector. For the ultimate in rear visibility, a flashing strobe light is tough to beat and virtually impossible to not see.

The Cat Eye's HL-500 is one example of a good light for road riding. It has a 2.4-watt bulb and runs on four AA batteries; for longer burn time, there's an optional auxiliary battery pack that holds four D batteries (the big flashlight size). The TL-LD500 Reflex taillight is unique in that the lens is also a reflector, thereby offering a rider rear visibility even with dead batteries. You can contact Cat Eye at 1-800-5-CATEYE or www.cateye.com.

For off-road riding, flashlight-type lights are usually a waste. They're fine for road use where their real job is to make cyclists more visible to motorists, but on pitch-black trails, a couple of D-cells just can't provide enough illumination for a safe and enjoyable trail ride. For road rides on darkened backroads, you're also going to want more candlepower. The answer is to get one of the systems commonly used for after-dark mountain bike riding.

Several companies make suitable night-riding light systems. Among them are Niterider, NiteSun, Cycgolite, and Schwinn. Most make systems with rechargeable nickel-cadmium or "NiCad" batteries made in the same size and shape as a water bottle, which means the battery can be carried on the bike in a water bottle cage. NiCad batteries can store far more energy than alkaline or lead acid batteries. And they hold up to repeated rechargings.

Miles of Experience

Although many lighting system batteries are designed to fit into a water bottle cage, because these batteries weigh a bit more than a water bottle, a water bottle cage may not quite be up to the task. I discovered this one night after accidentally riding over a deep rut; the jolt launched my battery into the woods. Luckily, I was also wearing a helmet light (with the battery tucked securely in a zippered jersey pocket) and was able to quickly find my battery. Otherwise, I might have been searching in the dark until morning. Since then, I've used a pedal toe-strap wrapped around the battery to keep it from bouncing out of the water bottle cage.

There are two ways to light the trail:

1. Lights mounted on the handlebars
2. Lights mounted on the helmet

Helmet lights are great for shining into corners and down hills because the light shines where you're looking. But they also create a tunnel-vision effect and a flat perspective that alters depth perception, making it tough to make out what you're seeing and to judge distances. If you're following in another rider's dust, a helmet light can glare off the airborne particles. It's like using high beams in fog—the light shines right back at you.

A handlebar light with its lower position spreads a broader beam that glares less and also forms shadows on rocks, roots, ruts, and so on, making them easier to spot. However, handlebar lights only shine where the bars are pointed. That's why I like to use both a handlebar light and a helmet light. Also, because it's not unusual for an off-road ride to include a few stretches of pavement, you should have at least a rear reflector or a rear flashing strobe light on your mountain bike.

For a unique experience that will add hours to your riding schedule, consider night riding. To find night rides, look to those now-familiar sources: the local bike shop, local clubs, and local race teams. If there are no rides, schedule your own. How? Read on.

Together at Last: Organizing a Ride

Suppose there is no shop ride, training ride, club ride, or night ride in your area. Or perhaps you'd just like to start another ride to better suit your schedule or riding appetite. Getting a new ride started is fairly easy.

First decide if your ride is going to be a one-time thing, or a weekly or monthly affair. If it's going to be a continuing thing, decide if it's going to follow the same route each time or if it's going to be a "Where-do-you-all-want-to-go-this-time?" type of thing. If you want to follow a set route, consider printing up maps or route sheets so that no one gets lost and the front riders won't have to wait on stragglers. Permits and such for these casual rides is rarely an issue as long as you're not charging a fee.

The next step is to put out the word about your new ride. Make up a flyer listing the time, date, and destination of your ride. Here are several ways to spread the news of your new ride:

Cycology

If you are trying to organize a new ride and meet resistance from your local shop about starting the ride at the shop, point out the fact that each ride will effectively deliver a number of enthusiastic riders to the shop's door. It's likely that many of those riders will buy inner tubes, sports bars, and so on before heading out.

➤ Again, your local bike shop is your number-one resource. Most shops will welcome the idea of a scheduled ride. Many shops have bulletin boards for posting race flyers and cycling announcements, so see whether you can post your flyer there.

➤ Print up extra flyers and post them at other shops. (I recommend mailing them to shops in neighboring towns, because it's quicker and cheaper than driving.)

➤ College bulletin boards are another means of reaching your potential riders.

➤ If there are any bike-oriented companies in your area, by all means send them a few flyers. People in the bike industry are usually enthusiastic riders themselves.

➤ Contact your local newspaper to get your ride listed in the community or sports activities section.

Most of all, tell all your riding friends and ask them to do the same. As useful as flyers and announcements can be, word-of-mouth is usually more effective at spreading the news of a good ride. As the scheduled day of your first ride approaches, get a few friends to commit to going. You want to have a few "for-sure" participants. If ride day arrives and only you and your few for-sures come, don't worry about it. Just go ahead and do the ride and enjoy it. The few that did show up will talk about it to other friends, who may well say, "Oh yeah, I saw a flyer on that." Before you know it, you have a full-fledged ride.

Miles of Experience

Some years ago I started a Thanksgiving morning mountain bike ride. All it took to get it started was telling a few friends and mailing about 30 flyers to a few bike shops and to a few companies in the bike industry. At least 40 riders showed for the "First Annual Thanksgiving Morning Appetite Seminar" ("Three hours of working up an appetite before you go to mom's to chow down"). In the following years, although I still only sent out the same number of flyers, the ride continued to grow. I've since moved away from where that ride took place and haven't sent out flyers in years. Yet the ride continues, and I understand that 60 or more riders still show each year. Recently, I asked someone about that ride. "Oh yeah, I've done it the last three years," was his quick response. When I asked him if he knew the ride's origin, he answered, "Geez, who knows?" I like that.

Who Needs an Amusement Park? The Fun Rides

How would you like to spend a weekend morning going for a ride with a few hundred other cyclists? It sure would be fun if that ride was well-organized and had a well-marked course and each rider was given an accurate route slip with every turn clearly described. How about if the ride had lots of rest stops where riders could refill their bottles with water or sports drink and help themselves to cookies, bananas, and peanut butter sandwiches. Wouldn't it be nice if those rest stops had porta-potties so riders wouldn't have to find strategically placed bushes? I'm sure you'd also like it if at the end of that ride a big spread of food was waiting to be devoured by hungry cyclists.

Fun rides like the one just described happen every weekend across the United States. Road rides are the most common, but as mountain bike festivals grow in popularity, more and more off-road fun rides are offered each year.

Speed isn't the idea behind these rides. Fun rides are aimed at those riders content to ride the day's distance at an enjoyable pace. The organizers of fun rides almost always stress "this is not a race." Just don't waste your breath trying to tell that to the riders at the front who invariably blast away from the start, skip the rest stops, and reach the end in a sprint finish. Although these rides are "just for fun," riding them as races can be fun, too. Before entering my first real road race, I rode a few fun rides at race pace. The experiences I learned riding in a pack and pacing myself on those fun rides certainly helped when I began racing for real.

The promoters of these fun rides usually offer two or three distance options. On road fun rides, the events are sometimes called *century* rides, with a longest option of 100 miles. Sometimes the shorter option is a *metric century* of 100 kilometers (62 miles). Distances as short as 10 or 20 miles are sometimes offered to give beginner riders a chance to join in the fun. On mountain bike fun rides, it's unusual for the longest option to be more than 35 miles, and short-distance options of 10 to 15 miles are usually scheduled.

Another type of fun ride is a *poker run*. These rides have a series of stops along the route where riders draw a playing card. At the end of the ride, the rider with the best poker hand wins prizes or cash. Poker runs are more common at mountain bike festivals, but there are road poker runs, too.

To find out about fun rides, check with your bike shop. (See a trend here?) Enthusiastic shops usually know about these rides, and promoters of fun rides usually send flyers to bike shops. Check with regional cycling publications as well. Once you've done a fun ride, you'll be on that promoter's mailing list. Expect your mailbox to receive a steady supply of flyers on fun rides forever after.

Fun rides usually cost about $25 to $60. Considering the logistics involved with a promoter getting city and highway permits, scouting and marking the course, making route slips, setting up the rest stops, recruiting and paying course workers, and supplying the food at the finish, the cost is usually quite reasonable for a day of fun. Few promoters get rich from their rides, but do expect good value for your money. If you're paying top dollar, you should expect good food and at least a commemorative T-shirt or water bottle.

Cyclebabble

To **poach** is to ride with a race or fun ride without paying the entry fee or to ride on trails that are closed to bicycle use.

If the fee for a fun ride is more than you want to spend, look around for another ride. Whatever you do, don't *poach* rides. Every fun ride seems to have those individuals who didn't pay their entry fee, but just "happen" to be riding the same route as the fun ride. These poachers are, in effect, stealing from every paying rider. Poachers often offer the excuse, "But I don't use the rest stops and don't take any of the food or water." Some of the riders who paid don't either—particularly those who ride at race pace. It takes countless hours of planning and work to put on a fun ride, so be fair and pay the promoter his or her just due.

Do Good, Feel Good: The Fund-Raising Rides

Going for long rides is good for you, but wouldn't it be nice if you could also benefit others while you add to your annual mileage totals? You can, thanks to myriad charity rides. These rides vary from one-day rides of 50 to 100 miles to month-and-a-half-long rides such as the American Lung Association's Big Ride, a U.S. coast-to-coast ride.

Charity rides raise funds for such causes as AIDS, cancer, and other nasty diseases. National as well as local charities promote these fund-raising rides. The handicapped ski school in my hometown, for instance, does an annual ride. Sometimes rider entry fees generate the money, but more often the riders raise money by soliciting pledges from supporters. To ride in one of the famed Tanqueray American AIDS Rides (there are five), for instance, a rider pays an entry fee of $45 and must raise donations of $1,500 to $2,500, depending on the length of the ride.

These charity rides have proven to be tremendous fund-raisers. The 1998 Big Ride raised over $6 million, and the 1998 California AIDS Ride raised $9.5 million, with each of the other four AIDS rides also raising funds in the millions. Yet the money raised by these charity rides is only part of what makes them so successful for their causes. Charity rides are also a wonderfully successful means of spreading public awareness.

Consider the dozens and even hundreds of towns along the routes of these rides, and each of those towns has newspapers and radio and TV stations. It quickly becomes apparent that media coverage of a ride can spread the message of a cause in ways unattainable by other means. Having hundreds or even thousands of cyclists riding through a town makes quite an impact as well. The Boston-to-New York AIDS Ride has seen years with over 3,000 riders.

A long, unbroken line of hundreds or even thousands of cyclists can have a tremendous impact on spreading awareness for a cause.

Closing ceremonies for Tanqueray's American AIDS Rides include the procession of the riderless bike, symbolizing those that have lost their battles with AIDS and those that can't ride for themselves.

Most of these rides have fully staffed rest stops spaced out along each day's route where riders can fill water bottles, grab lunch or a snack, and give tired bodies a well-deserved break. On the multiday rides, evenings are usually spent in tent cities provided by the organizers. Camping in tents and all-you-can-eat dinners and breakfasts are the usual means of lodging and feeding the multitudes. No, doing a charity ride isn't your usual bike vacation. These rides are a far cry from going on an outfitted tour with gourmet meals and five-star hotels, but there's more to doing these rides than just a vacation or an excuse for several days of quality miles.

Participating in one of these rides can be a rewarding experience, one that's punctuated with a full range of emotions. Riders have the personal satisfaction of covering the distances and of helping a worthy cause. To challenge yourself while raising funds for a worthy cause, consider doing a charity ride. These are a few of the larger rides, and there are probably other rides for local charities in your area:

➤ American Diabetes Society, 800-TOUR-888, www.diabetes.org

➤ Big Ride Across America, American Lung Association, 877-BIG RIDE, www.bigride.com

➤ Heartprints Across America, The Journey for the Cancer Cure, 888-349-2418

➤ Multiple Sclerosis Society, 212-476-0461

➤ Tanqueray American AIDS Ride, 800-825-1000

➤ Ride for a Reason, 888-89-RIDES

The Least You Need to Know

➤ Riding alone can be relaxing, but riding in a group can be big fun.

➤ You don't have to rely on the sun to light your ride.

➤ If there's no regularly scheduled ride in your area, it's easy to start one.

➤ The best way to learn to ride in a pack is to ride in a pack.

➤ You can do your part for charity while also enjoying a day or 10 of riding.

Chapter 21

Tandemonium!

> **In This Chapter**
>
> ➤ What's tandem cycling all about?
>
> ➤ How to ride a tandem
>
> ➤ Riding a tandem on the road
>
> ➤ Riding a tandem in the dirt
>
> ➤ Buying a tandem

They're big. They're fast. They're tons of fun, and they're becoming increasingly popular. What are they? They're tandems, or "bicycles built for two." For serious fun, on- or off-road, a tandem is a great way for two people to enjoy riding together. And they're the ultimate solution for couples of varying ability who otherwise would never ride together. "When we ride together on our single bikes, he's always having to wait for me," says my permanent tandem partner, Kathy. "On our tandems, we're always together. It's so much fun." Yes, she did say "tandems" plural. We have a road tandem and a mountain tandem with front and rear suspension and disc brakes. We love tandem riding that much.

In writing this chapter, I asked Kathy what she likes most about riding on the back of a tandem. Without hesitation, she replied, "I get to look around and enjoy the scenery." Unlike the rider on the front (called the *captain*), the rider on the back (the *stoker*) doesn't have to concentrate on watching the road. True, the view to the front is the captain's backside, but the stoker has free reign to look to either side.

Over the years, Kathy has spotted quite a few deer, coyotes, and other critters that I've missed. On the tandem, Kathy also becomes the official keeper of the snacks. It's nice being able to have her unwrap the PowerBars and peel the bananas. Jobs such as those are easy for stokers; their hands are free, and the captain's jersey pockets make a handy "glove compartment" for various snacks and incidental items. "It's great back there," she said, "I can reach for a Chapstick or put on or take off a jacket. I've fixed my ponytail, and a few times I've reached out and picked flowers and stuck them in my sweetie's hair," she said. On one occasion, she reached out, picked a wild raspberry, and popped it in my mouth. Lucky me.

Cyclebabble

The rider on the front of a tandem bicycle is called the **captain**, and the rider on the back is called the **stoker**.

Tandem-inspired smiles aren't limited to those who are astride them. On single bikes, we've often encountered hostility from motorists, but we've found that motorists and pedestrians alike are often roused into a friendly smile and wave by a passing tandem. While it's rare to have motorists strike up conversations with you at rest stops when you're riding a single bike, it's routine on a tandem. People like tandems, even if they don't quite understand them. A common comment we hear is, "The rider on the back has to pedal harder, doesn't she?" I don't know where this impression comes from. And nearly every aspiring comedian says something about Kathy putting her feet up and taking a break.

Miles of Experience

Being a tandem stoker can teach a rider a lot about riding a single bike. "I never shifted enough on my own bike before we started tandem riding," says my permanent stoker, Kathy. "It's a great way to learn by example," she added. "And it's helped me learn what a bike can really do. We've gone down nasty trails that I wouldn't have tried on my own bike, but doing them on the tandem gives me the confidence to later do them on my own bike."

Pilot and Co-Pilot

With a few quick pointers, most anybody can ride a tandem. Since steering a tandem requires the front rider to overcome the inertia of both riders' weight, putting the larger rider in front will make that job easier. For tandem teams where both riders are similar in size, putting the more experienced rider on the front is good idea.

To get started, the front rider, the captain, should straddle the bike and steady it by applying both brakes. With the captain steadying the bike, the rear rider, the stoker, climbs on and clicks into both pedals. Note that the captain should keep his or her feet splayed out to avoid getting smacked in the shins by the pedals as the stoker climbs aboard. Once the stoker is ready, the captain can count one, two, three, and push off.

During turns, the stoker needs to lean with the captain. A stoker who tries to be a backseat driver can throw the bike off balance. In turn, because the stoker has limited visibility of the road or trails ahead, an attentive captain calls out the ruts and potholes. Hitting them unexpectedly can give a stoker a pretty hard jolt. That's why suspension seat-posts are so popular among tandemites, even for road tandems. An attentive mountain bike captain also picks his or her lines very carefully when turning around rocks, stumps, or logs. A tandem's rear wheel follows a vastly different line than the front wheel, so that hunk of granite that just missed the captain's foot might be right in line to hit the stoker's foot. Captains need to remember that their back is a large stationary target for the stoker's fist should the stoker wish to seek revenge.

While the stoker position may at first seem like the raw end of this team deal, in reality the rider on the back enjoys many advantages over captaining or solo riding. While the stoker is enjoying the views and dishing out snacks, the captain is busy wrestling with the handlebars. Steering a tandem can be quite an arm workout, especially on a mountain tandem.

Cycology

While most tandems are the proverbial "bicycle built for two," bicycle builders have built tandems for three and more riders throughout the history of cycling. The record is a bicycle built for 10. Imagine seeing 10 riders barreling down a mountain trail!

Cycology

Riding a tandem involves learning to work as a team, dividing the workload, and compromising. For example, a captain who likes to spin high rpms and a stoker who likes to push big gears had better arrive at a happy medium, or their tandem rides will be constant arguments over when to shift gears. Like any good relationship, riding a tandem is all about give-and-take and being considerate of the other person.

Two for the Road

A road tandem can do practically everything that a single road bike can do. Tandem lovers take their two-seaters on club rides, weekend fun rides, and even on loaded tours. For sheer fun and exhilaration, the shared thrills aboard a good road tandem are hard to beat.

On flat sections or downhills, a tandem is faster than a single bike because it has twice the "motor," yet it still has only two wheels and is punching only one hole in the wind. That's how two reasonably fit riders on a tandem can ride away from a stronger single rider. A tandem can sometimes outrun a pack of single riders.

A road tandem offers the open road, exhilarating speed, and the opportunity for two people to enjoy that fun together.

I remember one Sunday morning ride with Kathy on southern California's Pacific Coast Highway. It was a typical sunny southern California day, and we were enjoying ocean views and a strong ocean tailwind. We were cruising along at nearly 30 miles an hour when I heard the distinct click of another bike shifting gears behind us. I turned around to see that we'd picked up a group of five riders following in our draft. "You guys want to come around?" I asked. The lead rider glanced back at his partners, looked back at me, and shook his head, "No." "Oh well," I thought. We towed them along for another five miles until we turned and they continued on—probably a little slower without us.

Two for the Trail

To many, the thought of riding a tandem on dirt trails is scary stuff. But in many ways, tandeming in the dirt is not much different than trail riding on a regular mountain bike. While it takes a bit more effort and planning to turn a tandem because of its length, that length is what gives tandems their phenomenal stability—they're the stretch limos of the bicycle world.

A bump that would send a single bike swapping sideways hardly causes a twitch on a tandem. You can take steep downhills at speed with confidence; the bike will stay straight. You can use the front brake aggressively with impunity—a tandem is not going to flip forward. Climbing is usually slower on a tandem, but when traction is limited, a tandem's extra weight allows it to dig in and climb where single bikes are getting wheelspin.

Cycology

Tandems are usually faster than a single bike, so imagine the speed of a pack of tandems in a race. That happens every year at the tandem-only Duet Cycling Classic in Eugene, Oregon. Many other regional races offer racing categories for tandems. Tandem racing also makes it possible for sight-impaired athletes to race. In fact, some of the strongest stokers in tandem racing are partially or completely blind.

In recent years, some of the greatest advancements in bicycle technology have been developed for downhill race bikes. Much of that new hardware has found its way to mountain tandems. Stout, long-travel downhill suspension forks do a fine job on the front of a mountain tandem. Oversize downhill hubs are perfect for mountain tandems because they can handle a tandem's weight and horsepower. With their weight and speed capabilities, mountain tandems make serious demands on brakes. The disc brake systems that work so well for downhill racers work splendidly on tandems. Take a mountain tandem with rear suspension, bolt on all the latest bits of downhill technology, and you'll have about the most sophisticated piece of machinery on the trail. For riders who love hardware and tinkering nearly as much as riding, a mountain tandem is a great way of satisfying both passions.

Cycology

Off-road riding on a tandem requires the captain to pay a bit more attention to the trail than when he or she is riding a single bike. A tandem has to maneuver around or plow over the bumps and ruts that a single rider would negotiate with a simple flick of the handlebar or a slight wheelie.

Miles of Experience

The braking needs of a tandem are many times those of a single bike. So when mountain bike disc brakes first became available, I had them installed on the front wheel of my old mountain tandem. It worked well, and Kathy and I finally had enough stopping power. However, on one particular ride, the disc brake tossed a brake pad, leaving us with only a standard rear brake. Being careful to keep our speed in control, I continually dragged the rear brake. Suddenly, the rear tire blew out. When I stopped to investigate, I discovered that the rear rim was as hot as a stove burner and that the inner tube had melted away!

For the most part, a mountain tandem can go anywhere a single bike can. Kathy and I have taken ours on group rides and on a five-day, off-road trip of the north rim of the Grand Canyon. We've ridden it on everything from fast fireroads to tight single-track trails. It's funny how skeptical other riders can be when they see we're joining them on a tandem. It doesn't take long for their skepticism to turn to sheer amazement when they see what kind of terrain a tandem can handle. We may lose some time on the climbs and have a little trouble with tight switchback turns, but we can hold our own most anywhere else. Give us a long, steep downhill, and we usually end up at the next crossroad, waiting for everyone else to catch up.

Tandem Shopping

Tandems come in a wide range of prices. If all you ever plan on doing is leisurely spins around the local park, then you might be happy with one of the budget models that sell for as little as $400. But if you try to go fast or off-road on a low-dollar tandem, you'll soon discover how flexible the frame is and how inadequate the brakes and drivetrain are. For anything beyond casual cruising, figure on budgeting at least $1,500. Of course, tandems are available at many price points beyond that amount, including some titanium models that nudge the $10,000 mark.

A good tandem is obviously not a minor investment—those behemoths can be expensive. So before laying out your hard-earned coin, carefully consider what type of tandem fits your style. Will you ride only on the road? If off-roading is in your plans, remember that mountain tandems are very versatile. Although off-roading on a road tandem is just inviting a spill, swapping a mountain tandem's knobby tires for road tread allows them to do just fine on paved surfaces. Although even that isn't entirely necessary because simply increasing the air pressure in knobbies does wonders to decrease their rolling resistance. Just be aware that knobbies don't do particularly well on paved corners. Some tandem aficionados prefer a mountain tandem for road use because the slightly smaller wheels are stronger.

Manufacturers specializing in tandems include Santana, Co-Motion, and da Vinci. They're the ones to see if you're interested in custom sizing or custom features and paint. Some of the mainstream manufacturers also have tandems in their line. The advantage to buying from these manufacturers is quick delivery and service from your local bike dealer. For serious mountain tandems, da Vinci, Ventana, or Santana are the companies to see. All have models with rear suspension.

Trek has two tandem models. The T200 with road bars, narrow tires, and a full complement of mounting brackets for racks makes a fine choice for pleasure riding, touring, or even racing. The lower-priced T100 is a hybrid design with a more upright rider position. It has 700c wheels, however, so it wouldn't be a good choice for off-road riding.

KHS has an extensive line of tandems in road models and mountain bike models. The Roma road tandem is especially nice with an aluminum frame, Campagnolo Mirage shifter/brake levers, and a suspension seat-post for the stoker. In 1998, KHS had a flagship off-road model, the aluminum-frame Tandemania FXT. For suspension, it had a Fox Vanilla shock and a Bullet USA ZZYZX fork up front. It was dropped for 1999, but if you can find a leftover, it's a great-performing bike and an

Cycology

Riding a road tandem in the dirt is an invitation to disaster, but a mountain tandem can do quite well on the road. For a real Cadillac ride, swap the knobby tires for some big, fat, 26" × 2" slicks such as Continental's Avenue tires. These large tires aren't as fast as narrow tires, but the ride and added control and stability are well worth the very slight loss of top speed.

excellent value. The Tandemania Alite, another aluminum model, comes with road tires and a rigid fork, but a switch to knobby tires and a suspension fork would make it a fine off-road machine.

Cannondale also has a full line of tandems. For roadies, the RT1000 or RT3000 both deserve consideration. Both have stoutly built aluminum frames. The RT1000 has a selection of Shimano XT and RSX drivetrain components and Avid Arch Rival 50 brakes; the RT3000 steps up to a mix of Shimano XTR and Ultegra drivetrain components and also a set of Avid Arch Rival brakes. Both road models have Cannondale's own Coda suspension seat-posts in the rear.

For off-road riding, Cannondale has the MT2000 and the MT3000, again with stout aluminum frames. The MT2000 has a rigid fork, a Shimano LX and XT drivetrain, Avid Arch Rival 50 brakes, and a Coda suspension seat-post for the stoker. The MT3000 has greater off-road potential than its MT2000 sibling thanks to Cannondale's own suspension fork, the HeadShok Moto FR with 100 mm of travel. Shimano XTR components handle shifting duties, and Magura hydraulic brakes provide plenty of stopping power. A Coda suspension seat-post for the stoker completes the package. Cannondale's Super V suspension bikes are excellent singles, but so far Cannondale hasn't responded to my prods to build a Super V rear-suspension tandem. Perhaps in 2000?

The Least You Need to Know

➤ For two people of diverse riding abilities, a tandem can be the great equalizer that enables them to finally ride together.

➤ The backseat of a tandem offers some of bicycling's best fun.

➤ A tandem can be the fastest people-powered vehicle on the road.

➤ There's not much that a single mountain bike can do that's beyond the capability of a mountain tandem.

Chapter 22

Wanna Race?

In This Chapter

➤ Race? Who me?

➤ Joining the pavement racers society

➤ Getting down and dirty

➤ The road to better racing results

Sooner or later most cyclists are asked, "Do you race?" Even if you bought your bike "just for exercise," admit it, the main reason you bought it was for fun. Take it from me, racing is more fun than you can imagine, and it's not as difficult to get started as you might think. In this chapter, I'll give you the low-down on racing. Get ready, get set, GO!

Are You Ready?

Yeah, I hear some of you. "But I'm not fast enough or strong enough to race!" Can you ride your road bike 10 miles? That's about the average length for most time-trial events. Can you ride in a road pack for just over a half-hour? In a lot of amateur road criterium events, the duration is scheduled as "one half-hour plus one lap." If mountain bikes are your thing, can you ride 10 miles of moderately challenging terrain? That's about the length of many beginner-class cross-country races. If downhill racing is more your cup of tea, can you get down your favorite downhill trail without crashing? If you can, then you're probably ready to do it against the clock.

All the different types of racing have categories for rank beginners. No one expects you to go out and challenge the pros and experts. As a new member of the clan of racers, simply finishing the event is often reward enough. Racing involves more than simply going out and riding as fast as you can. You must prepare yourself and your equipment, learn tactics, and develop skills, and the best way to learn about racing is to race.

Miles of Experience

Don't believe yourself when you say, "I'm too old to start racing." I know a man who didn't even start riding until he was 54. Two years later, he spent the summer traveling in his motor home to every NORBA National Championship mountain bike race. He came home with an armload of medals and a lifetime of memories. I also know a woman who took up racing at age 45. Ten years later, she's still going strong. Al Piemme took up sailboat racing upon his retirement. A few years later, he saw a photo of himself in his boat, asked, "Who's the fat guy?" and took up cycling. He races on the road and does mountain bike racing, too. At age 67, he spent the summer of '98 racing mountain bike downhill.

Taking It on the Road: Your First Road Race

Maybe you are one of those rare gifted individuals who'll go out and win your first road race and land a huge pro contract by the end of your first season. Or perhaps

Cyclebabble

DNF stands for Did Not Finish in the racing world.

you're like the vast majority of new racers: You'll make some mistakes, possibly score a few *DNFs*, and may even find yourself mid-race wondering why you ever decided to sign up in the first place. In practically every race I've ever done, somewhere along the way I thought about pulling out. Going beyond those thoughts and getting yourself to the finish line is what makes bike racing such a rewarding sport. Whether you finish first or thirty-first, there's always a feeling of accomplishment waiting at the end of a race. And racing is big fun!

A License to Speed

You're convinced: "Racing is fun; it's fast! Sign me up!" Well, there is a little red tape involved. In the United States, road racers and track racers need to be licensed by the USCF (United States Cycling Federation). In recent years, the USCF has made the licensing procedure quick and easy. Gone are the days of sending in a birth certificate and waiting weeks. Now, you can get licensed the day of an event and even get a $5, one-day license—a good option if you're not sure you'll race again or often.

An annual license is $35. Twenty dollars of that amount covers membership in USA Cycling. The USA Cycling fee is waived for racers under age 15. Mountain bike racers who are NORBA (National Off-Road Bicycle Association) members are already USA Cycling members, so adding a USCF license only costs $15.

USCF racers are divided into categories. New licensees start out at Category 5. Upgrades are based on experience and race results. Category 4 is the next step for novice riders; Category 3 is for intermediate riders with one to three years of experience. Category 2 is made up of advanced riders, and Category 1 riders are national-caliber amateurs who often compete with the pros.

There are also age-based categories for "masters" age 30 and above. Typically, race promoters offer masters categories divided into 5- or 10-year age ranges. For mass-start events, masters racing is the way to go for those of age. Those riders will feel a lot more comfortable knowing that everyone else out there also has to be at work on Monday.

Could you be the next Greg LeMond? You'll never know for sure unless you go out and mix it up. Try racing. I'll bet you'll love it.

Racing on Pavement: Time Trial, Road Race, Criterium, or Track?

Time-trial racing has been called "the race of truth." In this form of road racing, riders start individually in a race against the clock, so there's no team tactics or hiding in a pack.

For riders unsure of their racing forte or those who feel unprepared to mix it up in a tight pack, time trials are the perfect way to start racing. You can compare your speed against other riders without having to ride elbow to elbow. Many areas have weekly or monthly time trials on the same course, providing a perfect way to gauge fitness progress.

Time-trial specialists use aerodynamic bars, frames, wheels, and even helmets, but don't fret about your own lack of aero-exotica. For starting out, a standard bike will do fine. You can make a big improvement with just an aero bar extension, something that costs as little as $40.

Long-distance road racing is what most people think of as bicycle racing. Racing in a large pack of riders and covering 50 or 100 miles is quite a thrill. If you're already used to riding in a tight group, don't hesitate to jump into road racing. If bumping elbows sounds sketchy, go along on some club rides to get better accustomed to close formations.

With the logistic challenges of closing long stretches of road for road races, closed-course criterium racing is the most common type of road racing in the United States. Criterium races are multilap events held on courses ranging from a half-mile to two or three miles per lap. They're generally held in parks, streets of industrial parks, or parking lots.

Criterium racing is very intense with little or no climbing, so speeds remain high, and the pack tends to stay bunched. With so many corners, occasional bumping and jostling for position is normal. To be good in criteriums requires a strong sprint and feeling at ease while bumping elbows and occasionally buzzing tires.

Cycology

There are a few reasons that track bikes don't have brakes. One is actually a safety issue—with the tight formations that track racers ride in having a rider slow down abruptly could result in a multi-rider crash. And the same direct drive that prevents coasting also allows a rider to apply back pressure on the pedals for subtle reductions in speed, making brakes unnecessary.

For those fortunate enough to live close to one of the few velodromes in the United States, track racing is one of the most exciting and intense forms of racing imaginable. The ultra-smooth surface and steep banked corners of a velodrome create a riding experience that's hard to describe.

Track bikes are unique in that they're direct drive, which means no coasting, no derailleurs, and no brakes. Track events range from short sprints to multilap distances. There are team events, individual events, and the highly tactical match sprint events with one-on-one action.

Now that you know what kind of races are out there, where do you go about finding a race? Contact the USCF to find out about road races or a velodrome in your area. Racing-oriented shops are another source of racing info. While your average mom-and-pop bike shop would probably be able to dig for information on local races, a race-oriented shop will probably have race flyers posted on the wall. Heck, you can probably mooch a ride to a race from someone there. Wherever you live, there's probably a racing club nearby. USCF clubs promote activities such as training rides, clinics, races, and social events. After you sign up, it's time to prepare.

Before Race Day

If you've already sent for a USCF license, it's a good idea to pre-enter upcoming events by mail to minimize race-day hassle. Prior to race day, give your bike a thorough going-over. At most events, your bike will be inspected before you will be allowed on the course. Check that the handlebars and stem are tight and that the handlebars have plugs in the ends. Inspect the tires for cuts or sidewall damage. Check that the cranks and pedals are tight and that the wheels spin straight.

To reduce the chance of forgetting essentials, pack your gearbag at least a day before the event. Remember to bring your license (I've forgotten mine a time or two). Don't forget to bring along a towel for cleaning up after the race and a change of clothes to avoid hanging around in a clammy chamois. The night before, pack an ice chest or sack lunch; food service isn't usually available.

Cycology

The night before a race can be a night of nervousness, especially for a new racer. That anxiety can make it easy to forget essential items. Avoid the frustration of getting all the way to a race only to discover that you've forgotten your shoes, helmet, or license. Make a list of everything you'll need and check off each item as you gather up your race day supplies. Do this at least a day before the race, so if something turns up missing, you'll have plenty of time to find it.

The Big Day

Arrive early for your race and get right to registration, even if you've pre-entered—entries sometimes get lost in the mail. Besides, it's a good idea to get your race numbers before the last-minute rush. Double-check the scheduled time of your event. Pay careful attention to where the promoters want you to place your numbers. Placement will vary with the race depending on where the scorekeepers are located.

Usually there's a mandatory riders' meeting. Be there. Riders' meetings often have important information such as warnings of a gravelly corner, instructions on the day's free-lap policy, or announcements of *primes*.

Cyclebabble

A **prime** (pronounced *preem*) is a prize or cash award given for being the leader of the pack across the line on a given lap during a race.

If the race is a criterium, ride a few laps of the course during open warm-up. Often, packs will form during warm-ups. Jump into one to learn the flow of the course. Which side of the road does the pack tend to stay on? What are the pack-lines through the corners (a group of riders will often follow a vastly different route than a solo rider)? Are there any potholes or manhole covers to cause concern?

Mass-start road events sometimes start out easy, building speed gradually; then again, they often start as though the pack were fired from a cannon. You should do a thorough warm-up prior to racing in case of early attacks. For a warm-up, ride at least a half-hour, gradually picking up the tempo so that you'll reach your racing heart rate at least once. Better still, warm up on rollers or a stationary trainer (see Chapter 13, "Spinning Wheels: Indoor Workouts") to avoid getting distracted by roadside chats or getting a last-minute flat.

Get to the starting line early; there may be last-minute instructions. If it's a time trial, watch the riders ahead of you to learn the starting drill. If it's a mass-start event and you're feeling confident, arrive early to get a front position. When the race gets going, look for smooth riders and stick to them, avoiding those weaving, sloppy riders who might cross a wheel and go down, taking you with them. Throughout the race, remember that you're surrounded; stay smooth and hold your line through the corners.

Before you know it, your first race will be over. Whether you won, flatted, crashed, or came in thirty-ninth, realize that no matter the outcome, your day's experiences have been shared countless times by racers everywhere. Congratulations, you're now a member of the few, the proud, the racers. For more information on the USCF and racing, call 719-578-4949.

Get Down and Dirty: Your First Mountain Bike Race

So you think that you're the next hot downhill racer, and you're ready to teach Missy Giove or Shaun Palmer the fine art of mountain bike racing? Want to show Kirk Molday or Ruthie Matthes a thing or three about cross-country? Maybe you just like to race against your riding buddies. Whatever your racing ambitions, you have to start somewhere.

Most mountain bike races are sanctioned by NORBA and require a NORBA license. Licenses are available at most events, but I recommend getting one by mail prior to your first race—the line to get a license can be awfully long on race day. A one-year license is $35. Twenty dollars of that is membership in USA Cycling. USCF members already are USA Cycling members, so adding a NORBA license is only $15. A one-day license is $5.

New licensees and novices race as Beginners. The next step is Sport, for intermediate riders. Advanced riders race as Expert. A few years ago, NORBA created a new category called Elite that fits between Expert and Pro. It's now called Semi-Pro and provides means for aspiring riders to move up from Expert without getting massacred by the Pros. The highest category is Pro, for national- and world-caliber riders.

Choosing Your Course

The two most common types of mountain bike races are cross-country and downhill. Cross-country courses vary. Some are held on a small course of three to eight miles, and riders do multiple laps. Other courses make one big lap of 15, 20, or even 30 or more miles. The rare courses (and sometimes the most fun) are the point-to-point races where riders leave from the starting line and then need to be shuttled back from the finish line.

A cross-country race isn't just a Sunday morning ride. It's intense, exhilarating, sometimes grueling, and always fun.

Race promoters generally offer a shorter course for Beginners, perhaps 9 to 12 miles. Sport racers usually go longer; Experts go longer still. Promoters try to keep the Semi-Pros and Pros racing for about three hours, or roughly 30 miles, depending on the terrain. Within the different classes, promoters divide up the field by age group. A 30-year-old rider doesn't usually have to race against 20-year-olds, for instance. There might be a 30 to 39 or 30 to 35 age group, for example.

The format for downhill racing is simple: Riders start individually for a solo run against the clock. Courses vary. Some of the best courses are at ski resorts. Ski resort owners quickly figured out that their otherwise dormant chair-lifts could be put to use in the off-season by shuttling mountain bike riders to the top of the mountain. Factor in the steep terrain of your average ski resort, and it's obvious why Big Bear, Mammoth, Mt. Snow, and Breckenridge all host national championship downhill events.

In the early days of downhill racing, the typical course was a high-speed blast down dirt access roads with wide, sweeping corners. The famed Kamikaze

Cycology

For a time, the courses in Europe were far more difficult than U.S. courses. Over the past couple of seasons, however, promoters have risen to the European level of difficulty. Part of that change is that the promoters have begun building pro-only courses and offering easier, safer courses to amateur riders.

course at Mammoth ski resort in California typified the old style with speeds beyond 60 mph being common and there being only one moderately tight corner. Gradually, the courses have become more and more technical. Today's courses often have steep drop-in pitches that are only a few degrees short of qualifying as a cliff. Plunges between huge rocks are common, as are drop-off jumps and motocross-style jumps. Courses now have 50 or more corners compared to the nine corners of the Kamikaze.

Miles of Experience

Winning is fun, of course. But each race has only one winner, which isn't to say that the rest of the racers didn't have fun—far from it. Some of the most fun I've ever had has been in fierce battles in the middle of the pack. One particular mountain bike race comes to mind where three other riders and myself waged an intense struggle for position. We passed back and forth with some pulling ground on the uphills; others pulled passes with their downhill skills or cornering prowess. We stayed together for most of the 20-mile event. In the end, the fastest of our quartet managed to finish twenty-third that day; I was twenty-fifth. Even though I've finished much better than twenty-fifth place many times before and since, I count that fierce battle for twenty-fifth as one of the most fun racing days of my life.

Trials is another form of mountain bike competition. Trials isn't a contest of speed; it's one of sheer skill. Riders ride individually through short sections of the most technically difficult terrain imaginable as observers score them. Each time a rider puts a foot down, or *dabs* as it's called, the rider is assessed one point. Falling is five points. Lowest score after all the sections wins. It's common for a section to require a rider to hop up onto a log 40 inches high, and then hop onto another log three feet away. Going up steep cliffs or riding over cars or boulders are common obstacles for trials riders. Trials are extremely entertaining to watch and are very difficult to master. It's always been a small fringe sport within mountain biking.

In the early days of mountain bike racing, nearly every race had a hillclimb event. Usually a mass-start event, the course typically ran from the bottom of the ski resort to the top. Elevation gains of 1,000 to 2,000 feet were common. These days, hillclimbs are a rarity with only a few nationals and classic events still hosting them, and that's too bad. Hillclimbs were and still are the purest test of mountain biking fitness.

Cyclebabble

Dabbing is when a rider in a mountain bike trials competition puts his or her foot down.

Downhill racing offers thrills, excitement, and a chance to test your riding skills.

Race-Day Countdown

Whether your first race is cross-country or downhill, you'll race much faster, safer, and with more confidence if you ride the course before the race. Often, promoters will mark the courses or at least be able to tell you the course a week or more before the race.

For downhill practicing, take it slow the first time to learn the course and to avoid surprise obstacles that could cause a crash. Carefully analyze any difficult sections. Getting off and walking through often helps in finding the good line. Watch other riders to see what works and what doesn't. If possible, follow a faster rider down.

Pre-riding a cross-country course is especially valuable. Knowing what's around the next corner can make the difference between slowing down for it or upshifting and pedaling through. Just as in downhilling, learning how to ride the tricky sections can save time and prevent crashes. Perhaps the most valuable aspect of pre-riding is knowing just how long the race is. I've often heard racers say, "I could have pushed harder, but I didn't know how much further it was." Knowing the end is near is helpful in putting out that last bit of effort.

During the week before the race, make sure that your bike is in good working order. If your bike needs any new parts, be sure to ride the bike again after installing them to avoid last-minute adjustments on race day. Pack up your riding gear and equipment early and double-check that everything is there. After you drive to a race site in the boonies, you don't want to discover that essential equipment is back in the garage.

The night before the race, drink plenty of water and eat a normal-sized dinner. Avoid overdoing the "carbo-loading." You'll sleep better without a bloated belly.

The Big Day

Wake up early if necessary so that you can eat a good breakfast about three to five hours before your race. Continue snacking all morning. Choose snacks such as bananas, grapes, bagels, or sports bars. Continue taking in plenty of water, especially if the weather is hot or the race is at a high altitude. Arrive early and go directly to registration. You can save time by pre-registering by mail. But still go directly to registration upon arrival just in case your entry got lost in the mail. Check your start time and install your numberplate.

Whether you're racing cross-country or downhill, take the bike out for a short ride to make sure everything is still working well. Many races will have a booth offering tech support provided by a local bike shop or component manufacturer. If you discover problems and they're beyond your mechanical ability, get to the tech support booth as early as possible. The lines can get long.

If you're racing downhill, get in a few practice runs. Go easy on the first run, even if you know the course—the course may have been changed since you last rode it. Try not to go all out in practice. Instead, concentrate on going as quickly and smoothly as you can while expending as little effort as possible. Go ahead and hammer a section or two during each run; just don't go race pace the whole time.

Warming up is important for cross-country racers and downhillers. Downhillers should get to the top of the course with plenty of time to warm up. Although you can warm up by simply riding around, experienced riders bring along a stationary trainer just for warming up (see Chapter 13). Spend 15 to 30 minutes on the trainer. Gradually build speed to reach your racing heart rate. Time your warm-up so that you'll reach your peak just a few minutes before your start time. You want to get on the start good and sweaty, with your heart still pumping hard.

Cross-country races start out hard and fast, so being warmed up is especially important. It's a good idea for cross-country racers to ride the first mile or so of the course. What happens in those first few minutes can affect the entire race, especially if a single-track is near the beginning of the course. For a good, thorough warm-up, it's tough to beat a session on a stationary trainer. Not

Cycology

One of the best ways to learn a course is to walk the course. Most pros will hike up or down the course sometime in the days leading up to a race. Seeing the course on foot often provides vantage points and possible lines to take that you would miss while riding. And don't forget to look up at the course, too. You'll often spot good lines that you'll miss by only looking down at the course.

only can you get your heart up to racing rate, you can also do it without losing warm-up time to socializing. Racing buddies can still visit while you spin on the trainer next to your car, and you don't have to stop pedaling.

Whether the day's race is downhill or cross-country, a thorough warm-up before competing is very important.

Racers to the Line

If you've followed this book's advice, you'll arrive at the starting line well-hydrated, well-fed, well-warmed up, and well-prepared. So you should do … well.

Downhill racers should watch riders ahead of them to learn the starting drill. You can gain a second or more with good starting technique. Many downhill races have an automatic starting gate with a series of beeps that count down the last few seconds before your start. Do I go on the fourth beep or the fifth beep? Keep a cool head throughout your run. I've seen racers do excellently in practice only to throw it all away in the race by trying to go too fast. Concentrate on the lines you used in practice. Anticipate your gear changes and braking points and pedal like mad whenever possible. It'll all be over in just a few minutes!

Cross-country riders should arrive early to get a starting position near the front—it's hard to do well if you start in sixty-third place. Listen for any last-minute instructions, especially those concerning the number of laps or turn-offs for beginners. When the whistle blows, it's time to go. Go at your own pace, and don't worry too much about the jackrabbit racers ahead of you. You might catch and pass a lot of them later by keeping your pace. Drink plenty of water throughout the race. If you have to walk a steep

329

section, remember that racers still on their bikes have the right-of-way, so step off the good line to let them by. If you catch a slower rider on the single-track, by NORBA rules the command "Track" is your signal for that rider to let you by as soon as it's safe.

When it's all over, whether you crashed and burned or annihilated your class, hang around, clean up, and change into your casual clothes. Find some friends, join them for lunch, and wait for the results to be posted. If none of your friends are there, make some. Mountain bike racers are friendly people, and you're one of us now! For more information on NORBA and racing, call 719-578-4949.

Improving Your Racing Results

Hold this book out at arm's length. Kinda heavy, isn't it? There are several books at least as big as this one devoted entirely to cycling training, so over the next few pages I'm only going to touch on the highlights.

We've all heard that old saying, "What doesn't kill you will make you stronger." There's much truth to that. Going through everyday life, a human being's body grows accustomed to a certain level of activity and exertion. Push that body beyond its normal level through exercise and then give it a period of rest to recover, and that body will adapt itself for future episodes of increased exertion by making itself stronger. Simple, eh? As a bike racer, you must ask yourself what type of strength you wish to increase. Do you want greater endurance? Do you want a faster sprint? Do you want to climb better? If you're like most riders, you want to develop a balance of all these strengths.

Thumps Per Minute

Virtually all top trainers use their riders' heart rates as a means of quantifying effort. Measured in beats per minute, heart rate is a reliable indicator of how hard a rider is working. By tracking heart rate daily during training and during rest time, a rider can gauge improvement. Heart rate is also a valuable tool in recognizing the early signs of fatigue and overtraining. Although it's possible to calculate heart rate by taking a pulse, that's not always practical during training. That's why many racers use electronic heart-rate monitors. For more on heart-rate monitors and their use, refer to Chapter 12 under "Getting Technical: Heart Monitors."

Miles of Experience

I like to wear a heart-rate monitor during a race. I know what heart rate I can maintain and what heart rate has me on the verge of "blowing up." Knowing this, I can increase or decrease my efforts accordingly.

Many pro racers compete wearing heart-rate monitors that store data to later be downloaded to a computer. After a race, the racer and his/her trainer can make a minute-by-minute graph of the efforts throughout the race. A knowledgeable trainer can use this data to identify strengths and weaknesses and to help the athlete in creating a training program to build those strengths and eliminate those weaknesses.

Here's something interesting. John Tomac, a professional racer who has won in nearly every type of cycling, is now concentrating on downhill racing. His heart-rate download routinely shows heart rates of 200+ beats per minute. (Don't think for a moment that downhill racing is easy!)

Piles of Miles

Many new racers get the impression that the key to racing success is to pile on as many miles as humanly possible. This is true to a point. Amassing a good foundation of base miles is important to prevent stress injuries to muscles and connective tissues.

Equally important is the quality of the miles you ride. Although easy pace rides are an important means toward recovering from races and hard training, riders who spend most of their training plodding along at slow to medium speeds are training for plodding along at slow to medium speeds. Make sure you ride at race pace as part of your training.

Climb Like a Goat

On mountain bikes or road bikes, it's usually the little riders who excel at going uphill. A slight build, virtually zero body fat, and an exceptional cardiovascular system characterize the body types of the best climbers in the business. However, not all of these riders' climbing abilities came as gifts from nature. To truly shine as climbers, these riders have also followed specific training and have learned certain skills. Although a larger rider can't make up for not having the climber's genes, bigger riders can certainly improve their climbing ability by applying the same training and skills.

Climbing works your muscles differently than most other aspects of cycling do. The slower cadence and intensity of the effort makes climbing one of the most strenuous cycling activities. The main muscles used in climbing are the gluteus maximus (butt muscles), the quadriceps (muscles on the front of the thighs), the calf muscles, the hamstrings, and the lower back muscles. Strengthening these muscles will improve your climbing performance.

The most basic way to enhance the muscles used in climbing is to climb hills often and as quickly as possible. Most successful climbers devote at least one day of their weekly training schedule to hill work. Those who want to do more than that should have at least one day of no hill work between climbing sessions to give the muscles a chance to recover. Before starting a regular schedule of hill climbing work, be sure that you have a good foundation of base miles in your legs. Hard climbing work can damage knees and tear muscles if you don't work up to it.

Another means of strengthening the climbing muscles is weight training and floor exercises. An effective method of working the glutes and thigh muscles is doing *squats*, a weight exercise where a barbell is placed across the shoulders and the person squats down until the buttocks are about even with the knees. Lowering to that level may be difficult at first. If so, try working up to it by squatting down to whatever level is comfortable and gradually work your way lower.

When doing squats, you should have a partner watching. Injuries from squats are common because once fatigue sets in, the person may find that they don't have enough strength to rise back up from the full squatted position. Many weight facilities have special *squat racks*, a rectangular frame with adjustable crossbars to support the barbell should a person find themselves stuck in that position.

Cycology

When weight training, bear in mind that you want to build endurance and strength, not bulk. Added muscle mass is just more weight to haul up the hills. So avoid lifting heavy weight loads and ignore the tips of well-meaning friends or weight room trainers who want to pass on body-building tips. Low- to medium-weight loads and multiple repetitions are what you want.

Steer Clear

Don't place your chin on your chest when you're doing sit-ups. Doing that makes you prone to curling to the up position instead of sitting up, thus not working the muscles as well.

Step-ups are an exercise that are nearly as effective as squats and are safer to do alone or without a squat rack. To do step-ups, find a solid bench or crate about a foot high, take a barbell of perhaps only a third of the weight you would use for squats, and place the barbell across your shoulders. Place one foot on the platform and then step up with the other foot. Step back down. Repeat the exercise 10 to 20 times, and then repeat it with the other foot.

Most exercises that strengthen the back muscles also work the abdominal muscles. Strong abs help a rider support the upper body and take some of the load off the back muscles, which are already being exerted with climbing. Sit-ups, those old stand-bys from high school gym class, are still an effective means of toning up soft tummies and weak backs. Do sit-ups with bent knees to avoid back injury. If you don't have a sit-up board, have a partner hold your feet. Slipping them under the low opening of a couch or cabinet works, too. You can place your arms behind your head, but in that position many people can't resist using the arms to help them rise up. That's why I recommend folding them across your chest. I like to do sit-ups with my back bolt straight for added back muscle work. As the weeks pass and sit-ups become easier, you can increase their effectiveness by holding a weight across your chest as you sit up or by raising your slant board, if you have one.

Riders who put their bikes on a stationary trainer for workout sessions during inclement weather may be surprised to learn that they don't have to just pedal along. They can work on climbing, too. By placing a block under the front wheel to raise the front of the bike, you can duplicate the body position of climbing. Pedaling in that position works the muscles slightly differently than when you pedal on level ground. Use higher resistance and/or higher gears, and your body will be convinced it's heading up a mountain road.

All that training will make you a stronger climber, but what can you do to make use of the strength you have? Try these climbing tips:

➤ **Shift early.** Many riders get overly ambitious, try to climb in too high of a gear, and stubbornly keep pedaling in that gear until their cadence drops too low. By shifting before your cadence and speed drop, you can keep your momentum. Also, trying to shift at a low rpm and a high power output is hard on the shifting system. The drivetrains of old almost wouldn't shift under power; the fact that the modern ones do is a wonder of new technology. Still, if anything will make a modern drivetrain malfunction, this will.

➤ **Stand and deliver.** Standing up and using your body weight can be very effective for short climbs. It's also good for unleashing a quick burst of speed to pass other riders or to pull away from them at the top of a hill. It's not very efficient for very long, however, because it quickly tires you out.

➤ **Follow the straightest line between two points.** Traversing back and forth on a hill can make climbing it a little easier by effectively making it less steep. The added distance won't help you go any faster, though. By keeping the bike pointed straight, you'll travel only the minimum distance.

➤ **Pull on the brake hoods or bar-ends.** Road riders can generate a little more power by climbing with the hands on the brake hoods and pulling upward on the hood as the leg on the same side goes downward. Mountain bikers can accomplish the same thing by using handlebar bar-ends.

➤ **Vary your riding position.** Changing riding position will combat the fatigue of climbing by giving a rest to some muscles while others take the load. On a long climb, standing for short periods can give your back and buns a break. As efficient as it is for road riders to climb with their hands on the brake hoods, it's also tiresome on the arms and shoulders; these riders can give their arms a break by moving their hands to the top of the handlebars or even stretch their backs by putting their hands down in the hooks.

Many riders sit forward on the saddle when climbing, which can make the downward portion of the pedal spin a bit more efficient, but it's also hard on the crotch. Give the tender bits a break by occasionally sliding back in the saddle. You can help make up the power difference by putting a little more effort into pedaling over the top of your spin.

➤ **Pick a pacer.** It's all too easy to become preoccupied with the effort and strain of climbing and forget to concentrate on keeping your rhythm and pace. If you're in a race or group ride, pick a rider (known as a *pacer*) about your speed or perhaps a little faster and do your best to stick with that rider on climbs. You'll know immediately if your speed is dropping because your pacer will begin to pull away from you. You may even want to match your pacer's cadence.

➤ **Use your computer's cadence function.** If you have a cyclometer that shows cadence, monitor that function instead of speed. A drop in rpms will show long before the computer registers a drop of one mile per hour.

Many feel that climbing is the true test of a rider's strength and determination.

Become a Speed Demon

By now, you can probably guess that to develop more riding speed, you must push yourself to ride faster. But going out and trying to go as fast as you can for an entire ride will only exhaust you—quite quickly, I might add. To train for increased top-speed potential, most racers do *intervals*. Don't confuse intervals with sprints. A sprint is going 100 percent, as fast as you can; an interval is going about 90 percent, keeping some effort in reserve so that you can keep that speed longer.

There's no set formula for creating a good interval workout. Different riders and coaches use successfully varying distances and efforts. The following is but one example of an interval workout for a beginner racer.

Our beginner's interval example is for a 20-mile ride. Our beginner knows that by keeping a fairly hard pace, perhaps with a heart rate of about 80 percent of his maximum, he can ride that distance in about an hour. He starts out by riding perhaps 15 mph for the first mile or so until he's broken a sweat. In the next couple of miles, he picks up his speed so that his heart rate is at about 65 percent of his maximum. By about the fifth mile, he wants to have increased his speed to have his heart rate up to about 75 percent of his maximum.

He keeps that pace until mile 10, when the intervals begin. He rides mile 11 at 90 percent of his maximum heart rate. In mile 12, he slows down so that his heart rate drops back down to 75 percent. Mile 13 is another 90 percent effort, and mile 14 is another 75 percent recovery period. Mile 15 is yet another hard effort, and on mile 16, he drops back to 75 percent, where he stays for the rest of the ride, with that last four miles being a cool-down and recovery. A beginner who does this workout once or twice a week will see improved speed quickly. As fitness improves, the total mileage of the session and the number of intervals can increase for even more speed gain.

Speed Courtesy of Honda

Riding in the slipstream of a motorcycle has long been a training method for cyclists to improve their speed. By riding closely behind the motorcycle, the bicyclist isn't fighting the wind and can ride much faster. This type of training is called *motorpacing*. A rider who can maintain a speed of perhaps 20 mph can probably ride at 30 mph while motorpacing. Motorpacing develops the leg speed, which translates into higher bike speeds.

Motorpacing is relatively safe as long as you do it away from traffic and certainly not on busy city streets. The legalities of motorpacing on public roads are vague. I've seen motorpacing riders zip by highway patrol without receiving so much as a glance from the officer, and I've heard of riders being cited for following too closely. Perhaps you can find some private property suitable for motorpacing, such as a large parking lot.

Cyclebabble

Intervals are a series of hard, fast efforts divided by periods of moderate speeds and efforts for recovery.

Cycology

Sprinting ability is dependent on a rider's fast-twitch muscles. These muscles are the ones that perform during short, fast efforts, as opposed to the slow-twitch muscles that contribute to a rider's endurance. Whether you have more fast-twitch or slow-twitch muscles is largely a matter of genetics. So if you can't sprint to save your life, the blame rests solely on your parents and grandparents. (There's a rousing topic for your next family gathering: "Pass the gravy, Grandpa. And by the way, Gramps, did you know that's it's your fault that I got passed at the finish line at the state finals?") But all is not lost. You can make up for lousy genetics with specific training.

The Sprint of a Cheetah

Many different racing situations call for a strong sprint. A mountain bike racer needs a sprint for open sections and a sprint from lower speed to accelerate out of corners. The sprint that a road racer wants for the high-speed free-for-all at the finish line is different from the sprint needed to close the gap when another rider tries to pull away.

To practice your sprints, try to find a loop of perhaps a $1/2$ to $3/4$ mile, one that has a hill that takes about a half minute of hard riding to climb. If you can't do it as a loop, find a straight stretch of suitable road with an appropriate hill and do your sprints as an out-and-back route.

Do sprints when you're fairly fresh, but make sure you get in a good warm-up first, perhaps five miles. Hard efforts on cold legs can lead to injuries such as pulled muscles and tendons. An effective warm-up is a good 15 to 20 minutes of riding, gradually increasing the pace. Start riding your sprint course at a hard level of effort, perhaps 80 to 85 percent of your maximum heart rate. If you don't have a heart-rate monitor, gauge the effort by how hard you're breathing and whether you feel you could speak more than a few words.

Cycology

Whether you sit or stand for the sprint is up to you. I recommend doing it both ways, perhaps alternating on each sprint. The physical requirements of standing sprints and sitting sprints are slightly different, but both are valuable. Develop them both.

At the bottom of the climb, begin your all-out, 100-percent effort. At the crest of the hill, drop back to the 80- to 85-percent effort. Repeat the sprint six times. Take a 10-minute break by continuing to spin along at a low effort, and then do another series of sprints. Do five sets of six sprints, taking a 10-minute recovery period after each set.

A less structured means of improving your sprint is to work a few sprints into your rides. Sprint for a city limit sign or a cross street. Vary the distance from perhaps 100 feet to 100 to 200 yards and even more. Working in a few sprints can make group rides a little more fun and little more interesting: "Last one to the speed-limit sign buys the bagels!"

Few riders are gifted with the ability to unleash a sudden burst of speed to be able to pull away like this rider. Developing a strong sprint takes training.

Group Speed Work on the Road

Throughout the United States in areas where road racing is popular, you can usually find regularly scheduled fast training rides. Joining in on one of these rides is an ideal way to develop speed. The workout is much the same as motorpacing, and you'll also learn how to ride in a pack. To find these training rides, check with a race-oriented bike shop. Regional bike publications are another good source for scheduled training rides, as are cycling clubs.

There are many types of training rides. Some are basically a practice criterium race with an hour of laps around a small course in a park or on unused streets. Others are 50 or 100 miles with hills and varying terrain. The organizers of rides that attract large numbers of riders will often divide the riders into separate groups according to their speed and ability. On rides where they don't divide the riders, division usually happens by natural selection in the first few miles. Regardless, don't be intimidated about having to try to keep up with riders much faster than you. One way or another, you'll end up with riders going your own pace.

Group Speed Work in the Dirt

Finding a regularly scheduled mountain bike training ride is much the same as finding a road training ride; check with shops, clubs, and regional cycling publications. The rides themselves usually aren't as structured, however. Most of the road training rides I've attended have started promptly at the scheduled time, but mountain bike riders tend to be a more casual bunch. I used to do a Saturday morning ride that was scheduled for 8 a.m., but it never got going before 8:30. It eventually became the "Saturday 9 o'clock ride." It's still going. I'll bet it leaves at 10 a.m. now.

The route of a mountain bike training ride usually depends on the available terrain. In urban areas, it might be the same trail every week, using whatever limited trails and dirt roads are available. In an area with several different trail options, the ride might be different every week. Usually the fastest riders determine the day's route with a "Follow us." It's something of a mountain bike tradition that those fast riders rocket away and then wait at the top of a hill or at the next fork in the road. When the last straggler catches up, they take off again.

Riding with a fast group will improve your fitness as you work to keep up; it will also help you to learn bike-handling skills. By following another rider over difficult terrain, you get a visual demonstration on how to ride each section of trail. Often you'll find yourself riding much faster than you would if you were riding alone.

The Least You Need to Know

➤ You don't need to be an awesome rider to enjoy racing.

➤ An individual time trial against the clock is an ideal way of gauging your speed without having to ride in a crowded pack of riders.

➤ The difference between a downhill course and cliff is that the downhill course has banners running down each side.

➤ Riding lots of miles at slow speeds will prepare you only for long, slow races.

➤ To develop climbing, speed, and sprinting ability, you must practice.

Chapter 23

Beyond a Three-Hour Tour

In This Chapter

➤ How to take a vacation by bike

➤ Destination and route planning

➤ Edibles on two wheels

➤ A Hudson's Bay start

➤ Touring by gold card

Before the popularity of mountain biking began to boom in the mid- to late '80s, bicycling in the United States had been enjoying another type of boom: bicycle touring. Throughout the '70s and '80s, thousands of cyclists took to the roads aboard bikes laden with camping gear.

For those seeking adventure and for those wishing to truly experience a destination, bicycle touring is a blast. Aboard a bike, you're out in the world and able to really see the sights, smell the air, and get in touch with your surroundings in ways that are unimaginable when you're traveling inside a four-door, air-conditioned cocoon.

There are many ways to tour. Some like to do it on the road; others enjoy *bike-packing*, which is backpacking aboard mountain bikes. Whether you prefer being completely away from civilization on a wilderness trip or prefer riding on pavement, there's a touring destination that's right for you.

Loaded with camping gear and provisions, this bike is ready to take on the world (or at least a small corner of it).

Plan Your Play; Play Your Plan

Going on a bicycle adventure with an outfitted tour doesn't fit everyone's personality or budget. Some would rather go it alone or with a small group without the rigid structure and expense of an outfitter. To have an enjoyable extended tour without the benefit of support vans and support staff takes careful planning and forethought.

Destinations for a bicycle adventure are virtually endless. First, decide on whether yours will be a road quest or a mountain bike quest. Of course, there is the option of having a trip be both by using a mountain bike and mounting road tires for the paved portions. Next, consider whether you want to do a point-to-point trip and carry all supplies and equipment on the bike or drive or fly to a destination and take in different local rides.

Take an honest assessment of your own fitness and riding level. Someone who rides a flat bike path every other weekend shouldn't fool himself or herself into thinking he or she would enjoy a mountain bike trip to the Continental Divide or a road bike trip to the Swiss Alps. It's an expensive lessen to learn. Remember, too, that budgeting funds for a trip is only part of the equation. You also want to budget time before the trip to log some miles. Being exhausted and toppling over with cramps aren't conducive to an enjoyable trip.

Help on gathering data to help decide on a destination is as close as your nearest travel agent, who can provide toll-free numbers for tourist bureaus. Spend a little time on the phone, and within weeks your mailbox can be stuffed with full-color catalogs from every state and practically any country.

It's very important to go into such an adventure fully prepared to toss your well-engineered plans right out the window. There are so many things that can disrupt a schedule: a crash, a riding partner who falls ill, a mechanical breakdown, realizing that your mileage projections were too ambitious or too cautious. Or you could meet up with another group of riders and decide that their itinerary sounds like more fun. Whatever the reason, don't become upset by a change in plans. Go with it and realize that even the most disastrous situations usually seem funny when reflected upon after the trip.

Where in the World Should I Go?

A road map is just the beginning in planning a tour route. The major highways are best avoided; having Peterbilts and Winnebagos whizzing by at 70 mph is hardly conducive to peaceful riding. Look for the secondary roads that parallel the highways. They're sure to be less traveled and are probably more scenic. Chances are, they'll take longer than the highways, but on a tour, the experience of the ride takes priority over reaching the destinations.

A good source of information on good rides and routes is local bike shops. A shop staffed by enthusiastic cyclists and racers is your best source for local rides and suitable touring routes. They may even be able to provide information about local club rides or even invite you on their own shop ride. The chambers of commerce in the areas in which you plan to ride can usually provide the names and numbers of the shops. Realize that for some shops, especially in rural areas, bikes are only a sideline. Although Earl's Lawnmowers, Bikes, and Locksmithing may not necessarily know much about local rides, Earl can probably steer you to a nearby shop that does.

Or you can learn from the pros. With so many tour companies operating, there's a good chance that one or more of them has a trip in your chosen area. Their brochures will offer good hints on what routes are scenic and are lightly traveled enough to be ridden safely and enjoyably.

Where to Get Dirty

Finding the good dirt takes a little more digging than finding good road rides. Again, the best source for local riding knowledge is usually a local shop. It's always a treat to find a shop with regularly scheduled rides. Joining in with a group that knows all the trails is much more fun than trying to navigate those same trails by map. The local phone book's Yellow Pages can be a big help. Shops with ad listings showing mountain bike brand names can probably help more than Bob's Small Appliances and Bicycles. Following are some more suggestions about where you can find good mountain bike rides:

➤ The IMBA (International Mountain Bike Association), an organization dedicated to mountain bike trail access, is great source for finding the trails. If IMBA doesn't have specific trail information for an area, it can probably still help you find bike shops with knowledge on the local dirt. Any shop that belongs to IMBA is definitely one staffed by hard-core cyclists who'll know the local trails as well as anyone. IMBA can also provide information on its club affiliations. A mountain bike club with an IMBA membership is at least as good a source as a bike shop.

Steer Clear

Cattle ranchers often operate under permit on public lands. Gates in such areas usually indicate a bovine presence. Close these gates behind you so you don't let Bessie and company get out of their grazing pasture. Show Bessie some consideration; she and the rest of her herd have probably made some good cow trails for you to ride on. They've also made some other things that you don't want to ride on. Keep a close watch on the trail—the fresh ones splatter.

➤ The local U.S. Forestry ranger station is another good source. The rangers are sure to have maps of the area and may even be able to offer advice on suitable rides. There's even a chance that they'll have information on a local mountain bike club, because trail work is usually coordinated through the local ranger station.

➤ Trails that are good for off-road motorcycles and ATVs are also good for mountain bikes. So a motorcycle shop is yet another potential source of trail data. Some motorcycle shops even carry mountain bikes, so don't overlook this valuable source.

➤ Surprisingly, a road map can often offer clues on off-road adventures. Some maps will show the dirt roads that cross over the public lands, which can harbor good rides. On those maps that don't, look for the paved roads that dead-end into blank spots. Those blank spots are either undeveloped land or public land. Be sure that an area is okay to ride in before venturing out.

Gear Up

If you're going on a self-supported trip, practically everything that you need for daily existence will be strapped to or hauled by your bike. Decide how you'll haul your gear. Racks, panniers (saddlebags), and bags are one way. Gaining popularity are the cargo trailers, such as those made by B.O.B., Burley, Pac-Dog, and Wheele. They can easily tote as much freight as panniers and don't make the bike top-heavy and clumsy. They're especially suited for off-road trips where a heavily laden bike would be hard to maneuver over rough terrain. Another advantage of trailers is they're easily and quickly detached, leaving you with a bare bike for casual exploring of trails or roads without having to haul everything.

For long self-supported trips, consider mailing some items ahead. A cache of food, stove fuel, and spare tires waiting at a post office care of general delivery can be a welcome self-care package. This can work both ways. If you realize partway through the tour that you brought too many clothes and too much equipment, pack up some of it and send it home.

An alternative to packing everything on the bike is to pack it on a trailer. The bike will be far more maneuverable, and packing and unpacking will be easier, too.

The equipment list for a self-supported bike tour is the same as a backpacking trip, plus the tools and spares needed for the bike. At the top of the list are your camping and sleeping equipment:

➤ **Sleeping bag.** Choosing a sleeping bag is always a compromise between light-weight and warmth. What's more miserable: shivering all night or having to haul an extra few ounces?

➤ **Sleeping pad.** Make sleeping on the ground or in a tent a bit more comfy with a self-inflating pad, such as Therm-a-Rest, or a slab of foam.

➤ **Tent or bivvy sack.** A bivvy sack is almost a pup tent, providing limited protection from the elements. If you're absolutely positive that your trip is going to have only good weather, going minimal with a bivvy sack might be the way to go. Personally I prefer the added comfort, warmth, and room of a real tent. Some weigh as little as two pounds.

➤ **Ground cloth.** Whether you're sleeping in a tent, bivvy sack, or just in a sleeping bag, placing your sleeping quarters on a ground cloth will protect it from dirt, rocks, and twigs and add an extra layer between yourself and the cold ground. Ground cloths are available at any camping supply store. A vinyl tarp works well, too.

➤ **Inflatable pillow/pillow case.** Some people like to minimize by bringing a pillowcase and stuffing it with clothing. Realize that a few days into your trip most of your clothes may be wet, stinky, or both—hardly something you want to rest your head on all night. A small inflatable pillow weighs practically nothing and is very comfy.

➤ **Camp stove and fuel.** Camping and backpacking magazines have done an endless number of articles debating the merits of different types of camp stoves. Some people love the versatility of liquid fuel stoves that can burn anything from kerosene to plain old gasoline. I prefer not to pack flammable liquids—they can be dangerous, and if they leak, they can ruin a lot of equipment. I like propane stoves. They can burn a long time on a single canister and are clean and easy to light, and you can find canisters at hardware stores, sporting goods stores, and even grocery stores and gas stations.

A simple stove such as this can boil water for your tea or cook a meal for your whole party.

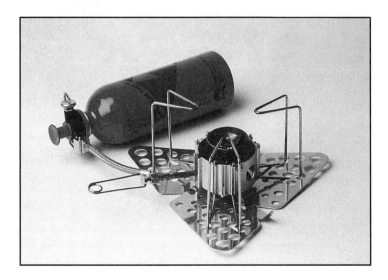

➤ **Cooking/eating utensils.** You can go simple and rob your own kitchen of a small pot, a knife, fork, and spoon, or go high tech and get a complete set of stainless steel, aluminum, or titanium cookware. I firmly straddle the middle ground with a spork (a spoon with fork tongs), a knife, a small stainless steel pot for cooking and eating out of, and a small stainless steel teakettle for heating/boiling water.

➤ **Compass.** Combine unfamiliar roads or trails with a few twists and turns, and it's easy for anybody to lose his or her sense of direction. A compass can prevent you from getting lost or riding in the wrong direction.

➤ **Headlamp/flashlight.** Unless you enjoy trying to cook or work on a bike with a flashlight clenched in your teeth, I strongly recommend a headlamp. Having a lamp strapped to your forehead makes it easy to work with your hands, do your bedtime reading, and so on. A flashlight makes a good backup, or use your bike's headlight. Be sure to bring extra batteries, and don't scrimp on the bargain brands—get the good ones.

➤ **Camp soap.** Unless you're able to wash your dishes and such in a campsite sink, bring liquid biodegradable soap that won't leave a lasting residue of soap scum on your campsite. You can also use it on your body.

A Little Dab'll Do Ya

As far as toiletries go, there are a few items you should bring to make your trip as comfortable and clean as possible:

➤ **One small bottle of shampoo.** Just because you're roughing it doesn't mean you have to go barbaric. A clean head of hair after a long day or two in the saddle is a nice touch of civility.

➤ **One bottle of liquid soap.** You never know where you're going to be able to wash up. If you're lucky, it'll be in a campsite shower, but it might also be in a gas station rest room sink or out of a small pan of hot water. Liquid soap is easier to use than bar soap when water is limited.

➤ **One can/stick deodorant.** You'll feel cleaner and your companions will be grateful.

➤ **One bottle of rubbing alcohol.** This item has many uses; use it to wipe down when a shower or sponge bath isn't possible, clean chain grime from your legs and hands, or sprinkle it on your towel and washcloth as a disinfectant.

➤ **One towel and one washcloth.** Bring a washcloth for showering and sponge bathing and a small towel for drying yourself after a wash. Be sure to hang them to dry immediately after use so they won't develop mildew or bacteria. A sprinkle of rubbing alcohol every couple of days will keep them fresh a little longer.

➤ **Two rolls of toilet paper.** You won't always find it at campsites and "borrowing" it from gas stations is just plain rude. Don't run short.

➤ **One toothbrush and one tube of toothpaste.** Used sparingly, a small tube of paste can go a long way.

➤ **One box dental floss.** Riding all day with an annoying bit of jerky or popcorn husk in your teeth is no fun. You can also use floss instead of thread to repair clothing, packs, tents, and so on.

➤ **Sunscreen.** When most of your time is going to be spent outdoors, UV protection is very important. Bring plenty of the highest SPF rating you can find and use it each and every day. Apply it at least twice a day, because even the waterproof varieties can sweat off.

Clara Barton on Wheels

Ride day in day out for any length of time and chances are you're going to take a spill, get scratched by branches, get jabbed by thorns, or get stung by a bee. Bring along a first-aid kit that includes at least the following items:

345

➤ One roll adhesive tape

➤ Four to six gauze pads

➤ Four to six bandages

➤ Two to six butterfly bandages

➤ One pair tweezers

➤ One bottle disinfectant (iodine, Mercurochrome, Bactine, Neosporin, and so on)

Day after day of riding can diminish your immune system, making you susceptible to colds and other illnesses. Sore muscles and joints are likely, too. Because drugstores can be hard, if not impossible, to find in the woods or on isolated back roads, I recommend putting together a mini medicine chest to get you though whatever ailments may decide to afflict you during your trip:

➤ **Anti-diarrheal medicine.** Strange water and food often bring on this inconvenient malady, especially to those traveling to foreign locales. Immodium or Lomotil can keep you on the saddle instead of the john.

➤ **Antihistamine.** You never know what might set off allergies when visiting a new locale. Try to find a nondrowsy type. If you're prone to allergies, perhaps your doctor will write a prescription for Claratin.

➤ **Anti-inflammatory.** Use this for tendonitis, sore knee joints, and so on.

➤ **Decongestant.** Colds strike when you're fatigued, as you'll surely be on a tour.

➤ **Aspirin.** Take this for headaches, fever, and so on.

➤ **Echinacea.** Its antibiotic properties are well known. A dose or two a day can help fight off an early onset of infection.

➤ **Throat lozenges/cough drops.** They can make a cough or sore throat a little easier to bear.

➤ **Pepto-Bismol.** This old standby for upset stomach is effective for diarrhea, too. Get a bottle if space isn't an issue, or get the tablets if it is.

➤ **Tylenol or other acetaminophen.** For those who have trouble with aspirin, this is the way to go.

➤ **Vitamin C.** This helpful vitamin is another means of warding off the evils of a cold.

Cycology

Contact lens wearers should add a few items to their medicine chests: wetting solution, cleaning solution, distilled water, and so on. Also bring an extra case, and, if you have one, an extra set of lenses. Don't let a lost lens ruin your trip. If you're extra-sensitive to dust, consider wearing goggles instead of just sunglasses.

You Wear It Well

Of course, you won't be packing for fashion, but that doesn't mean you don't have to pack. The following list of threads should keep you clothed and comfortable:

➤ **Two to three pairs of cycling shorts.** Two pairs are the minimum. That way, each evening you can wash that day's pair and have plenty of time for it to dry. If inclement weather is likely, take a third pair.

➤ **One pair short-fingered gloves.** These provide comfort and palm protection.

➤ **One helmet.** If you're getting a new helmet for your trip, wear it a few times beforehand to get it adjusted properly.

➤ **One set helmet pads.** Pads get lost, and they get stinky after several days of consecutive use.

➤ **Two short-sleeve shirts or jerseys.** Whether you prefer to ride in T-shirts or jerseys, take at least two, so that one can be drying from being washed while you wear the other.

➤ **One pair jeans or casual pants.** Even the warmest climates can get chilly at night. Having some warm pants to change into can be a blessing. They're also handy for those times when you want to go shopping or splurge on a restaurant meal and don't want to wear Lycra.

➤ **One to two pairs eyewear/sunglasses.** You always want to protect your eyes from sun, grit, and insects. By taking a dark pair and a light pair, you'll be prepared for changes in weather. Or get one pair with interchangeable lenses and bring dark and light lenses.

➤ **One sewing kit.** You'll need this to repair your cycling wear after a fall or a snag on a fence or bush.

In addition, unless you're absolutely, positively sure that you'll only encounter warm weather every day and night of your trip, bring cold-weather wear. Even in summer months, temperatures can drop, and weather can get ugly, especially if you're going to spend any time at higher elevations or along a coast. A selection of cold-weather wear doesn't weigh that much or take up much space.

➤ **One pair of long-fingered, cold-weather gloves.** Your hands have more veins and capillaries than just about any part of your body. When exposed to cold, they act like little radiators, shedding body heat with every gust of cold air. Keeping them warm goes a long way toward keeping the rest of you warm.

➤ **Two long-sleeve shirts or jerseys.** Longer sleeves are always warmer. And even if you don't encounter chilly riding conditions, a long-sleeve jersey can be cozy to wear around camp or for sleeping in.

➤ **One pair of tights.** Any time you're riding in temperatures below 60 degrees you want to have your knees covered, and tights are comfortable for lounging around camp or for sleeping.

➤ **One pair rain pants and one rain jacket.** It doesn't have to be raining for you to appreciate the warmth of rain pants or a rain jacket. They're also a nice extra layer against cold. Be sure you get pants and a jacket that are truly waterproof and not just water-resistant. The latter can get soaked and soggy in a hard rain.

➤ **One balaclava/scarf.** Most helmet companies proudly tout the ventilation qualities of their wares. Ventilation is a great feature in summer, but once the temperature drops, you want to save every iota of body heat. Wear a balaclava or scarf under your helmet to keep your skull and face from freezing.

What to Bring for Your Bike

Murphy of "Murphy's Law" fame must have taken a bicycle tour or two. I doubt that there's a single long-distance bicycle tourist who can't say, "I never broke a _____ until I started touring." Somehow a bike part seems to know when it's the only one of its kind for a hundred miles. You have to assume that local towns aren't going to have a bike shop or, if they do, that they won't have the part you need. Self-sufficiency is the goal for your bicycle equipment list:

➤ **Four to six inner tubes.** This amount may sound excessive, but nothing can replace an inner tube. If your bike uses presta tubes, consider drilling out your rims to accept shrader tubes. Shraders are much easier to find; they're available at most department stores and even drug stores and automotive stores.

➤ **Two complete patch kits.** Even with a large stash of tubes, a patch kit can save the day—getting four or five flats in a day isn't that uncommon. Take two kits, so you'll be sure to have plenty of glue. The extra patches may come in handy, too.

➤ **Two foldable tires.** Tires with Kevlar casings were originally designed to be light-weight, but the fact that they're foldable makes them a great spare. They can be stuffed into a pannier without taking up much space.

➤ **One chain.** Some riders feel safe in only carrying a few extra links to use to repair a broken or kinked chain. However, it's common for a broken chain to launch itself to parts unknown, especially when you're riding on a rough trail. Some-times a tossed chain gets wrapped up between the cogs and spokes or the cogs and rear dropouts and ends up as a twisted, kinked, unusable mess. Nothing can replace a lost or ruined chain except another chain.

➤ **Chain tool.** Of all the countless creative ways I've seen riders repair bikes in a pinch, I've never seen anyone come up with a way to fix a broken chain without a chain tool. When you need one, it's the only thing that will do.

➤ **Tools.** Make sure you take 4 mm, 5 mm, 6 mm, and 8 mm Allen wrenches, a Phillips screwdriver, and a standard screwdriver. Have a tool for every size and type of nut and screw on your bike. Better still, have two.

➤ **Extra rack mountain screws.** Considering the weight that a rack carries and the vibration it's subjected to, it's a wonder that the little 4 mm attachment screws hold up. They sometimes don't. They break, and they rattle loose. Have some spares.

➤ **One to two brake cables.** As strong as they are, brake cables still break occasionally. If you break a rear cable, don't toss it. It's probably still long enough to use as a spare front cable.

➤ **One to two shifter cables.** Although shifter cables are thinner and more delicate than brake cables, they seldom break. They do get kinked from getting snagged on things, which can effect shifting. Just as with a rear brake cable, don't toss a broken or kinked rear shifter cable without first checking to see whether it's still long enough to use as a spare front cable.

➤ **Three feet of shifter cable housing.** Getting snagged and kinked can ruin shifter housing and your bike's shifting. Three feet should be plenty to replace the longest section on your bike and the vulnerable loop at the rear derailleur.

➤ **Two to three feet brake cable housing.** Kinked brake cable can ruin a bike's braking action.

➤ **Four to six housing ferrules.** Ferrules (cable housing metal end caps) get bent, smashed, and sometimes don't want to come off of an old housing when you want to replace it. Having a stash of extra ferrules will allow you to simply snip off a stubborn one.

➤ **Four to six cable end caps.** Lose a cable end-cap, and the cable will unravel, making it difficult to adjust the shifter or brake and making it easy to stab your finger on the sharp little cable strands.

➤ **Two spokes of each size.** On most bikes, all the spokes in the front wheel are the same size. On the rear wheel, the spokes on the drive side are shorter than the nondrive side. Take your wheels or bike to your local shop and have them check your spoke sizes and get two of each size.

➤ **Four spoke nipples.** Sometimes when you try to straighten a badly bent wheel, a spoke nipple will round off or break. When you buy your spare spokes get some nipples, too.

➤ **One spoke wrench.** An adjustable wrench will work in a pinch, but a real spoke wrench in the right size will make the job go easier. Add this to your shopping list when you get your spare spokes and nipples.

➤ **Duct tape.** The only limitation to what can and can't be fixed with duct tape is your own imagination. Use it to fix a broken rack, boot a tire, or mend a torn pannier, tent, or sleeping bag.

➤ **Six to 10 zip-ties in assorted sizes.** If it can't be fixed with duct tape and zip-ties, it's truly broken.

➤ **Baling wire.** Bring along a good 10 to 12 feet coil of the stuff. If duct tape and zip-ties didn't work, maybe, just maybe…

Meals on Wheels

Planning for, packing for, and preparing meals on a self-supported trip can be a challenge. Those taking off-road trips are pretty much committed to bringing along all of their grub. Sure, if there are promising lakes or streams on the way, you can bring along a fishing pole. But the day you count on pulling in a nice rainbow trout for dinner is the day your dinner menu will be a choice between a Berry PowerBar and a bag of stale M&Ms.

Those taking road trips have a lot more freedom. You can go the self-sufficient route, or in populated areas you can get away with only carrying your snacks and stopping at markets or restaurants at mealtime. Even if you plan on going the restaurant and grocery store route, it's a good idea to still take along enough provisions for a meal or two. You never know what circumstances might strand you far away from the nearest town.

Just Add Water

Any of the foods meant for backpacking are also suitable for touring. Visit a well-equipped camping store such as REI or Campmor or check their catalogs, and you'll find a wide menu from which to plan your meals. Everything from vegetarian pizza to beef chow mien and dessert items such as pudding and apple cobbler are available as pre-packaged, freeze-dried meals—just add boiling water. Most are quite good; however, they can also be expensive, costing $5 to $8 per meal.

You can find alternatives to expensive freeze-dried backpacker chow at any grocery store. Good, nutritious menus can be assembled from such items as pre-packaged pasta meals, ramen, pancake mix, instant oatmeal, instant rice, cereal, powdered milk, instant breakfast, crackers, cookies, nuts, and so on.

Other Sundry Choices

Dried fruit is available at grocery stores, too. Raisins are an old standby. You can usually find banana chips in the bulk food section along with dried figs, apricots, pears, and apples.

Don't overlook fresh food. Many fruits and vegetables, such as potatoes, carrots, onions, apples, and oranges, keep quite nicely for several days. Other produce, such as bananas, melons, avocados, figs, tomatoes, peppers, and mushrooms, can stand being packed in your panniers for a day or three if you put them in something sturdy so they don't bruise.

Canned foods usually aren't worth the weight, although there's something about a nice bowl of chili and beans around a campfire. Sure, you could bring dried beans, but they take so long to cook that you'd use up all of the stove fuel in no time. Resorting to a few limited canned items is worth considering for your protein sources. Beef stew, tuna, or chicken can help meet your body's protein needs. If you do resort to cans, remember to pack out your empties.

A good source of protein is jerky. This type of dried meat is tasty, nutritious, and weighs practically nothing. Beef is the most common type, and turkey is also becoming popular. Avoid the types of jerky found on the counter of your local convenience store or in packets at your supermarket. These types are laced with preservatives and flavorings. Seek meat markets and delis that make their own. It's usually better-tasting, cheaper, and isn't full of chemicals.

Drink Up

Water should be a main concern. You're going to need two to four liters per day for drinking (more in hot weather), and you need it for cooking. Those taking domestic road trips through populated areas don't have much to worry about finding water. But when you're riding through a third-world country or on a wilderness trip, water is a worry indeed.

Never, ever drink from streams, lakes, or rivers without first boiling the water, adding iodine tablets, or filtering it. Boiling is always effective. Despite what it says in your Boy or Girl Scout Handbook, there's no need to boil it for 5 or 10 minutes, just bringing your water to a boil is enough to wipe out anything insidious in the water.

The second method is to purify your water with chemicals, such as chlorine or iodine. A drawback to these chemicals is that iodine makes your water taste like a medicine chest, and chlorine makes it taste like a swimming pool. One way to make chemically purified water more palatable is to add drink mix to mask the flavor, or you can use a neutralizer tablet. These tablets are ascorbic acid (vitamin C). You need to let the water sit for a while after adding a tablet, but it sure tastes better for it. You can find neutralizer tablets, chlorine tablets, and iodine tablets, such as the Potable Aqua brand, at most camping supply stores.

Perhaps the most effective means of purifying water is to use a portable water filter. Most weigh little more than a pound, cost from $30 to $90, and are capable of filtering out bacteria, silt, and, most importantly, giardia spores. They're simple to use. With most, you drop the hose into the water source, place the spigot over a container, and pump away to fill the container with safe, drinkable water. There are several brands: PUR, MSR, First Need, and others. Again, your camping supply store is your best source.

With one of these filters and a nearby stream, you can have all the safe-to-drink water you need.

A Hudson's Bay Start

During the 1700s heyday of the famed Hudson's Bay Company, the frontiersmen of the celebrated fur trading company had a unique way of beginning their expeditions. The first night of the journey was spent but a short distance from home. That way, all the provisions and equipment could be thoroughly checked out and arranged in real-life circumstances. Yet if some detail had been overlooked or a supply forgotten, it wasn't a big problem to send someone back. That's a smart way to begin an arduous journey.

Sure, going touring by bicycle is far more civilized than an eighteenth century trapping expedition, but it's still a major adventure by today's standards. Following the lead of the Hudson's Bay Company makes good sense. Gather all of your touring equipment and do a weekend or overnight test well before your trip. You want to get a feel for riding a loaded bike or pulling a trailer, and it's better to find out beforehand that your rack rattles or that some other piece of equipment has problems. Pitch your tent at home before the trip to make sure all the stakes and poles are there and that you know how to put it up. Test any mechanical equipment at home. Figuring out how to use your new camp stove when you're already tired and hungry practically guarantees frustration, as does learning to use a water filter when you're already parched.

Credit Where Credit Is Due

Heavily burdened bikes and roadside camping can sound like so much drudgery to some people. For those who would rather ride unencumbered, credit card touring is the way to go. With this type of touring, you carry just a change of clothes and the usual road/trailside emergency tools and supplies. Instead of packing a tent and dried fruit, you stay in hotels and eat at restaurants.

As free and spontaneous as this type of trip may sound, it calls for careful planning of the route, with realistic mileage schedules and confirmed lodging reservations. Remember that you won't have your tent and sleeping bag, so there's no back-up system should you not reach your planned hotel. You also can't count on finding other accommodations. You might ride into a town and find that all the rooms are booked by the annual toenail clipper manufacturers' convention.

Fly the Friendly Skies

There are some great places on this planet to ride a bike: Hawaii, Bolivia, the Grand Canyon, and on and on. For many destinations, the only practical way to get there is to fly. It's easy enough to get yourself there, but taking your bike aboard an airline flight can be a real hassle. The following sections provide some tips on getting your precious scoot there for the least amount of money and, hopefully, damage-free.

Bike Air Fare

On international flights, a boxed bike counts as one piece of normal baggage and flies for free. On domestic U.S. flights, golf clubs fly free and huge mongo suitcases fly free. But bikes? Depending on the airline, they'll hit you up for anywhere from $20 to $50 each way.

Also, the airlines are only responsible for up to $1,250 for loss or damage. Those of you with full DuraAce Merlins or XTR Litespeeds can get added insurance called "excess declared valuation" for $5 per every $100 over $1,250.

There is a way around the bike surcharge that will only cost you $20 a year. Join IMBA (International Mountain Bicycling Association) and fly on American, America West, Delta, Frontier, Northwest, TWA, or USAirways. To have the bike fee waived, you need to make your airline reservation through Professional Travel, Inc., at 800-225-0655. Not all flights and fares are eligible.

Another option is to ship the bike to your destination. UPS, FedEx, or any of the other carriers can get a bike just about anywhere in the United States for a lot less than the airlines charge. Of course, you'll be without your bike for a few extra days before and after your trip, but you also won't have to lug a bike box around the airport or try to stuff it into a rental car. In either case, read on. The bike will still need to be boxed for shipment.

Damage Control

Remember the luggage commercial with the gorilla slamming a suitcase around his cage? That old TV spot wasn't very accurate. The truth is, most airline baggage handling crews can inflict far more damage than any 600-pound ape. Heck, just look at all the implements of destruction they have: conveyors, handcarts, luggage trailers, and forklifts.

353

Miles of Experience

One of my traveling companions on a European trip was a poor victim of bike brutality. He unpacked his beloved De Rosa on arrival, only to discover that the top of the seat-tube had been crimped inward. His cardboard bike-box must have fallen a long way to manage that kind of damage. The rest of the group and I made him look the other way while we reamed out the seat-tube with a rat-tail file.

Many bike travel cases are available that do a fine job of foiling the baggage primates. Although packing a bike in one of these cases requires some disassembly, it's nothing beyond the mechanical skills of the average cyclist. Usually all that's required are a few hex wrenches and maybe a pedal wrench.

Most cases are made of hard plastic with reinforced corners for added protection and wheels for easy maneuvering in the airport. Inside, they have clamp-on brackets to hold the fork and rear dropouts. Some have zipper-bags or padded dividers for the wheels. Prices are in the $300 to $400 neighborhood—well worth it for those who frequently travel with a bike.

Those on a budget can get by using standard cardboard boxes, such as the ones that new bikes come in. They can usually be had for free from a bike shop (or for a six-pack or a few orders of fries). But remember my friend's De Rosa? That's why I recommend double-boxing the bike for added protection; get a medium box and slip it inside of a large box.

Bikes packed from the factories come with all manner of shipping padding and protective pieces, such as plastic braces for the dropouts, plastic sleeves for the frame, plastic caps for the axles, and cardboard panels to protect the frame from the wheels. These all get tossed when the bikes get built at the bike shop, so your local shop should be happy to give you some. All these bits can provide added protection when you're using a hard case and are a real necessity when you're using a cardboard box.

Packing It In

When you're pack a bike, take off the wheels and press on some plastic axle caps. Take the frame wrapping pads that you got out of the bike shop's dumpster and tape them on the frame. Loosen the stem, wrap the handlebar with a frame pad, tuck it onto the down-tube, and tape it in place. Remove the pedals and drop them in a bag or box. Remove the rear derailleur, wrap it with a shop-rag or pad, and tape it to the inside of the chainstay. Before taking out the seat-post, take a felt-tip pen and mark it at the seat-tube to assure getting your saddle height right again. Put the plastic dropout braces in place on the fork and rear dropouts.

Set the bike in the box or travel case. Place the wheels in their bags, or set the cardboard panels in place alongside the frame, and slip the wheels in. Before closing the case or taping up the box, pile in whatever else is going in the box: bike clothes, bike shoes, and so on. Don't forget to include the tools needed for reassembling the bike and some tape for closing the cardboard box on the return trip.

Post time: Marking the seat-post will save time spent trying to find the right saddle height.

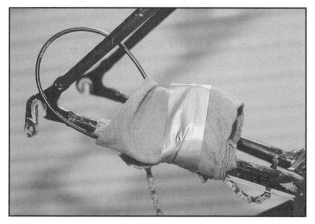

Derailleur retainer: Removing the rear derailleur and taping it safely to the frame will prevent damage to the derailleur and the derailleur hanger.

Plastic insurance: A simple pair of plastic dropout braces placed in the fork and frame will keep both from getting tweaked in transit.

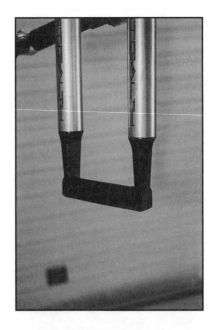

Armored protection: A travel case such as this one from Iron Case can protect a bike from just about anything short of a thermonuclear blast or a baggage handler on a four-ton forklift.

Underground Tips

Here are a few money-saving tips on taking a bike on the airlines. I've never tried any of these myself. In fact, I don't even know anyone who has. I just heard it all third-hand. Don't try this at home.

1. **Tip the skycap.** Curbside luggage check-in is a handy convenience. Skycaps, being out near the curb where they can help unload luggage from the car, have a long tradition of receiving tips. Give a skycap a thorough palm greasing and chances are your bike box will get checked right through to your final destination without ever being hit with the bike surcharge. Even if you tip the skycap $25, that can still be half the price the airline would charge you.

2. **Bike? What bike?** An oddity of airline luggage rules is that it's not the size or weight of a bike box that commands a surcharge, it's the fact that there's a bike in it. A box the same size and weight carrying say, bike parts, glass-framed artwork, exhibit materials, or a wheelchair would fly for free. Not that I or anybody I know would ever fib about the contents of a bike box. Nosiree.

3. **Divide and conquer.** Take off the wheels, seat-post, and saddle and put them in one box. Fill the box with whatever other incidentals or clothing that will fit. Put the frame in another box and fill it with stuff. Your bike and a good deal of your clothing and traveling stuff then qualify as two of your three pieces of checked luggage. If you also toss a couple of soft duffel bags in the box, you can transfer all your clothes into them and not have to use cardboard boxes as luggage at your destination.

Nice Outfit

If the logistics of planning and taking your own self-supported trip sounds like too much hassle, consider taking a trip with a commercial outfitter. Having someone else take care of the riding routes, lodging, ground transportation, and meals will allow you to concentrate only on riding, eating, sleeping, and having fun. There are dozens of outfitters and hundreds of destinations to choose from. Here are some of the more interesting destinations from a dozen outfitters who want to take you away from it all.

Alaska

The folks at Alaskan Bicycle Adventures call their Bicycle Alaska Tour, "one for those who love to bike!" This 8-day, 360-mile road bike trip stays far from the usual tourist destinations by following the scenic Richardson Highway from Fairbanks to Valdez. Along the way, riders experience nearly every climate zone that Alaska has to offer. They also enjoy the unsurpassed scenery of Nenana River Canyon, Paxson Lake, Summit Lake, the Copper River Basin, and the 12,000+ Alaska Range peaks of Mt. Deborah and Mt. Hayes.

Most daily rides are 60 to 70 miles. The last two rides of the trip are short (14 miles and 22 miles), with much of those days devoted to spotting whales, seals, bald eagles, and otters on a boat cruise of Prince William Sound and along the Turnagain arm route of the final ride.

> **Bicycle Alaska Tour**
> $2,295 for eight days
>
> **Alaskan Bicycle Adventures**
> 2734 Iliamna Ave.
> Anchorage, AK 99517
> Phone: 800-770-7242
> Fax: 907-243-4985
> E-mail: bicycle@alaskabike.com
> Web site: http://www.alaskabike.com

Secluded roads, breath-taking scenery—yeah, that's what it's all about.

Bolivia

Ready for some altitude? How does riding at 11,500 feet in the Bolivian Andes sound? Or how about a mountain bike trail with 12,000 feet of descending? That's all part of the itinerary with Explore Bolivia.

The first two of the nine days are spent in La Paz doing short rides to get acclimated to the altitude. Day three is spent exploring Jeep roads in the Cordillera Real and joining the canyons of the La Paz basin. Days four and five are spent exploring trails and Inca ruins around Lake Titicaca and Cohani Island. On day six, you climb out of the La Paz valley to the rocky rim of the Cumbre de Animas, with 21,260-foot Mt. Illimani looming above. On day seven, you travel more canyons and bucolic villages; on day eight, you take a trip across the Andes and into the tropical Yungas region with a thrilling 12,000-foot descent at the end. The trip ends back in La Paz with an early ride to the coffee regions.

Mountain Biking in Bolivia
$1,540 for nine days

Explore Bolivia
6551 S. Revere Parkway, #160
Englewood, CO 80111
Phone: 303-708-8810
Fax: 303-649-9017
E-mail: xplorbol@ix.netcom.com
Web site: http://www.explorebolivia.com

England, the Cotswolds, and South Downs

In this foreign trip, Americans already speak the language, more or less. Enjoy riding through the centuries-old towns of Bath, Winchester, and Salisbury, home of some of England's most colorful history and landscape. Discover historic castles, and be treated to a private tour of mysterious Stonehenge.

Vermont Bicycle Touring arranges all that, with stays in distinctive country inns, guesthouses, and European-style hotels. Each morning begins with a customary English breakfast before the day's easy-paced ride. Lunches are taken at the pubs and inns along the way. Group dinners are at the hotels and local restaurants. Three nights are set aside for guests to sample from a variety of suggested local fare.

The Cotswolds and South Downs
$1,895 for nine days/eight nights

Vermont Bicycle Touring
Monkton Rd. P.O. Box 711
Bristol, VT 05443
Phone: 800-245-3868
Fax: 802-453-4806
Web site: www.vbt.com

Grand Canyon North Rim

Although Arizona's Grand Canyon is one of the world's most popular tourist destinations, most visitors experience it from the crowded South Rim. Yet there's a whole other side to the canyon with blooming alpine meadows, exciting single-track, and no crowds.

Kaibab Tours takes mountain bike riders to the undeveloped North Rim. There awaits a forest of Douglas fir, ponderosa pine, and aspen. The rolling terrain offers a variety of riding, from the Arizona Trail, a 50-mile single-track through dense forests, to secluded fireroads among meadows of wildflowers. The dense forests give way to Marble Canyon and the Grand Canyon, which provide the scenery for the trip's campsites and lunch stops.

Most days have two route options, allowing guests to ride the graded fireroads or the challenging single-track. A guide leads the way on each route. The routes intersect with the support vehicle as the two groups meet for breaks and meals, making it a great tour to accommodate mountain bikers of varying levels. Another tour highlight is a hike down Thunder River Trail into the Grand Canyon, for a vantage point seen by few.

North Rim Grand Canyon
$745 for five days/four nights

Kaibab Tours
391 South Main St.
Moab, UT 84532
Phone: 800-451-1133
Fax: 801-259-6135
E-mail: kaibabtour@aol.com
Web site: http://www.kaibabtours.com

Although riding into the Grand Canyon itself is strictly forbidden, riding along the rim is an experience you'll never forget.

Hawaii, Molokai

Molokai is one of Hawaii's least developed islands. Save for 3,000 or so head of cattle and their attendants, only a few humans inhabit the island, so there's no fast food, traffic lights, or high-rises. Instead, there are miles of deserted beaches, lush tropical rain forests, and some of the best riding imaginable. Rides vary from the unique desert-like terrain on the west end of the island to the lush tropical rain forest on the east side. Molokai Ranch specializes in showing visitors the wonders of the island.

Anyone who has ever dreamed of camping on the beach of a tropical island will love Molokai Ranch. This is no rustic camp, however. The backcountry huts come complete with comfortable beds, solar heated showers, wooden decks, and access to trails. The rapidly developing mountain bike trail network is a work in progress, with 54,000 acres to work with. The camp is also unique in that guests are free to plan their own itineraries. Sign up to ride or set aside time to kayak, snorkel, body surf, hike, or just get lazy in the tropical sun.

Molokai Ranch
Experiences start at $185 a day

Molokai Ranch
P.O. Box 259
Maunaloa, HI 96770
Phone: 808-552-2791
Fax: 808-552-2773
Web site: www.molokai-ranch.com

Who hasn't dreamed of spending a vacation in the paradise that is Hawaii? What a life: camping near the beach, snorkeling, and riding through an emerald green landscape.

Italy: Veneto and Trentino

Realizing that riders who enjoy long rides and fast club rides appreciate longer miles and harder routes, La Corsa Tours is one of those few companies that caters to sport-minded cyclists. For hard-core riders, is there any better destination than Italy? Among La Corsa's many trips are two especially suited to Italophiles: Venetian Voyage and Discover the Dolomites.

Venetian Voyage is somewhat of a pilgrimage to those fond of Italian cycling hardware and history. With ride routes on roads used in the Giro de Italia and visits to the factories of Campagnolo components and Sidi cycling shoes, this trip through the ancient Venetian Empire is the stuff of dreams.

For advanced riders, there is little that can compare to the grueling climbs and exhilarating descents in the famed Dolomite Mountains of Northern Italy. Climb the classic switchbacks through the snow-capped granite peaks while remembering the feats of Coppi, Bartali, and Moser on some of the very roads on which these great racers earned their status as legends. La Corsa prides itself on comfortable hotels and sumptuous, bountiful meals that include local fare and plenty of vino.

Discover the Dolomites
$2,250 for nine days/eight nights

Venetian Voyage
$2,250 for 10 days/nine nights

La Corsa Tours
P.O. Box 30089
New York, NY 10011
Phone: 800-LACORSA
E-mail: info@lacorsa.com
Web site: www.lacorsa.com

Maine

Few riding routes in the United States are as charming and picturesque as the Maine coast. Bike Riders Tours' Down East in Camden and Castine tour follows the rocky Maine coast along Penobscot Bay. Small groups and quiet backcountry roads assure a relaxing experience.

Two days are spent in historic Castine at the old-fashioned Castine Inn. Founded in 1604, Castine is a step back in American history. The rides visit the artisan village of Blue Hill, with stops to feast on wild berries. A private boat takes guests to Isleboro Island to explore quiet coves and secluded beaches and watch lobstermen haul in their traps.

The last three days are spent in the beautiful port town of Camden. Two nights are spent in the town's finest inn, with beautiful rooms, original artwork, and sumptuous country breakfasts. Guests take leisurely rides or visit galleries, picnic at Lake Meguntiook, or hike up Mt. Battie. The final farewell dinner is set in an intimate turn-of-the-century home.

Down East in Camden and Castine
$1,095 for six days/five nights

Bike Riders Tours
P.O. Box 130254
Boston, MA 02113
Phone: 800-473-7040
Fax: 617-723-2355
E-mail: info@bikeriderstours.com
Web site: www.bikeriderstours.com

Mexico, Copper Canyon

In the northern Mexico state of Chihuahua, there's a canyon that's four times as big and 2,000 feet deeper than the Grand Canyon. World Trek Expeditions has a seven-day trip that takes guests on a phenomenal ride to the bottom of Copper Canyon and back.

The week begins with rides along the canyon rim. Then, you see waterfalls, meet the indigenous people of the Tarahumaras, and enjoy a hot-spring soak. After the indescribable 7,400-feet descent into the canyon, you camp in the village of La Bufa, which is perched on the side of the canyon walls. Hike the trails around La Bufa before riding deeper into the canyon to the tranquil village of Batopilas—a place that redefines the word "remote." See the 400-year-old Lost Mission of Satevo, built at the very bottom of the canyon. The ride to the village of Cerro Colorado is one of the best, with incredible single-track and multiple river crossings (some over narrow, wood-suspension bridges). On the final day in the village of Creel, guests can relax or expend whatever energy they have left on local single-track.

Copper Canyon
$899 for seven days

World Trek Expeditions
8700 West Colfax Ave, #L
Lakewood, CO 80215
Phone: 800-795-1142
Fax: 303-202-1145
E-mail: wrldtrek@ixnetcom.com
Web site: www.worldtrekexpeditions.com

Mexico's Copper Canyon is bigger and deeper than the Grand Canyon, and you can ride down into it.

New Mexico Single-Track

"Single-track" is a word that mountain bikers utter in hushed, reverent tones. Roads Less Traveled has a New Mexico single-track mountain bike trip that takes riders on over a hundred miles of the choicest trails of northern New Mexico's Sangre de Christo Mountains.

Starting in Santa Fe, you follow the Windsor Trail across aspen-lined Tesuque Creek. The next day, you are shuttled to Sangre de Christos, where you ride in Duran Canyon, climbing to 10,000 feet. That afternoon's exhilarating descent features stream crossings and extraordinary scenery. Day three is spent passing through alpine meadows on the South Boundary Trail. The afternoon is free to explore Taos's 600-year-old pueblos. The next three days are spent encircling the 13,000 feet of Mt. Wheeler. Pedal across the Sangre de Christos, winding through conifer forests. Then shuttle over Bobcat Pass to the trails of Enchanted Forest cross-country ski area. Ride to the bottom of Bobcat Pass and Red River, a gold mining boomtown. From high above Red River, enjoy an exhilarating descent along Cabresto Creek. The ride winds into a single-track trail along the Rio Grande River gorge. The fitting end of this trip is at La Junta Point, a viewpoint suspended high above the Rio Grande and Red River flows.

New Mexico Single-Tracker
$1,245 for six days/five nights

Roads Less Traveled
2840 Wilderness Pl. #F
Boulder, CO 80301
Phone: 800-488-8483
Fax: 303-413-0926
E-mail: fun@roadslesstravled.com
Web site: http://www.roadslesstraveled.com

New Zealand

There's practically no place farther to get away to than New Zealand. Escape The City Streets! has a tour that lets guests experience uncrowded mountain biking through secluded shepherds' fields, over high passes, through deep rainforests, and along tranquil ocean shores. Ever ridden on a volcano? Escape's guests get to experience that unique riding opportunity on this trip.

New Zealand Zeal-For-Adventure
$2,355 for 12 days/11 nights, includes all meals and snacks

Escape The City Streets!
8221 West Charleston Blvd. #101
Las Vegas, NV 89117
Phone: 800-596-2953

Fax: 702-838-6968
E-mail: escapethe@aol.com
Web site: www.adventurewest.com/escape/

Puget Sound

This eight-day trip is loved by hard-core cyclists and casual riders alike. They are sur-rounded by the blue Pacific and the snow-capped peaks of the Cascade and Olympic mountain ranges. For nearly traffic-free roads, it's tough to match the secluded San Juan Islands of the Pacific Northwest. That's why much of the trip is spent island-hopping to the nearly undeveloped islands of Vancouver, Orcas, San Juan, Fidalgo, and Whidbey to ride among the pastoral grazing land, wooded cliffs, and historic forts.

With whale watching, stays in quaint, small hotels, and a day devoted to kayaking and exploring inlets while watching for eagles and seals, this trip offers much more than an opportunity to pile on the miles. Those with a penchant for challenging pedaling can take the optional ride up Hurricane Ridge in Olympic National Park. This ride through majestic forests gains nearly a mile of altitude in just 18 miles, but the views at the top are fantastic.

Puget Sound
$1,824 for eight days

Bicycle Adventures
P.O. Box 11219
Olympia, WA 98508
Phone: 800-443-6060
Fax: 360-786-9661
E-mail: office@bicycleadventures.com
Web site: http://www.bicycleadventures.com

Spain

The name of this tour, Sabor of Spain, translates to "flavor of Spain," a fitting title for a tour that emphasizes the gastronomic delights of Spain along with the joys of its excellent cycling. Hosted by Camino Tours and taking place along Spain's northern coast, the ambiance of the trip is defined on the very first day with a ride in Bilbao, followed by an evening spent at the Hotel Karlos Arguinano. There, the most famous chef in Spain prepares a sumptuous meal with such regional specialties as Txangurro (stuffed spider crab).

The tour continues to beautiful San Sebastian along the Cantabrian Sea, where riders wind their way through the Basque country and more fine meals. One of the high-lights of the trip is the stay at the Parador de los Teyes Catolicos. Built in the fifteenth century by King Ferdinand and Queen Isabel (benefactors to Christopher Columbus), it's fitting lodging for guests who have already grown accustomed to eating like kings and queens.

Sabor of Spain
$1,655 for five days/four nights

Camino Tours
7044 18th Ave. NE
Seattle, WA 98115
Phone: 800-938-9311
Fax: 206-523-8256
E-mail: caminotour@aol.com
Web site: webtravel.com/caminotour

Roughing it isn't your game? How about bunking for the night in a fifteenth century Spanish castle?

Vermont Fall Colors

Vermont seems to be a state just made for cycling. Quiet back roads, few steep hills, and postcard settings among historic towns all make the state a perfect place for a bike vacation, especially in fall when the changing of the trees paints the landscape with a palette of red and orange hues.

Bike Vermont specializes in Vermont vacations, offering tours varying from two days to six days. Among its tours are the Dartmouth/Kezar Lake Region, Middlebury/Otter Creek, Shelburn/Lake Champlain, and many others. All trips include country breakfasts and stays at country inns.

Fall trips are offered in two-day trips for $335, three-day trips for $510, four-day trips for $680, five-day trips for $840, and six-day trips for $995.

Bike Vermont, Inc.
P.O. Box 207
Woodstock, VT 05091
Phone: 800-257-2226
Fax: 802-457-1236
E-mail: bikevt@bikevt.com
Web site: http://www.bikevt.com

The Least You Need to Know

➤ To have the best travel experience, take a bike tour.

➤ Bike touring doesn't have to be a long adventure; it can be a short weekend adventure, too.

➤ Self-sufficient touring can be arduous, strenuous, stressful, nerve-wracking, painful, uncomfortable, and the most fun you've ever had.

➤ If roughing it on your own isn't your cup of tea, a number of outfitters are ready to show you the world—and serve you your tea from a silver kettle into a china cup.

Chapter 24

The Cycling Life

In This Chapter

➤ Finding the road to adventure

➤ Advocates for cyclists' rights

➤ Trailside assistance and education

➤ The society of dirt: groups that get you out in the mud

➤ The trains don't run through here no more, but bikes do

➤ The society of pavement: groups that get you out on the road

➤ The big league: pro organizations

If you just can't wait to get out there and see and do all you can on two wheels, various cycling interest groups have a lot to offer to individual cyclists and the sport of cycling. In this chapter, I'll tell you about some of my favorites and how you can catch a ride with them.

Adventure Cycling Association

To enjoy cycling as a safe, pleasant experience, riders need quiet, scenic roads and trails. For over 25 years, the nonprofit Adventure Cycling Association has helped cyclists to find and enjoy these roads and trails. Founded in 1973 as Bikecentennial, the Adventure Cycling Association has inspired many, many cyclists to use bicycles for discovery and adventure. Today the organization boasts over 40,000 members and provides maps and directions to over 22,000 miles of riding opportunities.

Charting the Course

Many of the routes in Adventure Cycling's data bank began as part of Bikecentennial's 1976 TransAmerica Bicycle Trail. These routes usually aren't the most direct course to a destination, and they weren't meant to be. They're chosen to allow cyclists to see and experience rural America away from the busy and overcrowded highway routes. To build upon this vast network of routes, Adventure Cycling's staff carefully researches rural backroads to find low-traffic routes with an emphasis on scenic and interesting terrain.

Route maps cover 300- to 400-mile sections of these routes. The maps have details on road conditions, local history, and locations of bike shops, campgrounds, motels, and grocery stores. They're printed on waterproof paper and generally cost $9.95 each. Members of the Adventure Cycling Association receive the *Cyclosource*, a reference that lists the complete network of road routes and mountain bike trails. This information is also available on the Adventure Cycling Web site (www.adv-cycling.org).

Across the Great Divide

An example of the type of trip that can be planned using the association's maps is the Pacific Coast Bicycle Route. This 1,825-mile route follows the scenic West Coast from Vancouver, British Columbia, to San Diego, California. Follow the roads as detailed on five maps and enjoy the ever-changing scenery of redwood forests, lighthouses, rugged coastlines, and sheer cliffs that reveal glimpses of the beaches below.

Another popular route is the Great Parks Bicycle Route, a 2,115-mile trek that visits the jewels of the U.S. National Parks system, including Rocky Mountain, Grand Teton, Yellowstone, and Glacier national parks. For those with a taste for the south, the Southern Tier Bicycle Route is a 3,135-mile trip from San Diego, California, to St. Augustine, Florida, through Arizona, New Mexico, Texas, Louisiana, Mississippi, Alabama, and Georgia. Those of the Yankee persuasion may want to follow the Northern Tier Bicycle Route. In the course of this 4,395-mile journey, riders see Washington, Idaho, Montana, North Dakota, Minnesota, Wisconsin, Iowa, Illinois, Indiana, Ohio, Pennsylvania, New York, and Maine. Along the way, they enjoy the sights of Puget Sound and the mountain ranges of the Cascades, the Rockies, and the Adirondacks. They also get to see Glacier National Park, the headwaters of the great Mississippi River, and the Amish country of Pennsylvania.

Perhaps the ultimate mountain bike adventure is the Great Divide Mountain Bike Route. At 2,500 miles, it's touted as being the world's longest bicycle route. It follows the Continental Divide from Canada to Mexico, passing through Montana, Wyoming, Colorado, and New Mexico.

For those who thirst for adventure but prefer the peace of mind of going on an organized tour, Adventure Cycling also hosts supported trips of many of its routes. These trips involve mostly camping, but some nights riders enjoy the added comfort of a stay in a hostel. The groups are usually small (9 to 13 riders), and the participants are encouraged to break up into groups of only two or three for each day's ride. Included in these trips are three meals per day. The riders all share the cooking, cleaning, and food-shopping duties, and lunches are sack lunches packed by each rider each morning.

Membership to Adventure Cycling Association costs just $30 per year. Members receive nine issues of the association's magazine *Adventure Cyclist*, discounts on touring maps, a copy of the bicycle directory resource *The Cyclists' Yellow Pages*, and access to Adventure Cycling's special organized tours.

Write or call Adventure Cycling Association or visit its Web site for more information:

Adventure Cycling Association
P.O. Box 8308
Missoula, MT 59807
Phone: 406-721-1776
Fax: 406-721-8754
E-mail: ACABike@adv-cycling.org
Web site: www.adv-cycling.org

Miles of Experience

I've become fairly adept at choosing a riding route from a map. Still, my selected courses have many times turned out to be on a dangerously narrow road, or devoid of roadside services, or both. These fates could have been avoided had I referred to Adventure Cycling maps.

League of American Bicyclists

The more things change, the more things remain the same. When the League of American Bicyclists was founded back in 1880, rutted roads and antagonistic horsemen, wagon drivers, and pedestrians challenged the cyclists of the time. The league was founded to improve upon this situation for cyclists. Now, nearly 120 years later, the league continues to protect the rights of cyclists and to promote bicycles as a legitimate means of transportation through public education and by coordinating the efforts of affiliated bicycle clubs and advocacy groups.

This Road Was Made for You and Me

Currently, the league devotes itself to a program called the Safe Roads Movement. Interestingly, this 10-point action plan is fashioned after the league's Good Roads

Movement of the 1880s. Among the key points of the Safe Roads Movement is a plan of action to reduce the number of deaths and injuries to cyclists through education of cyclists and other road users and by advocating that roads be designed to safely accommodate cyclists. This action comes through the league's support of state and local bicycle activists through the National Coalition for Bicycle Advocacy, which functions as a clearinghouse for data, planning, and idea sharing between various cycling advocacy organizations.

The league's educational program, titled Effective Cycling, is taught by certified instructors. It combines the technical know-how needed to ride in traffic situations and includes curriculum on safe, responsible riding. The program has taught thousands of adults and children to become better and safer cyclists.

Each May, the league sponsors National Bike Month. This promotion serves to make the public better aware of the recreational, educational, and transportation aspects of bicycles. Much of the work of National Bike Month is done at the local level. The league facilitates this by providing Bike Month Organizer's Kits to bike clubs, environmental organizations, PTAs, local departments of parks and recreation, and other public organizations.

Cycology

Are unsafe cycling practices prevalent in your town? Do kids and adults continually ride against traffic, thinking that's the right way to ride? Perhaps your local PTA or city department of parks and recreation would like to do something about the situation by scheduling safety clinics or participating in National Bike Month. The League of American Bicyclists can help on both accounts.

A League of Their Own

One of the league's most high-profile endeavors is its involvement in training bicycle-mounted police patrols. In 1992, the league founded the International Police Mountain Bike Association (IPMBA). This association assists in providing information to municipalities wanting to start a police bike patrol as well as assisting in training officers for bike detail. Each year, IPMBA hosts the annual Police on Bikes Conference and has standardized the training of bike patrol officers throughout the United States through the Police Cyclist Training Course.

The cost of joining the League of American Bicyclists is as little as $30 per year. Those that travel by air and take a bike along can have that membership pay for itself with just one flight because members are entitled to free bike transport when flying on TWA, AmericaWest, Continental, Northwest, and USAirways. To take advantage of this program, members need to reserve their flights through Professional Travel Agency at 800-426-4055.

Members also receive six issues per year of *Bicycle USA* magazine. Among the publication's regular features are articles on government relations and education, cycling tips, cycling-related news, and even a calendar of rides from over 400 cycling clubs. Each year *Bicycle USA*'s March/April issue is published as a cycling almanac. This issue is chock-full of information about bicycling throughout the world and includes contact information for clubs and organizations and a state-by-state listing of bicycle resources and educational and advocacy information.

Contact the League of American Bicyclists or visit its Web site for more information:

> **League of American Bicyclists**
> 1612 K St., NW, Suite 401
> Washington, D.C. 20006
> Phone: 202-822-1333
> Fax: 202-822-1334
> Web site: www.bikeleague.org

IMBA

IMBA (International Mountain Bike Association) began in 1988 as a coalition of California mountain bike clubs who decided to work together to counter a trend of trail closure, assuring mountain bikers a place to ride. The organization was founded on the premise that trails were being closed without good reasons. Closures weren't based on environmental or safety data; closures were due to traditional trail users exerting their power.

Can't We All Just Get Along?

The role of IMBA is to advise and support local riders and advocates. The people who live in the communities have to get to know their local land managers, go to the public meetings, and do the trail work. IMBA helps with strategic advice, materials, tools, cash, credibility, and image making. All of these efforts are aimed at keeping trails open for mountain biking and in good condition for all trail users.

IMBA's work falls into three categories:

1. Encouraging responsible riding
2. Supporting volunteer trail work
3. Bringing mountain bikers together with land managers and other trail user groups

An increasing amount of IMBA's work is overseas. The same issues and roots of conflict that have been factors in the United States for the last 15 years unfortunately are at work in Europe, Asia, and Australia as well. The conflict mainly arises from the problem of crowded trails. In Austria, for instance, there are "no bikes" signs on 75 percent of the single-track trails. In Germany, mountain biking on anything narrower than two meters is illegal.

(Almost) Squeaky Clean

Part of the image-making task of IMBA is to dispel the perception of the mainstream public that mountain bikers are all adrenaline-charged Generation-Xers. Although IMBA recognizes that riding fast can be one of the basic appeals of the sport, responsible riding is all a matter of when and where.

IMBA's executive director Tim Blumenthal addresses the issue of nurturing the other side of IMBA's image: "Some people have a misconception about us, that we're the do-gooders, the people that worry about mountain biking. However, riding following IMBA's philosophy doesn't necessarily mean riding slow. It just means riding smart. Almost all of us here are avid riders. One of our staff is Pete Weber, one of the top 10 pro cross-country racers. One of our big challenges is getting people to realize that riding responsibly doesn't curtail your fun at all."

Cycology

When it comes to maintaining trails, the mountain bike community is possibly the most prolific of volunteer laborers. In 1998, IMBA members put in close to 250,000 hours of volunteer work. Over the years, IMBA members have built or help build a number of new trail miles, participating in the building of over 1,000 miles of new trails in 1998 alone.

Looking toward the future, IMBA sees four factors that should determine trail policies. The first and most important is environmental protection. A particular kind of trail use should only be permitted if it's environmentally sound. IMBA believes that mountain biking is almost always a sound trail use and that mountain biking on a well-designed and well-maintained trail is not going to cause excessive environmental damage. "The worst-case scenario is you may need to enact a seasonal closure during wet, muddy periods," Blumenthal said, "Not just to mountain biking, but to horses and hikers, too, as any of these users can leave tracks in muddy trails that, once the trail dries and hardens, can lead to excessive erosion."

The second factor of IMBA's long-term goals is public safety. IMBA's research shows that the incident of collisions as a percentage of mountain bike use is not significant. "We don't feel that mountain biking fundamentally threatens public safety," Blumenthal added, "Certain riders may be a danger to themselves and others. But that's a matter of education, which is a very large part of our work."

Cycology

Of IMBA's many victories in its fight for trail access, among the sweetest is the recent opening of a 13-mile, shared-use single-track from the north rim of the Grand Canyon to the border of the Kaibab National Forest.

The third factor is providing the types of trail experiences the public wants. "Increasingly, the public wants mountain biking," Blumenthal said. "The fourth thing is we should honor and respect traditional trail users," Blumenthal declared, "For instance, it's appropriate in a busy urban trail system to designate a couple of trails for foot travel only. A new idea for us is to advocate designating a trail or two for mountain biking only. If mountain biking is increasingly a trail experience that the public wants, and if you're going to create a separate trail for hiking, then you should do the same thing for mountain biking."

National Mountain Bike Patrol

Skiers are familiar with the National Ski Patrol—those guardian angels who come to the rescue when a skier is injured or lost. The National Mountain Bike Patrol (NMBP) is a sort of two-wheeled version of the Ski Patrol. In fact, many aspects of how the National Mountain Bike Patrol operates were directly copied from the Ski Patrol.

The objective of the Mountain Bike Patrol program is to maintain and advance trail opportunities for the sport through the support and education of regional mountain bike patrol groups. Patrol members provide an on-trail presence of trained mountain bikers able to inform, educate, and assist other mountain bikers and other trail users. Patrols urge other riders to be responsible mountain bikers by following the IMBA's philosophy of socially accountable and environmentally sound riding practices as suggested in IMBA's Rules of the Trail (see Chapter 11, "Rules of the Trail"). Above all, patrol members are there to provide emergency care, mechanical assistance, education on environmental concerns, trail user etiquette, and local expertise.

Patrollers are volunteers, and each puts in a minimum of 50 hours per year patrolling in addition to the time spent training. Patrollers are easy to spot, because they're required to wear the uniform of their patrol unit. For some units, the uniform is a T-shirt or jersey with a National Mountain Bike Patrol logo; other units wear uniform shirts similar to those used by forest rangers.

To become a patroller, applicants are required to have been trained in first aid and CPR and be knowledgeable in bike repair and minimum-impact riding skills. Patrollers also need to be aware of trail issues and environmental concerns pertaining to mountain bikes and need to have received training in interpersonal skills and conflict resolution.

For more information on the National Mountain Bike Patrol or to start a chapter in your area, contact:

> **IMBA—National Mountain Bike Patrol**
> Attention Jon Alegranti
> P.O. Box 7578
> Boulder, CO 80306-7578
> Phone: 303-545-9011
> Fax: 303-545-9026
> E-mail: imbambp@aol.com

Miles of Experience

A few years ago, I had the fortunate opportunity to spend a morning riding with the Mountain Bike Patrol in the mountain bike mecca of Moab, Utah. We spent a few hours riding on the redrock formations adjacent to the famed Slick Rock Trail. It was the week of the annual Moab Fat Tire Festival, and hundreds of riders swarmed the trails. In that short time, the patrol helped two riders with flat tires, gave directions to a few more, gave polite yet firm suggestions to helmetless riders to don head protection, and bandaged a rider's scraped elbow. The most memorable "customers" were a couple of guys who had convinced themselves that they were hopelessly lost—in reality, they were only a few hundred yards from the parking lot, but they couldn't see it from their location in a deep crevasse!

NORBA

NORBA (National Off-Road Bicycling Association) is the national governing body for mountain biking in the United States. Founded in 1983, this nonprofit entity provides mountain bike racing opportunities to members of all abilities, from beginner to professional. Because NORBA is the largest mountain bike racing sanctioning body in the United States, most racers compete under the sanction of NORBA and are licensed as racers through NORBA. The rules, racing formats, and criteria for earning a U.S. championship are established and governed by NORBA.

Cycology

NORBA doesn't sanction all U.S. mountain bike races; a few regional clubs and promoters put on races without NORBA. However, most race organizers choose to have a NORBA sanction because NORBA can provide trained race officials, a very competitive insurance package, and a well-established set of rules and regulations.

NORBA prides itself on its support of the grass-roots level of racing, and along with its membership services, NORBA sanctions over 1,000 events each year. At most of these events, racers/members earn points based on their results that are tallied for regional ranking. NORBA also conducts developmental clinics and hosts symposiums with race organizers, race officials, and coaches as efforts to improve U.S. mountain bike racing wherever possible.

Each year NORBA promotes the United States' premiere racing series, the NORBA National Championship Series (NCS). Taking place at six or seven venues across the country, this racing series determines the professional national champions in cross-country, downhill, dual-slalom, and trials. These events are highly popular, both as a spectator sport and for participants because each round of the series also schedules races for all amateur-racing categories.

A one-year NORBA membership/license is $35. Twenty dollars of that is membership in USA Cycling. USCF members already are USA Cycling members, so adding a NORBA license is only $15 for them.

Contact NORBA at:

> **NORBA (National Off-Road Bicycling Association)**
> One Olympic Plaza
> Colorado Springs, CO 80909
> Phone: 719-578-4581
> Fax: 719-578-4596
> Web site: www.usacycling.org

Cycology

Getting a NORBA (or USCF) license doesn't involve taking any kind of test. The only thing you need to be able to prove is your identity and age and your ability to fork over $35.

Rails-to-Trails Conservancy

Of all the places to enjoy cycling, among the most enjoyable and safest are the dedicated bike paths away from streets and highways. While some forward-thinking cities sometimes build these separated bikeways, in most instances they're simply alternate uses for access roads built for other purposes; river access roads, and flood-control channel access roads, and power-line service roads have all proven to be excellent bikeways.

Cycology

NORBA's logo, which depicts a bicycle wheel with a knobby tire, was originally drawn back in 1983 by one of mountain biking's founding fathers, Joe Breeze.

Across the United States, several bikeways have been built upon former railroad rights-of-way. Many of these owe their existence to the efforts of the Rails-to-Trails Conservancy, a nonprofit organization that works toward developing abandoned railroad corridors into multiuse trails. Since its inception in Washington, D.C. in 1986, the organization has had a hand in creating over 1,000 rail-trails, which together represent over 10,000 miles of trails.

These rail-trails vary in type and location. Some are urban trails surfaced with asphalt for the enjoyment of cyclists, pedestrians, roller-skaters, and others. In rural settings, rail-trails are often left as dirt or are finished with gravel or cinder. These types of trails are popular with equestrians, hikers, and mountain bike riders.

The function of the Rails-to-Trails Conservancy is not to perform the transformation from railway to trail, but to assist local concerns in the logistics of the process. This process involves far more than removing the rails and ties and putting up a few signs.

The conservancy helps start the process by informing local governments and trail advocates of upcoming railway abandonments. It further assists these public and private agencies in the complexities of acquiring rail corridors. After the land has been procured from the railroad company or lessor landowners, the conservancy provides technical assistance with trail design, development, and management.

Usually, a local public agency purchases the abandoned corridor, either the local parks and recreation department, the city, county, or state. That public agency usually builds or pays for the building of the trail. In some cases, citizen volunteers do the work. After the trail is built, its management falls to the local, state, or federal government. Some rail-trails are managed locally by nonprofit "friends of the trail" citizens' groups, community foundations, or land trusts.

To learn more about Rails-to-Trails, visit its Web site at www.railtrails.org/ or order "Rails-with-Trails: Sharing Corridors for Recreation and Transportation." To order this booklet, write to Rails-to-Trails Conservancy, 1100 17th St., NW, 10th Floor, Washington D.C. 20036.

As a nonprofit public organization, Rails-to-Trails is supported solely by its membership. Those wishing to become a part of Rails-to-Tails can join at the following levels: regular $18; supporting $25; patron $50; benefactor $100; advocate $500; and Trailblazer Society $1,000.

USA Cycling

USA Cycling is the United States' managing body for bicycle racing. Among the racing organizations that operate under the auspices of USA Cycling are the United States Cycling Federation (USCF), the National Off-Road Bicycle Association (NORBA), the U.S. Professional Racing Organization (USPRO), and the National Bicycle League (NBL), which governs U.S. BMX (bicycle motocross) racing. Each of the racing organizations operating under USA Cycling is run independently to focus on its individual sport's goals and directions, but it also shares the resources of the coalition of USA Cycling.

As a member of the United States Olympic Committee (USOC), USA Cycling is directly responsible for choosing racers to represent the United States in Olympic competition. As the overseeing entity of U.S. bicycle racing, USA Cycling is also a member of the international cycling governing body, the Union Cycliste Internationale (UCI), and as such has a voice in policies regarding international cycling competition. To further establish an international presence, several key members and officers of USA Cycling also hold strategic positions on international boards and committees. Membership in USA Cycling is automatic for riders joining NORBA, USCF, or NBL.

USCF

USCF (United States Cycling Federation) is another bike organization that has been around for a long, long time. Established in 1920, it was first called the Amateur Bicycle League of America. The current name of USCF has been in use since 1975.

Local clubs are the backbone of the USCF, promoting the sport at the local level. Clubs are behind such activities as training rides and clinics aimed at teaching the finer points of the sport to beginner and intermediate racers. Clubs also hold USCF-sanctioned races.

The USCF is involved in a wide variety of competition programs, including the development of junior riders (under age 18), a junior Olympic race series, and the selection of racers with the talent needed for membership on the national team. The coaching staff within the USCF works with juniors and in special programs, such as the Native American Sports Council Cycling Program and YMCA cycling clinics. The USCF also directs national championship races for all age categories and racing abilities and in all types of cycling (except mountain bike racing) including road racing, time-trials, all the various events of track (velodrome) racing, and cyclocross.

The 33,000+ USCF members include racers from all 50 states and range in age from 9 to 93, with the majority of racers being between age 19 and 39. An annual USCF license/membership is $35. Twenty dollars of that covers membership in USA Cycling. The USA Cycling fee is waived for racers under age 15. Mountain bike racers who are NORBA members are already USA Cycling members, so adding a USCF license only costs them $15.

Contact the USCF at:

> **USCF**
> One Olympic Plaza
> Colorado Springs, CO 80909
> Phone: 719-578-4581
> Fax: 719-578-4596
> Web site: www.usacycling.org

Cycology

USCF has taken steps to make its licensing procedure more user-friendly than it has been in the past. In years past, a rider had to send a birth certificate (original or certified copy only) to USCF and then wait several weeks to receive a license by return mail. Now an aspiring racer can be licensed at nearly any race and needs only some form of photo identification. Realizing that many riders are unsure of their racing aptitude and would like to be able to just give racing a try, USCF also offers one-day licenses for only $5.

USPRO

USPRO (United States Professional Racing Organization) is the most elite society of American bicycle racing. Of all the thousands of riders that take up racing, a rare few ever reach the pro ranks and become members of USPRO. Founded in 1981, USPRO is the sanctioning body of professional bicycle competition in the United States. It had operated as its own distinct, nonprofit organization until being acquired by the United States Cycling Federation (USCF) in June of 1994.

Among the many jobs of USPRO is to license professional racers and to manage the advancement, promotion, and rules administration of professional bicycle racing.

USPRO also serves as the intermediary between U.S. professional races and professional teams and Union Cycliste Internationale (UCI) and to assure that riders and teams adhere to UCI regulations.

USPRO also works closely with USA Cycling in developing and preparing racers for international competition. USPRO has been involved in choosing and sending riders to several world championship events and to the 1996 Olympics.

Don't worry about joining USPRO. Those very few racers who have their USCF licenses upgraded to pro are automatically contacted by USPRO. Membership is a classic case of "Don't call us; we'll call you."

The Least You Need to Know

➤ There's a whole world out there beyond your local bike path. The Adventure Cycling Association can help you find it.

➤ The League of American Bicyclists has been an advocate of cyclists' rights for over 100 years.

➤ IMBA has proven time and again that mountain bikers, hikers, and equestrians can coexist.

➤ Civic-minded mountain bike riders with a desire to serve the public can become members of the National Mountain Bike Patrol.

➤ Abandoned railways don't have to become corridors of blight; they can become multiuse trails instead.

➤ To race on the road, you need to join the USCF; to race mountain bikes, you need to join NORBA.

Resources

Recommended Reading

Backpacking: One Step at a Time, Harvey Manning, Vintage Books, New York, 1986.

Bear Aware: Hiking and Camping in Bear Country, Bill Schneider, Falcon Publishing Company.

Bicycling Magazine's Complete Guide to Bicycle Maintenance and Repair, Rodale Press, Emmaus, PA, 1994.

The Bicycle Repair Book, Robert Van der Plas, Motorbooks International, 1993.

The Bicycle Wheel, Jobst Brandt, Mountain Air Books, 1993.

Cycling Health and Physiology, Edmund Burke, Vitesse Press, Brattleboro, VT, 1997.

Eating for Endurance, Ellen Coleman, Bull Publishing Co., Palo Alto, CA, 1997.

Bicycling Medicine, Arnie Baker M.D., Simon & Schuster, New York, 1998.

Effective Cycling, John Forester, The MIT Press, Cambridge, MA, 1996.

Essential Touring Cyclist, Richard Lovett, G.P., McGraw Hill Co., New York, 1994.

A Gear Higher, Keith Code and David Gordon, Code Break Publishing, 1998.

Hearts of Lions, Peter Nye, W.W. Norton & Co., New York, 1989.

High-Tech Cycling, Edmund Burke, Human Kinetics Publishing, Champaign, IL, 1995.

How to Shit in the Woods: An Environmentally Sound Approach to a Lost Art, Kathleen Meyer, Ten Speed Press, Berkely, CA.1994.

Miles From Nowhere: A Round The World Cycling Adventure, Barbara Savage, The Mountaineers, Seattle, WA, 1985.

The Mountain Bike Way of Knowledge, W. Nealy, Menasha Ridge Press, Birmingham, AL, 1990.

The Road of Dreams, Bruce B. Junek, Images of the World, Rapid City, SD, 1991.

Self-Defense for Nature Lovers, Mike Lapinski, Stoneydale Publishing.

Serious Cycling, Edmund Burke, Human Kinetics, Champaign, IL, 1995.

Smart Cycling, Arnie Baker, M.D., Simon & Schuster, New York, 1997.

Training for Cycling, Davis Phinney and Connie Carpenter, Berkley Publishing Group, Berkley, CA.

The Ultimate Sports Nutrition Handbook, Ellen Coleman, Bull Publishing, Palo Alto, CA, 1996.

Weight Training for Cyclists, Fred Matheny and Stephen Grabe, Velo Press, Boulder, CO, 1998.

The Woman Cyclist, Elaine Mariolle and Michael Shermer, NTC Publishing Group, Lincolnwood, IL, 1987.

Bicycle-Related Web Sites

Adventure Cycling Association, touring information, maps, magazine, bicycle travel outfitter, www.adv-cycling.org

Airborne, titanium bicycles, www.airborne.net

Alaskan Bicycle Adventures, bicycle travel outfitter, www.alaskabike.com

Answer/Manitou, suspension forks, handlebars, components, clothing, helmets, www.answerproducts.com

Azonic, components, handlebars, accessories, www.oneal.com

AXO Cycling, cycling shoes, clothing, www.axocycling.com

Backroad Bicycle Tours, bicycle travel outfitter, www.backroads.com

Balance Bar Co., sports bars, www.balance.com

Barnett Bicycle Institute, bicycle mechanics school, www.bbinstitute.com

Bell Helmets, bicycle helmets, www.bellbikehelmets.com

Bicycle Adventures, bicycle travel outfitter, www.bicycleadventures.com

Bike Pro USA, travel cases, www.bikeprousa.com

Bike Riders Tours, bicycle travel outfitter, www.bikeriderstours.com

Blackburn Designs, accessories, pumps, trainers, www.blackburndesign.com

BLT Light Systems, bicycle lighting systems, www.norco.com

B.O.B., bicycle trailers, www.bobtrailers.com

Breezer Cycles, bicycles, www.breezerbikes.com

Burley Design Cooperative, tandems, child trailers, www.burley.com

CamelBak, hydration systems, www.camelbak.com

Camino Tours, bicycle travel outfitter, www.webtravel.com/caminotour

Campagnolo, bicycle components, www.campagnolo.com

Cannondale Corp., bicycles, components, accessories, clothing, child trailers, www.cannondale.com

Cat Eye, bicycle lights, cyclometers, www.cateye.com

Chris King Cycle Group, headsets, hubs, www.chrisking.com

Clif Bar, sports bars, www.clifbar.com

Cratoni Helmets USA, bicycle helmets, www.cratoni.com

Cycle Italia, bicycle travel outfitter, www.cycleitalia.com

Dave's Wheel Designs, custom bicycle wheels, www.speeddream.com

da Vinci Designs, tandems, www.teamspirit.com

Dirty Girls Activewear, women's cycling wear, www.dirtygirls.net

Dragon Optical, eyewear, www.dragonoptical.com

Escape The City Streets, bicycle travel outfitter, www.adventurewest.com/escape/

Explore Bolivia, bicycle travel outfitter, www.explorebolivia.com

Ellsworth Bicycles, bicycles, www.ellsworthbicycles.com

Exus, clipless pedals, cycling shoes, www.exus.com

Finish Line Technologies, lubricants, www.finishlineusa.com

Fit Kit, rider-to-bicycle fitting system, www.hdkcycles.com/fitkit.html

Fox Racing USA, bicycle clothing, www.foxracing.com

FSA, headsets, bottom brackets, cranksets, www.fullspeedahead.com

Gary Fisher Bicycles, bicycles, accessories, www.fisherbikes.com

Giant Bicycles, bicycles, accessories, www.giant-bicycle.com

Giro Sport Design, helmets, saddles, www.giro.com

Gore Ride On Cables, bicycle control cables, www.rideoncables.com

GT Bicycles, bicycles, accessories, clothing, www.gtbicycles.com

Hanebrink Bicycles, suspension forks, www.hanebrinkforks.com

Hayes, disc brakes, www.hayesbrake.com

Hollywood Engineering, bicycle carrying systems, www.hollywoodracks.com

Hope Technology USA, disc brakes, components, www.hopetech.com

Hurricane Components, components, rack adapters, clothing, www.hurricanecomponents.com

Intense Cycles, suspension bicycles, www.intensecycles.com

IRC Tire, bicycle tires, www.irc-tire.com

Jet Designs, bicycle lighting systems, www.jetdesigns.com

K2 Bike, bicycles, suspension forks, www.k2bike.com

Kaibab Tours, bicycle travel outfitter, www.kaibabtours.com

KHS Bicycles, bicycles, www.khsbicycles.com

Kona USA, bicycles, www.konaworld.com

Kreitler Rollers, training rollers, www.kreitler.com

Kryptonite Corp., bicycle locks, www.kryptonitelock.com

La Corsa Tours, bicycle travel outfitter, www.lacorsa.com

Litespeed, titanium bicycles, www.litespeed.com

Magura USA, hydraulic brakes, disc brakes, www.magura.com

Marin Bicycles, bicycles, www.marinbikes.com

Marzocchi USA, suspension forks, shock absorbers, www.marzocchi.com

Mavic USA, rims, wheel systems, www.mavic.com

Michelin Two Wheel, tires, inner tubes, www.michelin.com/bike

Minoura, stationary trainers, www.minoura.co.jp

Molokai Ranch, Hawaiian mountain bike resort, www.molokai-ranch.com

Mongoose Bicycles, bicycles, www.mongoose.com

More Than Bikes, bicycle socks, www.sockguy.com

Mountain Bike Resource, web magazine, www.mtbr.com

Mountain Bike, magazine, www.mountainbike.com

Nightsun Performance Lighting, bicycle lighting systems, www.night-sun.com

Niterider, bicycle lighting systems, www.niterider.com

NORBA (National Off Road Bicycle Association), U.S. mountain bike racing sanctioning body, www.usacycling.org/mtb/

OF3 Worldwide, clothing, shoes, www.of3usa.com

Pace Sportswear, bicycle clothing, www.pacesportswear.com

Panaracer, bicycle tires, www.panaracer.com

Park Tool Co., bicycle tools, www.parktool.com

Pearl Izumi, bicycle clothing, www.pearlizumi.com

Pedros USA, lubricants, www.pedros.com

Polar Electro, heart-rate monitors, www.polarusa.com

PowerBar, sports bars, www.powerbar.com

Pro-Dynamix, eyewear, www.prodynamix.com

Qranc USA, helmets, clothing, accessories, www.qranc.com

Race Face Performance Components, components, www.raceface.com

Racermate, computerized stationary trainers, www.computrainer.com

Raleigh USA, bicycles, www.raleighusa.com

Rhode Gear, accessories, tools, www.bellsports.com

Ritchey Design, bicycles, components, www.ritchey.com

Roads Less Traveled, bicycle travel outfitter, www.roadslesstraveled.com

RockShox, suspension forks, shock absorbers, disc brakes, www.rockshox.com

Rocky Mountain Bicycles, bicycles, www.bikes.com

Rudy Project, eyewear, www.rudyproject.it

Santa Cruz Bicycles, bicycles, www.santacruzbicycles.com

Santana Cycles, tandems, www.santanainc.com

SDG (Speed Defies Gravity), saddles, www.sdgusa.com

Schwinn Bicycles, bicycles, www.schwinn.com

Selle Italia, saddles, www.selleitalia.com

Serfas, saddles, accessories, www.serfas.com

Seven Cycles, bicycles, www.sevencycles.com

Shebeest Products, women's cycling wear, www.shebeest.com

Shimano, components, cycling shoes, www.shimano.com

Sidetrak, accessories, components, www.sidetrak.com

Sidi, cycling shoes, www.sidiusa.com

Sigma Sport USA, cyclometers, www.sigmasport.com

Slime, flat prevention goop, www.slimesealant.com

Smith Sport Optics, eyewear, www.smithsport.com

Societe de Tour de France, Tour de France information, www.letour.fr

Softride, bicycles, www.softride.com

Speedplay, clipless pedals, www.speedplay.com

Sprocket Head, cycling jewelry, clothing, www.sprockethead.com

Spy, eyewear, www.spyeyes.com

SRP, titanium fasteners, www.srp-usa.com

SR Suntour, components, www.srsuntour.com

SRAM/GripShift, bicycle shifters, derailleurs, brakes, brake levers, www.sram.com

Sugoi, bicycle clothing, www.sugoi.ca

Sun Ringle', rims, wheels, components, www.sunrims.com

Tamer Bicycle Components, shock-absorbing seat-posts, www.tamerusa.com

Tandem Magazine, magazine, www.tandemmag.com

Tandem Tours, tandem bicycle travel outfitter, www.tandemtours.com

Thule Car Rack Systems, bicycle carrying systems, www.thule.com/

Time Sport, clipless pedal systems, www.bianchi.it.com

Tioga, tires, headsets, accessories, www.tiogausa.com

Tomac, bicycles, www.tomac.com

Trek, bicycles, components, clothing, accessories, www.trekbikes.com

Tri All 3 Sports, bicycle travel cases, www.triall3sports.com

Troy Lee Designs, accessories, clothing, helmets, www.troyleedesigns.com

Turbocat, bicycle lighting systems, www.turbocatusa.com

United Bicycle Institute, bicycle mechanic school, www.bikeschool.com

USCF (United States Cycling Federation), U.S. road racing sanctioning body, www.usacycling.org/road/

Velo News, bicycle news magazine, www.velonews.com

Vermont Bicycle Touring, bicycle travel outfitter, www.vbt.com

Video Action Sports, bicycling-related videos, www.video-action-sports.com

Voodoo Cycles, bicycles, www.voodoo-cycles.com

Vredestein Tires USA, bicycle tires, www.vredesteinusa.com

Waterford, bicycles, www.waterfordbikes.com

Wellgo Pedals, clipless pedal systems, www.wellgo.com.tw

White Brothers, suspension forks, handlebars, www.whitebros.com

Wilderness Trail Bikes, tires, components, wheel systems, www.wtb.com

Wrench Force, bicycle tools, www.wrenchforce.com

The WWW Bicycle Lane, bicycle Web site resource, www.bikelane.com

WOMBATS (Women's Mountain Bike and Tea Society), women's mountain bike advocacy, fun rides and training, www.wombats.org

World Trek Expeditions, bicycle travel outfitter, www.worldtrekexpeditions.com

Yakima Products, bicycle carrying systems, www.yakima.com

Yeti Cycles, bicycles, www.yeticycles.com

Zeal Optics, eyewear, www.zealmaniak.com

Cyclebabble Glossary

animal   Unhuman rider; that is, someone who rides up mountains on the big chainring or rides unbelievably fast.

baked   Overtired or overtrained.

bar-ends   Short extensions clamped onto the ends of a mountain bike handlebar to provide extra hand positions and to allow the rider to put more weight over the front wheel.

biff   Crash.

blow up   A term describing when a rider overexerts himself or herself, is unable to recover, and succumbs to fatigue.

bonk   Running out of energy while riding.

bottom bracket   The assembly onto which a bicycle's cranks are bolted. The bottom bracket includes the spindle, the bearings, and any bearing cups or cartridge assembly.

bottom bracket shell   The portion of a bicycle frame that contains the bottom bracket.

bottom out   When all the travel of a suspension is used, as from the impact from a very large bump.

brain bucket   Helmet.

brake levers   The controls that actuate the brakes. A rider pulls a brake lever to apply a brake.

breakaway   (noun) A group of riders that has managed to get ahead of the main pack. (verb) The act of riding away from the main pack.

bug gag   What happens when a bug resists being swallowed.

bug gulp   Swallowing a flying insect whole, without chewing.

bunny hop   To spring upward and lift the bike off the ground. This move is useful in jumping over railroad tracks, potholes, curbs, or other riders.

bushing   A part that reduces the friction between two moving parts. Bushings are used in the connecting points of suspension pivots or in the sliders of a suspension fork.

Campy   Short for Campagnolo, an Italian manufacturer of fine road bike components.

Camp Granola   Slang for Campagnolo.

chainrings   The front sprockets connected to the crankarms.

chainstays   The two portions of a bike frame that extend back from the bottom bracket shell to the rear dropouts.

click in   The act of engaging into the mechanism of a clipless pedal.

clipless pedals   Pedals that use mechanisms similar to ski bindings to firmly attach a rider's feet to the pedals.

clunker   A term used by the first mountain bikers to describe their fat-tired bikes that were heavy and clunky compared to their light, sleek road bikes.

CNC-machined   A manufacturing method whereby a computer-controlled machine carves a component out of a solid chunk of material.

cogs   The rear sprockets connected to the hub of the rear wheel.

coil spring   A metal spring, usually steel, used in some suspension forks and rear shocks.

Cramp-and-go-slow   Yet another slang term for Campagnolo.

crankset   The arms onto which the pedals are attached. Turning the crank transfers power via the chain to the rear wheel.

cyclocross   An off-road competition using bikes that are similar to road bikes equipped with narrow knobby tires.

derailleur   A mechanism that causes a bike to shift gears by guiding the chain sideways onto another cog or chainring.

derailleur hanger   The portion of a bike frame that the rear derailleur attaches to.

DNF   An abbreviation found on racing results; it stands for Did Not Finish.

down-tube   The portion of a bike frame that runs from the head-tube to the bottom bracket shell.

dropouts   The notches on the rear of a bike frame or on the end of a bike fork into which the wheels' axles are placed.

elastomer   A type of suspension spring made of urethane or rubber.

electrolytes   In the human body, substances such as sodium, potassium, and chlorides that carry electrical charges in the blood and to the cells around them, allowing the cells to "talk" to and respond to each other.

fired out the back   When a slower rider drops behind the main pack of riders.

floor pump   A standard air pump, consisting of a long cylinder and a horizontal handle.

fork   The metal tubes that hold the front wheel and attach the wheel to the rest of the bike.

frame pump   A small bicycle tire pump designed to be carried on a bike for road-side flat repair and tire inflation.

front derailleur   The mechanism that carries the chain sideways to move it from one chainring to another.

fried   Overtired or overtrained.

glycogen   The compound in which sugar is stored in the liver for release to other parts of the body.

granny gear   A bike's lowest gear with a ratio so low that the rider moves at about the pace of an elderly, gray-haired woman.

grind   Pedal slowly in a high gear.

hammer   To ride at a hard, fast pace.

hammer-fest   A group ride with a very fast pace.

hammerhead   One who hammers.

hit the wall   Bonking.

handlebar   The component on a bicycle where a rider rests his or her hands. It is also the control for steering.

headset   The bearing mechanism on a bike's head-tube. The headset enables the handlebar and fork to turn in unison for steering.

head-tube   The front vertical tube at the very front of a bicycle frame. Look at the front of your bike. See the front portion of the frame proudly wearing a brand logo? That's your head-tube.

hub   The centermost component of a wheel where the spokes are attached.

inner plates   The links of a bike chain that fit inboard of the outer plates.

inner tube   An inflatable rubber balloon-like piece contained within a tire.

invisible hill   A headwind.

lactic acid   An acid formed in the body as a by-product of metabolizing sugars, as from hard exercise.

lube   (noun) Short for lubricant. (verb) Short for lubricate; for example, to apply lubricant to a bicycle component.

mash   To pedal by pushing downward on the pedals. Also a term used to describe pedaling in a very high gear.

minute man   The man in front of you in a road time trial or mountain bike downhill event.

monocoque   A construction method whereby a structure is not made up of joined-together subcomponents, but rather the structure is made as one singular shape.

organ donor   A helmetless rider.

outer plates   The hourglass-shaped metal pieces as seen from the side of a bike chain.

pace line   A pack of riders riding in a single-file formation. A pace line rotates with each rider taking a turn fighting the wind at the front of the line for a short duration before dropping back to the back of the line.

pivot   The hinged point connecting a swingarm to the frame or to the linkage or shock.

poach   1. To ride in a race or fun ride without paying the entry fee. 2. To ride on trails that are closed to bicycle use.

rebound   The act of a compressed spring bouncing back.

rigid   A bike frame or fork with no suspension; for example, a rigid fork or a hard-tail frame.

rim   The outermost component of a bike wheel. The tire attaches to the rim.

roadie   Road cyclist.

road rash   Skin abrasion from sliding on the ground during a crash.

rollers   A device used to ride a bike in place. Rollers consist of three horizontal drums held within a metal frame. Two drums are placed at the rear wheel, and the third is placed at the front wheel. A belt runs from one of the rear drums to the front drum so that the spinning of the rear wheel will also turn the front drum and the front wheel. A rider remains upright on rollers by balance and by the gyroscopic effect of the spinning wheels.

saddle   Seat.

seat-post   The long pillar that the saddle is attached to.

seat-stay   The two parts of a bike frame that extend back and downward from the seat-tube to the rear dropouts.

seat-tube   The portion of the frame that extends upward from the bottom bracket shell. The seat-post slips into the seat-tube.

shift levers   The controls a rider manipulates to shift gears.

single-track   A narrow off-road trail.

skip and jump   When a bike chain slips off the teeth of worn cogs.

slider   The large-diameter, lower-leg portion of a conventional telescopic suspension fork. On upside-down designs, the upper-leg tube has the larger diameter.

spin   The act of pedaling in a circle smoothly and efficiently.

spoke   The thin metal wires that connect a wheel's hub to the rim.

spoke nipple   The threaded fittings on the end of a spoke that are used to adjust the tension on that spoke.

spring   Any of the several different means of returning a shock absorber to its original position after compression. Types of springs used for mountain bikes are metal coil springs, air, or urethane elastomers made of microcellular foam.

spring rate   The measurement of a spring's stiffness, measured by the amount of weight needed to compress it one inch. Example: Applying a 150-pound weight to a 150-pound spring will compress the spring one inch.

Spuds   Specifically Shimano "SPD" (Shimano Pedaling Dynamics) clipless pedals, although the name is sometimes used generically for any brand of clipless mountain bike pedal.

stanchion   The small-diameter, upper-leg portion of a conventional telescopic fork. On upside-down design forks, the lower-leg tube has the smaller diameter.

stationary trainer   A device that allows a standard bicycle to be ridden in place as an exercise bike. Usually consists of a frame to hold the bicycle upright and some means of positioning the rear wheel onto a roller.

stem   The gooseneck into which a bike's handlebar is bolted.

swag or **schwag**   Items such as bike parts or accessories given as prizes or provided free to sponsored racers.

swingarm   The part of a rear suspension system that is connected by a pivot to the frame. The rear wheel is attached to the swingarm.

ti   Titanium. A very light and very strong material that is sometimes used in making bicycle frames or components. It is also very expensive.

toe-clip   A device that attaches a rider's feet to the pedals. A toe-clip consists of a metal or plastic basket that is attached to a pedal and loops over the toe of a rider's shoe. A leather or nylon strap threads through a loop in the toe-clip over the rider's instep. Pulling that strap tight against its buckle firmly secures the foot to the pedal.

top-tube   The horizontal tube at the top of a bicycle frame. Sit on your bike and look down between your knees. That tube you see is your top-tube.

travel   The distance that a suspension system allows a wheel to move.

triple-clamp fork   A term from motorcycle design referring to having the two stanchions and the steerer tube slipped into an assembly that clamps all three parts in place.

tubeset   The various tubes of material (aluminum, steel, carbon fiber, titanium, Scandium) that a manufacturer joins together to build a bike frame.

unattached   Racers who are not members of any race team.

unified rear triangle   A suspension design that has the swingarm pivot placed so that the entire drivetrain is on the swingarm.

unobtanium   The newest doodad that only the pros and sponsored riders can get.

V-Brakes   Although the term V-Brakes is a Shimano trademark, the term is often used to refer to any brand of brake that uses long brake arms and is actuated via a side-mounted cable.

wafo   (*wah-fo*) 1. An individual experiencing difficulty in understanding the motivation of another's leisure activities. 2. One who asks "Wafo?" as in "Wafo you ride those mountain bikes?"

waterbottle cage   A plastic or metal basket-like device designed to hold a water bottle.

wheel suck   To follow closely behind another rider, taking advantage of the slipstream, while also refusing to take a turn fighting the wind at the front.

workstand   An upright support used to hold a bike in place to be worked on while allowing the wheels to spin and the drivetrain to fully function. A workstand also brings the bike up to a comfortable working level so the mechanic doesn't have to stoop over.

Index

Symbols

A

B

C

401

405

We've been manufacturing bicycles in our Bedford, Pennsylvania factory for more than 15 years. In a unique process that combines edge-of-the-art production techniques with old-world hand-craftsmanship, we create some of the lightest, fastest and most innovative bicycles on the planet. Tested and proven in the world's toughest road and mountain bike races, Cannondale bikes are the ride of choice for cyclists who insist on the ultimate in quality and performance.

www.cannondale.com

1 800 BIKE USA

cannondale
HANDMADE IN USA

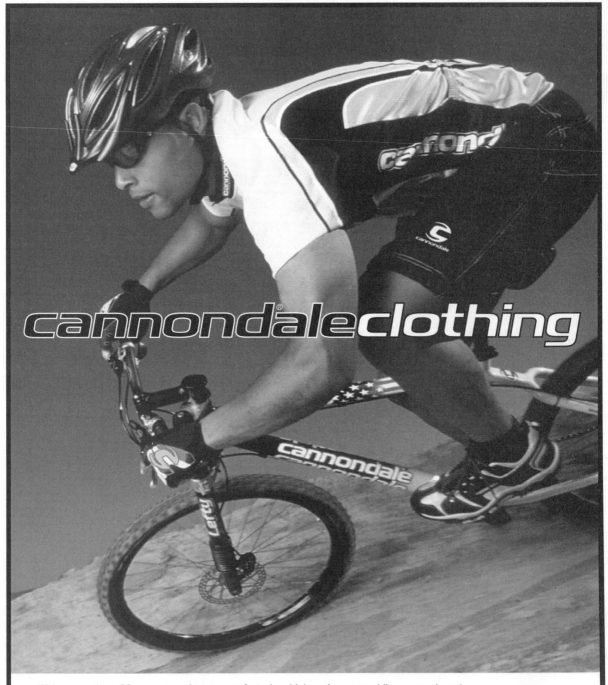

cannondale®clothing